CAM .DGE GREEK A

CICERO

PRO SEXTO ROSCIO

EDITED BY

ANDREW R. DYCK

Professor Emeritus of Classics, University of California, Los Angeles

CAMBRIDGE UNIVERSITY PRESS
Cambridge, New York, Melbourne, Madrid, Cape Town, Singapore,
São Paulo, Delhi, Dubai, Tokyo

Cambridge University Press
The Edinburgh Building, Cambridge CB2 8RU, UK

Published in the United States of America by Cambridge University Press, New York

www.cambridge.org
Information on this title: www.cambridge.org/9780521708869

First published 2010

Printed in the United Kingdom at the University Press, Cambridge

A catalogue record for this publication is available from the British Library

Library of Congress Cataloguing in Publication data
Cicero, Marcus Tullius.
[Pro Roscio Amerino. English & Latin]
Pro Sexto Roscio / Cicero ; edited by Andrew Dyck.
p.   cm. – (Cambridge Greek and Latin classics)
Includes bibliographical references and index.
ISBN 978-0-521-88224-8 (hardback)
1. Cicero, Marcus Tullius. Pro Roscio Amerino. 2. Cicero, Marcus Tullius – Criticism and
interpretation. 3. Roscius Amerinus, Sextus. 4. Speeches, addresses, etc., Latin – Translations
into English. 5. Trials (Murder) – Rome. I. Dyck, Andrew R. (Andrew Roy), 1947 –
II. Title. III. Series.
PA6307.R7   2010
875′.01 – dc22   2009040946

ISBN 978-0-521-88224-8 Hardback
ISBN 978-0-521-70886-9 Paperback

TO JANIS

CONTENTS

PREFACE

When young Cicero rose to plead the case of Sextus Roscius, the prosecutor was visibly relieved that this unknown was his opponent and not one of the established advocates (§60). Once the trial was concluded, there was no case to which he was thought unequal (*Brut.* 312). This career-making speech contains an almost fully formed approach to juror persuasion and to the psychology of criminality. It is also a risky speech in which the young C. excoriates a favorite of the powerful Sulla besides taking rhetorical risks, especially the purple passage about the parricide's punishment that embarrassed him in later years (*Orat.* 107). If, like Desmoulins' teacher at the Collège Louis-le-Grand, one is put off by the domineering figure of C. the senior statesman,[1] this speech shows instead a modest and struggling young orator of great appeal. It deserves to be widely read.

Conditions for anglophone readers of the speech have not been ideal. G. Landgraf's detailed German commentary ([2]1914) is a masterpiece of philological erudition but is more for scholars than for students and shows its age; there is also a recent edition with French translation and notes (Hinard and Benferhat 2006).[2] Most English students, however, have probably made the acquaintance of this text in the company of a reprint of E. H. Donkin's 1916 school edition based upon K. Halm's commented edition (1877) updated in consultation with A. C. Clark. The study of the text, of Roman institutions and law and of the historical actors has, however, moved considerably forward in the intervening ninety-odd years; the whole approach has had to be rethought with reference to the needs and questions posed by today's students and other readers.

It is my happy task to thank those persons and institutions who have made this work possible. I begin with the Editors E. J. Kenney, Philip Hardie and Stephen Oakley for their support for this project and meticulous attention to improving my drafts; I must add Michael Sharp and his staff for their unfailing patience and helpfulness during the production process. My greatest debt is indicated in the dedication.

---

[1] Highet 1949: 393; Parker 1937: 32.
[2] Cf. Dyck 2009.

ABBREVIATIONS

CITED EDITIONS

K. Halm[8]. Berlin, 1877
F. Richter and A. Fleckeisen. Leipzig–Berlin, 1906
E. H. Donkin[2]. London, 1916 (largely based on Halm)
H. Kasten. Leipzig, 1968
F. Hinard and Y. Benferhat. Paris, 2006

STANDARD WORKS

A–G	Allen and Greenough's *New Latin grammar*, ed. J. B. Greenough et al. Boston 1903.
Berger, A.	*Encyclopedic dictionary of Roman law*. Philadelphia 1953.
CAH	*The Cambridge ancient history*,[2] 14 vols. Cambridge 1984–2005.
Ernout and Meillet	Ernout, A., and A. Meillet, *Dictionnaire étymologique de la langue latine. Histoire des mots*.[4] Paris 1959.
G–L	Gildersleeve, B. L., and G. Lodge, *Latin grammar*[3]. London 1895.
H–S	Hofmann, J. B., and A. Szantyr, *Lateinische Syntax und Stilistik*. Munich 1965.
K–S	Kühner, R., and C. Stegmann, *Ausführliche Grammatik der lateinischen Sprache*, II: *Satzlehre*. 2 vols. With corrections to the 4th edn by A. Thierfelder. Darmstadt 1966.
Lausberg, H.	*Handbook of literary rhetoric: a foundation for literary study.* Tr. M. T. Bliss, A. Jansen, D. E. Orton. Ed. D. E. Orton, R. D. Anderson. Leiden 1998.
LIMC	*Lexicon iconographicum mythologiae classicae*. 18 vols. Zurich 1981–99.
LSJ	Liddell, H. G. and R. Scott, *A Greek-English lexicon*. Rev. H. S. Jones. Oxford 1940.
LTUR	Steinby, Eva Margareta, ed., *Lexicon topographicum urbis Romae*. 6 vols. Rome 1993–2000.
MRR	Broughton, T. R. S. *Magistrates of the Roman Republic*. 3 vols. New York 1951–Atlanta 1986.

NLS   Woodcock, E. C. *A new Latin syntax*. Cambridge,
                 Mass. 1959.
OLD   *Oxford Latin dictionary*, ed. P. G. W. Glare. Oxford 1982.
PHI   Database of Latin authors to AD 200: cd rom 5.3
                 produced by Packard Humanities Institute. Palo
                 Alto, Calif. (source of statements about nos. of
                 attestations and the like).
Richardson, L. J. Jr.   *A new topographical dictionary of ancient Rome*. Baltimore
                 and London 1992.
Roby   Roby, H. J. *A grammar of the Latin language*. 2 vols.
                 London 1871–4.
RS   Crawford, M. H., ed. *Roman statutes*. 2 vols. London
                 1996.
TLL   *Thesaurus linguae Latinae*. Leipzig 1900–.
TLRR   Alexander, M. C. *Trials in the late Roman Republic, 149
                 BC to 50 BC*. Toronto 1990.

MAPS

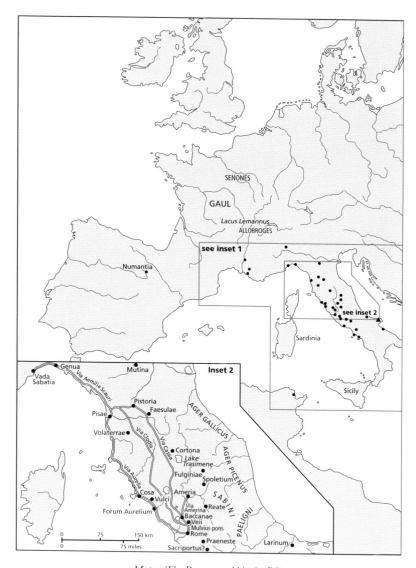

Map 1 The Roman world in 80 BC

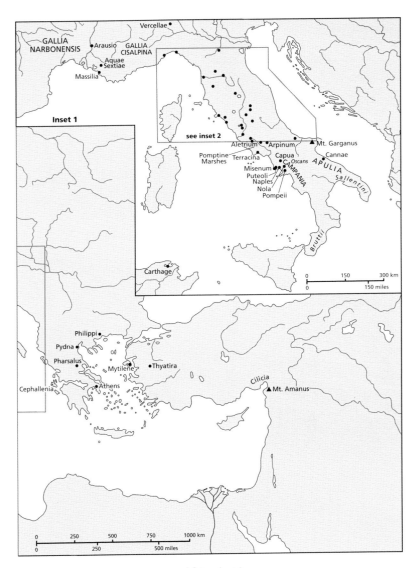

Inset 1

Vercellae

GALLIA
NARBONENSIS
Arausio   GALLIA
           CISALPINA
   Aquae
   Sextiae
Massilia

see inset 2

Aletrium   Arpinum   ▲ Mt. Garganus
                                  Cannae
Pomptine   Terracina   Capua
Marshes   Oscans   APULIA
           Misenum   CAMPANIA
           Puteoli
           Naples   Sallentini
           Nola
           Pompeii   Bruttii

Carthage

0   150   300 km
0   150 miles

Philippi
Pydna
Pharsalus
      Mytilene   Thyatira
                      Cilicia
Cephallenia Athens   ▲ Mt. Amanus

0   250   500   750   1000 km
0   250   500 miles

Map 1 (cont.)

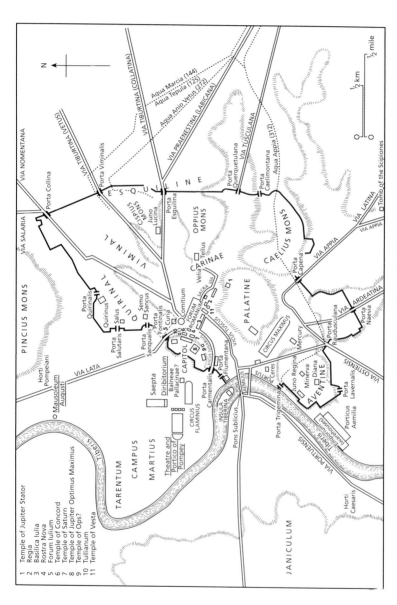

1 Temple of Jupiter Stator
2 Regia
3 Basilica Iulia
4 Rostra Nova
5 Forum Iulium
6 Temple of Concord
7 Temple of Saturn
8 Temple of Jupiter Optimus Maximus
9 Temple of Ops?
10 Tullianum
11 Temple of Vesta

Map 2 Rome in the late Republic

CHRONOLOGICAL TABLE

INTRODUCTION

1 THE CHARGE[1]

de parricidio causa dicitur, C. reminds the jurors to galvanize attention (§61). Under *parricidium* C. understands the murder of a parent, as is clear from his characterization of this case (ibid.) and the examples he cites in §§64–6 and 70.[2] It was a crime that filled Romans with horror and was, on available evidence, rare at Rome.[3] Although the second element clearly derives from the root for killing (*caedo*, *cid-* in *occidere* etc.), the first element remains, in spite of much discussion, obscure.[4] By the late Republic *parricidium* could also include the murder of other close relatives as well as patrons.[5]

Being an abomination at Rome, the *parricida* was subject to a gruesome and unique punishment: *insui uoluerunt in culleum uiuos atque ita in flumen deici* (§71). C. makes no mention of the inclusion in the sack of a snake, an ape, a dog, and a cock, alluded to by Justin. *Inst.* 4.18.6 and Modest. *Dig.* 48.9.9 pr. but evidently not practiced in his time. In spite of C.'s claim (§70) that it was invented as a deterrent, the punishment was probably originally a ritual procedure for removing a *prodigium* from the community; the drowning of hermaphrodites, likewise regarded as *prodigia*, is the closest parallel in historical times.[6] The *poena cullei* is referred to as early as Pl. *Epid.* 359–61.[7] One Malleolus was thus executed (for matricide) in 101 (*Rhet. Her.* 1.23; cf. *Inv.* 2.148–9). Q. Cicero inflicted it on provincials in 59 (*Q.fr.* 1.2.5). A *lex Pompeia*, probably of 55 or 52, appears to have subsumed *parricidium* under the regular punishment for murder in cases tried before the standing courts (*quaestiones*),

---

[1] C. stands for Cicero; references to this speech are by paragraph number alone; names of other Latin authors and works are abbreviated as in *OLD* or otherwise *TLL*; all references to Quint. are to *Inst.*; all dates are BC unless otherwise indicated.

[2] Cloud 1971: 15n16 argues for a wider sphere of application of the term even before the *lex Pompeia* (see below), but the case is not clear. Thomas 1981 emphasizes the father as the victim of primary concern.

[3] Cf. Saller 1986: esp. 9 and 19 and 1987: esp. 21–2 and 34.

[4] Cf. Ernout and Meillet s.v.; Cloud 1971: 5n5; Lovisi 1999: 83–7. Likewise unclear is the relation of the *parricida* of the late Republic to *paricidas* in an alleged law of Numa, where the word designates a murderer in general; cf. Festus 247.10L with Cloud 1971: 2–18; Thomas 1981: 659–79, suggesting that the passage be bracketed out from discussions of *parricida/parricidium*; Magdelain 1984.

[5] Marcian. *Dig.* 48.9.1: the *lex Pompeia*; see below.

[6] A closer parallel would be the sewing of the religious offender L. Atilius in a *culleus* and casting him into the sea by Tarquinius Superbus (V. Max. 1.1.13), if historical; Briquel 1984: 231 is skeptical. For the hermaphrodites cf. Livy 31.12.8 and other testimonies cited by Cloud 1971: 35. See further Radin 1919; Briquel 1980: 89.

[7] Cf. Cloud 1971: 32–6.

namely exile (Marc. *Dig.* 48.9.1).[8] The traditional punishment was, however, occasionally inflicted in other types of court under the Empire,[9] though Suet. *Aug.* 33.1 states that it was applicable only if the defendant confessed. It has also, bizarrely, been revived in modern times.[10]

2 THE COURT

In early times such matters were handled by families extrajudicially. In the early first century BC *parricidium* could be tried by the court *de ueneficiis* (*Inv.* 2.58); presumably the court *de sicariis*, attested from 142 onward,[11] was also available if that were the means used. The two murder courts were amalgamated by Sulla's judicial legislation;[12] hence the *quaestio de sicariis et ueneficiis* is the venue of our trial. A case of *parricidium* was, however, treated as special in that it was put on to a fast track ahead of other cases (*Inv., loc. cit.*). Our case was therefore the first following the interruption of judicial activity entailed by the civil war and proscriptions (§11n. and the next sections).

3 THE PROSCRIPTIONS[13]

The atmosphere and, to some extent, the content of Roscius' trial were determined by Sulla's recent proscriptions. C. claims that the prosecutor C. Erucius owes his standing to the recent bloodbath among prosecutors (§§89–90). Moreover, the pervasive activities of cutthroats (*sicarii*: §§80–1, 93–4) were invoked by both the prosecution and defense to help account for the elder Roscius' murder. C. expresses the hope that the court will help to put an end to the recent excesses (§11) rather than unleash a new proscription (§153); and he speaks of the right and wrong uses of the victory of the nobility (§§141–2 and 149). In framing his case this way C. clearly hopes to tap into widespread revulsion over recent events. Some background will help readers appreciate the resonance of his approach.

   The proscriptions were state-sanctioned plunder and killing of political enemies. Historians usually distinguish two sets of proscriptions, those of

---

[8] Rotondi 1912: 406–7; cf. Cloud 1971: 47–66; Justin. *Inst.* 4.18.6, however, claims that the *lex Pompeia* reaffirmed the traditional punishment.
[9] Cf. Cloud 1971: 58.
[10] Cf. Egmond 1995: 160, noting occurrences in the German-speaking countries, France, Spain and Italy between AD 1200 and 1750.
[11] Cf. Riggsby 1999: 50.
[12] *RS* §50; cf. Ferrary 1991 with literature.
[13] For the material in this section cf. in general Hinard 1985a; Keaveney 1982: ch. 8; Seager, *CAH* IX ch. 6; Letzner 2000: ch. 9.1.

Sulla (82– 1) and those of Antony, Octavian, and Lepidus (43), but the reality is more complex. Sulla's excesses of 82–1 were preceded by acts of the same kind but on a smaller scale in 88 and 87, and Julius Caesar's enemies in the civil war of 49 to 45 suffered a similar fate.

The 80s were a period of great turmoil and violence in Roman politics. C. speaks, not without reason, of the danger of a deadening of sensibility (§§3 and 150). Though the Social War was, apart from the siege of Nola, concluded by the end of 89, the practical question yet remained of how the new citizens should be distributed among Rome's 35 traditional voting tribes. This issue drove a wedge between P. Sulpicius, tribune of the plebs, and the two consuls Sulla and Q. Pompeius Rufus, Sulpicius proposing to distribute the new citizens among all 35 tribes, the latter to keep their influence to a minimum by placing them in a handful of tribes voting last. After a violent clash in which Pompeius' young son was killed, Sulla left Rome to join his troops destined for the campaign in Asia against Mithridates. But while he was still in Italy, he received word that a bill had been passed by which C. Marius was to supersede him in the command. Thereupon Sulla marched his troops on Rome and took possession of the city. The following day, with troops posted throughout the city, the senate met and declared Marius, his son, Sulpicius, and nine others public enemies. Sulpicius was betrayed by a slave and killed (Livy *ep.* 77; V. Max. 6.5.7), the others fled. This was the first but not the last instance of the senate's stepping in to legitimize one side in a political vendetta and delegitimize the other.

The fate of the new citizens continued to be a divisive issue, setting the consuls of 87, Cn. Octavius and L. Cornelius Cinna, at odds. Rioting by the new citizens led to a bloodbath in which many of them were killed by Octavius' supporters. Thereupon Cinna, who had championed the cause of the new citizens, left Rome to gather support; Marius joined him from his African exile, and together they mounted an attack on Rome. When the attackers entered the city, they proceeded to settle scores with no pretense of legality. A number of leading men were cut down, including the orator M. Antonius, C. and L. Caesar, and P. Crassus and his elder son. Sulla himself was outlawed and stripped of his priesthood, his property confiscated or destroyed.

But even these vengeful acts pale by comparison with those wreaked by Sulla upon his enemies after he patched together a peace with Mithridates and marched on Rome for the second time in 82. After his victory at Sacriportus, the city opened its gates to him, and his enemies fled; they were hunted down and killed, their property forfeit. The killings and confiscations were

so numerous that even Sulla's supporter Q. Catulus asked whether anyone
was to be left alive.[14] To satisfy such concerns, Sulla began publishing lists
(*proscribere*) of those targeted. The scale can be gauged from reports that the
first list contained the names of 40 (or 80) senators, the next two 220 each;[15]
Appian (*BC* 1.95.442) states that the first list included the names of 1,600
equites, though possibly this was the total number of them killed.[16] The heads
of the victims were at first brought to Sulla's house (V. Max. 3.1.2b; Plut. *Cat.
min.* 3); the confiscated property was sold at auction in the forum under his
personal supervision (Plut. *Sull.* 33.2). Punishment also fell on the sons and
grandsons of the proscribed, who were excluded from holding office, though
those of senatorial rank still had to assume the corresponding burdens (Plut.
Sull. 31; Vel. 2.28.4); such sanctions, unprecedented in Roman law, were felt
to be especially harsh (see further §152n.).

4 THE DATE OF THE TRIAL

The elder Sex. Roscius was murdered "some months" after 1 June 81 (*aliquot
post menses*: §128); news of the murder was carried to Sulla's camp at Volaterrae
within four days of the murder (§20). Thereby a chain of events was set in
motion including (apparently) the addition of the deceased to the list of
those killed among the enemy, confiscation of his property, and sale of the
same at auction. The dispossession of Sex. Roscius jun. occurred while the
funeral ceremonies were still incomplete (§23), i.e. within about nine days
of the death (cf. §23n.). After this event some time passed during which the
younger Roscius perceived danger to his life and, on advice of his relatives,
fled to his father's friends at Rome for protection (§26). It was in light of this
development and to assure themselves of a firm hold on their newly acquired
property that his adversaries filed charges of parricide (§6). In §139 C. refers
to Sulla's supreme authority and legislative work in the past tense (similar
use of the past tense at §91). The laying down of the dictatorship and normal
functioning of the organs of state would fit early 80 as the date of the speech
(see further on §11); and this would also accord with Quintilian's statement
(12.6.4) that C. delivered the speech at age 26 as well as with the consular
year indicated at Gel. 15.28.3.[17]

---

[14] Oros. 5.21.2; similarly C. Metellus at Plut. *Sull.* 31.
[15] Figures from Plut. *Sull.* 31; App. *BC* 1.95.442 gives the figure 40 instead of 80.
[16] So Seager, *CAH* IX 197.
[17] Cf. Kinsey 1967: 61–2 and 66–7.

5 THE PRINCIPAL CHARACTERS

The central character in the case is **Sex. Roscius jun.**, who stands accused of parricide. He is a puzzling figure: he is above forty years of age (§39) yet apparently has no wife or children. His father was a *domi nobilis* in the Umbrian town Ameria, wealthy (§6) and well connected to the nobility at Rome (§§15–16). Since after his death the father's property was sold under the law governing the proscriptions (see §125n.), those family connections are the son's sole remaining legacy (§15).

The prosecution characterized the defendant as *ferus atque agrestis* (§74), a loner without social skills (§52). Moreover, they claimed that he did not enjoy the favor of his sociable father (§40) and that the alienation was shown by the fact that Roscius sen. kept his other son (since deceased) always with him, whereas he relegated the defendant to work on his farms (§42). Moreover, the son organized the murder in order to forestall his father's plan to disinherit him (§53). The prosecution also raised the side-issue of embezzlement of public property (*peculatus*): the claim was presumably that he held back some of his father's property that was destined for public auction (§82 with n.).

C. does not so much contradict as reinterpret the prosecution's picture. He puts a positive face on Roscius' rustic life, emphasizing his skill at and devotion to agriculture (§49); the failure to appear in society is the inevitable concomitant (§52). Nor does the son's relegation to farm work show the father's dislike; rather, this is the old Roman way, still observed in the Italian *municipia* (§§48–51). The other side of the coin of Roscius' thoroughgoing rusticity is his utter unfamiliarity with the city and its ways: he would, so C. claims, have been helpless to organize a murder at Rome (§§74 and 79). Moreover, his rural values are utterly at odds with the city values that underlie such a murder (§75). It is, however, notable that the only individual relative of the defendant mentioned as present in court is T. Roscius Magnus, seated on the prosecution side (§§17, 84, 104), even though the defendant appears to have had a number of living relatives (§§49 and 96 with nn.). One wonders whether he was really so approved by his family as C. claims (*probatum suis filium* §152).

Both pictures have their weaknesses: the plan to disinherit would require proof, as C. points out (§58). On the other hand, C.'s use of the town/country stereotype[18] to paint Roscius as utterly naïve is suspect. A man over forty acquainted with his father's habits could surely have organized his murder if

---

[18]   Here he is playing variations on a theme that had great resonance in Rome going back to Cato the Censor; cf. §39n.

he put his mind to it. In addition, the *cui bono?* argument, of which C. makes so much (§§84–5), would point to the son, the presumptive beneficiary at the moment of the murder.[19]

In his extremity, Roscius turned to his father's noble friends at Rome for support. He received it, in the first place, from the well-born and influential **Caecilia Metella**, who offered him refuge when he perceived his life to be in danger (cf. §§26–7 with n.; §147). But her sphere is defined as *domi*; the legal defense was organized (probably) by **M. Valerius Messalla Niger**, a young noble who secured C.'s services as advocate with promises of *amicitia* and *beneficia* and himself appeared in court as an *aduocatus* (§4 and 149 with n.). Two other young nobles assisted Roscius' cause at an earlier stage: on several occasions (*aliquotiens*) **M. Metellus**, a cousin of Caecilia, and **P. Cornelius Scipio Nasica**, one of whose sons was adopted by the Caecilii Metelli, acted as Roscius' agents in requesting that the slaves who witnessed the murder be made available for judicial inquiry (by torture) but were refused by T. Roscius Magnus in behalf of Chrysogonus (§77).

Cicero himself is the last but not least important figure on the defense side. An *eques*, aged twenty-six, from the *municipium* Arpinum, he had devoted himself to studies in rhetoric, the *De inuentione*, a later source of embarrassment (*De orat.* 1.5), being the extant product,[20] as well as philosophy and law. After a brief interruption for military service in the Social War (89), the studies continued through the 80s, with C. emerging in 81 as a last-minute substitute for M. Junius as advocate for P. Quinctius in a civil case (*Quinct.* 3). No wonder the prosecutor seemed to breathe a sigh of relief when C. rose to speak for the defense (§60). He presents himself as a modest young man, aware of his inferior *dignitas* to others seated on the defense side (§§1–5) and to the senatorial jurors (§8) and keen to enlist their sympathy and support (§§9–10). At first he claims merely that his client has not been abandoned (§5), later, upon gaining confidence, that he is being defended *diligenter* (§148). At §§33–4 he gives an early signal that, though, like C. Marius, a native of Arpinum, he has no sympathy for the recent *popularis* excesses. Only toward the end of the speech does he clarify his own stance in the recent civil war (§§136, 142) and venture some political commentary on the case (§§150–4).

C. calibrates his attacks on the four men of the prosecution so as to effect a crescendo from C. Erucius through the T. Roscii to Chrysogonus.

<hr />

[19] Cf. F. Richter *apud* Landgraf on §84; similarly Kinsey 1980: 181. A counterargument can be drawn, however, from the embassy of the *decem primi* of Ameria (§§24–6), which implies community sympathy for the position of Roscius jun.; cf. Hutchinson 2005: 184n10.

[20] To be dated to the 80s; cf. MacKendrick 1989: 30; *aliter* Corbeill 2002: 28.

C. Erucius was a professional prosecutor whom C. also faced in the defense of Varenus. He appears to be a local Umbrian personality, since in Varenus' case he worked beside C. Ancharius Rufus, who hailed from the Umbrian municipality Fulginiae (fr. 3 Crawford); and indeed in that case, too, the defendant and the victim(s) were Umbrians.[21] There C. described Erucius as an imitator of M. Antonius (*Antoniaster*), one of the two leading orators of the previous generation (fr. 10 Crawford). In our speech C. clears his rival counsel of any personal animus against Roscius (§55). He quotes Erucius as saying that he was prosecuting in Chrysogonus' interest (§132) and supposes that, when he was hired, Chrysogonus promised there would be no *patronus* on the other side and no mention of the *societas* [sc. among himself and the T. Roscii: §58]. C. ascribes to Erucius *humanitatis non parum* and *studium doctrinae* (§46), but this is merely to smooth the way for the introduction of a literary example. In general, the attacks on Erucius are by C.'s later standards crude: he implies that he is of servile origin (§46) and attributes his status as an "adequate" (*sat bonus*) prosecutor to the recent bloodbath among members of the profession (§89); he repeatedly castigates him for failing to provide a plausible motive or proofs (§§42–5, 52–4, 61–2), to specify the precise means by which the crime was committed (§§73–4), or in general to come into court adequately prepared (§72); and he warns him against falling foul of the law against unfounded prosecution (*lex Remmia*: §§55–7).

The next targets of C.'s invective are the T. Roscii, bearing respectively the sobriquets Magnus and Capito, probably related to each other and to the defendant; C. leaves the precise relations unclear.[22] C. is keen to link the two T. Roscii together (§§17, 107). He first presents them as (gladiatorial) master and student (§17; cf. §119). In fact, however, the only palpable link between the two is the fact that Magnus' freedman Mallius Glaucia brought word of the death of Roscius sen. to Capito before anyone else in Ameria (§§19, 96–9). But, particularly if Glaucia, as seems likely, went on to report the news at other homes,[23] the initial stop at Capito's may be a contingent fact without the deeper significance with which C. seeks to invest it (see further on §19). Yet that fact is C.'s sole evidence for the existence of a *societas* between Capito and Magnus prior to the murder.

Mallius Glaucia's immediate knowledge of the murder would tend to cast suspicion on his former master, **Magnus**. C.'s speech makes it clear that

[21] Cf. also (on his name) Alexander 2002: 303n9.
[22] Cf. on §§17 and 96; C. mentions that the defendant is Magnus' *cognatus* at §87.
[23] This is suggested by *primo* at §96; cf. Kinsey 1980: 176.

Magnus had no previous criminal record (§17).[24] He had, however, a property
dispute with the deceased (§87) and, like Roscius sen., was constantly at Rome
during the time prior to the murder (§18); later C. alleges that Magnus was
a purchaser of property of victims of the proscriptions (*sector*), and it has
been suspected that the habitual presence in the forum of Roscius sen. at
this time points to similar activity on his part.[25] Shortly after Chrysogonus'
purchase of the dead man's property, he installed Magnus as his agent on
the spot (§23); as such, he took charge of the dispossession of Roscius jun.
(§21). In the trial he sits prominently on the prosecution side (to keep an eye
on the proceedings in Chrysogonus' interest? (§§17, 84, 87, 95)). The real link
appears to be between Magnus and Chrysogonus, and it existed even before
Capito was awarded three farms during the embassy of the leading men of
Ameria (see below). Within about nine days of the death Magnus, acting
as Chrysogonus' agent, took possession of the younger Roscius' property
(§23). Moreover, C. seems keen to conceal the Magnus–Chrysogonus nexus,
describing Magnus' dispossession of his client as if he were acting in his
own interest, not Chrysogonus' (§23), and he speaks as if Magnus enjoyed a
windfall by the elder Roscius' death on the same scale as that of Chrysogonus
and Capito (§§86, 93 *qui nostra pecunia diues es*, 107 with n.). All of this is to
insulate Chrysogonus from the charge of murder even though the *cui bono?*
argument carried to its logical conclusion points to him as the first and major
beneficiary of the three. C. implicitly concedes that Magnus was incapable
of organizing the murder on his own; he feels therefore that he must, even in
default of hard evidence, have Capito in the picture as soon as possible.

C. accords the elder Sex. Roscius an encomiastic obituary, stressing his
wealth, his connections to the nobility, and his reliability in its cause (§§15–
16). He introduces **Capito** in far different terms (§17), but Capito, too, was a
leading citizen of Ameria, as is shown by his inclusion in the embassy of the
decem primi of that municipality to defend the reputation of Roscius sen. before
Sulla; this suggests that no one at Ameria connected him with the murder.
C.'s claims of past criminality on Capito's part are notably vague (§§17 and
100; see on the latter); and the link that he seeks to establish between Capito
and the crime (via Mallius Glaucia) is not by itself cogent (see above). Capito
is expected to testify for the prosecution (to the enmity between Sex. Roscius
jun. and his father?), and C. accordingly deploys typical tactics for witness
intimidation (see on §§100–1). The *decem primi* of Ameria were sent to Sulla
at Volaterrae to plead that the posthumous treatment of Roscius sen. as an

---

[24] In spite of C.'s attempt to class him among the *sicarii* at §§93–4.
[25] Cf. Loutsch 1979: 108.

enemy of Sulla be rescinded (§25). C. uses Capito's rôle in the embassy as the occasion for a lengthy homily on *fides* and the moral bankruptcy of those who betray a trust (§§109–17). But if the case were that simple, surely some at least of the *decem primi* would have volunteered to testify for the defense; as it was, however, they refused to testify unless compelled by the prosecution (§110 with n.). Perhaps they were bribed to keep silent. But there is another possibility: perhaps Capito himself was the *spiritus mouens* behind the embassy. He may have been the only relative of the Roscii in the group. If the cause of his enmity with the elder Roscius (§§17, 19) was property (as it was in the case of Magnus: §87), then his only hope of realizing his claims was for Roscius' name to be removed from the list of those killed among Sulla's enemies. When the embassy arrived at Volaterrae and Chrysogonus blocked access to Sulla, Capito saw an opportunity to cut a deal: he pressed his claims, and Chrysogonus acquiesced, granting him three of the thirteen farms (§§17, 21, 108, 115);[26] in return Capito fobbed off the delegates with assurances, and they left (§26). With Capito satisfied, there was no move to revive the embassy, a further mark of his influence at Ameria. C.'s conception of a *societas* formed among Magnus, Capito, and Chrysogonus during conversations at Volaterrae when the murder was first announced there (§20) is therefore a chimaera; Chrysogonus yielded three farms to Capito only later under pressure of the embassy; a benefit accruing to Capito from the murder was at first by no means assured, his involvement in the murder thus doubtful.

C. has set Sulla's Greek-born freedman **Chrysogonus** at the center of the case. According to C., this move came as a great surprise and unleashed a flurry of activity on the prosecution side (§60). Erucius had, to be sure, mentioned that he was prosecuting for Chrysogonus' sake (§132) but yet had failed to mention the factor *quae conflauit hoc iudicium* (§5), i.e., in C.'s view, the protection of Chrysogonus' property interests (§6). C. cites as shocking the price paid by Chrysogonus for the elder Sex. Roscius' property (2,000 HS) compared with the true value (6 million HS) (§6), but such contrasts must have been commonplace during the proscriptions. The real issue was whether the seizure and sale were legitimate or not. C.'s argumentation at §§125–8 shows just how tricky this question was; in default of indication in the relevant public records C. even expresses doubt that the sale occurred (§128 with n.). The proscriptions were essentially extra-legal acts of revenge and banditry indulged in by Sulla and his supporters against political opponents (see above); the senate, of course, was keen to set a limit to them (cf. Plut.

---

[26] *Pace* C. §110 Capito is most unlikely to have confessed any part in the murder to Chrysogonus; doing so would have made him vulnerable, not given him leverage.

Sull. 31). If C. is right that 1 June (81) was fixed by statute as the closing date of the proscriptions (§128), then the killing of the elder Roscius could only have been justified as having occurred *in aduersariorum praesidiis* (§126), though surely, *pace* C., sale of enemy property after 1 June was still possible since military action was ongoing; see §128n. Whether or not Sulla was aware that Roscius' name was added to the list of his enemies on a fraudulent pretext may be left open; C.'s assurances that he was unaware carry no weight (cf. §21n.). In any case, the transfer of property occurred so quickly as to interrupt the younger Roscius' funeral observances for his father (§21 with n.); this suddenness strongly suggests a preconcerted plan, with Chrysogonus as the beneficiary and Magnus as his agent. If that is so, one need hardly look further to find those responsible for planning and executing the murder.[27] Indeed, the kind of *scrupulus* that, according to §6, drove Chrysogonus to instigate the prosecution looks more like a murderer's guilty conscience than the concern of a mere beneficiary after the fact. Yet C. is keen, not only to insulate Sulla from Chrysogonus' corruption of the proscription list, but also to insulate Chrysogonus from the murder, which he claims pertains only to Magnus and Capito; Chrysogonus' rôle is merely to deploy his *potentia* against the defendant (§35 *Chrysogonus . . . potentia pugnat*; cf. §122). Even as Sulla's power waned,[28] Chrysogonus still retained some power, and provoking him beyond a certain point could be a fatal mistake for a young orator. At the same time, however, Chrysogonus is too choice a target to be abandoned altogether: if C. can canalize all the pent-up resentment of the senatorial jurors against this one figure, he can save his client and earn himself a distinguished reputation. Already in this early speech C. shows himself a master at fanning the flames of *inuidia*; standard topics of abuse are tricked out with details of luxurious living, expensive gadgetry, noisy nightly parties, elaborate personal grooming and subservient *togati* in such a way as to effect a crescendo of resentment (§§133–5).

6 THE ADVOCATE'S RÔLE

At Athens and elsewhere in the Greek world, the defendant in court was allowed a συνήγορος, literally a "with-speaker," to collaborate in presenting the case.[29] The Roman term for the advocate in court, *patronus*, suggests

---

[27] Cf. Fuhrmann 1997: 56–7, who makes the suggestion in view of the frailty of the connection between Magnus and Capito.

[28] Sulla is thought to have laid down his dictatorship by the end of 81, albeit he then served as consul in 80; cf. on §§11 and 139; Seager, *CAH* ix 205 with n73.

[29] Cf. Crook 1995: 32–4.

a fundamentally different relation, namely the *patronus/cliens* relation that pervaded Roman society.[30] In early Rome, before advocacy was profession-alized, the *patronus* was expected to exert his *auctoritas* and force of personality in advocating his client's case before the bar. Continuing as a factor in C.'s time, this element is marked in the oratory of his maturity, when he seeks, on the strength of his longstanding ties to the client, to vouch for him as a worthy citizen and invest him with the aura of his consular *auctoritas* (especially in *Mil.*). In our defense, one of his first, C. speaks, however, as a young man who has not yet held public office, so this type of persuasion is not yet open to him.

The *iudicia publica* of Rome, as an arm of the government, took it as their brief to maintain public order in a broad sense. Hence larger public issues, including political ones, play a rôle in Roman judicial oratory to an extent inconceivable in most Western courts today.[31] This fact provides C. the opportunity to raise his voice as a concerned citizen against the evils that he detects in Roman society of the time and seeks to connect with those behind the prosecution.[32] In this regard he claims that his junior status is actually an advantage in that a more senior figure's criticisms would carry greater weight and thus entail greater risk: §3.

The Roman jury of this period, usually about 75 strong, was composed exclusively of senators; indeed, for this trial the jurors were chosen from within the senate by a special procedure (cf. §8 with n.). The senatorial jury conditions the kinds of arguments C. deploys. He is careful to place himself on the side of the nobles (and Sulla) in the recent civil war (§136). He likewise assumes the rôle of the spokesman for Roman tradition and the traditional values of hard work (above all in agriculture) and against the vices of the city (§§39, 50–1, 70–1, 75). He presents his client as a man devoted to agriculture and country life and utterly unfamiliar with the city and its ways (§§49, 74, 81). The senatorial jury is also, at least to a degree, open to persuasion by means of examples drawn from literature (§§45–6, 66–7) and history (§§50,70, 84). In seeking to drive a wedge between the jury and members of the prosecution C. used to great effect the figure of Sulla's Greek freedman Chrysogonus, whose behavior made him an easy target of satire and channel for the resentment of those who had come out of the civil wars and proscriptions less well off (see above).

[30] Cf. Badian 1958: 1–11.
[31] Cf. Riggsby 1999: 11–20.
[32] Especially §§11, 55–7, 136–42, 150–4; for association of prosecution members with the *sicarii/percussores* cf. §§93, 94, 103, 151.

Finally since a Roman trial took place out of doors in a part of the forum, it would attract a crowd of spectators looking to be informed and entertained (called by Roman writers the *corona*); the crowd at Roscius' trial was sizable (*quanta multitudo hominum conuenerit . . . uides*: §11). An estimable element of the Roman judicial "theatre," the reactions of the *corona* could powerfully influence the jurors' perceptions of the case, and C. missed this factor when he later had to plead before Caesar behind closed doors.[33] It tended to favor an impassioned style,[34] and the young C., as he later saw it, went perhaps too far to win their shouts at our trial.[35]

7 LANGUAGE AND STYLE

In general outline the style of *Sex. Rosc.* is similar to that of C.'s other speeches. One finds the periodic structure with careful balancing of parallel clauses, the explicit connection of sentences, and pronounced rhythmical preferences (especially at the end of the clause or sentence), though the avoidance of the hexameter ending is not as thoroughgoing as it would later become.[36] The exploitation of the verbal properties of the participle is still exceptional and will remain so until C.'s last period (cf. §27n.). At the same time there are differences from C.'s fully mature style, as some hints thrown out by C. himself lead one to expect.

At *De orat.* 2.88 C. has Antonius describe his first impression of the oratory of young Sulpicius: *oratione autem celeri et concitata . . . sed uerbis efferuescentibus et paulo nimium redundantibus, quod erat aetatis.* He goes on to declare that the overheated, superabundant style is no great vice in a youth: *uolo enim se efferat in adulescente fecunditas. nam facilius sicut in uitibus reuocantur ea quae se nimium profuderunt quam, si nihil ualet materies, noua sarmenta cultura excitantur, item uolo esse in adulescente unde aliquid amputem. non enim potest in eo sucus esse diuturnus, quod nimis celeriter est maturitatem assecutum.* The metaphor from grapes emphasizes the need for there to be "juice" early on; otherwise the process of maturation will leave the fruit desiccated and useless for the vintage. The young C. was similarly endowed to Sulpicius in this regard, as he reveals in the autobiographical passage *Brut.* 316.[37] Here he describes his training in

---

[33] Cf. *Deiot.* 6.
[34] Cf. *Brut.* 317 *acrem . . . oratorem, incensum et agentem et canorum concursus hominum forique strepitus desiderat.*
[35] *Orat.* 107 *quantis illa clamoribus adulescentuli diximus, quae nequaquam satis deferuisse post aliquanto sentire coepimus* (he goes on to cite from §72 *quid enim tam commune . . . mortui conquiescant*).
[36] Cf. the Appendix n. 6.
[37] Or was he so at least partly under the influence of Sulpicius, whose public speeches he studied closely (*Brut.* 306)?

Asia with the rhetor Molon of Rhodes: *is dedit operam . . . ut nimis redundantes nos et supra fluentes iuuenili quadam dicendi impunitate et licentia reprimeret et quasi extra ripas diffluentes coerceret.* This was during C.'s study tour of Greece and Asia from 79 to 77[38] and thus subsequent to our speech.[39] We should thus expect our speech to show traces of that youthful (over)enthusiasm and abundance that Molon's training enabled C. to control. The obvious example is the purple passage about the parricide's punishment (§§71–2), which C. himself, looking back from a distance of more than thirty years, found "insufficiently 'simmered down.'"[40]

Examples of abundance in diction are not difficult to find in our speech, including *magnam uim, magnam necessitatem, magnam . . . religionem* (§66); *sua quemque fraus et suus terror maxime uexat, suum quemque scelus agitat* (§67); *iussis atque oraculis* (§66); *impie scelerateque* (§67); *probro atque dedecore* (§68).[41] But such use of synonyms serves *amplificatio* and is not alien to C.'s later style. If there is an element in our speech that C. toned down later on, it was rather the exuberant use of wordplay, the young C. reveling in the Latin language itself and its multivalent expressive powers.[42]

Other marks of a youthful and not yet fully mature style are the acceptance of clichés drawn from legal Latin such as the overdetermination of the concessive relation with *tametsi . . . tamen* (§§49, 56, 73, 85, 117, 123) or the repetition of the antecedent within the relative clause (§§8, 28, 72, 140); similarly the formulaic phrase for respectful mention *quem honoris causa nomino,* which he himself later parodied (§6 with n.). A whole host of connectors destined for abandonment appears in the early speeches, C. later coming to regard *propterea quod, eo quod, quemadmodum, idcirco, tametsi, uerum tamen* and *uerum* itself (apart from such combinations as *non solum . . . uerum*) and *usque eo* as too clumsy.[43] Other early stylistic choices later abandoned are *pertimesco,* later replaced by *extimesco,* the glossing formula *hoc est,* which gives way to *id est,*[44] and *quiuis potest intellegere,* for which C. later prefers *intellegi potest.*[45] Alliteration is a powerful means of creating emphasis in Latin (see below); C. makes use of it in all his speeches; but such alliterative pairs as *oro atque obsecro* and *commendo atque concredo* are characteristic of our speech and *Quinct.* but

---

[38] Cf. Marinone 2004: 59–60, who places the stay in Rhodes in 78.

[39] Subsequent also to *Quinct.*; for a comparison of the two speeches cf. della Morte (1977).

[40] Cf. n. 35 above.

[41] These are among the examples cited by Falco 1982: 224–5.

[42] Examples are collected in the Index s.vv. *distinctio,* wordplay.

[43] Cf. von Albrecht, *RE* Suppl. 13 1302.29–37 (all of these forms are found in our speech).

[44] Cf. Parzinger 1910: 115–16 and 129–33.

[45] Cf. §132 with Landgraf's n.

used less later on.[46] In general C. is at pains to achieve balance and parallelism of form,[47] but in this speech there is an occasional mismatch between the formal division and the underlying content; cf. §3n.

Morphology and diction are still a bit rough-hewn. Thus we find such archaisms as the genitive *pernicii* (§131),[48] *abs te*, which was banished from the speeches after *Rab. Post.* 30 in favor of *a te* (cf. §12), or *ad uillam* for *in uilla* (§44); *nisi me fallit animus* likewise occurs (§48), whereas C. elsewhere prefers the elliptical *nisi me fallit*. The speech also shows a number of colloquialisms, including *numquid* and *numquisnam* (§§52, 107), the use of the emphatic *nullus* for *non* (§§55, 59), *mihi ausculta* (§104), verbal paraphrases with *facere* (§§2 and 146), the use of *se* to refer to the subj. of a different clause though not suboblique (§6n.), and such expressions as *summe* (§13), *nullo negotio* (§§20, 28), *mori malle* (§26), *hercules* (§31), *annos natus* (§39), *age* (§48), *nullo modo* (§§53, 123), *operae pretium esse* (§59), *id aetatis* or *temporis* (§§64, 97), the imperative of *facio* + subj. as an emphatic command (§74), *molestus esse* (§82), *id erit signi* (§83), the diminutive *paululum* (§115), *male loqui* (§140), *moleste ferre* (§148), and *molestia* as a euphemism (§154). Loan words from Greek are very sparingly used, as is C.'s general practice before the bar,[49] the exceptions being *architectus*, borrowed as early as Plautus (cf. §132n.) and *authepsa*, which occurs at §133 for the only time in classical Latin; it assists C.'s effort to depict Chrysogonus as addicted to exotic luxuries. C. has also enlivened his diction by taking over a few words from comedy: he applies *uociferor* and *uociferatio* to the advocate's appropriate response to his client's desperate plight (§§9 and 12) and *nebulo* to Chrysogonus, depicted as a stage villain (§128).

As one expects, C. takes full advantage of the expressive potential of Latin. Though he is usually associated with the periodic style, he can use short clauses to good effect, as in §60, where the short descriptive sentences (*perorauit aliquando, adsedit; surrexi ego* etc.) alternate with lengthier interpretative comments. Moreover, the flexible word order of Latin enables him to exploit the initial and final positions in the clause or sentence for emphasis. Thus initial placement can serve to signal a new subject, e.g. §55 *accusatores multos esse in ciuitate utile est*; on the other hand, the frequent appearance of Chrysogonus' name in final position focuses attention (and odium) on the man;

[46] *oro atque obsecro*: Quinct. 10, Sex. Rosc. 9 and 77; *commendo atque concredo*: Quinct. 62; Sex. Rosc. 113; cf. von Albrecht, *RE* Suppl. 13 1303.61–1304.4.

[47] See General Index s.vv. balance, parallelism. The tendency is tempered in his later oratory; cf. e.g. Manuwald on *Phil.* 3.8 (*neque enim Tarquinio*): "The contrasting pairs do not consist of parallel phrases but of constantly varied expressions . . ."

[48] This has been smoothed out in the medieval transmission to *pernicie* but is restored with certainty from Gel. 9.14.10 and Non. 486.28 (Charis. *GL* 1 69.10 reads *pernicies*).

[49] On the entire topic cf. Oksala 1953.

cf. §21 n. Though the verb is expected to occupy the final position, C. sometimes leads with a verb to emphasize surprising or drastic actions (e.g. §18
occiditur ad balneas Pallacinas, §37 *occidisse patrem Sex. Roscius arguitur*, §70 *insui
uoluerunt in culleum uiuos*) or to give vent to indignation (§146 *facis iniuriam, Chrysogone*). Another means of confounding expectations and thus lending emphasis
is the separation of words that would normally be expected together (hyperbaton); thus instead of the expected *nihil aliud agitur* C. writes *aliud agitur nihil*
(§8). Sometimes the noun appears first and one must await the intensifying
adjective, e.g. §24 *mors... crudelissima*; §38 *audaciam... singularem*; §97 *necessitas... tanta*; elsewhere the ominous noun itself is held in abeyance: §153 *noua
et multo crudelior... proscriptio.*[50] Word order can also be used to mirror the
sense, as in §27, where the referent and actions of Caecilia enfold Roscius
and his attributes just as she afforded him protection in life: *ea Sex. Roscium
inopem, eiectum domo atque expulsum ex suis bonis, fugientem latronum tela et minas
recepit domum.*

C. ordinarily makes explicit connections between sentences or clauses
by means of verbal repetition (cf. §10n.), conjunctions, or relative pronouns;
he likewise uses correlatives to mark units within the sentence. This speech
provides many examples, though some of the choices are at odds with C.'s
later preferences (see above and §130n.). This general practice enables C.
to exploit the absence of a connector (asyndeton) for expressive purposes.
Major uses are at the beginning of a narrative, to mark a strong contrast,
and to append an explanation; for the onset of a narrative cf. §84 *L. Cassius
ille... in causis quaerere solebat*; for adversative asyndeton cf. e.g. §54 *uerum
concedo tibi ut ea praetereas... illud quidem, uoluisse exheredare, certe tu planum facere
debes*; for explicative asyndeton §6, where *sese hoc incolumi non arbitratur huius
innocentis patrimonium... posse obtinere* explains the reason for Chrysogonus'
previously described suspicion and fear. Asyndeton can also be used to list
items; thus at §30 a series of complaints bursts forth in an asyndetic torrent.
Polysyndeton, too, can emphasize the sheer number of items on a list, as e.g.
the accumulation of intimidating factors that beset the young advocate at §9
et uestra dignitas et uis aduersariorum et Sex. Rosci pericula.[51]

Our speech is rich in examples of another device serving emphasis, namely
the recurrence of the same word at the head of a series of clauses (anaphora).
It effectively stresses magnitude or quantity: §66 *magnus*; §§104 and 118 *multus*.
Anaphora of the negation yields a powerful denial, as in §121 and especially
§98, where *non* occurs 8x; on the other hand, an affirmation is stressed at §142

[50] For other examples see the General Index s.v. hyperbaton.
[51] See the General Index s.vv. asyndeton, polysyndeton for further examples.

(*fateor . . . fateor*) and an urgent appeal at §140 (*desinant* 4x). The individualized punishment of parricides is emphasized by *suus* at §67 (4x), the qualities of the ideal nobles are detailed with *qui* (4x: §149); and the besetting problem of *domestica crudelitas* is singled out at §154 (*hanc tollite ex ciuitate . . . hanc pati nolite diutius in hac re publica uersari*).

Since the earliest texts alliteration and assonance have been used as expressive devices in Latin. C., too, draws upon them to good effect. Thus he calls attention to the elder Roscius' property, the disposition of which he uses as an index of guilt, as *pecuniam tam plenam atque praeclaram* (§6); similarly §133 *plura praeterea praedia neque tamen ullum nisi praeclarum et propinquum*; or again Chrysogonus' rôle is described this way: *is qui plurimum potest potentia pugnat* (§35). At §131 the puffs of breath needed to pronounce the phrase *uentis uehementioribus* seem to mimic the described phenomenon. Assonance is typically used to connect two halves of a compound expression, sometimes with a pun involved, as in §5 *non electus . . . sed relictus*; cf. §16 *in foro et in ore omnium*; §67 *agitat amentiaque afficit*; §87 *qui . . . os tuum non modo ostenderes sed etiam offeres*; §103 *sector . . . et sicarius*.

Even in this early speech C. works with a full palette of rhetorical figures. He dramatizes by apostrophizing the absent Chrysogonus (§144 *rogat oratque te, Chrysogone*; §146 *facis iniuriam, Chrysogone*). He adds color by personifying the *populus Romanus* (§154) and kindred entities (§70 *ciuitas Atheniensium*). Not only the state but also qualities can, however, be treated as personal agents (§143 *res publica et dolor meus et istorum iniuria*, all of which impelled his preceding argument); *terror et formido* are depicted as acting upon potential advocates (§5); the *uis belli ac turba* have consequences (§91); *luxuries* and other undesirable qualities might have been expected to motivate murder (§39); C. pins his hopes on the permanence of *uestra pristina bonitas et misericordia* (§150).

Since C. makes every effort to imprint his arguments vividly in the mind of the reader/listener, metaphors and similes abound in this speech. Obvious sources include the animal kingdom, which furnishes the memorable comparison of dogs to prosecutors, including the first application of *latro* "bark" to human speech (§57). On the other hand, the growth of moral qualities is conceived in agricultural terms at §75. Another profession, that of the architect, provides a metaphor for Chrysogonus at §132, whereas C. finds military/gladiatorial metaphors best suited to Magnus and Capito (§§17 and 100; cf. also the use of *spolia* at §§8, 145, and 146).[52] C.'s client, on the

---

[52] See further Imholtz 1971-2.

other hand, is memorably compared to the naked survivor of a shipwreck
(§147); other nautical metaphors include the already well worn "ship of state"
metaphor *ad gubernacula rei publicae sedere* (§51) and the comparison of the prosecution case to a ship at sea hoping to make it to port but instead running
into a reef (§79); the metaphor *iudicio perfundere* ("flood with litigation") in §80
is still under the influence of the previous seafaring images. Hovering over
the trial is the figure of the *quondam* dictator and current consul L. Cornelius
Sulla; Sulla's position is compared to that of the supreme deity Jupiter Optimus Maximus; this enables C. to encapsulate Sulla's supreme position and at
the same time insulate him from criticism, just as damage from storms and
the like is not ascribed to divine providence (§131 with n.).

8 CICERO'S ACHIEVEMENT

C. criticizes the prosecutor, C. Erucius, for presenting a weak case; he also
hints that the weakness of the prosecution makes it difficult for him to organize a refutation (§42). In fact, C. himself did not have much material; the
only evidence he adduces is a decree passed by the decurions of Ameria
declaring that the elder Roscius was wrongly proscribed and the son should
receive his property back (§25). He holds no witnesses in prospect, merely trying to intimidate a prospective prosecution witness (§§100–1) and criticizing
Chrysogonus, the current owner, for declining to make the slaves who witnessed the murder of the elder Roscius available for testimony under torture
(§§77–8, 119–23). In fact, C.'s lengthy speech in defense of his client is mostly
the product of his imagination, deployed to derive maximum advantage from
scanty materials.[53]

Treating the same material from different viewpoints can add weight
and persuasiveness. Thus at §24 the just narrated facts of the elder Roscius'
death and his son's dispossession are reviewed from the point of view of
the ordinary citizens of Ameria, the outrage of these third-party observers
reinforcing the jurors' feelings. A little later, at §§29–31, C. goes over the
facts that have just been disclosed in the *narratio* from his own point of view
as defense counsel: the situation is fraught with peril, but he will screw up
his courage to plead the case freely. Then to intensify still further and appeal
for pity, C. adds a restatement of the position from his client's point of view,
giving him a fictive speech (*sermocinatio*: §32); similarly, toward the end of the

---

[53] Canter 1931: 352 counts five digressions in our speech, a total exceeded only by *Ver.* 2.4
(eight); *pace* Canter (356–7) they are not to be explained by the weakness of the opposing case.

speech C. adds a fresh infusion of pathos with another *sermocinatio* by his client (§145).

C. differentiates his own point of view from that of Roscius jun. at §§130 and 143: the intervening criticism of Chrysogonus is purely his own, not his client's.[54] He similarly steps out of the *narratio* to add editorial comment exculpating Sulla from the proscription of the elder Sex. Roscius at §21–2. Elsewhere he likes to assume the rôle of the omniscient narrator, reporting as facts what are merely inferences. Thus he infers that the partnership (*societas*) for sharing the elder Roscius' goods was formed as soon as word of the murder was brought to Chrysogonus and imagines the reasoning that lay behind the plan (§20), even though it becomes clear in the course of the speech that one of the principals, T. Roscius Capito, only managed to extract his share under pressure of the embassy of the ten leading men of Ameria, who were later sent to complain to Sulla (§110). C. imagines another conversation among the members of the *societas* at §28 leading up to the decision to prosecute. Then at §110 he imagines the negotiations between Capito and Chrysogonus. All of these are constructed with great verisimilitude if one accepts C.'s premises; but to the skeptic they are plausible ways of portraying the opposing side as covering up murder (§110) and victimizing a vulnerable heir (§20).

C.'s problem is that his alternative suspect to his own client, namely Capito, was not at Rome on the day of the murder; and C. seeks to exculpate his client precisely on the grounds that he was not at Rome and lacked city connections (§§18, 74). The only connection he can construe between Capito and the murder is the fact that Mallius Glaucia, who brought word of the murder to Ameria, first stopped at Capito's house (§19). But stronger evidence points to a plot hatched between Magnus and Chrysogonus (see sec. 5 above). While ostensibly speaking freely (§§3, 30, 61), C. is, in fact, very careful to avoid giving serious offense to the *adulescens uel potentissimus* Chrysogonus (§6) by shielding him from the charge of murder (§§35, 122); and he is likewise careful to insulate Sulla from the charge he does level against Chrysogonus, namely that of improperly adding the elder Roscius' name to the list of those "killed in enemy fortifications" (§§21–2, 126–7, 131).

The *corona* and the senatorial jury fell under the spell of the young, impassioned orator, bursting into shouts of approbation at the overheated description of the parricide's punishment (§72; *Orat.* 107, cited n.35 above). Thus prepared, they probably also accepted C.'s vivid imaginative reconstruction

---

[54] Similarly, at *Clu.* 143–60 C. raises on his own the argument that Cluentius as an *eques* does not fall within the scope of the law on judicial murder; see further §129n.

of the crime and its immediate aftermath (§98) as the genuine article. Plutarch states that the defense of Roscius "succeeded" (*Cic.* 3.6), and in the sequel there was no case to which C. was thought to be unequal (*Brut.* 312). The speech made C.'s career.

9 THE AFTERLIFE OF THE SPEECH

Like C.'s other speeches, ours will have been published shortly after delivery to advertise his success and attract potential clients.[55] Though in later years he was slightly embarrassed by the purple passage about the parricide's sack (*Orat.* 107), representing the speech as a stroke *contra L. Sullae dominantis opes*,[56] he recommended it as reading for his son (*Off.* 2.51). The scholars Cornelius Nepos and Fenestella both tried their hand at placing the speech chronologically within C.'s career; both failed, however, and had to be corrected by Asconius Pedianus, whose remarks on the question probably derive from his (non-extant) commentary on the speech.[57] *Sex. Rosc.* was a staple of the rhetorical schools, as citations by Quintilian and others attest;[58] and there are the usual grammarians' quotations.[59] Unlike the *Verrines* or *Philippics*, however, the speech was not among the works used in set order by Nonius Marcellus.[60] The Gronovian scholia, quoting from material now in a lacuna, show that a fuller text was available to the end of antiquity.

The Middle Ages were not kind to *Sex. Rosc.*, inflicting damage at §132; and the speech fails to appear on lists of medieval set-books. Indeed, its survival hung by a single thread, the eighth-century Cluny MS (see below). Once the text was printed,[61] its history is largely the story of successive generations of editors laboring to purify and explain it. In the aftermath of the French Revolution, however, it contributed a word to political discourse: Desmoulins adapted the comparison of prosecutors to dogs (§§56–7); this struck a chord

---

[55] *aliter* Berry 2004 arguing for post-Sullan revision; but cf. on §§3, 22, 131, and 153.

[56] Plutarch's view that C. embarked on his study trip to Greece from 79–77 for fear of Sulla (*Cic.* 3.6–7) is to be rejected: C. remained in Rome after the trial and defended at least two other clients in 79 (cf. Marinone 2004: 59); and if that was his motivation, he might have been expected to return shortly after Sulla's death in 79; more convincing is C.'s own physiological explanation (*Brut.* 313); see also §6n.

[57] Gel. 15.28.1–4; cf. Wissowa, *RE* II 2.1525.38–60.

[58] Quint. *Inst.* 4.2.3 and 19; 9.2.53; 12.6.4; for citations by Fortunatus, Victorinus, Julius Victor, Martianus Capella, Rufinus, and Grillius cf. Kasten's collection of testimonies.

[59] Charisius, Diomedes, and Arusianus, all cited by Kasten.

[60] Cf. Schmidt 2000: 107–8.

[61] The Rome and Venice editions, both dated 1471.

with the public so that during the Terror "barker" (*aboyeur*) became a code-word for "informer."[62] In the mid-nineteenth century the British statesman and author Thomas Babington Macaulay showed a fine appreciation when he wrote in his journal: "read Cicero's Pro P. Quinctio Pro Rosc Amer and Pro Rosc Com skipping here and there – Liked the three speeches much. They are inferior in magnificence, no doubt, but superior, I think, in force and sharpness to the more celebrated orations of his manhood. They are capital speeches to juries."[63]

10 THE TEXT

Sex. Rosc. is one of a group of speeches that owe their preservation to a single MS, housed by AD 1158–61 in the monastery at Cluny. It was the merit of A. C. Clark to raise this witness (**C**), as it were, from the dead and show its importance.[64] By the date of the Council of Constance (AD 1414–17) C seems to have become known among French scholars, one of whom, Jean de Montreuil, called it to the attention of Poggio Bracciolini, who brought it to Italy, where it was copied and lost. But before it left, Nicolas de Clamanges made a copy at Paris (**Σ** = Paris. 14749). In addition, Poggio's traveling companion Bartolomeo da Montepulciano copied excerpts from C; these are preserved in Laurentian 54.5 (**B**).[65]

Before its disappearance C also spawned a number of Italian offspring; whether all derive from a lost intermediary or some directly from C remains to be clarified.[66] Editors divide the major ones between two families, the first consisting of Laurentian 68.10 (**A**), Perugia E71 (**π**), and Laurentian 52.1 (**φ**); the second of Pistoia A.32 (**σ**), Laurentian 48.25 (**χ**), and Laurentian 90 sup. 69 (**ψ**). In addition, a palimpsest fragment of the 5th century preserved in Vatican Pal. lat. 24 (**P**) gives access to an earlier stage of tradition for §§1–5. Quotations in scholia, grammarians, and rhetoricians also provide some control over the medieval tradition; see the previous section. The following are, apart from orthographica, the divergences of this edition from the last critical edition, that of F. Hinard, to whose critical apparatus reference is made for variants:

---

[62] Cf. Highet 1949: 398.
[63] Macaulay 2008: II 233 (12 April 1850).
[64] Clark 1905.
[65] Cf. Rouse and Reeve in Reynolds 1983: 88–91; Maslowski 1995: xliv–vi; Hinard and Benferhat 2005: lxxvii–lxxxviii.
[66] Rouse and Reeve in Reynolds 1983: 89.

Hinard	Dyck
2 si quis	si qui
7 aequa et	aequa ea et
8 uel hoc	hoc uel
11 sanguini dimissui	sanguine dimisso uirtutis
	ostentui
21 manceps	cuius bonorum manceps
22 reparet	sanet
24 flagitiosa, flagitiosa	flagitiosa,
24 audere	ardere
30 Roscio	T. Roscio
desunt	[desunt]
32 aut iuguletis aut condemnetis	iam iuguletis
33 quae tantum potuit	qui tantum potuit
ipse ab eis	ab iis ipsis
35 accusator Erucius	C. Erucius
38 et denique	[et] denique
39 luxurie	luxuria
40 et plurimis	plurimis
42 relegarat	relegauit
47 Veienti	Veiente
nostram	[nostram]
49 maximae	maxime
56 uenerint et . . . tametsi	uenerint . . . et tametsi
61 confitere huc	aut confitere te huc
62 uel maxime	et maxime
64 reperiebatur	reperiretur
73 ita	et ita
Eruci quomodo	Eruci [quomodo]
74 si Ameriae . . . si Romae	si Ameria . . . si Roma
hi	ii
77 et te, Metelle	te, M. Metelle
80 tamen	tandem
81 fuerit . . . nesciret	fuit . . . nesciuit
90 Mammios	Memmios
96 Roscio Capitoni[1]	T. Roscio Capitoni

(cont.)

(cont.)

Hinard	Dyck
98 capienda sit	capienda est
99 uoluerit	uellet
102 atque adeo	atque [ad]
an	ac non
106 suspicionem	suspicione me ponere
108 Roscius	T. Roscius
112 posse	non posse
quod maxime uidetur graue	quod minime uidetur leue
114 ille qui	illeque
115 Roscio	T. Roscio
117 legationis offici	[legationis] offici
120 neque enim	neque [enim]
124 Chrysogoni	[Chrysogoni]
se esse	sese
126 quo modo	quo more
129 mihi	mihi ipsi
quae ad huius uitae casum	quae ad huius uitam
causamque pertinent	causamque pertineant
132 <... > hoc iudicium	[hoc iudicium]
Deriuat crimen et expedit se	deriuat tamen et ait se
133 quid praeco enumeraret	praeconem numerare
137 in isto bello	isto bello
141 exspectata	spectata
142 prope	probe
149 Messalla	M. Messalla
151 ne hoc	ut hoc
154 horis	omnibus horis

M. TVLLI CICERONIS
ORATIO PRO SEXTO ROSCIO

ORATIO PRO SEXTO ROSCIO

[1] Credo ego uos, iudices, mirari quid sit quod, cum tot summi oratores **1** hominesque nobilissimi sedeant, ego potissimum surrexerim, is qui neque aetate neque ingenio neque auctoritate sim cum his qui sedeant comparandus. omnes enim hi quos uidetis adesse in hac causa iniuriam nouo scelere conflatam putant oportere defendi, defendere ipsi propter iniquitatem temporum non audent. ita fit ut adsint propterea quod officium sequuntur, taceant autem idcirco quia periculum uitant. quid ergo? audacissimus ego ex **2** omnibus? minime. an tanto officiosior quam ceteri? ne istius quidem laudis ita sum cupidus ut aliis eam praereptam uelim. quae me igitur res praeter ceteros impulit ut causam Sex. Rosci reciperem? quia, si qui istorum dixisset quos uidetis adesse, in quibus summa auctoritas est atque amplitudo, si uerbum de re publica fecisset, id quod in hac causa fieri necesse est, multo plura dixisse quam dixisset putaretur. ego autem si omnia quae dicenda sunt libere **3** dixero, nequaquam tamen similiter oratio mea exire atque in uulgus emanare poterit. deinde quod ceterorum neque dictum obscurum potest esse propter nobilitatem et amplitudinem neque temere dicto concedi propter aetatem et prudentiam, ego si quid liberius dixero, uel occultum esse propterea quod nondum ad rem publicam accessi, uel ignosci adulescentiae meae poterit; tametsi non modo ignoscendi ratio uerum etiam cognoscendi consuetudo iam de ciuitate sublata est. accedit illa quoque causa quod a ceteris forsitan **4** ita petitum sit ut dicerent ut utrumuis saluo officio se facere posse arbitrarentur; a me autem ii contenderunt qui apud me et amicitia et beneficiis et dignitate plurimum possunt. quorum ego nec beneuolentiam erga me ignorare nec auctoritatem aspernari nec uoluntatem neglegere debebam. [2] his **5** de causis ego huic causae patronus exstiti, non electus unus qui maximo ingenio sed relictus ex omnibus qui minimo periculo possem dicere, neque uti satis firmo praesidio defensus Sex. Roscius uerum uti ne omnino desertus esset.

Forsitan quaeratis qui iste terror sit et quae tanta formido quae tot ac tales uiros impediat quominus pro capite et fortunis alterius quemadmodum consuerunt causam uelint dicere. quod adhuc uos ignorare non mirum est, propterea quod consulto ab accusatoribus eius rei quae conflauit hoc iudicium mentio facta non est. quae res ea est? bona patris huiusce Sex. Rosci, **6** quae sunt sexagiens, quae de uiro fortissimo et clarissimo L. Sulla, quem honoris causa nomino, duobus milibus nummum sese dicit emisse adulescens uel potentissimus hoc tempore nostrae ciuitatis, L. Cornelius Chrysogonus. is

a uobis, iudices, hoc postulat ut, quoniam in alienam pecuniam tam plenam
atque praeclaram nullo iure inuaserit quoniamque ei pecuniae uita Sex.
Rosci obstare atque officere uideatur, deleatis ex animo suo suspicionem
omnem metumque tollatis: sese hoc incolumi non arbitratur huius innocentis patrimonium tam amplum et copiosum posse obtinere, damnato et eiecto
sperat se posse quod adeptus est per scelus, id per luxuriam effundere atque
consumere. hunc sibi ex animo scrupulum, qui se dies noctesque stimulat
ac pungit, ut euellatis postulat, ut ad hanc suam praedam tam nefariam
adiutores uos profiteamini.

7   Si uobis aequa ea et honesta postulatio uidetur, iudices, ego contra breuem
postulationem affero et, quomodo mihi persuadeo, aliquanto aequiorem. [3]
primum a Chrysogono peto ut pecunia fortunisque nostris contentus sit,
sanguinem et uitam ne petat; deinde a uobis, iudices, ut audacium sceleri
resistatis, innocentium calamitatem leuetis et in causa Sex. Rosci pericu-
8 lum quod in omnes intenditur propulsetis. quodsi aut causa criminis aut
facti suspicio aut quaelibet denique uel minima res reperietur quamobrem
uideantur illi nonnihil tamen in deferendo nomine secuti, postremo si praeter
eam praedam quam dixi quicquam aliud causae inueneritis, non recusamus
quin illorum libidini Sex. Rosci uita dedatur. sin aliud agitur nihil nisi ut iis
ne quid desit quibus satis nihil est, si hoc solum hoc tempore pugnatur ut ad
illam opimam praeclaramque praedam damnatio Sex. Rosci uelut cumulus
accedat, nonne cum multa indigna tum hoc uel indignissimum est, uos idoneos habitos per quorum sententias iusque iurandum id assequantur quod
antea ipsi scelere et ferro assequi consuerunt? qui ex ciuitate in senatum
propter dignitatem, ex senatu in hoc consilium delecti estis propter seueritatem, ab his hoc postulare homines sicarios atque gladiatores, non modo
ut supplicia uitent quae a uobis pro maleficiis suis metuere atque horrere
debent, uerum etiam ut spoliis ex hoc iudicio ornati auctique discedant?

9   [4] His de rebus tantis tamque atrocibus neque satis me commode dicere
neque satis grauiter conqueri neque satis libere uociferari posse intellego. nam
commoditati ingenium, grauitati aetas, libertati tempora sunt impedimento.
huc accedit summus timor quem mihi natura pudorque meus attribuit et
uestra dignitas et uis aduersariorum et Sex. Rosci pericula. quapropter uos
oro atque obsecro, iudices, ut attente bonaque cum uenia uerba mea audi-
10 atis. fide sapientiaque uestra fretus plus oneris sustuli quam ferre me posse
intellego. hoc onus si uos aliqua ex parte alleuabitis, feram ut potero studio
et industria, iudices; sin a uobis — id quod non spero — deserar, tamen
animo non deficiam et id quod suscepi, quoad potero, perferam. quod si
perferre non potero, opprimi me onere offici malo quam id quod mihi cum

fide semel impositum est aut propter perfidiam abicere aut propter infirmi-
tatem animi deponere. te quoque magnopere, M. Fanni, quaeso ut qualem **11**
te iam antea populo Romano praebuisti, cum huic eidem quaestioni iudex
praeesses, talem te et nobis et rei publicae hoc tempore impertias. [5] quanta
multitudo hominum conuenerit ad hoc iudicium uides; quae sit omnium mortalium exspectatio, quae cupiditas ut acria ac seuera iudicia fiant intellegis.
longo interuallo iudicium inter sicarios hoc primum committitur, cum interea
caedes indignissimae maximaeque factae sunt; omnes hanc quaestionem te
praetore manifestis maleficiis cotidianoque sanguine dimisso uirtutis ostentui
sperant futuram.

Qua uociferatione in ceteris iudiciis accusatores uti consuerunt, ea nos hoc **12**
tempore utimur qui causam dicimus. petimus abs te, M. Fanni, a uobisque,
iudices, ut quam acerrime maleficia uindicetis, ut quam fortissime hominibus
audacissimis resistatis, ut hoc cogitetis, nisi in hac causa qui uester animus
sit ostendetis, eo prorumpere hominum cupiditatem et scelus et audaciam ut
non modo clam uerum etiam hic in foro ante tribunal tuum, M. Fanni, ante
pedes uestros, iudices, inter ipsa subsellia caedes futurae sint. etenim quid **13**
aliud hoc iudicio temptatur nisi ut id fieri liceat? accusant ii qui in fortunas
huius inuaserunt, causam dicit is cui praeter calamitatem nihil reliquerunt;
accusant ii quibus occidi patrem Sex. Rosci bono fuit, causam dicit is cui non
modo luctum mors patris attulit uerum etiam egestatem; accusant ii qui hunc
ipsum iugulare summe cupierunt, causam dicit is qui etiam ad hoc ipsum
iudicium cum praesidio uenit ne hic ibidem ante oculos uestros trucidetur;
denique accusant ii quos populus poscit, causam dicit is qui unus relictus
ex illorum nefaria caede restat. atque ut facilius intellegere possitis, iudices, **14**
ea quae facta sunt indigniora esse quam haec sunt quae dicimus, ab initio
res quemadmodum gesta sit uobis exponemus, quo facilius et huius hominis
innocentissimi miserias et illorum audacias cognoscere possitis et rei publicae
calamitatem.

[6] Sex. Roscius, pater huiusce, municeps Amerinus fuit, cum genere et **15**
nobilitate et pecunia non modo sui municipi uerum etiam eius uicinitatis
facile primus, tum gratia atque hospitiis florens hominum nobilissimorum.
nam cum Metellis, Seruiliis, Scipionibus erat ei non modo hospitium uerum
etiam domesticus usus et consuetudo, quas, ut aequum est, familias honestatis
amplitudinisque gratia nomino. itaque ex suis omnibus commodis hoc solum
filio reliquit; nam patrimonium domestici praedones ui ereptum possident,
fama et uita innocentis ab hospitibus amicisque paternis defenditur. hic **16**
cum omni tempore nobilitatis fautor fuisset tum hoc tumultu proximo, cum
omnium nobilium dignitas et salus in discrimen ueniret, praeter ceteros in

ea uicinitate eam partem causamque opera, studio, auctoritate defendit. etenim rectum putabat pro eorum honestate se pugnare propter quos ipse honestissimus inter suos numerabatur. posteaquam uictoria constituta est ab armisque recessimus, cum proscriberentur homines atque ex omni regione caperentur ii qui aduersarii fuisse putabantur, erat ille Romae frequens atque in foro et in ore omnium cotidie uersabatur, magis ut exsultare uictoria nobilitatis uideretur quam timere ne quid ex ea calamitatis sibi accideret.

17 Erant ei ueteres inimicitiae cum duobus Rosciis Amerinis, quorum alterum sedere in accusatorum subselliis uideo, alterum tria huiusce praedia possidere audio; quas inimicitias si tam cauere potuisset quam metuere solebat, uiueret. neque enim, iudices, iniuria metuebat. nam duo isti sunt T. Roscii — quorum alteri Capitoni cognomen est, iste qui adest Magnus uocatur — homines eiusmodi: alter plurimarum palmarum uetus ac nobilis gladiator habetur, hic autem nuper se ad eum lanistam contulit, quique ante hanc pugnam tiro esset, quod sciam, facile ipsum magistrum scelere audaci-

18 aque superauit. [7] nam cum hic Sex. Roscius esset Ameriae, T. autem iste Roscius Romae, cum hic filius assiduus in praediis esset cumque se uoluntate patris rei familiari uitaeque rusticae dedisset, iste autem frequens Romae esset, occiditur ad balneas Pallacinas rediens a cena Sex. Roscius. spero ex hoc ipso non esse obscurum ad quem suspicio malefici pertineat; uerum id quod adhuc est suspiciosum, nisi perspicuum res ipsa fecerit, hunc affinem culpae iudicatote.

19 Occiso Sex. Roscio primus Ameriam nuntiat Mallius Glaucia quidam, homo tenuis, libertinus, cliens et familiaris istius T. Rosci, et nuntiat domum non fili sed T. Capitonis inimici; et cum post horam primam noctis occisus esset, primo diluculo nuntius hic Ameriam uenit; decem horis nocturnis sex et quinquaginta milia passuum cisiis peruolauit, non modo ut exoptatum inimico nuntium primus afferret sed etiam cruorem inimici quam recentissi-

20 mum telumque paulo ante e corpore extractum ostenderet. quadriduo quo haec gesta sunt res ad Chrysogonum in castra L. Sullae Volaterras defertur; magnitudo pecuniae demonstratur; bonitas praediorum — nam fundos decem et tres reliquit qui Tiberim fere omnes tangunt —, huius inopia et solitudo commemoratur; demonstrant, cum pater huiusce Sex. Roscius, homo tam splendidus et gratiosus, nullo negotio sit occisus, perfacile hunc hominem incautum et rusticum et Romae ignotum de medio tolli posse; ad eam rem operam suam pollicentur. ne diutius teneam, iudices, societas

21 coitur. [8] cum nulla iam proscriptionis mentio fieret, cum etiam qui antea metuerant redirent ac iam defunctos sese periculis arbitrarentur, nomen refertur in tabulas Sex. Rosci, hominis studiosissimi nobilitatis, cuius bonorum manceps fit Chrysogonus; tria praedia uel nobilissima Capitoni propria traduntur, quae hodie possidet; in reliquas omnes fortunas iste T. Roscius nomine Chrysogoni, quemadmodum ipse dicit, impetum facit. haec omnia, iudices, imprudente L. Sulla facta esse certo scio. neque enim mirum, cum **22** eodem tempore et ea quae praeterita sunt sanet et ea quae uidentur instare praeparet, cum et pacis constituendae rationem et belli gerendi potestatem solus habeat, cum omnes in unum spectent, unus omnia gubernet, cum tot tantisque negotiis distentus sit ut respirare libere non possit, si aliquid non animaduertat, cum praesertim tam multi occupationem eius obseruent tempusque aucupentur ut, simul atque ille despexerit, aliquid huiuscemodi moliantur. huc accedit quod, quamuis ille felix sit, sicut est, tamen in tanta felicitate nemo potest esse in magna familia qui neminem neque seruum neque libertum improbum habeat. interea iste T. Roscius, uir opti- **23** mus, procurator Chrysogoni, Ameriam uenit, in praedia huius inuadit, hunc miserum, luctu perditum, qui nondum etiam omnia paterno funeri iusta soluisset, nudum eicit domo atque focis patriis disque penatibus praecipitem, iudices, exturbat, ipse amplissimae pecuniae fit dominus. qui in sua re fuisset egentissimus, erat, ut fit, insolens in aliena: multa palam domum suam auferebat, plura clam de medio remouebat, non pauca suis adiutoribus large effuseque donabat, reliqua constituta auctione uendebat.

[9] Quod Amerinis usque eo uisum est indignum ut urbe tota fletus gemi- **24** tusque fieret. etenim multa simul ante oculos uersabantur: mors hominis florentissimi Sex. Rosci crudelissima, fili autem eius egestas indignissima, cui de tanto patrimonio praedo iste nefarius ne iter quidem ad sepulcrum patrium reliquisset, bonorum emptio flagitiosa, possessio, furta, rapinae, donationes. nemo erat qui non ardere omnia mallet quam uidere in Sex. Rosci, uiri optimi atque honestissimi, bonis iactantem se ac dominantem T. Roscium. itaque decurionum decretum statim fit ut decem primi profi- **25** ciscantur ad L. Sullam doceantque eum qui uir Sex. Roscius fuerit, conquerantur de istorum scelere et iniuriis, orent ut et illius mortui famam et fili innocentis fortunas conseruatas uelit. atque ipsum decretum, quaeso, cognoscite.

DECRETVM DECVRIONVM

legati in castra ueniunt. intellegitur, iudices, id quod iam ante dixi, imprudente L. Sulla scelera haec et flagitia fieri. nam statim Chrysogonus et ipse ad eos accedit et homines nobiles allegat qui peterent ne ad Sullam adirent et omnia Chrysogonum quae uellent esse facturum pollicerentur. usque adeo **26** autem ille pertimuerat ut mori mallet quam de his rebus Sullam doceri. homines antiqui qui ex sua natura ceteros fingerent, cum ille confirmaret

sese nomen Sex. Rosci de tabulis exempturum, praedia uacua filio traditurum, cumque id ita futurum T. Roscius Capito, qui in decem legatis
erat, appromitteret, crediderunt; Ameriam re inorata reuerterunt. ac primo
rem differre cotidie ac procrastinare isti coeperunt, deinde aliquanto lentius
nihil agere atque deludere, postremo, id quod facile intellectum est, insidias
uitae huiusce Sex. Rosci parare neque sese arbitrari posse diutius alienam
27 pecuniam domino incolumi obtinere. [10] quod hic simul atque sensit, de
amicorum cognatorumque sententia Romam confugit et sese ad Caeciliam,
Nepotis sororem, Baliarici filiam, quam honoris causa nomino, contulit, qua
pater usus erat plurimum. in qua muliere, iudices, etiamnunc, id quod omnes
semper existimauerunt, quasi exempli causa uestigia antiqui offici remanent.
ea Sex. Roscium inopem, eiectum domo atque expulsum ex suis bonis,
fugientem latronum tela et minas recepit domum hospitique oppresso iam
desperatoque ab omnibus opitulata est. eius uirtute, fide, diligentia factum
est ut hic potius uiuus in reos quam occisus in proscriptos referretur.
28   Nam postquam isti intellexerunt summa diligentia uitam Sex. Rosci cus-
todiri neque sibi ullam caedis faciendae potestatem dari, consilium ceperunt
plenum sceleris et audaciae ut nomen huius de parricidio deferrent, ut ad
eam rem aliquem accusatorem ueterem compararent qui de ea re posset
dicere aliquid in qua re nulla subesset suspicio, denique ut, quoniam crimine non poterant, tempore ipso pugnarent. ita loqui homines: quod iudicia
tam diu facta non essent, condemnari eum oportere qui primus in iudicium
adductus esset; huic autem patronos propter Chrysogoni gratiam defuturos;
de bonorum uenditione et de ista societate uerbum esse facturum neminem;
ipso nomine parricidi et atrocitate criminis fore ut hic nullo negotio tolleretur,
29 cum ab nullo defensus esset. hoc consilio atque adeo hac amentia impulsi
quem ipsi, cum cuperent, non potuerunt occidere, eum iugulandum uobis
tradiderunt.
    [11] Quid primum querar aut unde potissimum, iudices, ordiar aut quod
aut a quibus auxilium petam? deorumne immortalium, populine Romani
uestramne qui summam potestatem habetis hoc tempore fidem implorem?
30 pater occisus nefarie, domus obsessa ab inimicis, bona adempta, possessa,
direpta, fili uita infesta, saepe ferro atque insidiis appetita. quid ab his tot
maleficiis sceleris abesse uidetur? tamen haec aliis nefariis cumulant atque
adaugent, crimen incredibile confingunt, testes in hunc et accusatores huiusce
pecunia comparant; hanc condicionem misero ferunt ut optet utrum malit
ceruices T. Roscio dare an insutus in culleum per summum dedecus uitam
amittere. patronos huic defuturos putauerunt; qui libere dicat, qui cum fide
31 defendat, id quod in hac causa satis est, non deest profecto, iudices. et
forsitan in suscipienda causa temere impulsus adulescentia fecerim; quoniam quidem semel suscepi, licet hercules undique omnes in me terrores

periculaque impendeant omnia, succurram ac subibo. certum est deliberatumque quae ad causam pertinere arbitror, omnia non modo dicere uerum
etiam libenter audacter libereque dicere; nulla res tanta exsistet, iudices, ut
possit uim mihi maiorem adhibere metus quam fides. etenim quis tam disso- **32**
luto animo est qui haec cum uideat tacere ac neglegere possit? 'patrem meum,
cum proscriptus non esset, iugulastis, occisum in proscriptorum numerum
rettulistis, me domo mea per uim expulistis, patrimonium meum possidetis.'
quid uultis amplius? etiamne ad subsellia cum ferro atque telis uenistis ut hic
iam iuguletis Sex. Roscium?

[12] Hominem longe audacissimum nuper habuimus in ciuitate C. Fim- **33**
briam et, quod inter omnes constat, nisi inter eos qui ipsi quoque insaniunt
insanissimum. is cum curasset in funere C. Mari ut Q. Scaeuola uulner-
aretur, uir sanctissimus atque ornatissimus nostrae ciuitatis, de cuius laude
neque hic locus est ut multa dicantur neque plura tamen dici possunt quam
populus Romanus memoria retinet, diem Scaeuolae dixit posteaquam com-
perit eum posse uiuere. cum ab eo quaereretur quid tandem accusaturus
esset eum quem pro dignitate ne laudare quidem quisquam satis commode
posset, aiunt hominem, ut erat furiosus, respondisse: quod non totum telum
corpore recepisset. quo populus Romanus nihil uidit indignius nisi eiusdem
uiri mortem, qui tantum potuit ut omnes occisus perdiderit et afflixerit; quos
quia seruare per compositionem uolebat, ab iis ipsis interemptus est. estne **34**
hoc illi dicto atque facto Fimbriano simillimum? accusatis Sex. Roscium.
quid ita? quia de manibus uestris effugit, quia se occidi passus non est. illud,
quia in Scaeuola factum est, magis indignum uidetur, hoc, quia fit a Chrysogono, non est ferendum. nam per deos immortales! quid est in hac causa
quod defensionis indigeat? qui locus ingenium patroni requirit aut oratoris
eloquentiam magnopere desiderat? totam causam, iudices, explicemus atque
ante oculos expositam consideremus; ita facillime quae res totum iudicium
contineat et quibus de rebus nos dicere oporteat et quid uos sequi conueniat
intellegetis.

[13] Tres sunt res, quantum ego existimare possum, quae obstent hoc tem- **35**
pore Sex. Roscio, crimen aduersariorum et audacia et potentia. criminis confictionem C. Erucius suscepit, audaciae partes Roscii sibi poposcerunt, Chrysogonus autem, is qui plurimum potest, potentia pugnat. de hisce omnibus
rebus me dicere oportere intellego. quid igitur est? non eodem modo **36**
de omnibus, ideo quod prima illa res ad meum officium pertinet, duas autem
reliquas uobis populus Romanus imposuit: ego crimen oportet diluam, uos
et audaciae resistere et hominum eiusmodi perniciosam atque intolerandam
potentiam primo quoque tempore exstinguere atque opprimere debetis.

Occidisse patrem Sex. Roscius arguitur. scelestum, di immortales! ac **37**
nefarium facinus atque eiusmodi quo uno maleficio scelera omnia complexa

esse uideantur! etenim si, id quod praeclare a sapientibus dicitur, uultu saepe
laeditur pietas, quod supplicium satis acre reperietur in eum qui mortem
obtulerit parenti, pro quo mori ipsum, si res postularet, iura diuina atque
38 humana cogebant? in hoc tanto, tam atroci, tam singulari maleficio, quod ita
raro exstitit ut, si quando auditum sit, portenti ac prodigi simile numeretur,
quibus tandem tu, C. Eruci, argumentis accusatorem censes uti oportere?
nonne et audaciam eius qui in crimen uocetur singularem ostendere et mores
feros immanemque naturam et uitam uitiis flagitiisque omnibus deditam,
denique omnia ad perniciem profligata atque perdita? quorum tu nihil in
Sex. Roscium ne obiciendi quidem causa contulisti.

39   [14] Patrem occidit Sex. Roscius. qui homo? adulescentulus corrup-
tus et ab hominibus nequam inductus? annos natus maior quadraginta.
uetus uidelicet sicarius, homo audax et saepe in caede uersatus? at hoc ab
accusatore ne dici quidem audistis. luxuries igitur hominem nimirum et aeris
alieni magnitudo et indomitae animi cupiditates ad hoc scelus impulerunt?
de luxuria purgauit Erucius cum dixit hunc ne in conuiuio quidem ullo fere
interfuisse. nihil autem umquam debuit. cupiditates porro quae possunt esse
in eo qui, ut ipse accusator obiecit, ruri semper habitarit et in agro colendo
uixerit? quae uita maxime disiuncta a cupiditate et cum officio coniuncta est.

40   Quae res igitur tantum istum furorem Sex. Roscio obiecit? 'patri' inquit
'non placebat.' patri non placebat? quam ob causam? necesse est enim eam
quoque iustam et magnam et perspicuam fuisse. nam ut illud incredibile est,
mortem oblatam esse patri a filio sine plurimis et maximis causis, sic hoc
ueri simile non est, odio fuisse parenti filium sine causis multis et magnis et
41 necessariis. rursus igitur eodem reuertamur et quaeramus quae tanta uitia
fuerint in unico filio quare is patri displiceret. at perspicuum est nullum
fuisse. pater igitur amens, qui odisset eum sine causa quem procrearat? at
is quidem fuit omnium constantissimus. ergo illud iam perspicuum profecto
est, si neque amens pater neque perditus filius fuerit, neque odi causam patri
neque sceleris filio fuisse.

42   [15] 'Nescio' inquit 'quae causa odi fuerit; fuisse odium intellego quia
antea, cum duos filios haberet, illum alterum qui mortuus est secum omni
tempore uolebat esse, hunc in praedia rustica relegauit.' quod Erucio accidebat in mala nugatoriaque accusatione, idem mihi usu uenit in causa optima:
ille quomodo crimen commenticium confirmaret non inueniebat, ego res tam
43 leues qua ratione infirmem ac diluam reperire non possum. quid ais, Eruci?
tot praedia, tam pulchra, tam fructuosa Sex. Roscius filio suo relegationis
ac supplici gratia colenda ac tuenda tradiderat? quid? hoc patres familiae
qui liberos habent, praesertim homines illius ordinis ex municipiis rusticanis,
nonne optatissimum sibi putant esse filios suos rei familiari maxime seruire

et in praediis colendis operae plurimum studique consumere? an amandarat **44**
hunc sic ut esset in agro ac tantummodo aleretur ad uillam, ut commodis
omnibus careret? quid? si constat hunc non modo colendis praediis prae-
fuisse sed certis fundis patre uiuo frui solitum esse, tamenne haec a te uita
eius rusticana relegatio atque amandatio appellabitur? uides, Eruci, quantum distet argumentatio tua ab re ipsa atque a ueritate: quod consuetudine
patres faciunt, id quasi nouum reprehendis; quod beneuolentia fit, id odio
factum criminaris; quod honoris causa pater filio suo concessit, id eum supplici causa fecisse dicis. neque haec tu non intellegis, sed usque eo quid arguas **45**
non habes, ut non modo tibi contra nos dicendum putes uerum etiam contra
rerum naturam contraque consuetudinem hominum contraque opiniones
omnium.

[16] 'At enim, cum duos filios haberet, alterum a se non dimittebat, alterum
ruri esse patiebatur.' quaeso, Eruci, ut hoc in bonam partem accipias; non
enim exprobrandi causa sed commonendi gratia dicam. si tibi fortuna non **46**
dedit ut patre certo nascerere ex quo intellegere posses qui animus patrius
in liberos esset, at natura certe dedit ut humanitatis non parum haberes; eo
accessit studium doctrinae ut ne a litteris quidem alienus esses. ecquid tandem tibi uidetur, ut ad fabulas ueniamus, senex ille Caecilianus minoris facere
Eutychum filium rusticum quam illum alterum, Chaerestratum — nam, ut
opinor, hoc nomine est — alterum in urbe secum honoris causa habere,
alterum rus supplici causa relegasse? 'quid ad istas ineptias abis?' inquies. **47**
quasi uero mihi difficile sit quamuis multos nominatim proferre, ne longius
abeam, uel tribules uel uicinos meos qui suos liberos, quos plurimi faciunt,
agricolas assiduos esse cupiunt. uerum homines notos sumere odiosum est,
cum et illud incertum sit uelintne ii sese nominari, et nemo uobis magis
notus futurus sit quam est hic Eutychus, et certe ad rem nihil intersit utrum
hunc ego comicum adulescentem an aliquem ex agro Veiente nominem.
etenim haec conficta arbitror esse a poetis ut effictos nostros mores in alienis personis expressamque imaginem uitae cotidianae uideremus. age nunc, **48**
refer animum sis ad ueritatem et considera non modo in Vmbria atque in
ea uicinitate sed in his ueteribus municipiis quae studia a patribus familias maxime laudentur; iam profecto te intelleges inopia criminum summam
laudem Sex. Roscio uitio et culpae dedisse. [17] ac non modo hoc patrum
uoluntate liberi faciunt sed permultos et ego noui et, nisi me fallit animus,
unus quisque uestrum qui et ipsi incensi sunt studio quod ad agrum colen-
dum attinet, uitamque hanc rusticam, quam tu probro et crimini putas esse
oportere, et honestissimam et suauissimam esse arbitrantur. quid censes hunc **49**
ipsum Sex. Roscium quo studio et qua intellegentia esse in rusticis rebus?
ut ex his propinquis eius, hominibus honestissimis, audio, non tu in isto

artificio accusatorio callidior es quam hic in suo. uerum, ut opinor, quoniam ita Chrysogono uidetur, qui huic nullum praedium reliquit, et artificium obliuiscatur et studium deponat licebit. quod tametsi miserum et indignum est, feret tamen aequo animo, iudices, si per uos uitam et famam potest obtinere; hoc uero est quod ferri non potest, si et in hanc calamitatem uenit propter praediorum bonitatem et multitudinem et quod ea studiose coluit, id erit ei maxime fraudi, ut parum miseriae sit quod aliis coluit, non sibi, nisi etiam quod omnino coluit crimini fuerit.

50   [18] Ne tu, Eruci, accusator esses ridiculus, si illis temporibus natus esses cum ab aratro arcessebantur qui consules fierent. etenim qui praeesse agro colendo flagitium putes, profecto illum Atilium quem sua manu spargentem semen qui missi erant conuenerunt hominem turpissimum atque inhonestissimum iudicares. at hercule maiores nostri longe aliter et de illo et de ceteris talibus uiris existimabant itaque ex minima tenuissimaque re publica maximam et florentissimam nobis reliquerunt. suos enim agros studiose colebant, non alienos cupide appetebant; quibus rebus et agris et urbibus et nationibus rem publicam atque hoc imperium et populi Romani nomen auxerunt.

51   neque ego haec eo profero quo conferenda sint cum hisce de quibus nunc quaerimus, sed ut illud intellegatur, cum apud maiores nostros summi uiri clarissimique homines, qui omni tempore ad gubernacula rei publicae sedere debebant, tamen in agris quoque colendis aliquantum operae temporisque consumpserunt, ignosci oportere ei homini qui se fateatur esse rusticum, cum ruri assiduus semper uixerit, cum praesertim nihil esset quod aut patri gratius aut sibi iucundius aut re uera honestius facere posset.

52   Odium igitur acerrimum patris in filium ex hoc, opinor, ostenditur, Eruci, quod hunc ruri esse patiebatur. numquid est aliud? 'immo uero' inquit 'est; nam istum exheredare in animo habebat.' audio; nunc dicis aliquid quod ad rem pertineat; nam illa, opinor, tu quoque concedis leuia esse atque inepta: 'conuiuia cum patre non inibat.' quippe qui ne in oppidum quidem nisi perraro ueniret. 'domum suam istum non fere quisquam uocabat.' nec mirum, 53   qui neque in urbe uiueret neque reuocaturus esset. [19] uerum haec tu quoque intellegis esse nugatoria; illud quod coepimus uideamus, quo certius argumentum odi reperiri nullo modo potest. 'exheredare pater filium cogitabat.' mitto quaerere qua de causa; quaero qui scias; tametsi te dicere atque enumerare causas omnes oportebat, et id erat certi accusatoris officium qui tanti sceleris argueret explicare omnia uitia ac peccata fili quibus incensus parens potuerit animum inducere ut naturam ipsam uinceret, ut amorem illum penitus insitum eiceret ex animo, ut denique patrem esse sese obliuisceretur; quae sine magnis huiusce peccatis accidere potuisse non arbitror.

uerum concedo tibi ut ea praetereas quae, cum taces, nulla esse concedis; **54**
illud quidem, uoluisse exheredare, certe tu planum facere debes. quid ergo
affers quare id factum putemus? uere nihil potes dicere; finge aliquid saltem
commode ut ne plane uidearis id facere quod aperte facis, huius miseri fortunis et horum uirorum talium dignitati illudere. 'exheredare filium uoluit.'
quam ob causam? 'nescio.' exheredauitne? 'non.' quis prohibuit? 'cogitabat.'
cogitabat? cui dixit? 'nemini.' quid est aliud iudicio ac legibus ac maiestate
uestra abuti ad quaestum atque ad libidinem nisi hoc modo accusare atque
id obicere quod planum facere non modo non possis uerum ne coneris quidem? nemo nostrum est, Eruci, quin sciat tibi inimicitias cum Sex. Roscio **55**
nullas esse; uident omnes qua de causa huic inimicus uenias; sciunt huiusce
pecunia te adductum esse. quid ergo est? ita tamen quaestus te cupidum
esse oportebat ut horum existimationem et legem Remmiam putares aliquid
ualere oportere.

[20] Accusatores multos esse in ciuitate utile est ut metu contineatur
audacia; uerum tamen hoc ita est utile ut ne plane illudamur ab accusatoribus.
innocens est quispiam, uerumtamen, quamquam abest a culpa, suspicione
tamen non caret; tametsi miserum est, tamen ei qui hunc accuset possim
aliquomodo ignoscere. cum enim aliquid habeat quod possit criminose ac
suspiciose dicere, aperte ludificari et calumniari sciens non uideatur. quare **56**
facile omnes patimur esse quam plurimos accusatores, quod innocens, si
accusatus sit, absolui potest, nocens, nisi accusatus fuerit, condemnari non
potest; utilius est autem absolui innocentem quam nocentem causam non
dicere. anseribus cibaria publice locantur et canes aluntur in Capitolio ut
significent si fures uenerint. at fures internoscere non possunt, significant
tamen si qui noctu in Capitolium uenerint quia id est suspiciosum, et tametsi
bestiae sunt, tamen in eam partem potius peccant quae est cautior. quodsi luce
quoque canes latrent cum deos salutatum aliqui uenerint, opinor, eis crura
suffringantur, quod acres sint etiam tum cum suspicio nulla sit. simillima **57**
est accusatorum ratio. alii uestrum anseres sunt, qui tantummodo clamant,
nocere non possunt, alii canes, qui et latrare et mordere possunt. cibaria
uobis praeberi uidemus; uos autem maxime debetis in eos impetum facere
qui merentur; hoc populo gratissimum est. deinde, si uoletis, etiam tum cum
uerisimile erit aliquem commisisse, in suspicione latratote; id quoque concedi
potest. sin autem sic agetis ut arguatis aliquem patrem occidisse neque dicere
possitis aut quare aut quomodo, ac tantummodo sine suspicione latrabitis,
crura quidem uobis nemo suffringet, sed, si ego hos bene noui, litteram
illam cui uos usque eo inimici estis ut etiam Kalendas omnes oderitis ita
uehementer ad caput affigent ut postea neminem alium nisi fortunas uestras
accusare possitis.

58 [21] Quid mihi ad defendendum dedisti, bone accusator? quid hisce autem ad suspicandum? 'ne exheredaretur ueritus est.' audio, sed qua de causa uereri debuerit nemo dicit. 'habebat pater in animo.' planum fac. nihil est; non quicum deliberarit, quem certiorem fecerit, unde istud uobis suspicari in mentem uenerit. cum hoc modo accusas, Eruci, nonne hoc palam dicis: 'ego quid acceperim scio, quid dicam nescio; unum illud spectaui quod Chrysogonus aiebat neminem isti patronum futurum; de bonorum emptione deque ea societate neminem esse qui uerbum facere auderet hoc tempore'? haec te opinio falsa in istam fraudem impulit; non mehercules uerbum fecisses, si tibi quemquam responsurum putasses.

59 Operae pretium erat, si animaduertistis, iudices, neglegentiam eius in accusando considerare. credo, cum uidisset qui homines in hisce subselliis sederent, quaesisse num ille aut ille defensurus esset; de me ne suspicatum quidem esse, quod antea causam publicam nullam dixerim. posteaquam inuenit neminem eorum qui possunt et solent, ita neglegens esse coepit ut, cum in mentem ueniret ei, resideret, deinde spatiaretur, nonnumquam etiam puerum uocaret, credo, cui cenam imperaret, prorsus ut uestro con-**60** sessu et hoc conuentu pro summa solitudine abuteretur. [22] perorauit aliquando, assedit; surrexi ego. respirare uisus est quod non alius potius diceret. coepi dicere. usque eo animaduerti, iudices, eum iocari atque alias res agere antequam Chrysogonum nominaui; quem simul atque attigi, statim homo se erexit, mirari uisus est. intellexi quid eum pepugisset. iterum ac tertio nominaui. postea homines cursare ultro et citro non destiterunt, credo qui Chrysogono nuntiarent esse aliquem in ciuitate qui contra uoluntatem eius dicere auderet; aliter causam agi atque ille existimaret, aperiri bonorum emptionem, uexari pessime societatem, gratiam potentiamque eius neglegi, **61** iudices diligenter attendere, populo rem indignam uideri. quae quoniam te fefellerunt, Eruci, quoniamque uides uersa esse omnia, causam pro Sex. Roscio, si non commode at libere dici, quem dedi putabas defendi intellegis, quos traduturos sperabas uides iudicare, restitue nobis aliquando ueterem tuam illam calliditatem atque prudentiam, aut confitere te huc ea spe uenisse quod putares hic latrocinium, non iudicium futurum.

De parricidio causa dicitur; ratio ab accusatore reddita non est quam ob **62** causam patrem filius occiderit. quod in minimis noxiis et in his leuioribus peccatis quae magis crebra et iam prope cotidiana sunt et maxime et primum quaeritur, quae causa malefici fuerit, id Erucius in parricidio quaeri non putat oportere. in quo scelere, iudices, etiam cum multae causae conuenisse unum in locum atque inter se congruere uidentur, tamen non temere creditur, neque leui coniectura res penditur, neque testis incertus auditur, neque accusatoris ingenio res iudicatur. cum multa antea commissa maleficia, cum uita hominis perditissima, tum singularis audacia ostendatur necesse est, neque audacia solum sed summus furor atque amentia. haec cum sint omnia, tamen exstent oportet expressa sceleris uestigia, ubi, qua ratione, per quos, quo tempore maleficium sit admissum. quae nisi multa et manifesta sunt, profecto res tam scelesta, tam atrox, tam nefaria credi non potest. magna est enim uis humanitatis; multum ualet communio sanguinis; **63** reclamat istius modi suspicionibus ipsa natura; portentum atque monstrum certissimum est esse aliquem humana specie et figura qui tantum immanitate bestias uicerit ut, propter quos hanc suauissimam lucem aspexerit, eos indignissime luce priuarit, cum etiam feras inter sese partus atque educatio et natura ipsa conciliet.

[23] Non ita multis ante annis aiunt T. Cloelium quendam Tarracinensem, **64** hominem non obscurum, cum cenatus cubitum in idem conclaue cum duobus adulescentibus filiis isset, inuentum esse mane iugulatum. cum neque seruus quisquam reperiretur neque liber ad quem ea suspicio pertineret, id aetatis autem duo filii propter cubantes ne sensisse quidem se dicerent, nomina filiorum de parricidio delata sunt. quid poterat tam esse suspiciosum aut tam inauditum? neutrumne sensisse? ausum autem esse quemquam se in id conclaue committere eo potissimum tempore cum ibidem essent duo adulescentes filii qui et sentire et defendere facile possent? erat porro nemo in quem ea suspicio conueniret. tamen, cum planum iudicibus esset factum **65** aperto ostio dormientes eos repertos esse, iudicio absoluti adulescentes et suspicione omni liberati sunt. nemo enim putabat quemquam esse qui, cum omnia diuina atque humana iura scelere nefario polluisset, somnum statim capere potuisset, propterea quod qui tantum facinus commiserunt non modo sine cura quiescere sed ne spirare quidem sine metu possunt.

[24] Videtisne quos nobis poetae tradiderunt patris ulciscendi causa sup- **66** plicium de matre sumpsisse, cum praesertim deorum immortalium iussis atque oraculis id fecisse dicantur, tamen ut eos agitent Furiae neque consistere umquam patiantur, quod ne pii quidem sine scelere esse potuerunt? sic se res habet, iudices: magnam uim, magnam necessitatem, magnam possidet religionem paternus maternusque sanguis; ex quo si qua macula concepta est, non modo elui non potest uerum usque eo permanat ad animum ut summus furor atque amentia consequatur. nolite enim putare, quemadmodum in **67** fabulis saepenumero uidetis, eos qui aliquid impie scelerateque commiserunt agitari et perterreri Furiarum taedis ardentibus. sua quemque fraus et suus terror maxime uexat, suum quemque scelus agitat amentiaque afficit, suae malae cogitationes conscientiaeque animi terrent; hae sunt impiis assiduae domesticaeque Furiae quae dies noctesque parentium poenas a consceleratissimis filiis repetant. haec magnitudo malefici facit ut, nisi paene manifestum **68**

parricidium proferatur, credibile non sit: nisi turpis adulescentia, nisi omnibus flagitiis uita inquinata, nisi sumptus effusi cum probro atque dedecore, nisi prorupta audacia, nisi tanta temeritas ut non procul abhorreat ab insania. accedat huc oportet odium parentis, animaduersionis paternae metus, amici improbi, serui conscii, tempus idoneum, locus opportune captus ad eam rem; paene dicam, respersas manus sanguine paterno iudices uideant oportet, si tantum facinus, tam immane, tam acerbum credituri sunt.

69 Quare hoc quo minus est credibile, nisi ostenditur, eo magis est, si conuincitur, uindicandum. [25] itaque cum multis ex rebus intellegi potest maiores nostros non modo armis plus quam ceteras nationes uerum etiam consilio sapientiaque potuisse, tum ex hac re uel maxime quod in impios singulare supplicium inuenerunt. qua in re quantum prudentia praestiterint **70** iis qui apud ceteros sapientissimi fuisse dicuntur considerate. prudentissima ciuitas Atheniensium, dum ea rerum potita est, fuisse traditur; eius porro ciuitatis sapientissimum Solonem dicunt fuisse, eum qui leges quibus hodie quoque utuntur scripserit. is cum interrogaretur cur nullum supplicium constituisset in eum qui parentem necasset, respondit se id neminem facturum putasse. sapienter fecisse dicitur, cum de eo nihil sanxerit quod antea commissum non erat, ne non tam prohibere quam admonere uideretur. quanto nostri maiores sapientius! qui cum intellegerent nihil esse tam sanctum quod non aliquando uiolaret audacia, supplicium in parricidas singulare excogitauerunt ut, quos natura ipsa retinere in officio non potuisset, ii magnitudine poenae a maleficio summouerentur.

71 Insui uoluerunt in culleum uiuos atque ita in flumen deici. [26] o singularem sapientiam, iudices! nonne uidentur hunc hominem ex rerum natura sustulisse et eripuisse cui repente caelum, solem, aquam terramque ademerint ut, qui eum necasset unde ipse natus esset, caret iis rebus omnibus ex quibus omnia nata esse dicuntur? noluerunt feris corpus obicere ne bestiis quoque quae tantum scelus attigissent immanioribus uteremur; non sic nudos in flumen deicere ne, cum delati essent in mare, mare ipsum polluerent quo cetera quae uiolata sunt expiari putantur; denique nihil tam uile neque tam **72** uulgare est cuius partem ullam reliquerint. etenim quid tam est commune quam spiritus uiuis, terra mortuis, mare fluctuantibus, litus eiectis? ita uiuunt, dum possunt, ut ducere animam de caelo non queant, ita moriuntur ut eorum ossa terra non tangat, ita iactantur fluctibus ut numquam alluantur, ita postremo eiciuntur ut ne ad saxa quidem mortui conquiescant. tanti malefici crimen, cui maleficio tam insigne supplicium est constitutum, probare te, Eruci, censes posse talibus uiris, si ne causam quidem malefici protuleris? si hunc apud bonorum emptores ipsos accusares eique iudicio Chrysogonus **73** praeesset, tamen diligentius paratiusque uenisses. utrum quid agatur non uides, an apud quos agatur? agitur de parricidio, quod sine multis causis suscipi non potest; apud homines autem prudentissimos agitur qui intellegunt neminem ne minimum quidem maleficium sine causa admittere.

[27] Esto, causam proferre non potes. tametsi statim uicisse debeo, tamen de meo iure decedam et tibi quod in alia causa non concederem in hac concedam fretus huius innocentia. non quaero abs te quare patrem Sex. Roscius occiderit, quaero quomodo occiderit. et ita quaero abs te, C. Eruci, et sic tecum agam ut meo loco uel respondendi uel interpellandi tibi potestatem faciam uel etiam, si quid uoles, interrogandi. quomodo occidit? ipse percussit **74** an aliis occidendum dedit? si ipsum arguis, Romae non fuit; si per alios fecisse dicis, quaero: quos? seruosne an liberos? si liberos, quos homines? indidemne Ameria an hosce ex urbe sicarios? si Ameria, qui sunt ii? cur non nominantur? si Roma, unde eos nouerat Roscius, qui Romam multis annis non uenit neque umquam plus triduo fuit? ubi eos conuenit? qui collocutus est? quomodo persuasit? 'pretium dedit': cui dedit? per quem dedit? unde aut quantum dedit? nonne his uestigiis ad caput malefici perueniri solet? et simul tibi in mentem ueniat facito quemadmodum uitam huiusce depinxeris: hunc hominem ferum atque agrestem fuisse, numquam cum homine quoquam collocutum esse, numquam in oppido constitisse. qua in re praetereo illud **75** quod mihi maximo argumento ad huius innocentiam poterat esse, in rusticis moribus, in uictu arido, in hac horrida incultaque uita istius modi maleficia gigni non solere. ut non omnem frugem neque arborem in omni agro reperire possis, sic non omne facinus in omni uita nascitur. in urbe luxuries creatur, ex luxuria exsistat auaritia necesse est, ex auaritia erumpat audacia, inde omnia scelera ac maleficia gignuntur; uita autem haec rustica quam tu agrestem uocas parsimoniae, diligentiae, iustitiae magistra est.

[28] Verum haec missa facio; illud quaero, is homo qui, ut tute dicis, **76** numquam inter homines fuerit, per quos homines hoc tantum facinus, tam occultum, absens praesertim, conficere potuerit. multa sunt falsa, iudices, quae tamen argui suspiciose possunt; in his rebus si suspicio reperta erit, culpam inesse concedam. Romae Sex. Roscius occiditur cum in agro Amerino esset filius. litteras, credo, misit alicui sicario qui Romae nouerat neminem. arcessiuit aliquem. quem aut quando? nuntium misit. quem aut ad quem? pretio, gratia, spe, promissis induxit aliquem. nihil horum ne confingi quidem potest; et tamen causa de parricidio dicitur.

Reliquum est ut per seruos id admiserit. o di immortales, rem miseram et **77** calamitosam! quid? in tali crimine quod innocenti saluti solet esse ut seruos in quaestionem polliceatur, id Sex. Roscio facere non licet? uos qui hunc accusatis omnes eius seruos habetis; unus puer uictus cotidiani administer ex tanta familia Sex. Roscio relictus non est. te nunc appello, P. Scipio, te, M.

Metelle: uobis aduocatis, uobis agentibus aliquotiens duos seruos paternos in
quaestionem ab aduersariis Sex. Roscius postulauit; meministisne T. Roscium
recusare? quid? ii serui ubi sunt? Chrysogonum, iudices, sectantur; apud eum
sunt in honore et in pretio. etiamnunc ut ex iis quaeratur ego postulo, hic
78 orat atque obsecrat. quid facitis? cur recusatis? dubitate etiamnunc, iudices,
si potestis, a quo sit Sex. Roscius occisus, ab eone qui propter illius mortem
in egestate et insidiis uersatur, cui ne quaerendi quidem de morte patris
potestas permittitur, an ab iis qui quaestionem fugitant, bona possident, in
caede atque ex caede uiuunt. omnia, iudices, in hac causa sunt misera atque
indigna; tamen hoc nihil neque acerbius neque iniquius proferri potest:
mortis paternae de seruis paternis quaestionem habere filio non licet! ne
tam diu quidem dominus erit in suos dum ex iis de patris morte quaeratur?
ueniam, neque ita multo post, ad hunc locum; nam hoc totum ad Roscios
pertinet, de quorum audacia tum me dicturum pollicitus sum cum Eruci
crimina diluissem.

79   [29] Nunc, Eruci, ad te uenio. conueniat mihi tecum necesse est, si
ad hunc maleficium istud pertinet, aut ipsum sua manu fecisse, id quod
negas, aut per aliquos liberos aut seruos. liberosne? quos neque ut conuenire potuerit neque qua ratione inducere neque ubi neque per quos
neque qua spe aut quo pretio potes ostendere. ego contra ostendo non
modo nihil eorum fecisse Sex. Roscium sed ne potuisse quidem facere,
quod neque Romae multis annis fuerit neque de praediis umquam temere
discesserit. restare tibi uidebatur seruorum nomen, quo quasi in portum
reiectus a ceteris suspicionibus confugere posses; ubi scopulum offendis eiusmodi ut non modo ab hoc crimen resilire uideas uerum omnem suspicionem
80 in uosmet ipsos recidere intellegas. quid ergo est quo tandem accusator
inopia argumentorum confugerit? 'eiusmodi tempus erat' inquit 'ut homines
uulgo impune occiderentur; quare hoc tu propter multitudinem sicariorum
nullo negotio facere potuisti.' interdum mihi uideris, Eruci, una mercede
duas res assequi uelle, nos iudicio perfundere, accusare autem eos ipsos
a quibus mercedem accepisti. quid ais? uulgo occidebantur? per quos et
a quibus? nonne cogitas te a sectoribus huc adductum esse? quid postea?
nescimus per ista tempora eosdem fere sectores fuisse collorum et bono-
81 rum? ii denique qui tum armati dies noctesque concursabant, qui Romae
erant assidui, qui omni tempore in praeda et sanguine uersabantur, Sex.
Roscio temporis illius acerbitatem iniquitatemque obicient et illam sicariorum multitudinem in qua ipsi duces ac principes erant huic crimini putabunt
fore? qui non modo Romae non fuit sed omnino quid Romae ageretur nesciuit, propterea quod ruri assiduus, quemadmodum tute confiteris,
fuit.

Vereor ne aut molestus sim uobis, iudices, aut ne ingeniis uestris uidear **82** diffidere, si de tam perspicuis rebus diutius disseram. Eruci criminatio tota, ut arbitror, dissoluta est; nisi forte exspectatis ut illa diluam quae de peculatu ac de eiusmodi rebus commenticiis inaudita nobis ante hoc tempus ac noua obiecit. quae mihi iste uisus est ex alia oratione declamare quam in alium reum commentaretur; ita neque ad crimen parricidi neque ad eum qui causam dicit pertinebant. de quibus quoniam uerbo arguit, uerbo satis est negare. si quid est quod ad testes reseruet, ibi quoque nos, ut in ipsa causa, paratiores reperiet quam putabat.

[30] Venio nunc eo quo me non cupiditas ducit sed fides. nam si mihi **83** liberet accusare, accusarem alios potius ex quibus possem crescere; quod certum est non facere dum utrumuis licebit. is enim mihi uidetur amplissimus qui sua uirtute in altiorem locum peruenit, non qui ascendit per alterius incommodum et calamitatem. desinamus aliquando ea scrutari quae sunt inania; quaeramus ibi maleficium ubi et est et inueniri potest; iam intelleges, Eruci, certum crimen quam multis suspicionibus coarguatur, tametsi neque omnia dicam et leuiter unumquidque tangam. neque enim id facerem, nisi necesse esset, et id erit signi me inuitum facere quod non persequar longius quam salus huius et mea fides postulabit.

Causam tu nullam reperiebas in Sex. Roscio; at ego in T. Roscio reperio. **84** tecum enim mihi res est, T. Rosci, quoniam istic sedes ac te palam aduersarium esse profiteris. de Capitone post uiderimus si, quemadmodum paratum esse audio, testis prodierit: tum alias quoque suas palmas cognoscet de quibus me ne audisse quidem suspicatur. L. Cassius ille quem populus Romanus uerissimum et sapientissimum iudicem putabat identidem in causis quaerere solebat 'cui bono' fuisset. sic uita hominum est ut ad maleficium nemo conetur sine spe atque emolumento accedere. hunc quaesitorem ac **85** iudicem fugiebant atque horrebant ii quibus periculum creabatur ideo quod, tametsi ueritatis erat amicus, tamen natura non tam propensus ad miseri- cordiam quam applicatus ad seueritatem uidebatur. ego, quamquam praeest huic quaestioni uir et contra audaciam fortissimus et ab innocentia clemen- tissimus, tamen facile me paterer uel illo ipso acerrimo iudice quaerente uel apud Cassianos iudices, quorum etiamnunc ii quibus causa dicenda est nomen ipsum reformidant, pro Sex. Roscio dicere. [31] in hac enim causa **86** cum uiderent illos amplissimam pecuniam possidere, hunc in summa men- dicitate esse, illud quidem non quaererent, cui bono fuisset, sed eo perspicuo crimen et suspicionem potius ad praedam adiungerent quam ad egestatem. quid si accedit eodem ut tenuis antea fueris? quid si ut auarus? quid si ut audax? quid si ut illius qui occisus est inimicissimus? num quaerenda causa quae te ad tantum facinus adduxerit? quid ergo horum negari potest?

tenuitas hominis eiusmodi est ut dissimulari non queat atque eo magis eluceat
87 quo magis occultatur. auaritiam praefers qui societatem coieris de municipis
cognatique fortunis cum alienissimo. quam sis audax, ut alia obliuiscar, hinc
omnes intellegere potuerunt quod ex tota societate, hoc est ex tot sicariis,
solus tu inuentus es qui cum accusatoribus sederes atque os tuum non modo
ostenderes sed etiam offerres. inimicitias tibi fuisse cum Sex. Roscio et mag-
88 nas rei familiaris controuersias concedas necesse est. restat, iudices, ut hoc
dubitemus, uter potius Sex. Roscium occiderit, is ad quem morte eius diuitiae
uenerint, an is ad quem mendicitas, is qui antea tenuis fuerit, an is qui postea
factus sit egentissimus, is qui ardens auaritia feratur infestus in suos, an is qui
semper ita uixerit ut quaestum nosset nullum, fructum autem eum solum
quem labore peperisset, is qui omnium sectorum audacissimus sit, an is qui
propter fori iudiciorumque insolentiam non modo subsellia uerum etiam
urbem ipsam reformidet, postremo, iudices, id quod ad rem mea sententia
maxime pertinet, utrum inimicus potius an filius.
89 [32] Haec tu, Eruci, tot et tanta si nanctus esses in reo, quam diu diceres!
quo te modo iactares! tempus hercule te citius quam oratio deficeret. etenim
in singulis rebus eiusmodi materies est ut dies singulos possis consumere.
neque ego non possum; non enim tantum mihi derogo, tametsi nihil arrogo,
ut te copiosius quam me putem posse dicere. uerum ego forsitan propter multitudinem patronorum in grege annumerer, te pugna Cannensis accusatorem
sat bonum fecit. multos caesos non ad Trasimenum lacum sed ad Seruilium
90 uidimus. 'quis ibi non est uulneratus ferro Phrygio?' non necesse est omnes
commemorare Curtios, Marios, denique Memmios quos iam aetas a proeliis
auocabat, postremo Priamum ipsum senem, Antistium, quem non modo
aetas sed etiam leges pugnare prohibebant. iam quos nemo propter ignobi-
litatem nominat, sescenti sunt qui inter sicarios et de ueneficiis accusabant;
qui omnes, quod ad me attinet, uellem uiuerent. nihil enim mali est canes
ibi quam plurimos esse ubi permulti obseruandi multaque seruanda sunt.
91 uerum, ut fit, multa saepe imprudentibus imperatoribus uis belli ac turba
molitur. dum is in aliis rebus erat occupatus qui summam rerum administrabat, erant interea qui suis uulneribus mederentur; qui, tamquam si offusa rei
publicae sempiterna nox esset, ita ruebant in tenebris omniaque miscebant;
a quibus miror ne quod iudiciorum esset uestigium, non subsellia quoque
esse combusta; nam et accusatores et iudices sustulerunt. hoc commodi est
quod ita uixerunt ut testes omnes, si cuperent, interficere non possent; nam,
dum hominum genus erit, qui accuset eos non deerit; dum ciuitas erit, iudicia fient. uerum, ut coepi dicere, et Erucius, haec si haberet in causa quae
commemoraui, posset ea quamuis diu dicere, et ego, iudices, possum; sed
in animo est, quemadmodum ante dixi, leuiter transire ac tantummodo

perstringere unam quamque rem ut omnes intellegant me non studio accusare sed officio defendere.

[33] Video igitur causas esse permultas quae istum impellerent; uideamus **92** nunc ecquae facultas suscipiendi malefici fuerit. ubi occisus est Sex. Roscius? — 'Romae.' — quid? tu, T. Rosci, ubi tunc eras? — 'Romae. uerum quid ad rem? et alii multi.' — quasi nunc id agatur quis ex tanta multitudine occiderit, ac non hoc quaeratur, eum qui Romae sit occisus utrum uerisimilius sit ab eo esse occisum qui assiduus eo tempore Romae fuerit, an ab eo qui multis annis Romam omnino non accesserit. age nunc ceteras quoque facultates **93** consideremus. erat tum multitudo sicariorum, id quod commemorauit Erucius, et homines impune occidebantur. quid? ea multitudo quae erat? opinor aut eorum qui in bonis erant occupati aut eorum qui ab iis conducebantur ut aliquem occiderent. si eos putas qui alienum appetebant, tu es in eo numero qui nostra pecunia diues es; sin eos quos qui leuiore nomine appellant percussores uocant, quaere in cuius fide sint et clientela; mihi crede, aliquem de societate tua reperies; et, quicquid tu contra dixeris, id cum defensione nostra contendito; ita facillime causa Sex. Rosci cum tua conferetur. dices: **94** 'quid postea, si Romae assiduus fui?' respondebo: 'at ego omnino non fui.' — 'fateor me sectorem esse, uerum et alii multi.' — 'at ego,' ut tute arguis, 'agricola et rusticus.' — 'non continuo, si me in gregem sicariorum contuli, sum sicarius.' — 'at ego profecto qui ne noui quidem quemquam sicarium longe absum ab eiusmodi crimine.' permulta sunt quae dici possunt quare intellegatur summam tibi facultatem fuisse malefici suscipiendi; quae non modo idcirco praetereo quod te ipsum non libenter accuso uerum eo magis etiam quod, si de illis caedibus uelim commemorare quae tum factae sunt ista eadem ratione qua Sex. Roscius occisus est, uereor ne ad plures oratio mea pertinere uideatur.

[34] Videamus nunc strictim, sicut cetera, quae post mortem Sex. Rosci **95** abs te, T. Rosci, facta sunt; quae ita aperta et manifesta sunt ut medius fidius, iudices, inuitus ea dicam. uereor enim, cuicuimodi es, T. Rosci, ne ita hunc uidear uoluisse seruare ut tibi omnino non pepercerim. cum hoc uereor et cupio tibi aliqua ex parte quod salua fide possim parcere, rursus immuto uoluntatem meam; uenit enim mihi in mentem oris tui. tene, cum ceteri socii tui fugerent ac se occultarent, ut hoc iudicium non de illorum praeda sed de huius maleficio fieri uideretur, potissimum tibi partes istas depoposcisse ut in iudicio uersarere et sederes cum accusatore? qua in re nihil aliud assequeris nisi ut ab omnibus mortalibus audacia tua cognoscatur et impudentia. occiso Sex. Roscio quis primus Ameriam nuntiat? Mallius **96** Glaucia, quem iam antea nominaui, tuus cliens et familiaris. quid attinuit eum potissimum nuntiare quod, si nullum iam ante consilium de morte ac

de bonis eius inieras nullamque societatem neque sceleris neque praemi cum homine ullo coieras, ad te minime omnium pertinebat? — 'sua sponte Mallius nuntiat.' — quid, quaeso, eius intererat? an, cum Ameriam non huiusce rei causa uenisset, casu accidit ut id quod Romae audierat primus nuntiaret? cuius rei causa uenerat Ameriam? 'non possum' inquit 'diuinare.' eo rem iam adducam ut nihil diuinatione opus sit. qua ratione T. Roscio Capitoni primo nuntiauit? cum Ameriae Sex. Rosci domus uxor liberique essent, cum tot propinqui cognatique optime conuenientes, qua ratione factum est ut iste tuus cliens, sceleris tui nuntius, T. Roscio Capitoni potissimum nuntiaret?

97 occisus est a cena rediens; nondum lucebat cum Ameriae scitum est. quid hic incredibilis cursus, quid haec tanta celeritas festinatioque significat? non quaero quis percusserit; nihil est, Glaucia, quod metuas; non excutio te, si quid forte ferri habuisti, non scrutor; nihil ad me arbitror pertinere, quoniam cuius consilio occisus sit inuenio, cuius manu sit percussus non laboro. unum hoc sumo quod mihi apertum tuum scelus resque manifesta dat: ubi aut unde audiuit Glaucia? qui tam cito sciuit? fac audisse statim; quae res eum nocte una tantum itineris contendere coegit? quae necessitas eum tanta premebat ut, si sua sponte iter Ameriam faceret, id temporis Roma proficisceretur, nullam partem noctis requiesceret?

98 [35] Etiamne in tam perspicuis rebus argumentatio quaerenda aut coniectura capienda est? nonne uobis haec quae audistis cernere oculis uidemini, iudices? non illum miserum, ignarum casus sui redeuntem a cena uidetis, non positas insidias, non impetum repentinum? non uersatur ante oculos uobis in caede Glaucia? non adest iste T. Roscius? non suis manibus in curru collocat Automedontem illum, sui sceleris acerbissimi nefariaeque uictoriae nuntium? non orat ut eam noctem peruigilet, ut honoris sui causa laboret,

99 ut Capitoni quam primum nuntiet? quid erat quod Capitonem primum scire uellet? nescio, nisi hoc uideo, Capitonem in his bonis esse socium; de
100 tribus et decem fundis tres nobilissimos fundos eum uideo possidere. audio praeterea non hanc suspicionem nunc primum in Capitonem conferri; multas esse infames eius palmas, hanc primam esse tamen lemniscatam quae Roma ei deferatur; nullum modum esse hominis occidendi quo ille non aliquot occiderit, multos ferro, multos ueneno. habeo etiam dicere quem contra morem maiorum minorem annis LX de ponte in Tiberim deiecerit. quae, si prodierit atque adeo cum prodierit — scio enim proditurum esse

101 — audiet. ueniat modo, explicet suum uolumen illud quod ei planum facere possum Erucium conscripsisse; quod aiunt illum Sex. Roscio intentasse et minitatum esse se omnia illa pro testimonio esse dicturum. o praeclarum testem, iudices! o grauitatem dignam exspectatione! o uitam honestam atque eiusmodi ut libentibus animis ad eius testimonium uestrum iusiurandum accommodetis! profecto non tam perspicue nos istorum maleficia uideremus, nisi ipsos caecos redderet cupiditas et auaritia et audacia. [36] alter ex **102** ipsa caede uolucrem nuntium Ameriam ad socium atque magistrum suum misit ut, si dissimulare omnes cuperent se scire ad quem maleficium pertineret, tamen ipse apertum suum scelus ante omnium oculos poneret. alter, si dis immortalibus placet, testimonium etiam in Sex. Roscium dicturus est; quasi uero id nunc agatur utrum is quod dixerit credendum ac non quod fecerit uindicandum sit. itaque more maiorum comparatum est ut in minimis rebus homines amplissimi testimonium de sua re non dicerent. Africanus, qui **103** suo cognomine declarat tertiam partem orbis terrarum se subegisse, tamen, si sua res ageretur, testimonium non diceret; nam illud in talem uirum non audeo dicere: si diceret, non crederetur. uidete nunc quam uersa et mutata in peiorem partem sint omnia. cum de bonis et de caede agatur, testimonium dicturus est is qui et sector est et sicarius, hoc est qui et illorum ipsorum bonorum de quibus agitur emptor atque possessor est et eum hominem occidendum curauit de cuius morte quaeritur.

Quid? tu, uir optime, ecquid habes quod dicas? mihi ausculta: uide ne **104** tibi desis; tua quoque res permagna agitur. multa scelerate, multa audaciter, multa improbe fecisti, unum stultissime, profecto tua sponte non de Eruci sententia: nihil opus fuit te istic sedere; neque enim accusatore muto neque teste quisquam utitur eo qui de accusatoris subsellio surgit. huc accedit quod paulo tamen occultior atque tectior uestra ista cupiditas esset. nunc quid est quod quisquam ex uobis audire desideret, cum quae facitis eiusmodi sint ut ea dedita opera a nobis contra uosmet ipsos facere uideamini?

[37] Age nunc illa uideamus, iudices, quae statim consecuta sunt. ad Vola- **105** terras in castra L. Sullae mors Sex. Rosci quadriduo quo is occisus est Chrysogono nuntiatur. quaeritur etiamnunc quis eum nuntium miserit? nonne perspicuum est eundem qui Ameriam? curat Chrysogonus ut eius bona ueneant statim, qui non norat hominem aut rem. at qui ei uenit in mentem praedia concupiscere hominis ignoti quem omnino numquam uiderat? soletis, cum aliquid huiuscemodi audistis, iudices, continuo dicere: 'necesse est aliquem dixisse municipem aut uicinum; ii plerumque indicant, per eos plerique produntur.' hic nihil est quod suspicione me ponere hoc putetis. non **106** enim ego ita disputabo: 'uerisimile est Roscios istam rem ad Chrysogonum detulisse; erat enim eis cum Chrysogono iam antea amicitia; nam cum multos ueteres a maioribus Roscii patronos hospitesque haberent, omnes eos colere atque obseruare destiterunt ac se in Chrysogoni fidem et clientelam contulerunt.' haec possum omnia uere dicere, sed in hac causa coniectura nihil **107** opus est; ipsos certo scio non negare ad haec bona Chrysogonum accessisse impulsu suo. si eum qui indiciuae partem acceperit oculis cernetis, poteritisne

dubitare, iudices, qui indicarit? qui sunt igitur in istis bonis quibus partem Chrysogonus dederit? duo Roscii. numquisnam praeterea? nemo est, iudices. num ergo dubium est quin ii obtulerint hanc praedam Chrysogono qui ab eo partem praedae tulerunt?

108   Age nunc ex ipsius Chrysogoni iudicio Rosciorum factum consideremus. si nihil in ista pugna Roscii quod operae pretium esset fecerant, quam ob causam a Chrysogono tantis praemiis donabantur? si nihil aliud fecerunt nisi rem detulerunt, nonne satis fuit iis gratias agi, denique, ut perliberaliter ageretur, honoris aliquid haberi? cur tria praedia tantae pecuniae statim Capitoni dantur? cur quae reliqua sunt iste T. Roscius omnia cum Chrysogono communiter possidet? nonne perspicuum est, iudices, has manubias Rosciis Chrysogonum re cognita concessisse?

109   [38] Venit in decem primis legatus in castra Capito. totam uitam naturam moresque hominis ex ipsa legatione cognoscite. nisi intellexeritis, iudices, nullum esse officium, nullum ius tam sanctum atque integrum quod non eius scelus atque perfidia uiolarit et imminuerit, uirum optimum esse eum iudi-

110 catote. impedimento est quominus de his rebus Sulla doceatur, ceterorum legatorum consilia et uoluntatem Chrysogono enuntiat, monet ut prouideat ne palam res agatur, ostendit, si sublata sit uenditio bonorum, illum pecuniam grandem amissurum, sese capitis periculum aditurum; illum acuere, hos qui simul erant missi fallere, illum identidem monere ut caueret, hisce insidiose spem falsam ostendere, cum illo contra hos inire consilia, horum consilia illi enuntiare, cum illo partem suam depecisci, hisce aliqua fretus mora semper omnes aditus ad Sullam intercludere. postremo isto hortatore, auctore, intercessore ad Sullam legati non adierunt; istius fide ac potius perfidia decepti, id quod ex ipsis cognoscere poteritis, si accusator uoluerit

111 testimonium eis denuntiarc, pro re certa spem falsam domum rettulerunt. in priuatis rebus si qui rem mandatam non modo malitiosius gessisset sui quaestus aut commodi causa uerum etiam neglegentius, eum maiores summum admisisse dedecus existimabant. itaque mandati constitutum est iudicium non minus turpe quam furti, credo propterea quod quibus in rebus ipsi interesse non possumus, in eis operae nostrae uicaria fides amicorum supponitur; quam qui laedit, oppugnat omnium commune praesidium et, quantum in ipso est, disturbat uitae societatem. non enim possumus omnia per nos agere; alius in alia est re magis utilis. idcirco amicitiae comparantur ut commune

112 commodum mutuis officiis gubernetur. quid recipis mandatum si aut neglecturus aut ad tuum commodum conuersurus es? cur mihi te offers ac meis commodis officio simulato officis et obstas? recede de medio; per alium transigam. suscipis onus offici quod te putas sustinere non posse; quod minime uidetur leue iis qui minime ipsi leues sunt. [39] ergo idcirco turpis haec

culpa est quod duas res sanctissimas uiolat, amicitiam et fidem. nam neque
mandat quisquam fere nisi amico neque credit nisi ei quem fidelem putat.
perditissimi est igitur hominis simul et amicitiam dissoluere et fallere eum qui
laesus non esset, nisi credidisset. itane est? in minimis rebus qui mandatum **113**
neglexerit, turpissimo iudicio condemnetur necesse est, in re tanta cum is
cui fama mortui, fortunae uiui commendatae sunt atque concreditae, ignominia mortuum, inopia uiuum affecerit, is inter honestos homines atque adeo
inter uiuos numerabitur? in minimis priuatisque rebus etiam neglegentia in
crimen mandati iudiciumque infamiae uocatur, propterea quod, si recte fiat,
illum neglegere oporteat qui mandarit, non illum qui mandatum receperit;
in re tanta quae publice gesta atque commissa sit qui non neglegentia priua-
tum aliquod commodum laeserit sed perfidia legationis ipsius caerimoniam
polluerit maculaque affecerit, qua is tandem poena afficietur aut quo iudicio damnabitur? si hanc ei rem priuatim Sex. Roscius mandauisset ut cum **114**
Chrysogono transigeret atque decideret inque eam rem fidem suam, si quid
opus esse putaret, interponeret illeque sese facturum recepisset, nonne, si
ex eo negotio tantulum in rem suam conuertisset, damnatus per arbitrum
et rem restitueret et honestatem omnem amitteret? nunc non hanc ei rem **115**
Sex. Roscius mandauit sed, id quod multo grauius est, ipse Sex. Roscius cum
fama uita bonisque omnibus a decurionibus publice T. Roscio mandatus est;
et ex eo T. Roscius non paululum nescioquid in rem suam conuertit sed
hunc funditus euertit bonis, ipse tria praedia sibi depectus est, uoluntatem
decurionum ac municipum omnium tantidem quanti fidem suam fecit.

[40] Videte iam porro cetera, iudices, ut intellegatis fingi maleficium **116**
nullum posse quo iste sese non contaminarit. in rebus minoribus socium
fallere turpissimum est aequeque turpe atque illud de quo ante dixi; neque
iniuria, propterea quod auxilium sibi se putat adiunxisse qui cum altero
rem communicauit. ad cuius igitur fidem confugiet, cum per eius fidem
laeditur cui se commiserit? atque ea sunt animaduertenda peccata maxime
quae difficillime praecauentur. tecti esse ad alienos possumus, intimi multa
apertiora uideant necesse est; socium cauere qui possumus? quem etiam si
metuimus, ius offici laedimus. recte igitur maiores eum qui socium fefellis-
set in uirorum bonorum numero non putarunt haberi oportere. at uero T. **117**
Roscius non unum rei pecuniariae socium fefellit — quod tametsi graue est,
tamen aliquomodo posse ferri uidetur — uerum nouem homines honestis-
simos eiusdem muneris, offici mandatorumque socios, induxit, decepit, des-
tituit, aduersariis tradidit, omni fraude et perfidia fefellit; qui de eius scelere
suspicari nihil potuerunt, socium offici metuere non debuerunt, eius mali-
tiam non uiderunt, orationi uanae crediderunt. itaque nunc illi homines
honestissimi propter istius insidias parum putantur cauti prouidique fuisse;

iste qui initio proditor fuit, deinde perfuga, qui primo sociorum consilia
aduersariis enuntiauit, deinde societatem cum ipsis aduersariis coiit, terret
etiam nos ac minatur tribus praediis, hoc est praemiis sceleris, ornatus.

In eiusmodi uita, iudices, in his tot tantisque flagitiis hoc quoque malefi-
118 cium de quo iudicium est reperietis. etenim quaerere ita debetis: ubi multa
auare, multa audacter, multa improbe, multa perfidiose facta uidebitis, ibi
scelus quoque latere inter illa tot flagitia putatote. tametsi hoc quidem minime latet quod ita promptum et propositum est ut non ex illis maleficiis quae
in illo constat esse hoc intellegatur uerum ex hoc etiam, si quo de illorum forte
dubitabitur, conuincatur. quid tandem, quaeso, iudices? num aut ille lanista
omnino iam a gladio recessisse uidetur aut hic discipulus magistro tantulum
de arte concedere? par est auaritia, similis improbitas, eadem impudentia,
gemina audacia.

119   [41] Etenim, quoniam fidem magistri cognostis, cognoscite nunc discipuli aequitatem. dixi iam antea saepenumero postulatos esse ab istis duos
seruos in quaestionem. tu semper, T. Rosci, recusasti. quaero abs te: iine
qui postulabant indigni erant qui impetrarent, an is te non commouebat
pro quo postulabant, an res ipsa tibi iniqua uidebatur? postulabant homines
nobilissimi atque integerrimi nostrae ciuitatis quos iam antea nominaui; qui
ita uixerunt talesque a populo Romano putantur ut quicquid dicerent nemo
esset qui non aequum putaret. postulabant autem pro homine miserrimo
atque infelicissimo qui uel ipse sese in cruciatum dari cuperet dum de patris
120 morte quaereretur. res porro abs te eiusmodi postulabatur ut nihil interesset,
utrum eam rem recusares an de maleficio confiterere. quae cum ita sint,
quaero abs te quam ob causam recusaris. cum occiditur Sex. Roscius ibidem fuerunt. seruos ipsos, quod ad me attinet, neque arguo neque purgo;
quod a uobis oppugnari uideo ne in quaestionem dentur, suspiciosum est.
quod uero apud uos ipsos in honore tanto sunt, profecto necesse est sciant
aliquid quod, si dixerint, perniciosum uobis futurum sit. — 'in dominos
quaeri de seruis iniquum est.' — at non quaeritur: Sex. enim Roscius reus
est neque, cum de hoc quaeritur, in dominos quaeritur; uos enim dominos
esse dicitis. — 'cum Chrysogono sunt.' — ita credo; litteris eorum et urba-
nitate Chrysogonus ducitur ut inter suos omnium deliciarum atque omnium
artium puerulos ex tot elegantissimis familiis lectos uelit hos uersari, homines
121 paene operarios, ex Amerina disciplina patris familiae rusticani. non ita est
profecto, iudices; non est uerisimile ut Chrysogonus horum litteras adamarit
aut humanitatem, non ut rei familiaris negotio diligentiam cognorit eorum et
fidem. est quiddam quod occultatur; quod quo studiosius ab istis opprimitur
122 et absconditur, eo magis eminet et apparet. [42] quid igitur? Chrysogonus
suine malefici occultandi causa quaestionem de iis haberi non uult? minime,

iudices; non in omnes arbitror omnia conuenire. ego in Chrysogono, quod ad me attinet, nihil eiusmodi suspicor; neque hoc mihi nunc primum in mentem uenit dicere. meministis me ita distribuisse initio causam: in crimen cuius tota argumentatio permissa Erucio est et in audaciam cuius partes Rosciis impositae sunt. quicquid malefici, sceleris, caedis erit, proprium id Rosciorum esse debebit. nimiam gratiam potentiamque Chrysogoni dicimus et nobis obstare et perferri nullo modo posse et a uobis, quoniam potestas data est, non modo infirmari uerum etiam uindicari oportere. ego sic **123** existimo, qui quaeri uelit ex eis quos constat, cum caedes facta sit, adfuisse, eum cupere uerum inueniri; qui id recuset, eum profecto, tametsi uerbo non audeat, tamen re ipsa de maleficio suo confiteri.

Dixi initio, iudices, nolle me plura de istorum scelere dicere quam causa postularet ac necessitas ipsa cogeret. nam et multae res afferri possunt et una quaeque earum multis cum argumentis dici potest. uerum ego quod inuitus ac necessario facio neque diu neque diligenter facere possum. quae praeteriri nullo modo poterant, ea leuiter, iudices, attigi, quae posita sunt in suspicionibus de quibus, si coepero dicere, pluribus uerbis sit disserendum, ea uestris ingeniis coniecturaeque committo.

[43] Venio nunc ad illud nomen aureum sub quo nomine tota soci- **124** etas latuit; de quo, iudices, neque quomodo dicam neque quomodo taceam reperire possum. si enim taceo, uel maximam partem relinquo; sin autem dico, uereor ne non ille solus, id quod ad me nihil attinet, sed alii quoque plures laesos sese putent. tametsi ita se res habet ut mihi in communem causam sectorum dicendum nihil magnopere uideatur; haec enim causa noua profecto et singularis est. bonorum Sex. Rosci **125** emptor est Chrysogonus. primum hoc uideamus: eius hominis bona qua ratione uenierunt aut quomodo uenire potuerunt? atque hoc non ita quaeram, iudices, ut id dicam esse indignum, hominis innocentis bona uenisse — si enim haec audientur ac libere dicentur, non fuit tantus homo Sex. Roscius in ciuitate ut de eo potissimum conqueramur — uerum ego hoc quaero: qui potuerunt ista ipsa lege quae de proscriptione est, siue Valeria est siue Cornelia — non enim noui nec scio — uerum ista ipsa lege bona Sex. Rosci uenire qui potuerunt? scriptum enim **126** ita dicunt esse: ut aut eorum bona ueneant 'qui proscripti sunt' — quo in numero Sex. Roscius non est — aut eorum 'qui in aduersariorum praesidiis occisi sunt'. dum praesidia ulla fuerunt, in Sullae praesidiis fuit; posteaquam ab armis omnes recesserunt, in summo otio rediens a cena Romae occisus est. si lege, bona quoque lege uenisse fateor. sin autem constat contra omnes non modo ueteres leges uerum etiam nouas occisum esse, bona quo iure aut quo more aut qua lege uenierint quaero.

127　[44] In quem hoc dicam quaeris, Eruci. non in eum quem uis et putas; nam Sullam et oratio mea ab initio et ipsius eximia uirtus omni tempore purgauit. ego haec omnia Chrysogonum fecisse dico, ut ementiretur, ut malum ciuem Roscium fuisse fingeret, ut eum apud aduersarios occisum esse diceret, ut his de rebus a legatis Amerinorum doceri L. Sullam passus non sit. denique etiam illud suspicor, omnino haec bona non uenisse; id quod postea, si per **128** uos, iudices, licitum erit, aperietur. opinor enim esse in lege quam ad diem proscriptiones uenditionesque fiant, nimirum kalendas Iunias. aliquot post menses et homo occisus est et bona uenisse dicuntur. profecto aut haec bona in tabulas publicas nulla redierunt nosque ab isto nebulone facetius eludimur quam putamus, aut, si redierunt, tabulae publicae corruptae aliqua ratione sunt; nam lege quidem bona uenire non potuisse constat. intellego me ante tempus, iudices, haec scrutari et propemodum errare qui, cum capiti Sex. Rosci mederi debeam, reduuiam curem. non enim laborat de pecunia, non ullius rationem sui commodi ducit; facile egestatem suam se laturum putat, **129** si hac indigna suspicione et ficto crimine liberatus sit. uerum quaeso a uobis, iudices, ut haec pauca quae restant ita audiatis ut partim me dicere pro me ipso putetis, partim pro Sex. Roscio. quae enim mihi ipsi indigna et intolerabilia uidentur quaeque ad omnes, nisi prouidemus, arbitror pertinere, ea pro me ipso ex animi mei sensu ac dolore pronuntio; quae ad huius uitam causamque pertineant et quid hic pro se dici uelit et qua condicione contentus sit iam in extrema oratione nostra, iudices, audietis.

130　[45] Ego haec a Chrysogono mea sponte remoto Sex. Roscio quaero: primum quare ciuis optimi bona uenierint, deinde quare hominis eius qui neque proscriptus neque apud aduersarios occisus est bona uenierint, cum in eos solos lex scripta sit, deinde quare aliquanto post eam diem uenierint quae dies in lege praefinita est, deinde cur tantulo uenierint. quae omnia si, quemadmodum solent liberti nequam et improbi facere, in patronum suum uoluerit conferre, nihil egerit; nemo est enim qui nesciat propter magnitudinem rerum multa multos partim improbante, partim imprudente L. Sulla **131** commisisse. placet igitur in his rebus aliquid imprudentia praeteriri? non placet, iudices, sed necesse est. etenim si Iuppiter Optimus Maximus, cuius nutu et arbitrio caelum terra mariaque reguntur, saepe uentis uehementioribus aut immoderatis tempestatibus aut nimio calore aut intolerabili frigore hominibus nocuit, urbes deleuit, fruges perdidit, quorum nihil pernicii causa diuino consilio sed ui ipsa et magnitudine rerum factum putamus, at contra commoda quibus utimur lucemque qua fruimur spiritumque quem ducimus ab eo nobis dari atque impertiri uidemus, quid miramur, iudices, L. Sullam, cum solus rem publicam regeret orbemque terrarum gubernaret imperique maiestatem quam armis receperat tum legibus confirmaret, aliqua animaduertere non potuisse? nisi hoc mirum est quod uis diuina assequi non possit, si id mens humana adepta non sit. uerum ut haec missa **132** faciam quae iam facta sunt, ex iis quae nunc cum maxime fiunt nonne quiuis potest intellegere omnium architectum et machinatorem unum esse Chrysogonum? qui Sex. Rosci nomen deferendum curauit, cuius honoris causa accusare se dixit Erucius . . .

in uico Pallacinae
maxime metuit
deriuat tamen et ait se
manupretia praediis
hic ego audire istos cupio

[46] . . . aptam et ratione dispositam se habere existimant qui in Sallentinis aut in Bruttiis habent unde uix ter in anno audire nuntium possunt. alter **133** tibi descendit de Palatio et aedibus suis; habet animi causa rus amoenum et suburbanum, plura praeterea praedia neque tamen ullum nisi praeclarum et propinquum. domus referta uasis Corinthiis et Deliacis, in quibus est authepsa illa quam tanto pretio nuper mercatus est ut qui praetereuntes praeconem numerare audiebant fundum uenire arbitrarentur. quid praeterea caelati argenti, quid stragulae uestis, quid pictarum tabularum, quid signorum, quid marmoris apud illum putatis esse? tantum scilicet quantum e multis splendidisque familiis in turba et rapinis coaceruari una in domo potuit. familiam uero quantam et quam uariis cum artificiis habeat quid ego dicam? mitto hasce artes uulgares, coquos, pistores, lecticarios; animi et **134** aurium causa tot homines habet ut cotidiano cantu uocum et neruorum et tibiarum nocturnisque conuiuiis tota uicinitas personet. in hac uita, iudices, quos sumptus cotidianos, quas effusiones fieri putatis, quae uero conuiuia? honesta, credo, in eiusmodi domo, si domus haec habenda est potius quam officina nequitiae ac deuersorium flagitiorum omnium. ipse uero quemad- **135** modum composito et dilibuto capillo passim per forum uolitet cum magna caterua togatorum uidetis, iudices; uidetis ut omnes despiciat, ut hominem prae se neminem putet, ut se solum beatum, solum potentem putet.

Quae uero efficiat et quae conetur si uelim commemorare, uereor, iudices, ne quis imperitior existimet me causam nobilitatis uictoriamque uoluisse laedere. tametsi meo iure possum, si quid in hac parte mihi non placeat, uituperare; non enim uereor ne quis alienum me animum habuisse a causa nobilitatis existimet. [47] sciunt ii qui me norunt me pro mea tenui infirmaque **136** parte, posteaquam id quod maxime uolui fieri non potuit, ut componeretur, id maxime defendisse ut ii uincerent qui uicerunt. quis enim erat qui non uideret humilitatem cum dignitate de amplitudine contendere? quo in certamine perditi ciuis erat non se ad eos iungere quibus incolumibus et domi dignitas et foris auctoritas retineretur. quae perfecta esse et suum cuique honorem et gradum redditum gaudeo, iudices, uehementerque laetor eaque omnia deorum uoluntate, studio populi Romani, consilio et imperio et feli-

137 citate L. Sullae gesta esse intellego. quod animaduersum est in eos qui contra omni ratione pugnarunt, non debeo reprehendere; quod uiris fortibus quorum opera eximia in rebus gerendis exstitit honos habitus est, laudo. quae ut fierent idcirco pugnatum esse arbitror meque in eo studio partium fuisse confiteor. sin autem id actum est et idcirco arma sumpta sunt ut homines postremi pecuniis alienis locupletarentur et in fortunas uniuscuiusque impetum facerent, et id non modo re prohibere non licet sed ne uerbis quidem uituperare, tum uero isto bello non recreatus neque restitutus sed subactus oppressusque populus Romanus est.

138   Verum longe aliter est: nil horum est, iudices. non modo non laedetur causa nobilitatis, si istis hominibus resistetis, uerum etiam ornabitur. [48] etenim qui haec uituperare uolunt Chrysogonum tantum posse queruntur; qui laudare uolunt concessum ei non esse commemorant. ac iam nihil est quod quisquam aut tam stultus aut tam improbus sit qui dicat: 'uellem quidem liceret; hoc dixissem.' dicas licet. 'hoc fecissem.' facias licet; nemo prohibet. 'hoc decreuissem.' decerne, modo recte; omnes approbabunt. 'hoc

139 iudicassem.' laudabunt omnes, si recte et ordine iudicaris. dum necesse erat resque ipsa cogebat, unus omnia poterat; qui posteaquam magistratus creauit legesque constituit, sua cuique procuratio auctoritasque est restituta. quam si retinere uolunt ii qui reciperarunt in perpetuum poterunt obtinere; sin has caedes et rapinas et hos tantos tamque profusos sumptus aut facient aut approbabunt — nolo in eos grauius quicquam ne ominis quidem causa dicere, unum hoc dico: nostri isti nobiles nisi uigilantes et boni et fortes et misericordes erunt, iis hominibus in quibus haec erunt ornamenta sua

140 concedant necesse est. quapropter desinant aliquando dicere male aliquem locutum esse, si qui uere ac libere locutus sit, desinant suam causam cum Chrysogono communicare, desinant, si ille laesus sit, de se aliquid detractum arbitrari, uideant ne turpe miserumque sit eos qui equestrem splendorem pati non potuerunt serui nequissimi dominationem ferre posse. quae quidem dominatio, iudices, in aliis rebus antea uersabatur, nunc uero quam uiam munitet et quod iter affectet uidetis: ad fidem, ad iusiurandum, ad iudicia

141 uestra, ad id quod solum prope in ciuitate sincerum sanctumque restat. hicne etiam sese putat aliquid posse Chrysogonus? hicne etiam potens esse uult? o rem miseram atque acerbam! neque mehercules hoc indigne fero, quod uerear ne quid possit, uerum quod ausus est, quod sperauit sese apud tales uiros aliquid posse ad perniciem innocentis, id ipsum queror. [49] idcircone spectata nobilitas armis atque ferro rem publicam reciperauit ut ad libidinem suam liberti seruulique nobilium bona fortunas uitasque nostras uexare possent? si id actum est, fateor me errasse qui hoc maluerim, fateor insanisse qui cum illis senserim; tametsi inermis, iudices, sensi. sin autem uictoria nobilium ornamento atque emolumento rei publicae populoque Romano debet esse, tum uero optimo et nobilissimo cuique meam orationem gratissimam esse oportet. quod si quis est qui et se et causam laedi putet cum Chrysogonus uituperetur, is causam ignorat, se ipsum probe non nouit; causa enim splendidior fiet, si nequissimo cuique resistetur, ille improbissimus Chrysogoni fautor qui sibi cum illo rationem communicatam putat laeditur, cum ab hoc splendore causae separatur. **142**

Verum haec omnis oratio, ut iam ante dixi, mea est, qua me uti res publica et dolor meus et istorum iniuria coegit. sed Roscius horum nihil indignum putat, neminem accusat, nihil de suo patrimonio queritur. putat homo imperitus morum, agricola et rusticus, ista omnia quae uos per Sullam gesta esse dicitis more, lege, iure gentium facta; culpa liberatus et crimine nefario solutus cupit a uobis discedere; si hac indigna suspicione careat, animo aequo se carere suis omnibus commodis dicit. rogat oratque te, Chrysogone, si nihil de patris fortunis amplissimis in suam rem conuertit, si nulla in re te fraudauit, si tibi optima fide sua omnia concessit, annumerauit, appendit, si uestitum quo ipse tectus erat anulumque de digito suum tibi tradidit, si ex omnibus rebus se ipsum nudum neque praeterea quicquam excepit, ut sibi per te liceat innocenti amicorum opibus uitam in egestate degere. [50] 'praedia mea tu possides, ego aliena misericordia uiuo; concedo, et quod animus aequus est et quia necesse est. mea domus tibi patet, mihi clausa est; fero. familia mea maxima tu uteris, ego seruum habeo nullum; patior et ferendum puto. quid uis amplius? quid insequeris? quid oppugnas? qua in re tuam uoluntatem laedi a me putas? ubi tuis commodis officio? quid tibi obsto?' si spoliorum causa uis hominem occidere, spoliasti; quid quaeris amplius? si inimicitiarum, quae sunt tibi inimicitiae cum eo cuius ante praedia possedisti quam ipsum cognosti? si metus, ab eone aliquid metuis quem uides ipsum ab se tam atrocem iniuriam propulsare non posse? sin, quod bona quae Rosci fuerunt tua facta sunt, idcirco hunc illius filium studes perdere, nonne ostendis id te uereri quod praeter ceteros tu metuere non debeas, nequando liberis proscriptorum bona patria reddantur? facis iniuriam, Chrysogone, si maiorem spem emptionis tuae in huius exitio ponis quam in iis rebus quas L. Sulla gessit. quodsi tibi causa nulla est cur hunc miserum tanta calamitate affici uelis, si tibi omnia sua praeter animam tradidit nec sibi quicquam paternum ne monumenti quidem causa clam reseruauit, per deos immortales! quae ista tanta crudelitas est, quae tam fera immanisque natura? quis umquam praedo **143**

144

145

146

fuit tam nefarius, quis pirata tam barbarus ut, cum integram praedam sine
147 sanguine habere posset, cruenta spolia detrahere mallet? scis hunc nihil
habere, nihil audere, nihil posse, nihil umquam contra rem tuam cogitasse,
et tamen oppugnas eum quem neque metuere potes neque odisse debes
nec quicquam iam habere reliqui uides quod ei detrahere possis? nisi hoc
indignum putas, quod uestitum sedere in iudicio uides quem tu e patrimonio
tamquam e naufragio nudum expulisti. quasi uero nescias hunc et ali et uestiri
a Caecilia Baliarici filia, Nepotis sorore, spectatissima femina, quae cum
patrem clarissimum, amplissimos patruos, ornatissimum fratrem haberet,
tamen, cum esset mulier, uirtute perfecit ut, quanto honore ipsa ex illorum
dignitate afficeretur, non minora illis ornamenta ex sua laude redderet.

148   [51] An, quod diligenter defenditur, id tibi indignum facinus uidetur?
mihi crede, si pro patris huius hospitiis et gratia uellent omnes huic hospites
adesse et auderent libere defendere, satis copiose defenderetur; sin autem
pro magnitudine iniuriae proque eo quod summa res publica in huius periculo temptatur haec omnes uindicarent, consistere mehercule uobis isto in
loco non liceret. nunc ita defenditur, non sane ut moleste ferre aduersarii
149 debeant neque ut se potentia superari putent. quae domi gerenda sunt, ea
per Caeciliam transiguntur, fori iudicique rationem M. Messalla, ut uidetis,
iudices, suscepit; qui, si iam satis aetatis ac roboris haberet, ipse pro Sex.
Roscio diceret. quoniam ad dicendum impedimento est aetas et pudor qui
ornat aetatem, causam mihi tradidit, quem sua causa cupere ac debere intel-
legebat, ipse assiduitate, consilio, auctoritate, diligentia perfecit ut Sex. Rosci
uita erepta de manibus sectorum sententiis iudicum permitteretur. nimirum,
iudices, pro hac nobilitate pars maxima ciuitatis in armis fuit; haec acta res
est ut ii nobiles restituerentur in ciuitatem qui hoc facerent quod facere Mes-
sallam uidetis, qui caput innocentis defenderent, qui iniuriae resisterent, qui
quantum possent in salute alterius quam in exitio mallent ostendere; quod
si omnes qui eodem loco nati sunt facerent, et res publica ex illis et ipsi ex
inuidia minus laborarent.

150   [52] Verum si a Chrysogono, iudices, non impetramus ut pecunia nostra
contentus sit, uitam ne petat, si ille adduci non potest ut, cum ademerit
nobis omnia quae nostra erant propria, ne lucem quoque hanc quae communis est eripere cupiat, si non satis habet auaritiam suam pecunia explere,
nisi etiam crudelitati sanguis praebitus sit, unum perfugium, iudices, una
spes reliqua est Sex. Roscio eadem quae rei publicae, uestra pristina bonitas et misericordia. quae si manet, salui etiam nunc esse possumus; sin ea
crudelitas quae hoc tempore in re publica uersata est uestros quoque ani-
mos — id quod fieri profecto non potest — duriores acerbioresque reddit,
actum est, iudices; inter feras satius est aetatem degere quam in hac tanta

immanitate uersari. ad eamne rem uos reseruati estis, ad eamne rem delecti ut **151** eos condemnaretis quos sectores ac sicarii iugulare non potuissent? solent hoc boni imperatores facere cum proelium committunt, ut in eo loco quo fugam hostium fore arbitrentur milites collocent, in quos si qui ex acie fugerint de improuiso incidant. nimirum similiter arbitrantur isti bonorum emptores uos hic, tales uiros, sedere qui excipiatis eos qui de suis manibus effugerint. di prohibeant, iudices, ut hoc quod maiores consilium publicum uocari uoluerunt praesidium sectorum existimetur! an uero, iudices, uos non intellegitis nihil **152** aliud agi nisi ut proscriptorum liberi quauis ratione tollantur et eius rei initium in uestro iureiurando atque in Sex. Rosci periculo quaeri? dubium est ad quem maleficium pertineat, cum uideatis ex altera parte sectorem, inimicum, sicarium eundemque accusatorem hoc tempore, ex altera parte egentem, probatum suis filium, in quo non modo culpa nulla sed ne suspicio quidem potuit consistere? numquid hic aliud uidetis obstare Roscio nisi quod patris bona uenierunt?

[53] Quodsi id uos suscipitis et eam ad rem operam uestram profitemini, **153** si idcirco sedetis ut ad uos adducantur eorum liberi quorum bona uenierunt, cauete, per deos immortales! iudices, ne noua et multo crudelior per uos proscriptio instaurata esse uideatur. illam priorem quae facta est in eos qui arma capere potuerunt tamen senatus suscipere noluit, ne quid acrius quam more maiorum comparatum est publico consilio factum uideretur, hanc uero quae ad eorum liberos atque ad infantium puerorum incunabula pertinet nisi hoc iudicio a uobis reicitis et aspernamini, uidete per deos immortales! quem in locum rem publicam peruenturam putetis! homines sapientes et ista auc- **154** toritate et potestate praeditos qua uos estis ex quibus rebus maxime res publica laborat, iis maxime mederi conuenit. uestrum nemo est quin intellegat populum Romanum, qui quondam in hostes lenissimus existimabatur, hoc tempore domestica crudelitate laborare. hanc tollite ex ciuitate, iudices, hanc pati nolite diutius in hac re publica uersari. quae non modo id habet in se mali quod tot ciues atrocissime sustulit uerum etiam hominibus lenissimis ademit misericordiam consuetudine incommodorum. nam cum omnibus horis aliquid atrociter fieri uidemus aut audimus, etiam qui natura mitissimi sumus assiduitate molestiarum sensum omnem humanitatis ex animis amittimus.

COMMENTARY

His first criminal defense, that of Sex. Roscius of Ameria on charges of parricide, shows C. already a master in directing and controlling the jurors' emotions. He will have learned the technique more from observation than from handbooks, Antonius' defense of Norbanus, for example, having left a deep impression on him; cf. Solmsen 1968: 240–2; *TLRR* no. 86. There Antonius had succeeded in channeling the jurors' anger at Caepio, charged with losing the battle of Arausio; here C. makes such a lightning-rod out of Sulla's newly rich freedman Chrysogonus. In addition, to satisfy the virtual requirement of an alternative suspect for a murder (cf. §12n.), he fingers two apparent relatives of the defendant, T. Roscius Magnus and T. Roscius Capito. The case against them, especially Capito, is, however, thin and circumstantial. C. has very little to offer in the way of evidence, merely the decree passed by the *decuriones* of Ameria seeking restoration of the reputation of the deceased and the fortunes of his son (§25) and the fact that the son was not at the scene of the crime (Rome) when it was committed (§18); and he criticizes the other side for denying access to the testimony of slave witnesses (§§77, 119–22). He relies on the prosecution's own characterization of his client as a rustic, reinterpreted in a positive sense (§§39, 74–5), and the prosecution's inability to establish a convincing motive or *modus operandi* for the crime. C.'s mastery of the audience's emotions is shown by the shouts with which they greeted the purple passage on the parricide's punishment that slightly embarrassed the mature C. (§72; cf. *Orat.* 107) as well as his client's acquittal and C.'s own enhanced reputation at the bar (Plut. *Cic.* 3.6; *Brut.* 312). The major divisions of the speech are as follows; the detailed contents can be found under each individual head:

I *Exordium* (1–14)
II *Narratio* (15–29)
III *Digressio I* (29–32)
IV *Digressio II* (33–4)
V *Diuisio* (35–6)
VI *Refutatio / argumentatio*
    A   Erucius' charges (37–82)
    B   *Anticategoria* of Magnus and Capito (83–123)
    C   Chrysogonus (124–42)
VII *Peroratio* (143–54).

COMMENTARY 57

The speech is cited as *Pro Sexto Roscio Amerino* at *Off.* 2.51, and this form is often followed by editors (e.g. Donkin, Kasten); but the ethnic is weakly attested in the mss of our work (*Gs*) and so may not have formed a part of the title when published.

EXORDIVM (1–14)

The purpose of the exordium is to render the listener *beneuolus*, *attentus*, and *docilis* (Quint. 4.1.5). The tableau of the courtroom as C. depicts it is calculated to pique the jurors' interest, with a very junior, little known, and relatively inexperienced advocate rising to speak, rather than many other better qualified men sitting as *aduocati* in the benches (*subsellia*) reserved for the defense (§1). The description, especially when he speaks of the *periculum* deterring others, will command attention and perhaps begin to garner sympathetic support for himself and, ultimately, his client. The listeners' attention will be redoubled when he alludes to a more generalized *periculum quod in omnes intenditur* (§7). At the same time he begins the work of alienating the jurors from the prosecution, who are at first represented by a single figure, L. Cornelius Chrysogonus, who claims to have purchased the estate of the elder Sex. Roscius at auction (§6). Property interests are thus placed firmly at the center of the case from the beginning, and greed is said to be the motor driving the prosecution (§8). In general, even in this early case, C. shows himself astute at reading the public mood. This was the first case tried for a long time under the *lex Cornelia de sicariis et ueneficiis*; the civil war and Sullan proscriptions had intervened (cf. Introduction, secs. 2–3; §11n.); there was evidently a sense of revulsion at the sheer amount of killing and a desire to reassert the authority of the courts by firm handling of defendants on murder charges; the prosecution was evidently hoping to exploit this sentiment (cf. §28). But C., at the end of the exordium, surprisingly calls for severe treatment of malefactors himself (§12); for he will, in fact, turn the tables and charge that the murder was carried out by men associated with the prosecution (*anticategoria*; cf. on §§83–123). Thus, as in an operatic overture, the main themes are sounded in this exordium: the victimization of his client, the greed and violence of the prosecutors, and the times and citizens' proper response to them. This exordium is also remarkable for what C. does *not* do: he scarcely mentions his client; he does not justify his own rôle as advocate as the result of a long personal relationship with him or his family; nor does he allude to the prosecutor Erucius or to the charge of parricide; instead he piques the jurors' interest by oblique reference to dangers besetting the defense; cf. Loutsch 1994:

ch. 1, especially 172–3; Cerutti 1996: ch 2. The contents may be outlined as
follows:

  I C. as defense speaker (1–5)
     A   Others better qualified but deterred (1)
     B   His reasons for taking the case (2–4)
        (1) Can speak more freely than others about affairs of state
           (*a*) His youth will be pardoned
           (*b*) Has not yet held public office
        (2) Request made by persons of influence
     C   Summary of the position (5)
 II The deterrent: Chrysogonus (5–6)
     A   His status as purchaser of Roscius' property
     B   His "request"
III C.'s charge to the jury (7–8)
     A   Help Roscius
     B   Resist his adversaries
     C   Roscius to be condemned if any motive but greed underlies the
         prosecution
IV C.'s inadequacies as defense speaker but resolve to carry on (9–10)
 V The presiding magistrate and circumstances of the trial (11)
VI Reversal of rôles with defense calling for severity (12–14)

1 Credo ego uos . . . qui sedeant comparandus: an unusual opening:
only three times elsewhere does C. begin a speech with a first-person verb
(*Clu.*, *Ver.* 2.4, *Cat.* 4), here reinforced with the optional pronoun to effect
a contrast with *uos*; it is, in addition, a front-loaded period, with the main
clause trailed by a series of subordinate clauses; cf. Posch 1979: 314 and
n27. Though C.'s action and referent (*comparandus*) bookend the sentence,
the intervening qualifiers temper any implication of arrogance (though these
can be taken as ironic in view of the following criticism; cf. Haury 1955:
114n6). *Div. Caec.* begins similarly with the jurors' supposed wonderment: *si
quis uestrum, iudices, . . . forte miratur me . . . ad accusandum descendere . . .* ; cf. also
Sest. 1 *si quis antea, iudices, mirabatur . . .* The *topos* goes back to Isoc. *Archid.* 1,
which C. imitates and at the same time complicates; cf. Weische 1972: 21–
2; Loutsch 1994: 167–71. *iudices* is the standard address in a forensic speech
for the judges. *quid sit quod* "what is (the reason) that" or "why it is that."
summi oratores hominesque nobilissimi: the chiastically arranged
adj.-noun units create a sonorous block in contrast with the series of short
words with which the speech begins; cf. Posch 1979: 316. *summus orator* is a frequent combination in C.'s *rhetorica* (e.g. *Inv.* 1.75 *tantum inter summos oratores*

et mediocres interesse) but occurs only here in the speeches; the claim is contradicted, however, at §59; see *ad loc.* C. refers to those who have a consul among their ancestors as *homines nobiles*; cf. Berry on *Sul.* 37.5. Swarney 1993: 141–3 shows how C. uses the social eminence of Roscius' supporters to compensate for the defendant's own unattractive rusticity (and, it might be added, C.'s own lack of distinction). **sedeant:** i.e. they occupy the *subsellia* on the defendant's side of the court so as to show support as *aduocati*; the subjunctive is concessive ("while these sit"): G–L §587. *potissimum* "in particular," "of all people": *OLD* s.v. 1. **qui . . . sim . . . comparandus:** the subjunctive is generic, defining C.'s position ("the kind who . . . "); cf. G–L §§631.1; *NLS* §§155–6 and 230(3). **neque aetate neque ingenio neque auctoritate:** the polysyndeton emphasizes the sheer number of points. *ingenium* and *aetas* are among qualities contributing to *auctoritas* at *Top.* 73. All three are also valuable in a prosecutor; cf. *Div. Caec.* 35–9 (*ingenium*) and 70 (*aetas*); *auctoritas* is discussed (with reference to the Sicilians) ibid. 17–21; for *auctoritas* as viewed by the Romans cf. Heinze 1960: 43–58. Born in 106, C. was twenty-six at the time of the trial (an *adulescentulus* according to *Orat.* 107; cf. the reference to his *adulescentia* at §3; Introduction sections 5 and 6). **cum his qui sedeant:** *hic* refers, as usual, to what is actually present; cf. Roby §2258; K–S 1 621; the subj. is by attraction to the mood of the leading verb (G–L §§629 and 663).

omnes enim hi . . . non audent: C. often exploits to advantage what is visible to his audience; cf. in general Vasaly 1993: especially 15–26; Pöschl 1983: 34; here it is the persons seated in court (*hi quos uidetis*); the consensus is weaker than C. suggests, however; only later does he acknowledge that T. Roscius Magnus is present to support the prosecution (cf. §84 with n.). *nouus* often has negative connotations in Latin ("strange, unheard of": *OLD* s.v. 3). *scelus*, originally applied to physical deformity ("crookedness"), was transferred to the religious sphere as opposite of *pietas*, then broadened to "wickedness" generally; cf. Reichenbecher 1913: 7–9; Petersmann 1996: 272–3. *conflo* here is "invent, concoct": *OLD* s.v. 4; similarly *confingo* (§30). *ipsi* "in person"; cf. §§29 and 149; *TLL* s.v. *ipse* 335.75. Some of Roscius' *aduocati* are later identified: P. Scipio, M. Metellus (§77) and M. Messalla (§149); for the last-named a different excuse is given; see *ad loc.* The *iniquitas temporum* will be the topic at §§3 *fin.*, 11, and especially 150–4.

ita fit ut . . . quia periculum uitant: the desire to lend support to their erstwhile client's son (*officium sequi*) is in conflict, C. claims, with a perceived danger. This implicit criticism of cowardice was perhaps planted to encourage the jurors to want to do better (so Posch 1979: 316–17). The formula *ita fit ut* is characteristic of C.'s early and less formal writing (cf. Dyck on *Off.* 1.101); it occurs elsewhere in the speeches only at *Quinct.* 8 and *Pis.* 81. This sentence highlights the two sides of the behavior of the *homines nobilissimi* with the two heavy causal connectors *propterea quod* and *idcirco quia* lending weight to the antithesis. For *officium sequi* (where *sequor* = "use as a guide to conduct": *OLD* s.v. 10b) cf. *Leg.* 1.48, *Fin.* 2.58, *Div.* 1.27, *Fam.* 6.1.3. For the conative present (*periculum uitant*) cf. G–L §227.2. On the accumulation of words for danger and fear in the *exordium* cf. Benferhat 2003–4: 281. The criticism of the *homines nobilissimi* is blunted by the following description of C.'s less exposed position but prepares the way for the detailed critique of the *nobiles* and contrast to *uera nobilitas* at §§136–42; cf. Buchheit 1975a: 195–6.

2 quid ergo? . . . eam praereptam uelim: C.'s different behavior could be explained either by his being more willing to run risks (*audacissimus . . . ex omnibus*) or more devoted to duty (*officiosior*); cf. the supposition at *Quinct.* 72 that Quinctius' advocate would be *homo antiqui offici*. *audax* can mean "bold, daring" in a good sense but often, as here, shading toward "reckless, rash" (*OLD* s.v. 1–2); with thirty-one occurrences *audax / audacia / audac(i)ter* is a theme running throughout the speech. *minime* ("by no means") is often used in replies to questions (ibid. s.v. 2b). *tanto* is abl. of measure of difference (G–L §403; *NLS* §82). *ne . . . quidem* "not . . . either," emphatic: "I am not so eager for praise on that ground either." *cupidus* ("eager for, desirous of") is often used, as here, with the objective gen. *praeripio* "seize first, snatch" is accompanied by the dat. of disadvantage: *OLD* s.v. 1.

quae me igitur . . . reciperem?: *igitur* is postpositive here and elsewhere throughout this speech, as it usually is in C.; cf. Ramsey on *Phil.* 2.41.22. *causam recipere* is said of an advocate's "undertaking a case": *OLD* s.v. *recipio* 10a. In his early career C. was eager to take on work; at §31 he concedes *forsitan in suscipienda causa temere impulsus adulescentia fecerim*; cf. his decision-making in 74, as described at *Clu.* 49–50, when he (ill-advisedly) agreed to handle the murder case of the freedman Scamander at the request of citizens of Aletrium, located a little west of his native Arpinum.

quia, si qui istorum . . . quam dixisset putaretur: this is an account of C.'s reasoning at the time he took on the case (*quae me . . . res . . . impulit*) and so is framed in subjunctive and past sequence with *dixisset* for original *dixerit*, *fecisset* for *fecerit*, and *putaretur* for *putabitur*, as the sequel with the retained *dixero* and *poterit* shows; cf. Kinsey 1987b. *iste* is used of what the jurors (and others present) see; cf. *OLD* s.v. 1a. *quos uidetis adesse* was deleted by Fleckeisen as repeated from the second sentence; but *istorum* by itself might be taken as contemptuous (cf. *OLD* s.v. *iste* 3); hence Halm wanted to change it to *horum*, unnecessarily. For *auctoritas* cf. §1n.; when used of persons *amplitudo* is "distinction, eminence": *OLD* s.v. 2a. *uerbum facere* is to "speak a word" (ibid. s.v. *uerbum* 5c); such paraphrases of a verb using *facere* are colloquial and tend to be avoided in C.'s later work; cf. Hellmuth 1877: 40–2; von Albrecht 2003: 99; here *si uerbum . . . fecisset* varies *si . . . dixisset. res publica* is "affairs of state" (*OLD* s.v. 1a). **id quod in hac causa fieri necesse est:** the point is not obvious; the murder victim, the elder Sextus Roscius, is alleged to have been killed among the enemy (cf. §21n.), but that fact, though touched upon (§§125–8), is not going to be the basis for the defense because of "the extreme delicacy with which a legalistic defense had to be made" and the odious nature of parricide; see Alexander 2002: 161–4 (the quoted words at 163), who cites the previous literature. Politically sensitive points are broached (cf. Paterson 2004: 85), but C. advisedly reserves these for the last fifth of the speech, by which time he has assured himself of the jurors' sympathy: beginning at §124 criticism of Chrysogonus gradually broadens to warnings about a possible revival of the proscriptions; cf. on §§143–54. C. later claimed to have been placed in a similar position of having to discuss politically sensitive matter in his defense of C. Antonius in 59 BC; cf. *Dom.* 41; Paterson 2004: 87. **multo plura dixisse quam dixisset putaretur** could stand as a description of the pregnant style much admired and imitated in the early Empire; cf. Sen. *Ep.* 114.1 *abruptae sententiae et suspiciosae, in quibus plus intellegendum esset quam audiendum.* Cerutti 1996: 60 calls attention to the *susurratio* of C.'s sibilants here, by which Roscius' *aduocati* "are reduced to a whispering mass of huddled fear." At the same time C. contrives to present his deficiency in *auctoritas* as an advantage; cf. Paterson 2004: 87.

3 ego autem . . . in uulgus emanare poterit: emphatic placement of *ego* signals a contrast; for *si* with concessive force ("even if") cf. *OLD* s.v. 9; for the indicatives *dixero* and *poterit* cf. the preceding n. *libere* is often used with verbs of speaking in the sense "openly, frankly": *OLD* s.v. 3a; cf. §§31 and 61; *Clu.* 142; *Phil.* 3.5 and 5.19; for *libere dicere* as a right of the defense cf. Cerami 1998: especially 19–20. The emphatic *nequaquam* negates *similiter*, by litotes "far differently"; *tamen*, i.e. in spite of the public discussion. **exire atque in uulgus emanare:** the amplification *atque in uulgus emanare* serves clarity. *emano* originally is "pour forth" (of liquids) and hence metaphorically of facts "leak out" (*OLD* s.v. 1 and 3a); in the context of the dissemination of information *in uulgus* = "to the general public": ibid. s.v. *uulgus* 1b.

  deinde quod . . . et prudentiam: *deinde* presents this as a second reason parallel with the preceding *quia, si qui . . .* (§2), but it is more plausibly an explanation of the assertion *nequaquam . . . similiter oratio mea exire atque in uulgus emanare potest*; hence Bake's deletion of *deinde*. A further reason is introduced at §4 (*accedit illa quoque causa . . .*); and he refers back again to the chain of reasons at §5 (*his de causis . . .*). C. evidently inserted *deinde* in order to create smaller, more perspicuous units; but this passage illustrates the imperfect match between content and symmetry of form in the young C.; cf. von Albrecht, *RE* Suppl. 13 1251.16–18 with reference to *Quinct.* Instead of repeating the *si qui istorum dixisset . . .* construction, C. characterizes the *dictum* ("assertion") of others, though he then returns to the conditional mode (*ego siquid liberius dixero*). For *nobilitas* and *amplitudo* cf. on §§1 and 2 respectively. *temere* is to be taken closely with *dicto* and shows that, though *dictum* has been substantivized since Plautus, its verbal force is still felt: "a thing rashly said": cf. *OLD* s.vv. *temere, dictum. potest* is to be taken not only with *esse* but also with the impersonal *concedi*: "can concession be made to" (ibid. s.v. *concedo* 11a). *aetas* implies that the silent *homines nobilissimi* are older, but that is not true of all; cf. §149n.

ego si quid . . . adulescentiae meae poterit: as in the previous explanation, the emphatically placed pronoun *ego* provides the point of contrast; for the reference to C.'s *adulescentia* cf. *Q. Rosc.* 44 *mea adulescentia indiget illorum bona existimatione*; for his age at the time of the speech cf. §1n. **liberius** "too freely" (see the n. before last); in Latin the comparative of adjectives and adverbs is often used without explicit standard of comparison, in which case the general norm is understood: G–L §297. *occultum esse* [sc. *poterit*] varies the preceding *obscurum*, which does not apply to a statement by one of the *homines nobilissimi. accedere ad rem publicam* is "to begin to occupy oneself with affairs of state," i.e. to hold public office; cf. *OLD* s.v. *accedo* 9a; the combination recurs at *Rep.* 1.9; *Top.* 82; *Off.* 1.28; *Phil.* 5.50; *Q.fr.* 1.2.2. *ignosci* varies the preceding *concedi* and follows the same construction (impersonal passive + dat.).

tametsi non modo . . . de ciuitate sublata est: an aside prompted by the mention of pardon (*ignosci*). This criticism of the times is at odds with the preceding argument that he *will* receive pardon (hence the connection with the concessive *tametsi*, similarly used at §§53, 83, 118, 124, 135 and 141). **cognoscendi consuetudo** is "the habit of trying cases": *OLD* s.v. *cognosco* 4; this had indeed been eliminated (*sublata*), our case being the first murder trial after a long interval (§11; see *ad loc.*); there is a mild pun on the verb stem shared between *ignosco* and *cognosco*; cf. Holst 1925: 63. Berry 2004: 82–3 argues that this passage was added to the speech at the time of its publication. The statement would, however, have been true when the speech was delivered and is in keeping with other criticisms of the times that must have been part of the original speech; cf. §9n.

4 accedit illa quoque . . . uoluntatem neglegere debebam: Cicero characterizes himself as a young man deeply embedded in and respectful of the network of Roman social relationships; cf.

Kurczyk 2006: 140. Here *accedo* has a different sense (see the n. before last), namely "be added": *OLD* s.v. 15a. *ille*, as often, looks forward, to be defined by the *quod*-clause; cf. *OLD* s.v. 3. **petitum sit:** the cause is given in the subj. since C. is representing the (assumed) reasoning in the minds of others; cf. G–L §541. *saluo officio* is "without detriment to duty": ibid. s.v. *saluus* 7b; similarly *Fam.* 13.77.1 *non existimaui me saluo iure nostrae amicitiae multorumque inter nos officiorum facere posse . . .* The counterpoint is provided this time by *a me*. Here the more intense *contendo* ("ask for earnestly, press for": *OLD* s.v. 7) replaces *peto* used of the request of others. The polysyndeton *et . . . et . . . et* piles up the factors so as to make the pressure seem overwhelming. *amicitia, beneficia,* and *dignitas* are the relevant factors to be weighed; cf. the influencing factors listed at *Off.* 2.21. The first implies an established exchange of *beneficia* (cf. *Off.* 1.56 with Dyck's n.); *dignitas* opens up the prospect of desirable *amicitia* and associated *beneficia* for the future, an important consideration for an ambitious young man like C.; for another example of C.'s deciding such a matter cf. §2n. The following tricolon, by reversal, highlights the corresponding items of baggage entailed by a refusal: *beneuolentiam . . . ignorare . . . auctoritatem aspernari . . . uoluntatem neglegere. beneuolentia* would cover the case of previous *beneficia; ignoro* = "ignore," a relatively infrequent usage (*OLD* s.v. 4). *auctoritas* would follow from the *dignitas* of the petitioner, evidently M. Valerius Messalla Niger, acting on behalf of Caecilia Metella (cf. §§27 and 149); for the concept cf. §1n. *uoluntas* is "goodwill" (*OLD* s.v. 8b), not something a young *nouus homo* like C. can afford to take lightly (*neglegere*).

5 his de causis . . . ne omnino desertus esset: the summarizing formula *his de causis* rounds off the topic; *causa* appears in two senses, "reason" and "case," an example of *distinctio*; cf. Lausberg §804; Holst 1925: 56; similarly §149. *ego* again spotlights C. *patronus* is the influential person who affords protection to clients; since representation in court was one of the *officia* expected of the *patronus*, the word also comes to be used for the advocate (corresponding to Gk συνήγορος "with-speaker," implying a more equal relation); cf. *OLD* and LSJ s.vv.; Crook 1995: 32–4 and 39. C.'s modest affirmations are set against emphatic denials of more ambitious claims. **non electus . . . sed relictus:** for the wordplay with assonance cf. Holst 1925: 86. *unus* is used for emphasis with or without a superlative; cf. H–S 165 with literature. **qui . . . possem:** for the generic/defining subj. cf. §1n. Even in his maturity C. tried to be modest in any claims about his natural ability (*ingenium*); cf. e.g. *Arch.* 1 *si quid est in me ingeni, iudices, quod sentio quam sit exiguum . . . ;* here *maximum ingenium* (denied) forms a neat contrast with *minimum periculum. praesidium* is used of protection in various senses; the legal meaning found

here is not uncommon; cf. e.g. *Div. Caec.* 2. Roscius' need for *praesidium* recurs
in the literal sense at §§13 and 26–7; cf. also §§111, 126, and 151. This passage
provides the only two instances of the more archaic *uti* used instead of *ut* in
the speech; cf. H–S 632. *uerum* varies *sed*. Here C. begins the depiction of his
client as pitiable, developed especially at §§23, 27, and 145–7.

Forsitan quaeratis . . . facta non est: the use of synonyms (*terror,
formido*) here allows C. to qualify each in a certain way: *iste* refers back to
something already mentioned or otherwise known, here without implying
contempt; cf. *OLD* s.v. 3; the fear has been implied by *periculum uitare* (§1); *tanta
formido* prompts the relative clause with consecutive force; cf. G–L §631.1.
Kinsey 1980: 185 notes that "the *nobiles* themselves would hardly have told
Cicero that they were frightened to speak, so this must be Cicero's own
reason." He goes on to argue that since Sulla's violence was confined to the
earlier period, they could have spoken with impunity. **tot ac tales uiros:**
a shorthand version of §1 *tot summi oratores hominesque nobilissimi.* **pro capite
et fortunis:** *caput* is the head and stands for the person's life when at
risk as penalty for criminal offenses; though in the late Republic exile was
usually allowed as an alternative to the death penalty (cf. *OLD* s.v. *caput* 1,
4, 5; Mommsen 1899: 70–3), this was probably not the case in a trial for
parricide; cf. Cloud 1971: 44–5; Bauman 1996: 30; Santalucia 1999: 147–8;
C. will speak throughout of his client's *caput* or *uita* being at stake: §§6, 8,
15, 30, 128, 149. At the time of the trial the property the defendant stood to
inherit from his father is already in others' hands (§§21, 23, and 144–5); C.
will claim that his client is interested only in maintaining his innocence, not
in recovering property; cf. §§7, 49, 128, 143, and 146–7; as Vasaly 1993: 162
remarks, "this extreme humility forms part of the positive stereotype of the
young rustic." **quemadmodum consuerunt:** in his later style C. tends to
eliminate the cumbersome *quemadmodum* in favor of *ut*; cf. von Albrecht 2003:
100. This must have been their practice while the courts were still functioning
(cf. §11n.); hence Ernesti wanted to substitute plupf. *consueuerant*, but a good
clausula (trochee + spondee) is thereby destroyed. *quod* refers back to *terror
et formido*, the neuter being the strongest gender for inanimate entities; cf.
G–L §§614.5 and 286.1. *ignoro* is to "have no knowledge, be ignorant of"
(*OLD* s.v. 1; cf. the different sense at §4). For *propterea quod* cf. §1n. *consulto*
"deliberately" is emphatic: it was not a mere inadvertence; he thus suggests
the prosecution's deviousness; cf. Alexander 2002: 165. *eius rei* is emphasized
by separation from the limited noun *mentio*, an example of hyperbaton, and
is personified as implied subject of a verb (*conflauit*); C. thus shifts, somewhat
abruptly, from the *terror et formido* to what he presents as the cause underlying
the prosecution. For *conflo* cf. §1n.

6 bona patris huiusce . . . L. Cornelius Chrysogonus: *hic* is used by the speaker of himself or persons associated with him (cf. G–L §305.2); hence C. uses it regularly of his client in forensic speeches. As its genitive *huius* alternates with *huiusce*, in which the deictic force is strengthened by the suffix *-ce* (cf. *OLD* s.v. *-ce*; Leumann 1977: 468); this is the first of twelve instances in our speech (as against fifteen of *huius*); C.'s fondness for *huiusce* declines markedly, however; it occurs only five times in speeches subsequent to his consular year. Homonymous father and son are common among the Romans (so e.g. C., his father and his paternal grandfather all bore the same name), much less so among the Greeks, who preferred to name after the grandfather; cf. Ernst Fraenkel, *RE* xvi 2.1624.14 (s.v. Namenwesen). Like his son, the elder Sextus Roscius is known only from our speech; cf. Von der Mühll, *RE* ia 1.1116.54 (Roscius 6). **sexagiens:** 60x [sc. *sestertia* = 100,000 sesterces], i.e. six million sesterces, a substantial sum, in striking contrast to the purchase price of two thousand (the figure two thousand drachmas at Plut. *Cic.* 3 appears to be based on a misunderstanding; cf. Alexander 2002: 303n6). When one of Sulla's favorites was bidding, others no doubt stayed away; cf. Liebs 2007: 61. Rawson 1991: 215 and n40 compares this figure, divided among the thirteen farms (§20), with other known property values of the time. At such a rate of profit it is easy to see how Sulla's favorites amassed great riches; one centurion is reported to have exceeded a census of 10 million sesterces (Asc. p. 90c). **quae de uiro . . . sese dicit emisse:** a rare example of *oratio obliqua* in the exordium; cf. *Div. Caec.* 2–3; Wiesthaler 1956: 17n3; von Albrecht, *RE* Suppl. xiii 1290.45–9. **fortissimo et clarissimo:** C. often juxtaposes the terms; here the order *clarissimo et fortissimo* is also attested (both orders are also found elsewhere in his corpus); one suspects that in our passage military exploits will take precedence over social standing (for *clarissimus* being "generally reserved for prominent senators" cf. Berry on *Sul.* 3.2), and that is indeed the reading of the archetype (albeit contradicted by one early witness). For Sulla see in general Keaveney 1982; Hinard 1985b; Letzner 2000. **quem honoris causa nomino:** as a young man very unequal in rank C. must use this precautionary formula in naming the great and powerful; cf. §15 *quas . . . familias honestatis amplitudinisque gratia nomino*; §27 *quam honoris causa nomino*; Offermann 1974: 67; Moreau 2006: especially 296–7 and 299 and n28. Later he will mock the formula as used by Antony of Brutus (*Phil.* 2.30–1); cf. Parzinger 1910: 100–1; von Albrecht, *RE* Suppl. 13 1304.10–14 and 2003: 101. Sulla notoriously declared the property of the proscribed his personal booty (*Agr.* 2.56; *Off.* 2.27; Hinard 1985a: 51) and himself presided over auctions from the tribunal (Plut. *Sul.* 33.2); hence Chrysogonus' claim. *uel*, used with a superlative, means "quite, altogether";

cf. *OLD* s.v. 5c; though rare in archaic Latin and not found in this sense in *Inv.* or *Quinct.*, it will from now on be much used by C.; cf. Landgraf *ad loc.* This first mention of Chrysogonus, who was not present in court, came as a great surprise to the prosecutor, and subsequent allusions to him unleashed a frenzy of activity on the prosecution side (§60). He is identified with all three names, a mark of great formality (cf. Adams 1978: 164); this is seen as a form of mockery (*irrisio*) by sch. Gronov. p. 303.17 Stangl; cf. Offermann 1974: 69; Hinard 1979: 75; in the sequel he is referred to merely as Chrysogonus (C. plays on the meaning of the Gk name at §124; see *ad loc.*); for emphatic final placement of his name cf. §21n. He was evidently a freedman of Sulla (cf. Treggiari 1969: 183n1), though his precise function in Sulla's administration is unclear; he also appears in the list of powerful freedmen at Plin. *Nat.* 35.200; cf. Münzer, *RE* IV 1.1281.67 (Cornelius 101); C. will deal with him in detail at §§124–49. **adulescens . . . potentissimus:** Treggiari 1969: 260n1 suggests that the use of *adulescens* may be pejorative on the analogy of the use of *puer* of slaves of any age (cf. §59n.). *potens*/*potentia* is the leitmotif accompanying Chrysogonus throughout this speech; *potentia* is his weapon at §35 *Chrysogonus . . . is qui plurimum potest potentia pugnat*; C. imagines his conduct of the case being reported to Chrysogonus in these terms: *gratiam potentiamque eius neglegi* (§60); similarly the reference at §122 to *nimiam gratiam potentiamque Chrysogoni*; cf. Buchheit 1975a: 199–200. Few *adulescentes* were, however, powerful at Rome (cf. Afzelius 1942: 213; Vasaly 1993: 169), and his power was not absolute; he was dependent on the favor of Sulla, and he might be worth less to Sulla than some others (cf. Kinsey 1980: 183); hence C.'s tactic of censuring Chrysogonus while claiming that the criticism does not apply to the former (§§21, 131); thus C.'s later claim that this speech was a blow struck *contra L. Sullae dominantes opes* (*Off.* 2.51) is overstated; it was at most a blow struck against Chrysogonus, and even he is shielded from the charge of murder.

   is a uobis . . . metumque tollatis: in the absence of the presiding officer's formal charge to the jury, the ancient advocates formulated their own charges, sometimes even, as here, pretending to speak for the other side; C. will set his own *postulatio* against this at §7; cf. Riggsby 1999: 15, 27–33, and 55–9. *is* refers back to and focuses on the just mentioned Chrysogonus: *OLD* s.v. 1; similarly *ea* in §27; *is cum curasset* in §33. *postulo* is ordinarily used of requesting something to which one is entitled (*OLD* s.v. 1; Don. on Ter. *An.* 422; cf. §77); here the irony is made even more palpable by the following *alienam pecuniam* and *nullo iure. pecunia*, a collective from *pecu* ("flock, herd"), can be "possessions, property" in a broad sense, not just "money"; *OLD* s.v. *pecunia*; here it varies *bona*. **tam plenam atque praeclaram** follows from the value indicated above; the alliteration lends emphasis (cf. §35n.); the expression is varied below: *patrimonium tam amplum et copiosum* and §8 *illam opimam praeclaramque praedam*. **nullo iure** is contestable: C. has just reported Chrysogonus' claim to have bought the property legitimately at auction (albeit he will cast doubt on it at §§127–8); cf. also on §23 (*insolens in aliena*). *inuado* (often, as here, with *in* + acc.) is to "lay hands on, seize possession of": *OLD* s.v. 6a; cf. §13 *accusant ii qui in fortunas huius inuaserunt*; §23 *in praedia huius inuadit*; similarly of Antony, *Phil.* 2.41; the process of violent dispossession is described in different terms at §21 (*impetum facit*). For the *uita* of Sextus Roscius as the issue cf. §5n. The use of the synonyms *obstare atque officere* strengthens the idea of blocking. The chiastic arrangement of verbs and objects (*deleatis . . . suspicionem . . . metumque tollatis*) seems to restore a sense of order, just as the denoted actions (from Chrysogonus' standpoint) would do; at the same time a fine concluding rhythm (cretic + trochee) is effected.

    sese hoc incolumi . . . effundere atque consumere: an example of explicative asyndeton, clarifying the basis for Chrysogonus' suspicion and fear; cf. H–S 830. **hoc incolumi** "while my client lives": since Latin as yet lacks a participle for *esse*, substantive and adj. function as abl. absolute in the classical period; cf. G–L §410.3N.5; here it is equivalent to a protasis and corresponds to the alternative *damnato et eiecto* below. For *hic* used of his client see above; *incolumis*, which shares a root with *calamitas*, is "unharmed" in various senses: it often means "undamaged in power, wealth, position," but Roscius' position and wealth are already compromised; it is his *uita* that is said to be Chrysogonus' obstacle, and C. will claim that his client's life is under direct threat (§§13 and 26–7); cf. *OLD* s.v. 1 and 2; similar wording at §26 *neque sese arbitrari posse diutius alienam pecuniam domino incolumi obtinere*. What had been the *bona* or *pecunia* of the elder Roscius now appears in a different light as the *patrimonium* of the son. On the economic model implicitly approved in this speech, by which wealth is created by *diligentia* and *parsimonia* and transferred from father to son, cf. Benferhat 2003–4: especially 267–8. This is the first of a number of passages referring to his client as *innocens* (§§7, 14, 15, 25, 77, 125, 141, 144, 149) or to his *innocentia* (§§73, 75; cf. also §152 *culpa nulla*), C. carefully planting the idea in the jurors' minds even before he has begun to prove his case. The description *tam amplum et copiosum*, reminding the jurors of the stakes, varies the previous *tam plenam atque praeclaram*. *obtineo* is "sustain one's claim to" property: *OLD* s.v. 8. **damnato et eiecto:** the asyndeton prior to these words is strongly adversative; cf. H–S 830. Supply *hoc*; the abl. absolute is parallel with the preceding *hoc incolumi*. The reference will hardly be to Roscius' removal from his property, which has already occurred (*pace* Pericoli 1993);

Mommsen 1899: 644n3 sees an allusion to his exile following conviction;
Thomas 1981: 708n242 and Santalucia 1999:148n20 think rather of Roscius'
being cast into a river if condemned for parricide; cf. §5n. The sentence could
have ended with *sperat se posse*, but in the fuller style of his youth C. misses no
opportunity to characterize an adversary, as he does here through the manner
of acquisition (*per scelus*; cf. §1n.) and the use to which the property will (he
claims) be put, both discreditable. C. will paint a vivid picture of Chrysogonus'
addiction to *luxuria* and means of self-enrichment at §§133–5. For the relative
clause preceding its "antecedent" (*id*), an old pattern in Hittite and Latin, cf.
Dyck on *Leg.* 2.19.2. A verb of remarkably varied application, *effundo* (lit. "pour
out") can mean to "squander" money (*OLD* s.v. 11a). The addition of *atque
consumere* both strengthens the idea and instantiates the equivalent of a double
cretic.

hunc sibi ex animo . . . adiutores uos profiteamini: *scrupus* is a
sharp stone, but *scrupulus* is used metaphorically of a "worry, source of uneasi-
ness" or the like: *OLD* s.vv. **qui se dies noctesque stimulat ac pungit:**
se refers, not to the grammatical subject of the clause, but to Chrysogonus,
even though the thought is not subobblique (with subj.), a colloquialism; cf.
Inv. 1.55 *quod ei qui sibi ex lege praetor successerat exercitum non tradidit*; Landgraf
1878: 37; K–S I 613–14. *dies noctesque*, recurring at §§67 and 81, appears to
be a set phrase for "constantly, unremittingly," the order varied *metri causa* at
Enn. *Ann.* 336 Sk. *sollicitari te, Tite, sic noctesque diesque* (cited at *Sen.* 1). *pungo*
("puncture, sting") has the metaphorical sense "trouble, vex" (*OLD* s.v. 1 and
4a) previously found in comedy (Pl. *Trin.* 1000, *Truc.* 853); cf. also §60 *intellexi
quid eum pepugisset.* The groundwork is laid for the comic depiction of this
antagonist at §§133–5. Why was Chrysogonus so worried? Was it that he
had no documented title to the property (cf. §128n.) or that he had himself
masterminded the murder (cf. the Introduction sec. 5) and feared legal or
extra-legal retribution if Roscius jun. lived? *euello* could apply to a little pebble
in the shoe ("pluck out") or metaphorically to a worry ("get rid of"): *OLD* s.v.
1 and 2; for the *iunctura* cf. *Clu.* 4 *euellam ex animis hominum tantam opinionem.* The
property at stake is no longer *bona, pecunia*, or the defendant's *patrimonium* but
is now, as possessed by Chrysogonus, *praeda* ("booty") and the man himself
and his agents implicitly *praedones* or *latrones*; cf. §15 *domestici praedones*; §24 *praedo
iste nefarius*; §27 *Sex. Roscium . . . fugientem latronum tela*; §146 *quis . . . praedo . . . quis
pirata?*; Opelt 1965: 209; Burian 1984. *nefas* refers to what is religiously imper-
missible; from that starting point the adj. *nefarius* comes to be a general term
for "wicked": Ernout and Meillet s.v. *fas*; Latte 1960: 38; *OLD* s.v. *nefarius.*
As *adiuuo* can be used with *ad* + the goal of action, so too the agent noun
adiutor; similar to our passage is Caes. *Gal.* 5.38.4 (Ambiorix to the Nervii) *se*

ad eam rem profitetur adiutorem; cf. *OLD* s.vv. *adiuuo* 6, *adiutor* 1. For this trial as a *latrocinium* rather than a *iudicium* cf. §61 with n.

7 Si uobis aequa ea . . . aliquanto aequiorem: *aequus* goes from "level, even" to "fair, just" (with reference to laws or actions): *OLD* s.v. 1 and 6; it is the quality expected of the courts; hence at *Cat.* 4.2 C. refers to the *forum in quo omnis aequitas continetur. ea* is Havet's insertion adding point to the contrast; in this position it can easily have dropped out; for the order cf. §25 *scelera haec et flagitia*; §121 *diligentiam . . . eorum et fidem. honestus* refers originally to one having recognition through the holding of public office (*honos*) but becomes a general term of approbation ("honorable"); cf. §16 of the elder Roscius *honestissimus inter suos numerabatur*; Klose 1933: 133–4. As in §1 and twice in §3 C.'s *ego* contrasts sharply (the contrast heightened here with *contra*). **breuem . . . et . . . aliquanto aequiorem:** C. sets his request off as modest in scope and moderate; similarly *Phil.* 1.27 *proponam ius, ut opinor, aequum . . . quid hac postulatione dici potest aequius?*

    primum a Chrysogono peto . . . ne petat: cf. §150, cross-referring to our passage. His request of Chrysogonus *ut pecunia fortunisque nostris contentus sit* gives nothing away. If Roscius is acquitted, the *decuriones* can renew their efforts to have his property restored (§25) or Roscius himself can institute a suit for restitution (*rei uindicatio*); cf. Liebs 2007: 61. **peto . . . ne petat** is another example of *distinctio* (cf. §5n.), the senses "ask" and "attack" being in question: *OLD* s.v. 8 and 2 respectively; Holst 1925: 59. *sanguis* adds vividness and horror to the previously mentioned threat to Roscius' life (cf. on §§5 and 30) and will be a significant, recurring symbol in this speech: the dark background of the proscriptions (§§11, 81), the familial ties Roscius is accused of violating (§63), the powerful inhibition against harming a parent (§66), the consequent high standard of proof by which one must virtually see the defendant with fouled hands (§68), and the unnatural and insatiable cruelty of Chrysogonus (146, 150; cf. Dufallo 2007: 41–2). *sanguis* occurs in combination with *uita* 5x elsewhere in the speeches; similar to our passage is *Quinct.* 46 *unde . . . fateatur se non pecuniam sed uitam et sanguinem petere.*

    deinde a uobis . . . propulsetis: this tricolon contains C.'s own charge to the jurors (cf. §6n.). *audax* is a substantive here; cf. *OLD* s.v. 2a; *ut audacium sceleri resistatis* is varied at §12 *ut . . . hominibus audacissimis resistatis*. The *audacia* of those behind the prosecution will be a major theme; cf. §35n. For *scelus* cf. §1n. For Roscius as *innocens* cf. §6n. *leuo* is to "lighten, alleviate"; cf. §10 *hoc onus si uos aliqua ex parte alleuabitis . . .* **periculum quod in omnes intenditur:** the defendant was, of course, always in danger (cf. §85n.); C. has alluded to this (§5 *pro capite et fortunis alterius*) and has also spoken of the avoidance of danger by the *homines nobilissimi* (§1), but this first hint at a more generalized danger should galvanize attention. *in omnes* is, of course, hyperbolic (cf. §129); at §§145 and 152–3 he broadens the topic by connecting Roscius' case with the fate of the children of the proscribed generally; see on §152. For the general tactic cf. *Clu.* 8 *permulta . . . de communibus inuidiae periculis dicenda esse uideantur*; *Flac.*1 *in maximis periculis huius urbis atque imperi*; *De orat.* 2.209 *timor incutitur aut ex ipsorum periculis aut ex communibus*. For *periculum propulsare* ("ward off danger") cf. *Clu.* 144, *Rab. perd.* 8, *Mur.* 45, *Sul.* 49, *Red. pop.* 24, *Phil.* 7.7.

8 quodsi aut causa criminis . . . Sex. Rosci uita dedatur: it is characteristic of C. to assume a seemingly overwhelming burden of proof early in the speech which later proves to be a bluff; similarly §§18 and 76; cf. Riggsby 1999: 30 and 56. In Latin of this period *crimen* is a "charge," not yet a "crime": *OLD* s.v. 1 and 4. *suspicio* is what leads a prosecutor to file charges; cf. §55 *suspicione tamen non caret*; ibid. *quod possit . . . suspiciose dicere*; §56 *quia id est suspiciosum;* ibid. *tum cum suspicio nulla sit*; §57 *in suspicione latratote*; ibid. *sin . . . sine suspicione latrabitis*; §64 *quid poterat tam esse suspiciosum?*; §76 *multa . . . quae . . . argui suspiciose possunt*. For *uel* + superlative cf. §6n. **res . . . quamobrem:** the antecedent is fussily repeated within the relative clause ("a thing . . . on account of which (thing)"); cf. §28 *de ea re . . . in qua re*; K–S II 283–4; H–S 563–4. *illi* are "the accusers," as usual; cf. §13 *ex illorum nefaria caede*. By litotes *nonnihil* = "something": *OLD* s.v. **tamen** = *saltem* "at least"; similarly §104; cf. *Phil.* 1.10.8 with Ramsey's n. *nomen deferre* is to indict a person on criminal charges; *OLD* s.v. *defero* 9d and *nomen* 21c; Mommsen 1899: 382–4; Robinson 1995: 5. For the use of *sequor* cf. §1 *officium sequuntur* (with n.); §34 *quid uos sequi conueniat*. **eam praedam quam dixi:** sc. §6. **quicquam aliud causae** "any other cause"; for the gen. of the rubric cf. *NLS* §72(5)(ii); Löfstedt 1956: 1 chs. 8 and 11. C. is fond of characterizing opponents by their salient qualities; thus *illorum libidini* substitutes for *illis*, just as *furor iste tuus* does for Catiline (*Cat.* 1.1) etc.; for Chrysogonus as a *bon vivant* cf. §§133–4; for the claim that Roscius' *uita* is at stake cf. §5n.

sin aliud agitur nihil . . . assequi consuerunt?: *sin* ("but if") introduces the second of two mutually exclusive conditions: G–L §592; further examples at §§10, 57, 93, 126, 137, 139, 142. *agitur* is to "be at stake, at issue": *OLD* s.v. *ago* 38b. *nihil* receives emphasis by its separation from *aliud* and its final position in its clause. **quibus satis nihil est:** the insatiable thirst for riches was a rich theme for moralizing and satire; cf. e.g. Hor. *Ep.* 1.2.46; Sen. *Ep.* 15.9 and 19.7; Mart. 12.10 *habet Africanus miliens, tamen captat.*| *Fortuna multis dat nimis, satis nulli. cupiditas* will, in fact, be claimed as a hallmark of the other side; cf. §§12 and 101. **opimam praeclaramque praedam:** this is now the third time that the prize has been adorned with two ornamental epithets (cf. §6 *pecuniam tam plenam atque praeclaram*; *patrimonium tam amplum et copiosum*), characteristic of the copious style. *cumulus* is the "finishing touch, crown": *OLD* s.v. 4. *cum* . . . *tum* effects a transition from general to specific. *hoc* is defined by the following *uos idoneos habitos* [sc. *esse*]. The juries were at this period composed exclusively of senators, who might well take umbrage at being thought suitable (*idonei*) to be used for such purposes; C. dilates on the point just below and at §151; sim. *Sest.* 2 *in quo cum multa sunt indigna, tum nihil minus est ferendum quam quod iam non per latrones suos . . . sed per uos nobis . . . periculum inferre conantur.* **per quorum sententias iusque iurandum id assequantur:** C. reminds the jurors of the solemn oath they had to swear to render a conscientious verdict; cf. Mommsen 1899: 219 and 395; Freyburger 1986: 213–17. The Romans generally took their oaths very seriously; cf. Latte 1968: 375–9 and §§10 and 101; C. aims to stir the jurors' resentment by framing the prosecution as an attempt to instrumentalize their verdict for unworthy ends. For the relative clause with consecutive force cf. §5n. **scelere et ferro:** a hendiadys ("with wicked sword" or the like); for *scelus* cf. §1n.; the two appear in the list at *Dom.* 5 *hunc tu ciuem ferro . . . et consulum scelere . . . cedere coegisti.* For the alleged "habit" of violence (*consuerunt*) of the prosecution side cf. §§17, 84, and 100. C. develops the idea of prosecution as an alternative to (thwarted) murder at §28–9.

  qui ex ciuitate . . . ornati auctique discedant?: for the relative clause preceding its "antecedent" cf. §6n. The double process of selection insures both *dignitas* and *seueritas*; cf. *Phil.* 1.20 *in iudice . . . spectari et fortuna debet et dignitas*, as well as the contrasting description of the jurors to be enrolled under Antony's law leading to the exclamation *o dignitatem consili admirandam!* (ibid. 5.12). The jurors' *dignitas* stands in contrast to the prosecution's expectations (*indigna . . . indignissimum*). The senate had been enlarged by Sulla to include ex-quaestors; besides election to public office, adlection by the censors remained an alternative path to senate membership; cf. *Leg.* 3.27 with Dyck's n. **ex senatu . . . delecti estis:** a *consilium* is any deliberative or advisory body; juries are regularly referred to as such; cf. §151; *OLD* s.v. 3c; Crook 1955: 5. Santalucia 1999 rightly insists on giving *delecti* its full weight: these are not merely jurors chosen by lot and not rejected by the prosecution (as in the other Sullan criminal courts); rather, they have been specially chosen. **propter seueritatem:** surprisingly speaking in the manner of a prosecutor (explicitly so in §12), C. sees the *seueritas* of judges as positive; cf. Bernardo 2000: 74–82. **ab his . . . gladiatores:** the acc. + inf. construction (following *tum uel hoc indignissimum est*) continues. *ab his* and *homines sicarios atque gladiatores* are contrasting poles held in precarious balance in this

clause; *hoc* is defined by the following *ut*-clause, a colloquialism serving struc-
tural clarity; cf. H–S 640. **homines sicarios atque gladiatores** has not
been adequately prepared by the preceding argument that *libido* underlies
the prosecution; the claim will be repeated at §§17, 87 and 100, in the last
passage with the added detail that Capito killed a man by throwing him from
a bridge into the Tiber. *homo* used with a defining term indicates the class or
group to which one belongs: cf. *OLD* s.v. 4b. The *sica*, a pointed dagger with
curved blade, was the preferred weapon of urban criminals, hence called
sicarii "gangsters": cf. Cloud 1969: 270–80. *sicarius* thus becomes the earliest
Latin word for "murderer" (*homicida* appearing first at *Phil.* 2.31; cf. Mommsen 1899: 613n2); the allusion will remind jurors of the *lex Cornelia de sicariis et
ueneficiis* under which this case is being tried; cf. Introduction sec. 2. *gladiator*
was (usually) a slave trained in the use of weapons and displayed in combat
for entertainment; the term is often used abusively, as here ("cutthroat"); cf.
Opelt 1965: 209 and (for C.'s later usage) 136. **non modo ut . . . horrere
debent:** for *non modo . . . uerum etiam* cf. §5n. Here C. gets ahead of himself,
speaking as if the supporters of the prosecution were guilty of *maleficia*, were
the defendants in the case and that punishments (*supplicia*) for them were
at issue; this is the first clear signal that he will turn the tables and claim
that those behind the prosecution were, in fact, the murderers. The addition
of *atque horrere* lends vividness to *metuere* and, followed by *debent*, yields a fine
clausula (trochee + spondee). **ut spoliis . . . discedant?:** the *bona* or *pecunia*
of the elder Roscius have figured successively as (potentially) the *patrimonium*
of his son and the *praeda* of Chrysogonus (§6); now continuing the metaphorical violence (*sicarios atque gladiatores*), C. calls them equipment stripped from
a fallen enemy (*spolia*: *OLD* s.v. 2–3); this is later varied with *manubiae* (§108).
ornati auctique "embellished and aggrandized"; the two are often paired,
e.g. *Fam.* 7.17.2 (to Trebatius) *semper te . . . augendum atque ornandum putaui*; again
the added synonym effects a good clausula (cretic + spondee).

9 His de rebus . . . sunt impedimento: *his de rebus* is a summarizing
formula (cf. §5 *his de causis*); *amplificatio* (cf. Lausberg §259) is achieved by spec-
ifying scope and quality (*tantis tamque atrocibus*), the latter expressive of visceral
dislike ("shocking, atrocious"); it is formed from *ater* ("black") with addition
of the *-ox/-ωψ* suffix that means "looking like"; cf. *OLD* s.v. 6; Ernout and
Meillet s.v. **commode dicere . . . grauiter conqueri . . . libere uociferari:** three actions, arranged to form a crescendo, that the defense case
would demand; it turns out that each adverbial qualifier is somehow blocked;
for *commode dicere* cf. §33 *quem pro dignitate ne laudare quidem quisquam satis commode
posset*; *uociferor* ("raise a loud cry") is first attested in comedy (Atta *com.* 7);

C. appears to have been the first to take it over into prose; cf. *OLD* s.v.; for its derived noun *uociferatio* cf. §12; for *aetas* and *ingenium* cf. §1n. C.'s first complaint about the times appeared in the aside at §3 *fin.*; see *ad loc.* At §61 C. will claim *causam pro Sex. Roscio si non commode at libere dici.*

huc accedit summus timor . . . Sex. Rosci pericula: *natura pudorque meus* "my modest nature," by hendiadys; this is, of course, appropriate to a young man of C.'s age; cf. §149 *pudor qui ornat aetatem*; *Off.* 2.46 *prima . . . commendatio proficiscitur a modestia*; for the relation of *pudor* and fear cf. Kaster 2005: 161n111. Anxiety at the beginning of the speech seems, however, to have been especially characteristic of C.: he confesses to it at *Clu.* 51 and in the exordium of *Mil.*; he attributes it to Crassus and other *summi oratores* at *De orat.* 1.121–2, where he adds: *fuit . . . mirificus quidam in Crasso pudor qui tamen non modo non obesset eius orationi sed etiam probitatis commendatione prodesset*; that is clearly the effect he aims at in our passage; for the *pudor* of a public speaker cf. Kaster 2005: 59–60. *attribuit* agrees with the nearer subject, as usual: G–L §211 R.1. The polysyndeton (*et . . . et . . . et*) gives the impression of an overwhelming accumulation. **uestra dignitas:** sc. as a panel specially selected from members of the senate; cf. §8 *qui ex ciuitate in senatum propter dignitatem . . . delecti estis* with n. **uis aduersariorum** has so far been hinted at metaphorically (§8 *sicarios atque gladiatores*; *spoliis . . . ornati auctique*); C. will provide details at §§13 and 26–7.

quapropter uos oro . . . uerba mea audiatis: C. shows fondness in his early speeches for such alliterative pairs as *oro atque obsecro*; cf. §77 *hic orat atque obsecrat*; *Q. Rosc.* 20; von Albrecht, *RE* Suppl. 13 1303.61–5 and 2003: 100. The inartistic way of achieving attentiveness (one of the goals of the exordium; see on §§1–14) is simply to ask for it, as in our passage; similarly *Clu.* 8, 66, and 89; cf. Lausberg §271a; an alternative is to suggest that the listener may have something at stake; cf. §7n. **bona . . . cum uenia** "with (your) indulgence" is a polite formula accompanying requests; cf. *OLD* s.v. *uenia* 3a.

10 fide sapientiaque uestra . . . me posse intellego: explicative asyndeton (cf. §6n.), clarifying the reason for the request. That the jurors' *fides* ("good faith": *OLD* s.v. 6a) is engaged follows from their oath; cf. §8n. **plus oneris:** for the common use of the partitive gen. with comparatives cf. G–L §372. The display of modesty, appropriate to C.'s years, continues from §9.

hoc onus si uos . . . quoad potero, perferam: repeating *onus* achieves a connection of ideas and at the same time lends focus; cf. von Albrecht 1989: 95 and 97. *aliqua ex parte* "in some degree"; cf. *OLD* s.v. *pars* 3c;

see §36 with n. **feram . . . perferam:** a chiastic frame with *feram ut potero* answered by *quoad potero perferam*. This is a good illustration of the force of the prefix *per*-: "bear" vs. "bear to the end"; cf. also Holst 1925: 70. C. claims to bring *studium* and *industria* to the case; he will deny even that much to the opposing counsel, Erucius (§§58–9, 61, 72). For *sin* cf. §8n. *animo* "in courage" is emphatic: *OLD* s.v. *animus* 13.

quod si perferre . . . deponere: the same indomitable spirit appears at *Leg.* 3.34 (Quintus is the speaker) *ui opprimi in bona causa est melius quam malae cedere*. C.'s handling of the *onus offici* forms an implicit contrast with Capito's (§112); cf. also *Div. Caec.* 5; *Sul.* 65; *Fam.* 3.13.1. C.'s *fides* is involved inasmuch as he has pledged his client the best defense he can muster; cf. §§83 and 95; Freyburger 1986: 160–4. The verbal play (*fides, perfidia*) recurs at §110; cf. Holst 1925: 70–1 and 72.

11 te quoque magno opere . . . hoc tempore impertias: M. Fannius was a plebeian aedile and moneyer in 86 and at the time of the trial a serving praetor. The homicide court was ordinarily presided over by an aedilician *iudex quaestionis*, as Fannius had done some time between 85 and 81; cf. Alexander 2002: 168–9 and 307n44 with literature, updating Münzer, *RE* VI 2.1993.16 (Fannius 15); Mommsen 1899: 187n4. *impertio* is to "give a share of" (< *pars*), here, unusually, with the reflexive (*OLD* s.v. 1); it is more or less equivalent to the previous *praebeo*. The true reading *r(ei) p(ublicae)* has been preserved in the indirect transmission alone (Arusianus), all the MSS carelessly repeating *p(opulo) R(omano)* from the preceding clause. C. will now dilate on the significance of the time (*hoc tempore*).

quanta multitudo hominum . . . intellegis: two similarly structured sentences in asyndeton summarizing the setting and the mood as (allegedly) observed by the praetor; the following sentence explains these phenomena. It is important for the orator to sniff out the jurors' sentiments in advance, as Antonius argues at *De orat.* 2.186; at §28 the prosecutors are depicted as relying on public sentiment to help their case. Instead of *homines* C. sometimes substitutes *mortales*, characteristic of the "high" style; cf. e.g. *Q. Rosc.* 18 *estne quisquam omnium mortalium . . . ?*; von Albrecht 1989: 68–9; here variety is also served, given the preceding *hominum*. **acria ac seuera:** *acer* in this context is "strict, stern": *OLD* s.v. 8; cf. *quam acerrime* in §12; *acre supplicium* at §37; L. Cassius as *acerrimus iudex* at §85. The reaction is represented as natural following a period of lawlessness (cf. §8 *propter seueritatem*); Riggsby 1999: 65 argues, however, that "an acquittal would be a surer sign of normalcy" after the previous uncontrolled bloodletting. The attitude described by C., if present, should *per se* benefit the prosecution (cf. §28 with n.); in the following chapters, however, C. is at pains to appropriate it for the defense.

longo interuallo... factae sunt: *longo interuallo*: how long? Berry 2004: 83 and n7, citing *Brut.* 306, dates the cessation from the beginning of the civil disturbances in 88 down to Sulla's reestablishment of the courts in 81. Hinard 1999 and Hinard and Benferhat 2006: xxiv think that this was merely the first case of the year 80, not the first since the cessation of the proscriptions, but it seems doubtful that that would qualify as a *longum interuallum* and with *caedes* on a large scale intervening. More plausible is the view of Kinsey 1987a, who argues from §§89–91 and *Brut.* 308 that there was some forensic activity under Cinna and C. here refers to the interval between our case and Sulla's seizure of power at the end of 82. **iudicium inter sicarios:** i.e. the court trying cases under the *lex Cornelia de sicariis et ueneficiis*; cf. §8n. C. seems not to use *iudicium committere* quite this way elsewhere; *committo* can mean to "bring about" generally; possibly he has in mind the analogy of *pugnam committere* or the like; cf. *OLD* s.v. 8 and 15. Why was this the first case? Citing *Inv.* 2.58, Santalucia 1999: 149 shows that a case of parricide was scheduled *extra ordinem*, i.e. ahead of all other cases, because the charge was so grave.

omnes hanc quaestionem... sperant futuram: the printed text is a conjectural restoration: "all hope that this court under your praetorship will be a manifestation of virtue with overt crimes and daily bloodshed banished." The hyperbole (*cotidiano sanguine*) is further accelerated in §154 (*omnibus horis*). The transmitted text concludes (after *sanguine*) with the words *dimissui sperant futuram*; *dimisso*, however, is the reading of the Gronovian scholiast 304.26 St. (the *o* is in an erasure). *dimissus* is elsewhere attested only at Charis. p. 245.22 Barw. Landgraf attempted to retain *dimissui* by changing *sanguine* to *sanguini*, thus restoring a double dative construction (G–L § 356); but in C. and Caesar one expects the personal dative ("personal object for whom": ibid. with examples); cf. K–S I 313–14; Jörgensen 1913. No more convincing is the insertion of *e* prior to *manifestis* (Madvig 1912 and earlier), since, in spite of Madvig, *dimissui* can hardly be equivalent to *liberationi*. The text adopted here is based on the assumption that, though a correction, the reading of the Gronovian scholiast (and his explanation *prae contemptu* (for the corrupt *contempto*) *relicto*) is right and the archetype already corrupt; *dimisso* agrees, as usual, with the nearer antecedent. On this analysis -*ui* will be the relic of a different but likewise attested deverbative noun *ostentus* ("demonstration, advertisement, display (of a quality)": *OLD* s.v. 2).

12 Qua uociferatione... qui causam dicimus: this justifies the expressed attitudes toward *seueritas, seuera iudicia* etc. (§§8 and 11), surprising in the defense counsel. *uociferatio* ("loud outcry" and hence "loud, energetic argument"), like the related verb (cf. §9n.), was a *uox comica* (Afran. *com.* 394)

turned to account by C.; cf. *OLD* s.v. C. achieves a careful chiastic balance
of agents (*accusatores* vs. *nos*) and circumstances (*in ceteris iudiciis* vs. *hoc tempore*).
causam dicere is "to plead a case, especially in defence" (*OLD* s.v. *causa* 3b).

petimus abs te . . . caedes futurae sint: for *quam acerrime* see § 11n.
(*acria ac seuera*). In spite of C.'s attribution of unspecified *maleficia* to supporters
of the prosecution (§8), only Roscius stands accused of *maleficium* in this court;
Chrysogonus has been said to have bought the estate of the elder Roscius at a
very low price (§6), but that is hardly a criminal offense. To judge from extant
examples, an alternative suspect was a virtual requirement of a successful
defense on charges of murder; cf. Stroh 1975: 59; Riggsby 1999: 38 and ch.
3; our passage helps prepare the jurors for such a claim. *scelus* and *audacia*
can be distinguished as criminality *per se* and the mentality that gives rise to
it; cf. §75 and Marchetti 1986: 110–11; for *audacia* and the prosecution side as
audaces cf. §§2 and 7 with nn.; it was a term applied to their opponents by
conservative politicians; cf. §33n.; Riggsby 1999: 64–5 and n48. *eo* or *usque
eo* ("to such an extent") commonly prompts a consecutive clause; cf. *OLD*
s.v. *eo²* 2; K–S II 248–9. *cupiditas* in the form of Chrysogonus' possession of
Roscius' property and determination to make his title to it secure has been
said to be behind the prosecution (§6); *scelus* (cf. §1n.) and *audacia* are yet to
be shown; they will recur together in §§17 and 28. For *non modo . . . uerum etiam*
cf. §5n. **hic in foro . . . futurae sint:** a *descriptio*, offering a vivid picture
of the consequences of conviction (cf. *Rhet. Her.* 4.51). C. begins with what is
visible in court (cf. §1n.), namely the magistrate's raised platform (*tribunal*, on
which cf. David 1995; Bablitz 2007: 29–31 and 56), the jurors' feet, and the
benches occupied by the litigants and witnesses (*subsellia*: Bablitz 2007: 53–6),
and imaginatively transforms this into the scene of a bloodbath; similarly
§32 *fin.* and the imaginative reconstruction of the crime scene at §98; cf. also
§91n. (burning of the *subsellia*). The addition of *tuum* and *uestros* with following
vocatives personalizes the vivid scene and aims to secure his listeners' close
involvement. *ipse* is reserved for the climactic term; cf. *TLL* s.v. 348.54.

13   etenim quid aliud . . . ut id fieri liceat?: an audacious claim; the
support for it follows.

accusant ii . . . ex illorum nefaria caede restat: for the explicative
asyndeton cf. §6n. C. offers four contrasting characterizations of prosecutors
and defendant, each unit set off by the formulas *accusant ii* and *causam dicit
is* (on which see §12n.). The first characterization of the accusers is repeated
from §6 (*Chrysogonus . . . in alienam pecuniam tam plenam atque praeclaram nullo iure
inuaserit*); but Chrysogonus, as we learn only at §60, is not in court and
thus is hardly a member of the prosecution team; cf. Levene 2004: 132; for

Magnus' occupation of the defendant's estates and relation to the prosecution cf. §§23, 94, and 104 with nn. For Roscius' *calamitas* cf. §7 with n. The second characterization breaks new ground by deploying the *cui bono?* argument destined for full elaboration at §§84–8; see *ad locos. ipsum* strengthens *hunc* and contrasts Roscius with his already murdered father; cf. *TLL* s.v. *ipse* 311.13. Perhaps originally from the realm of sacrifice or gladiatorial combat, *iugulo* is "kill by cutting the throat," hence generally "slaughter": *OLD* s.v. The adv. *summe* ("intensely"), perhaps colloquial, drops out of Ciceronian oratory after the *Verrines*. **cum praesidio:** *praesidium* is a (private) bodyguard or escort (cf. *OLD* s.v. 4b), no doubt supplied by Caecilia Metella (§27), a precaution characteristic of the disordered 80s: Marius created a slave escort, and Sulla followed suit; cf. Nowak 1973: 43–8. For the threat to Roscius' life see §26n. *hic ibidem* "in this very place," *ibidem* strengthening the local adv., just as *ipse* in this sentence has twice strengthened the pronoun *hic*; cf. *OLD* s.v. 1. **ante oculos** "in full view": *OLD* s.v. *oculus* 3b; similarly §§34 and 102. The idea of the jurors as spectators of murder in court is taken up from §12. *trucido*, like *iugulo*, is a particularly brutal word ("butcher" or the like: *OLD* s.v. 2). **accusant ii quos populus poscit:** *posco* here is "demand for punishment": ibid. s.v. 3b. But Capito's membership of the board of the *decem primi* of Ameria (§26) suggests that no one there connected him with the murder. C. probably means to identify the accusers with those responsible for the indiscriminate slaughter of the proscriptions; cf. §§93–4. **unus relictus ex illorum nefaria caede restat:** here finally, after the allusions to *maleficia* in §§8 and 12, is the claim that the prosecutors (*illi*; cf. §8n.) were behind the elder Roscius' murder; with *unus relictus . . . restat* C. makes it appear that the rest of the family has been wiped out, not just Roscius sen. For C.'s placement of the murder of Roscius sen. within the larger bloodbath of the proscriptions see above and §§152–3. For *nefarius* cf. §6n.

14 atque ut facilius . . . rei publicae calamitatem: a formulaic transition to the *narratio*; cf. *Quinct.* 10 *id quo facilius facere possitis, dabo operam ut a principio res quemadmodum gesta et contracta sit cognoscatis*; similarly *Ver.* 2.4.3. For degrees of outrageousness cf. §8 *cum multa indigna tum hoc uel indignissimum*. Stirring up indignation is a powerful weapon in court; cf. Arist. *Rhet.* 1387a6 and especially 22; Chrysogonus will be particularly vulnerable (§§133–5). For the narration *ab initio* cf. *Ver.* 1.1.16 *sed prius ut ab initio res ab eo constituta sit, quaeso, cognoscite. quo facilius* varies *ut facilius*, since *quo*, too, can introduce a final clause containing a comparative; cf. G–L §545.2. C. continues to accustom the reader/listener to thinking of Roscius as *innocens* (§6n.) and associating *audax/audacia* with the prosecution (cf. §§7 and 12); C. was fond of using abstract substantives in the plural; the commonest type is the one expressing repetition: *miseriae* = "woes" (*OLD* s.v. *miseria* b; cf. §49), matched by *audaciae* = "audacious behavior"; cf. Lebreton 1901: 32–8 especially 33–4. To crown the exordium, Roscius' individual *calamitas* (§§7 and 13) becomes *rei publicae calamitas* (cf. §7 *periculum quod in omnes intenditur*); C. attempts to connect this case with the larger issue of the fate of the *proscriptorum liberi* at §§152–3.

NARRATIO (15–29)

The three virtues of narrative according to rhetorical theory are that it be *simplex*, *aperta*, and *probabilis* (*Inv.* 1.28; cf. Lausberg §294). Despite Tacitus' criticism of the young C. as *longus in narrationibus* (*Dial.* 22), our narrative is modestly proportioned, amounting to only about 9% of the entire speech. It is also straightforward (*aperta*), carrying the story in a straight line from the character and death of the elder Roscius to his son's indictment for murder. If examined critically in light of the rest of the speech, however, it is seen to contain dubious arguments, though the defects in probability are more apparent to the reader than they would have been to a listener in court.

    C. alleges that the murder was carried out by two apparent relatives of the deceased, Capito and Magnus, and that Sulla's freedman Chrysogonus was an accessory after the fact. But how could they have hoped to succeed if the proscriptions were already concluded and Chrysogonus, who alone of the group could have seen to it that the name of the deceased was added to the proscription list, was not yet part of the plot? Cf. Stroh 1975: 57–8. C. conceals these difficulties when first narrating the murder by leaving the time vague (§18); indeed in light of §16 (*cum proscriberentur homines*) one might have thought it during the proscriptions; only at §21 does he clarify that it was after their conclusion; greater specificity (*aliquot post menses*) comes only later (§128); cf. Stroh 1975: 58n13.

    The link between Capito and the murder is a tenuous one: it consists in the fact that he was the first person in Ameria to receive the news. But Mallius Glaucia's speedy journey to Ameria with the news and first report of it to Capito may have a different explanation, namely that the *homo tenuis libertinus* (§19) expected a handsome reward for his efforts and that Capito's house was a convenient first stop; cf. Kinsey 1980: 176.

    The link between Magnus and the murder is not so very strong either. Nonetheless C. quickly narrows the field of suspects to just two, Magnus and his client, and expects the decision between them to hinge on which one was present in Rome at the time (§18); only later is a distinction drawn between mastermind and agent (§74).

C. also wants the *societas* of Capito, Magnus, and Chrysogonus to have been entered into as close to the murder as possible, at the very time when news of the murder first reached Sulla's camp at Volaterrae (§20). He wants the listener/reader to believe that the plan included from the start the pro-scription of Roscius sen., purchase of his property by Chrysogonus, and yielding of three farms to Capito. This version is contradicted, however, by C.'s own later account, by which it was only during the mission to Volaterrae of the *decem primi* that Capito managed to wring three farms from Chryso-gonus (§110). It would thus appear that Chrysogonus acted on his own in having the name of Roscius sen. added to the proscription list and buying the property; he was certainly active in the market in many other cases (§133).

C. wanted a local mastermind (Capito) and a local henchman (Glaucia, acting on orders from Magnus). But C.'s local mastermind was suspected by no one in Ameria, as is suggested by his presence among the *decem primi* on the embassy, and the willingness of the delegates to abandon the embassy on the basis of the assurances from Capito is better explained not by their naïveté (*homines antiqui qui ex sua natura ceteros fingerent . . .* : §26; cf. Stroh 1975: 58) but on the assumption that the embassy was undertaken not least on Capito's initiative, possibly with a view to salvaging his claims against the elder Roscius' holdings; cf. Dyck 2003: 240–1. The *societas*, if it existed, thus looks like an *ad hoc* formation for sharing the spoils and not the force behind the murder itself. If that is so, then C.'s client is by no means in the clear.

Other points, such as Capito's alleged criminal background (§17; cf. §100) and the claim of a threat to his client's life (§26), are notably lacking in substantiation. Finally, C.'s picture of the motives behind the prosecution (§§28–9) is, of course, pure imagination. The section can be outlined as follows:

I Roscius sen.
   A   Reputation and connections (15)
   B   Legacy to his son
   C   Attitude in the civil war (16)
   D   Enmity with the T. Roscii (17)
   E   Murdered near the Pallacinian Baths while returning from dinner (18)
II Report of his death (19)
   A   Brought to Ameria by Mallius Glaucia
       (1)   With extraordinary speed
       (2)   Capito first recipient
   B   Brought to Volaterrae four days later (20)

15–16 This section about the elder Roscius' connections and political align-
ment with the nobility serves ostensibly as background; it also, however,
prepares the argument about the illegality of his proscription at §§125–30; cf.
Berger 1978: 34.

15 Sex. Roscius, pater . . . hominum nobilissimorum: typical
beginning of a *narratio*, identifying the principal and his local affiliation;
cf. *Ver.* 2.4.3 *C. Heius est Mamertinus.* C. highlights the father's social and political connections; he has, however, remarkably little to say about his character
(in §41 he merely denies that he was insane and asserts that he was *omnium
constantissimus*); see §16n. For homonymous father and son and the form *huiusce*
cf. §6n. Ameria (mod. Amelia) was an old Umbrian *municipium* with territory
extending to the Tiber and a road, the *Via Amerina*, connecting it to the *Via
Cassia* a little north of Baccanae; it was famous for apples, pears, and pas-
tures; cf. Hülsen, *RE* i 2.1826.17; Lomas 2004: 104–5; Talbert 2000: 42c 3–4.
Two sets of distinctions appear (*cum . . . tum* and within the former another
marked by *non modo . . . uerum etiam*), gradually enlarging the sphere within
which the elder Roscius is to be judged or was active. Roscius sen. was one of
the local notables (*domi nobiles*) of his *municipium*; for the term cf. *Clu.* 23 and in
general Wiseman 1983. The distinction *genere* is shown by the selection of his
probable relation, Capito, as one of the *decem primi* on the embassy to Sulla
(§26); his financial position is indicated by the value quoted at §6. Beyond the
municipium, connections and reputation would spread first to the neighboring
communities (*uicinitas*); cf. e.g. *Clu.* 49 *quod mihi cum Aletrinatibus uicinitatem et
cum plerisque eorum magnum usum esse sciebat.* As usual, the point introduced
by *tum* is destined for elaboration. **gratia atque hospitiis:** the link with
atque lays emphasis on the stronger term: his popularity (*gratia*) advanced to
the point of reciprocal guest-host relations (*hospitia*); cf. Wiseman 1971: 33–8;

on Italian nobles' *hospitium* vis-à-vis their Roman counterparts degenerating
into *clientela* cf. Badian 1958: 11, 148–9 and 154–5. **florens** ("distinguished")
is a favorite characterization of C.'s in all periods; cf. *OLD* s.v. 3. **hominum
nobilissimorum** is strategically placed so as to linger in the mind: it will
continue as the leading idea through the end of the section; and *-issimorum*
forms a fine double trochee; for C.'s usage of *nobilis* cf. §1n.

 nam cum Metellis . . . amplitudinisque gratia nomino: pride of
place goes to the (Caecilii) Metelli, now a bit past the apex of their influence;
between 123 and 102 they had furnished six consuls, five *triumphatores*, and
four censors; cf. Münzer, *RE* III 1.1202.55; it was a Caecilia Metella who gave
refuge to the younger Roscius (cf. §27 with n.) and another Metellus who
tried to secure the testimony of slave witnesses to the murder (§77). An old
patrician family, the Servilii are attested since the Punic Wars, albeit one
branch, the Caepiones, never recovered from Q. Servilius Caepio's disaster
in the battle of Arausio (106); when C. spoke, the leading representative of
the family was P. Servilius Vatia (the cognomen Isauricus was added later);
a *triumphator* in 88, he staunchly supported Sulla in the civil war and went
on to be consul of 79; cf. Münzer, *RE* IIA 2.1759.15 and 1812.20 (Servilius
93). The Punic Wars also, of course, made the reputation of the (Cornelii)
Scipiones, of whom a P. Scipio joined with Metellus in the effort to secure
slave testimony (§77). One might also have expected mention of the Valerii in
view of the rôle taken by a Valerius Messalla in organizing the defense (§149).
The *domesticus usus et consuetudo* that Roscius sen. enjoyed with these families
went beyond mere *hospitium*. **ut aequum . . . nomino**: the naming formula
for these allies is noticeably more fulsome than in §6; see *ad loc.*; for *amplitudo*
of persons cf. §2n.

 itaque ex suis . . . amicisque paternis defenditur: *commoda* are
"advantages" in a broad sense: *OLD* s.v. *commodum* 1; C. goes on to distinguish
the material (*patrimonium*) from the abstract. **hoc:** i.e. the connection with
leading families. One is expecting the agents to be called *praedones* (§6 with n.)
and the means to be *uis* (§9 *uis aduersariorum*), but the epithet *domestici* is so far
unexplained; cf. §17n.; Levene 2004: 130–1. The adversative asyndeton before
fama et uita contrasts with the fate of the *patrimonium*; cf. §6n. For Roscius as
innocens cf. §6n. *hospites amicique* is a common combination; cf. e.g. *Ver.* 2.4.32. In
the Roman conception both friends and enemies were heritable; cf. Hinard
1980.

16 hic cum omni tempore . . . auctoritate defendit: *hic* is the elder
Roscius, the general subject of these sections. **nobilitatis fautor:** this posture is unsurprising in one with the property and connections previously
described; for the concept *nobilis* cf. §1n. *fautor* (< *faueo*) is attested since

Plautus; here it is a "political supporter, partisan": *OLD* s.v. 3; cf. §142 *ille improbissimus Chrysogoni fautor. tumultus* is an outbreak of violence, used of civil war since *Rhet. Her.* 4.38: *OLD* s.v. 2a; the terms *bellum domesticum* and *ciuile* are later (*Cat.* 2.11 and 3.19 respectively). **cum omnium nobilium . . . in discrimen ueniret:** similarly §136 *quis enim erat qui non uideret humilitatem cum dignitate de amplitudine contendere? discrimen* is a "crisis" involving a threat to safety or existence: *OLD* s.v. 5; *in discrimen uenire* ("be at risk") recurs 7x in C.'s corpus. For *pars* used of a party or side in politics cf. *OLD* s.v. 16b; Taylor 1949: 10–11. **opera studio auctoritate defendit:** cf. §10 *feram . . . studio et industria.* Badian 1958: 247 oddly claims that "the senior Roscius was apparently cautiously neutral" in the civil war; more accurately Lomas 2004: 105 ("clearly a Sullan partisan"). With our passage contrast *Clu.* 25, where C. paints a very dark portrait of activity by Oppianicus on Sulla's behalf in the *municipium* of Larinum.

  etenim rectum putabat . . . inter suos numerabatur: as a *domi nobilis*, the elder Roscius saw (or so it is claimed) a correlation between his own position as *honestissimus inter suos* and the public standing (*honestas*) of those at the top of the Roman social pyramid. *honestissimus* was often applied to the *equites* or individual members of that class; cf. §7n.; Hellegouarc'h 1963: 387–8 and 462–3; Achard 1981: 385.

  posteaquam uictoria . . . sibi accideret: *posteaquam . . . recessimus* establishes the general framework, the following *cum*-clause the relevant circumstances; here and elsewhere in the speech C. speaks of Sulla's victory as already won; cf. §135n. On the Sullan proscriptions cf. the Introduction sec. 3 with literature. **erat ille Romae frequens** prepares the reader/listener for his death at Rome (§18) but fails to explain the reason for his visits. C. wants the reader/listener to infer that he would not appear so conspicuously (expressed with nice assonance *in foro et in ore omnium*) and so frequently (*cotidie*) if he feared being targeted in the proscriptions; cf. §21 *cum etiam qui ante metuerant redirent.* **magis ut exsultare . . . sibi accideret:** C. heightens the ironic contrast between Roscius' "triumphalist behaviour" (Lomas 2004: 105) and his subsequent fate; for the addition of his name to the proscription list cf. §21. For the genitive of the rubric *quid . . . calamitatis* ("anything of the nature of disaster," i.e. anything disastrous) cf. §8n.; *ea* refers back to *uictoria. accido* ("happen to, befall") is usually used of a negative outcome (cf. Engl. "if anything should happen to me"): *OLD* s.v. 6.

17 This chapter forms a transition to the narrative of the murder (§18). It characterizes two men, T. Roscius Capito and T. Roscius Magnus, in such a way as to suggest that they must have been behind the crime (*spero . . . non*

esse obscurum ad quem suspicio malefici pertineat: §18); both are known only from
this speech. Given the identical family name in the small town of Ameria,
it is likely that they were relations of the elder Sextus Roscius (hence §15
praedones domestici), though C. describes them here merely as his *inimici*; at
§87 he acknowledges the family tie between Roscius sen. and Magnus (*de
municipis cognatique fortunis*); Capito's leading rôle in the embassy of the *decem
primi* to Sulla's camp (§26) suggests that he was acting for a kinsman. Kinsey
1985: 189n4 suggests that Capito was unrelated because at §96 C. expresses
astonishment that word of the murder was first brought to Capito although
the elder Roscius had in Ameria *domus, uxor liberique . . . tot propinqui cognatique
optime conuenientes*; but even if a *propinquus*, Capito would be excluded from this
list by the qualifier *optime conuenientes*.

   Erant ei ueteres inimicitiae . . . iniuria metuebat: the *inimicitiae*
are emphasized by use of the dative of possession; cf. Löfstedt 1963: 65; for the
pl. abstract cf. §14 (*audacias*) with n. **quorum alterum . . . uideo:** for the
subsellia cf. §12n.; C. treats Magnus' presence in support of the prosecution
as a provocation at §§84, 87 and 95. **alterum tria . . . possidere audio:**
Chrysogonus has been described as the purchaser of all of the property (§6);
this amounts to thirteen farms (§20); C. explains at §21 *tria praedia uel nobilissima
Capitoni propria traduntur quae hodie possidet*; he reconstructs the circumstances at
§§108–10; here he does not yet mention Capito's relation to the prosecution
(§§84 and 100–2). For the reference and form of *huiusce* cf. §6n. The elder
Roscius' difficulty was that he was not able to guard against (*cauere*) these
enmities, merely to fear (*metuere*) them. **uiueret** ("he would be alive") hints
strongly that these *inimicitiae* were his undoing, a further indicator after §8 (*ut
supplicia uitent*) of the *anticategoria* that will be developed at §§83–123. *iniuria* in
the abl. is used adverbially; with a negative added "rightly" (*OLD* s.v. 3b); for
neque iniuria cf. §116; *De orat.* 1.150.

   nam duo isti . . . audaciaque superauit: the pronoun *iste* refers back
to them as the two already mentioned but can also convey a note of contempt;
similarly the adj. regularly accompanies the name of T. Roscius (Magnus)
in the following chapters; cf. *OLD* s.v. 3 and 5; K–S 1 621–2. Each of the
two has an expressive nickname, Capito = Great Head; cf. Weise 1909: 32.
plurimarum palmarum "with many victories to his credit," the palm-
branch being the traditional victor's reward (*OLD* s.v. 5); the genitive of quality
characterizes (*NLS* §§72(6) and 84–5; G–L §365); the metaphor recurs, again
with reference to Capito, at §84. **uetus ac nobilis gladiator:** *uetus* denotes
a "veteran" in a particular line of work; cf. *OLD* s.v. *uetus* 2. *nobilis* here
is "renowned, famous": *OLD* s.v. 2. For *gladiator* cf. §8n. C. thus suggests
that Capito has a record of violence, though, apart from the assassination

claimed at §100, particulars are lacking; he similarly abuses Naevius at *Quinct.*
29 (*cum isto gladiatore uetulo*). The metaphor continues with *lanista*, the trainer in
gladiatorial schools (*OLD* s.v.), often used as a term of abuse; Antony would
later apply it to C. (*Phil.* 13.40); cf. Opelt 1965: 209; *magister* is substituted
in the sequel. Since Capito is scheduled to be a prosecution witness (cf.
§§84, 100–1, 102), this characterization aims to discredit him in advance,
perhaps even intimidate him; cf. Loutsch 1979: 111; Schmitz 1985: 35–6. *tiro*
is a military recruit and hence generally a novice, beginner; it is used of
a new gladiator at Suet. *Jul.* 26.3; cf. *OLD* s.v. 1–2. *quod sciam* "so far as I
know," a relative clause with limiting force; cf. K–S II 307–8; G–L §627 R.1.
By characterizing him as a *tiro* prior to this incident C. admits that he can
establish no previous wrongdoing on Magnus' part; cf. Stroh 1975: 68 and
n48. **facile ipsum . . . superauit:** C. may have in mind the Gk trimeter
he quotes at *Fam.* 9.7.2 πολλοὶ μαθηταὶ κρείσσονες διδασκάλων ("many
pupils are better than their teachers") = [Men.] *Sent.* 651. *scelere audaciaque*
"audacious wickedness," by hendiadys.

18 nam cum hic . . . rediens a cena Sex. Roscius: an artful sentence
beginning with two *cum*-clauses, the first explaining the whereabouts of two
principals at the time of the murder, the second relevant background information; the essential content (albeit without reference to Magnus) is repeated
in plain style at §76 (*Romae Sex. Roscius occiditur cum in agro Amerino esset filius*).
T. . . . iste Roscius will be Magnus (since Capito receives the news in Ameria
(§19)). *assiduus* "constantly present": *OLD* s.v. 2a. Acting *uoluntate patris* is a
major point in defense of a son under *patria potestas*; thus his father's support will play a prominent rôle in the defense of M. Caelius Rufus (§§3–5,
17–18, 79–80). C. later seeks to refute the prosecution's argument that the
son's *relegatio* to the country proves the father's dislike by claiming that it is
characteristic of an entire class of young men acting *patrum uoluntate* (§§42–8,
51), and in the peroration he calls his client *probatum suis filium* (§152). **iste
autem frequens Romae esset:** i.e. just like Roscius sen. (§16). The initial
placement of the verb in its clause (as here *occiditur*) emphasizes sudden or
surprising actions; cf. Marouzeau 1938: 69; the historical present, found as
early as Plautus, serves vividness and contrasts with the previous past narrative tenses: *erant . . . metuebat . . . superauit* (§17); cf. von Albrecht 1989: 30n115
and 41. *ad* + acc. gives an approximate location: "in the neighborhood of";
cf. G–L §386 R.2. The *balneae Pallacinae* are mentioned only here; see §132n.
rediens a cena (repeated at §§97, 98, and 126) economically adds the circumstances and makes it clear that the elder Roscius was merely following
his usual routine and thus the victim of ambush (*insidiae*); cf. §98; he was

hardly involved in a fight or the like. The murder occurred some months after 1 June 81, as C. explains at §128.

spero ex hoc ipso . . . affinem culpae iudicatote: C. has set up a comparison (σύγκρισις) of two potential suspects, his client and Magnus, and expects the reader/listener to conclude that suspicion attaches to the latter based purely on his presence at Rome at the time of the murder and the defendant's absence in Ameria. But absence from the scene of the crime would not necessarily clear his client since the applicable law seems to have included a clause that proscribed the arranging as well as the commission of the crime; cf. Riggsby 1999: 50 and 202n5 and 6; hence C. will later deny that Roscius had the city connections needed to organize the plot (§§73–6 and §92). For *suspicio malefici* cf. *Har.* 37 *multi enim sunt . . . in quos huius malefici suspicio cadat*; for *suspicio* as the starting point of prosecution cf. §8n. *affinis* (+ dat.) is "connected with, implicated in"; cf. Scaur. *orat.* 43 no. 11n. = V. Max. 3.7.8 *Aemilius Scaurus huic se affinem esse culpae negat*; *Clu.* 127; *Sul.* 70; *OLD* s.v. 4a.

nisi perspicuum res ipsa fecerit: i.e. without argumentation; similarly §82 *de tam perspicuis rebus*; §98 *in tam perspicuis rebus argumentatio quaerenda . . . ?*; §105 *nonne perspicuum est . . . ?*; cf. also §41; here there is a play on the shared root of *suspiciosus* and *perspicuus*; cf. Holst 1925: 83; Riggsby 1999: 58 and 59. *iudicatote* is the second or "future" imperative, characteristic of formal or legal writing, also found at §109; the singular form (*iudicato*) was inherited, the plural formed by analogy with the first imperative; cf. Meiser 1998 §143.3; for the semantics see further Risselada 1993: 122–38 and 163. Here C. pulls back from the suspicions he has been planting and once again assumes a large burden of proof; cf. §8n.; Berger 1978: 35.

19 Occiso Sex. Roscio . . . T. Capitonis inimici: the abl. absolute restates the main content of the previous narrative as background for the following scene. The chiastic *Ameriam nuntiat . . . nuntiat domum* assimilates *nuntio* to the construction of verbs of motion: G–L §337; *OLD* s.v. 1; transl. "brings word to Ameria . . . to the house." The historical present continues initially from *occiditur*: *nuntiat . . . et nuntiat . . . uenit* (present, rather than perfect, because of the cretic clausula). Mallius Glaucia, a freedman of Magnus and therefore his *cliens et familiaris*, is known only from our speech. *tenuis* is a description of his financial position ("poor"); cf. Hellegouarc'h 1963: 471 and n8; Achard 1981: 376; it may, however, suggest to the senatorial jury a man who can easily be suborned to crime, like the *egentes* who were solicited by Lentulus' agent to free him from custody (*Cat.* 4.17); even Glaucia's patron, Magnus, was *egens* before dispossessing Roscius jun. (§23); cf. also C.'s remarks on *tenuitas* at §86. After the description of Glaucia *et nuntiat* resumes the narrative (from the previous *nuntiat*), which now focuses on the first recipient of the news; C. draws out what he sees as the implications at §96. *inimici* is emphasized by its final position. In spite of the suspicions C. wants to arouse, the announcement to Capito may have a perfectly innocent explanation, e.g. that he was the relative of the deceased who lived closest to the highway to Rome; *primo* at §96 suggests that this was merely Glaucia's first stop in a series; and C. is likely to have such details as the length of the journey and mode of transport from his client; cf. Lincke 1890 195; Kinsey 1980: 176.

   et cum post horam . . . extractum ostenderet: the Romans divided day and night into twelve hours (*horae*) each, the exact duration depending on the time of year; cf. *OLD* s.v. *hora* 1; the vague chronological indicator at §128 places the event "some months" (*aliquot menses*) after 1 June, so it is unclear exactly when this occurred or how long the hours would have been. *primo diluculo* is "at daybreak": *OLD* s.v. *diluculum*. **decem horis nocturnis** "within ten hours of the night": G–L §393. The 56 Roman miles correspond to approximately 52 English miles or 84 km. *cisium* is a Gallic word borrowed along with the light, two-wheeled carriage it designates; cf. *Phil.* 2.77 (of Antony) *inde cisio celeriter ad urbem aduectus domum uenit capite inuoluto*; the use of the plural implies that the plot was so well organized that different vehicles were in readiness at several stages of the journey (so Landgraf *ad loc.*); cf. *OLD* s.v. *peruolo* "fly through" or "over" is here used hyperbolically of "rushing through" or "over": ibid. s.v. 1 and 3. At §§97–8 he dilates on the suspicion thus planted and strongly implies that Glaucia committed the murder (*non uersatur ante oculos uobis in caede Glauciae?*). *inimicus* is emphasized by repetition in this sentence; but even if they were enemies, it hardly follows that Capito hoped for (*exoptatum*) the death of the elder Roscius; C. here assumes the rôle of omniscient narrator; cf. Berger 1978: 35. He reserves for the end of the sentence the gruesome details *cruorem . . . telumque* with emphasis on the proximity to the deed.

   20 quadriduo quo haec . . . solitudo commemoratur: the Etruscan city Volaterrae is 130 miles from Rome as the crow flies; a center of resistance to Sulla, it was under siege at this time; he later planted a colony of his veterans there: Keaveney 1982: 183; Letzner 2000: 290 and n80. C.'s claimed knowledge that the news arrived at Volaterrae four days after the murder (*quadriduo quo haec gesta sunt res*) is evidently a guess based on estimated travel time and the date when Roscius jun. was ejected from his property (§23); see Kinsey 1980: 177–8; Berger 1978: 35. The time is repeated at §105 with the suggestion that Magnus despatched the messenger (see *ad loc.*), though our passage gives the impression that Magnus and Capito conferred with

Chrysogonus in person; see below. That Chrysogonus was the recipient accords with C.'s picture of the *societas* (see below); but he never establishes that Chrysogonus and Capito knew one another prior to the embassy of the *decem primi*, though he makes this claim at §106 (where see n.). Hinard and Benferhat 2006 *ad loc.* go further, doubting that either Sulla or Chrysogonus was at the camp either now or during the embassy of the *decem primi*, but this seems too radical a contradiction of C.'s account; cf. Dyck 2009. With *defertur . . . demonstratur . . . commemoratur* C. returns to historical present (cf. §18n.); the impersonal passive leaves the agent(s) vague. For the *magnitudo pecuniae* cf. §6n. The total number of farms is indicated also at §99. Location on the Tiber will facilitate transport of produce to market and thus enhance the value of land (cf. the description of the ideal farm at Col. 1.2.3 *nec procul a mari uel nauigabili flumine*); hence the inclusion of this detail. **huius inopia et solitudo:** for *hic* referring to the defendant cf. §6n. The (alleged) communication highlights the vulnerability of Roscius jun. *inopia* is "helplessness, defencelessness": *OLD* s.v. 3; cf. the tenth commonplace for moving pity at *Inv.* 1.109 *per quem inopia, infirmitas, solitudo demonstratur*; for our *iunctura* cf. *Quinct.* 5 *quod si tu iudex nullo praesidio fuisse uidebere . . . solitudini atque inopiae*; it recurs at *Q.fr.* 1.1.25 but not in later speeches. Roscius' *solitudo* is evidently inferred from his anti-social habits (§52); for the resulting vulnerability cf. *Leg.* 1.41 *quid in deserto quo loco nactus quem multo auro spoliare possit, imbecillum atque solum?*

demonstrant, cum pater . . . societas coitur: the subject of *demonstrant* and *pollicentur* is unspecified; the use of *oratio obliqua* hastens the narrative forward; cf. Wiesthaler 1956: 24–5 and 43; in view of the conclusion *societas coitur* and benefits accruing to Capito and Magnus (§22), the reader/listener assumes that these two are the informants; cf. Berger 1978: 40. In fact, however, there is no need to suppose that any such conversation took place (see the previous n.); and even if it did, C. could hardly have known about it, since neither he nor his client was privy to it; though purely a construct of his imagination, this narrative is the core of his interpretation of the case; cf. Wiesthaler 1956: 69. *splendidus* "illustrious" is an epithet appropriate to *equites*; cf. §133; §140 *equestrem splendorem*; *Cael.* 3; *OLD* s.v. 4; Hellegouarc'h 1963: 458–61; Achard 1981: 385 and n40. **gratiosus** is first attested in C. (*Quinct.* 2): *TLL* s.v.; for the idea cf. §15 *gratia atque hospitiis florens*. **nullo negotio** "with no trouble," perhaps colloquial: *OLD* s.v. *negotium* 3; the phrase recurs at §28. **perfacile** shows the "urbane" prefix *per-*, often preferred by C. to the fussier comparative or superlative endings; cf. André 1951. The following description elaborates on the *inopia et solitudo* of Roscius jun. *rusticus* is the key term: it explains both his incautious nature and his lack of connections at Rome; it is also the one point on which prosecution and defense agree; cf.

§§39–51 and 74. *de medio tollere* is "to get rid of, remove" (with the implication of killing): *OLD* s.v. *tollo* 13a. **ne diutius teneam:** *uos* is understood, as also at *Ver.* 2.1.34 (though it could easily have fallen out after -*us*). **societas coitur:** a *societas* is a partnership in a broad sense; *coeo* is transitive with *societas* or a similar object ("to form a partnership"), possibly legal jargon, first attested at *Quinct.* 76, recurring at §117 and found in the jurists; cf. *OLD* s.v. *coeo* 10; *TLL* s.v. 1420.19; Wegner 1969: 30–8 especially 35–6. This is, of course, merely C.'s inference from the demonstrable facts narrated in the following section; cf. Berger 1978: 35. C. later elaborates his picture of the *societas*: he claims that it consisted of gangsters (*sicarii*: §87) and qualifies it negatively: *si . . . nullam . . . societatem neque sceleris neque praemi . . . coieras* (§96).

21 cum nulla iam . . . manceps fit Chrysogonus: the act narrated (*nomen . . . Sexti Rosci*) is inserted between the *cum*-clauses that explain the (paradoxical) circumstances and the epithet that should have exempted him (*hominis studiosissimi nobilitatis*). *proscribo* is to "announce publicly in writing, post up," the derived noun *proscriptio* is used both of the process of posting and of the posted notice itself, here specifically of "the publication of the names of citizens who were declared outlaws and their goods confiscated"; cf. *OLD* s.vv. and on the history of the posting of public notices at Rome Hinard 1985a: 18–28; on the procedures used in the first proscription ibid. 52–9. *defungor* (+ abl.) is "to be done with, rid of": *OLD* s.v. 2a. *tabula* is a public notice board and hence proscription list: ibid. s.v. 4a; Hinard 1985a: 32–3. *studiosissimi nobilitatis* varies and intensifies *nobilitatis fautor* (§16). The impression left by this passage is deceptive, however; it turns out that, in fact, Roscius' property was seized not because his name was on a proscription list (the proscriptions were already closed before the date of his death) but, rather, on the grounds that he was slain among Sulla's enemies (*apud aduersarios*); cf. §§ 127–8 with nn. *cuius bonorum*, supplied by the editor, smoothes an otherwise abrupt transition; *cuius* can easily have dropped out after -*tatis*. *manceps* is the "purchaser," *mancipium* being "ownership" obtained by the legal form of laying hold of the property (*manu capere*) in the presence of witnesses; cf. *OLD* s.v. *mancipium* 1–2; Berger s.vv. *mancipium, mancipatio.* The one undoubted fact *manceps fit Chrysogonus* in final position lends apparent confirmation to the foregoing narrative; for the emphasis on the proper name cf. §6 *sese dicit emisse . . . L. Cornelius Chrysogonus*; §125 *emptor est Chrysogonus*; §132 *omnium . . . machinatorem esse Chrysogonum*; §141 *sese putat aliquid posse Chrysogonus?*; Baldo on *Ver.* 2.4.126.

tria praedia . . . impetum facit: for *uel* + superl. cf. §6n. Contrary to the implication of our passage, the transfer to Capito of three farms (cf. §17) was not immediate; cf. §110 with n. For *quemadmodum* cf. §5n.; *ipse* is Magnus, acting as Chrysogonus' agent (cf. §23 *procurator Chrysogoni*). *impetum facere in* varies *inuadere in* (§§6, 13, and 23) and likewise implies violence, as though there had been no sale (cf. §127 *illud suspicor, omnino haec bona non uenisse*); the process is described with pathetic embellishment at §23. After *impetum facit* the words *haec bona sexagiens HS emuntur duobus milibus nummum* are transmitted but were rightly deleted by Kayser as repeated from §6 and inserted here in the wrong place.

21–22   haec omnia . . . libertum improbum habeat: C. knew he could only win if he succeeded in separating, to the jurors' satisfaction, Sulla from the wrongs attributed to his freedman Chrysogonus; cf. Berger 1978: 37. Here accordingly, having brought the matter *in castra L. Sullae* (§20), he steps out of the *narratio* to add editorial comment on Sulla's relation to these events. The exculpation of Sulla will resume at §§91, 127, and 131; he cross-refers to our passage at §127 *nam Sullam . . . oratio mea ab initio . . . purgauit.* In the course of the speech, as Berger *loc. cit.* points out, there is a gradual broadening of Sulla's sphere of authority from the *paterfamilias* within the household in our passage to that of the general vis-à-vis his army (§91) to Jupiter's government of the world (§131).

21   haec omnia . . . certo scio: C. is in no position to know this; it proves to have been inferred from the handling of the embassy from Ameria (cf. §25n.). *imprudens* will refer to ignorance rather than foolishness; cf. Berry 2004: 86n8.

22   neque enim mirum . . . aliquid huiuscemodi moliantur: a long, involved period that contrives to hedge about Sulla's possible inadvertence (*si aliquid non animaduertat*) with circumstantial *cum*-clauses to such an extent that it is virtually without impact; the whole is capped with a fine ditrochaic clausula. C. begins with Sulla's responsibility for the polar opposites past and future, war and peace, then Sulla's rôle as sole governor (*unus*); the extenuation is then summarized *cum tot tantisque negotiis distentus sit ut respirare libere non possit*; only then does C. drop the reference to possible inattention, which he immediately follows up with the point that *tam multi* are looking to exploit any such moment. **et ea . . . et ea . . . et pacis . . . et belli:** the polysyndeton helps to articulate the parallel clauses and also gives the impression of a plethora of factors; cf. §9n.; for the frequency of polysyndeton in causal expressions cf. Amacker 2002: 36–7. A verb is clearly needed to govern *quae praeterita sunt*; Rinkes's *sanet* is the best so far offered; originally referring to the healing of disease or diseased bodies, the word comes to be used of correcting harmful tendencies in the body politic; cf. *OLD* s.v., especially 2b; for Sulla's appointment as *dictator legibus scribendis et rei publicae constituendae* cf. Keaveney 1982: 161; Hinard 1985b: 223–6 and 1988: 87–90; Letzner 2000: 247–8 and n7. *unus* is very often contrasted with *omnia*; cf. *Ver.* 1.1.20 *omnia in unius potestate ac moderatione vertentur*; §132 with n. *guberno* (< Gk κυβερνάω) originally refers to "piloting" a ship, but, like its Gk source, comes to be applied to "governing" the state: *OLD* and LSJ s.vv. *distineo* is to "draw the attention of in several directions, distract": *OLD* s.v. 3–4. **si aliquid non animaduertat:** the brief allusion to a possible lapse on Sulla's part is quickly extenuated in the next clause. For the danger of a leader's being distracted from business cf. *Phil.* 11.22 (on Pansa's possible appointment to command against Dolabella before the siege of Mutina is lifted). *occupatio* is one's "preoccupation (with business)": *OLD* s.v. 2b. *tempus* here, like Gk καιρός, is a "favourable time, opportunity" (*OLD* s.v. 9a). C. was fond of *aucupor*, a metaphor from bird-catching: "be on the look-out for": *OLD* s.v. 3a. *despicio* is "to look down, i.e. relax one's attention" (*OLD* s.v. 1c). For *huiusce* cf. §6n.; *molior* is to "set in motion (with some degree of effort)": *OLD* s.v. 5; similarly at §91.

huc accedit quod . . . libertum improbum habeat: *quamuis ille felix sit, sicut est*: an allusion to the epithet inscribed beside Sulla's name on his equestrian statue: App. *BC* 1.451; cf. Keaveney 1982: 160. This type of expression, affirming what is first raised as a theoretical possibility, occurs 60x in C.'s corpus. Berry 2004: 83 finds the qualification added to Sulla's epithet "impertinent: Sulla is genuinely fortunate — but not, however, as fortunate as he thinks." That would be impertinent, but is not what C. says; rather, the point is that no one, however fortunate, is immune from having *in magna familia* a crooked slave or freedman; the goal is to absolve Sulla of responsibility. C. returns to Sulla's *felicitas* at §136.

23 interea iste T. Roscius . . . pecuniae fit dominus: the irony of *uir optimus* is palpable; cf. Dyck on *Leg.* 1.21. In §21 Magnus was said to have taken possession of the estates of C.'s client *nomine Chrysogoni*; the relationship is now clarified: he is Chrysogonus' *procurator* ("property manager": *OLD* s.v. 2). Kinsey 1980: 177 remarks that the appointment of a local man was convenient for Chrysogonus. No doubt, but how did Chrysogonus come to choose him? On Capito's recommendation (so Loutsch 1979: 110)? But it is not clear that Capito and Chrysogonus were acquainted before the embassy of the *decem primi* (in spite of §106; cf. §110). Fuhrmann 1997: 57 suspects that Magnus was Chrysogonus' tool in the murder of Roscius sen. **Ameriam**

uenit: he was previously mentioned as being at Rome (on the day of the elder Roscius' murder: §18). For *inuadere in* cf. §21n. *miser* is among the words that "recur obsessively in perorations" (Winterbottom 2004: 223); in our speech C. deploys it early and often; besides this passage cf. §§30, 54, 119, 146; so too of his client's father (§98); cf. the appeal for pity (*misericordia*), which C. fears may be dying out (cf. §§150 and 154, as well as §3 on the *ignoscendi ratio*); for his *miseriae* cf. §14; cf. also §78 *omnia . . . in hac causa sunt misera*. **luctu perditum** "broken by grief" (*OLD* s.v. *perditus* 1a), a unique combination in classical Latin, intensifies the previous *cui . . . luctum mors patris attulit* (§13). **qui nondum . . . iusta soluisset:** *iusta* are the due observances, especially in the cult of the dead: *OLD* s.v. *iustum* 3. The son was presumably observing the *feriae denicales*, a nine-day period in which the bereaved family abstained from work or other activity following the burial; cf. Samter, *RE* v 1.219.59; Toynbee 1971: 50; Maurin 1984: 205; Belayche 1995: 167–8. **nudum eicit domo:** *nudum* ("destitute": *OLD* s.v. *nudus* 10) is emphatically placed, with intent to shock and stir sympathy; C. amplifies at §144 *si uestitum quo ipse tectus erat anulumque de digito suum tibi tradidit*; he compares his condition to that of a shipwreck at §147 (*quem tu e patrimonio tamquam e naufragio nudum expulisti*); cf. Corbier 2005: 125–9. The present *eicit* is generally accepted to match the following *exturbat* (*eiecit* is transmitted). *domus* is amplified by the reference to the *foci patrii* and *di penates* with their sacred associations; cf. *Dom.* 109 *quid omni religione munitius quam domus unius cuiusque ciuium? hic arae sunt, hic foci, hic di penates, hic sacra, religiones, caerimoniae continentur.* Emphatically placed before the inserted vocative, *praecipitem* ("headlong") intensifies the implied disorder, as at *Ver.* 2.4.67 *praeceps prouincia populi Romani exturbatus est*. For *exturbo* ("drive out, expel") with plain abl. cf. e.g. *Quinct.* 95 *miserum est exturbari fortunis omnibus.* *ipse* provides an emphatic point of contrast (similarly §115), as does *dominus*, emphatic by position; cf. §13n. C.'s narrative is calculated to arouse pity for his client and indignation at the procedure and outcome.

    qui in sua re . . . constituta auctione uendebat: *qui in sua re fuisset egentissimus* is concessive (cf. G–L §634) and stands, for contrast, in chiastic relation to *insolens* ("arrogant") *in aliena*, a summary of the behavior of *nouveaux riches*, already discussed by Aristotle (cf. §14n.). As he portrays the newly rich Magnus, C. may have in mind the mime entitled *modo egens, repente diues*: cf. Ramsey on *Phil.* 2.65.8 as well as *Phil.* 2.42 *tot dies in aliena uilla declamasti?*, where the charge of using another's property is as contestable as it is here; cf. Ramsey *ad loc.*; on §6 (*nullo iure*). C. proceeds to a kind of checklist of the various methods of disposal (*multa . . . plura . . . non pauca . . . reliqua*), expressed in clauses of approximately equal length (*isocola*) and with the same ending (*homoeoteleuton*). **palam . . . clam** often contrast procedures. Was the secrecy

perhaps motivated by perceived *inuidia* (see the next n.)? Or had the property not, in fact, been confiscated and sold (cf. §127 with n.)? **de medio**
"from the scene": *OLD* s.v. *medium* 3b. Magnus' helpers (*adiutores*) are mentioned only here; one assumes they include Mallius Glaucia (cf. §19). For
large effuseque cf. *effundere* as a goal of Chrysogonus (§6); *Cael.* 13 (of Catiline) *quis in largitione effusior?* Though Chrysogonus is unmentioned here, sch.
Gronov. p. 314.27–9 Stangl reports that he removed some objects to furnish
a villa he was building near Veii; if we had the full text of §132, possibly it
would clarify whether Magnus' plundering was separate or in the service of
that plan. **uendebat** "set about selling"; inceptive impf. (*NLS* §200(ii), G–L
§233).

24 Quod Amerinis . . . furta, rapinae, donationes: C., no doubt
deliberately, blends together two things, the grief over the death of Roscius
sen. and the reaction to the transfer of his property. He makes the grief
seem at first a reaction to the dispossession of Roscius jun. just narrated
(*Quod . . . usque eo uisum est indignum ut . . .*), but then clarifies that the reaction
was partly also to the father's death. **urbe tota:** *totus* + a designation of
place in the plain abl. indicates extension over: K–S I 351. The verbal nouns
fletus gemitusque ("weeping and groaning"; cf. *Ver.* 2.4.110 *gemitus fletusque*) serve
vividness as does the following description of events that passed before the
eyes (*ante oculos uersabantur*) of the Amerians. The list begins with the fates
of the two principals, father and son, both qualified with superlative adjs.
(*crudelissima . . . indignissima*), and goes on to the events leading to the latter's
plight. This narrative from the Amerians' point of view both elicits pity
(perhaps more effectively since they are third-party observers; cf. Berger
1978: 38) and also motivates the decree of the decurions and the embassy of
the *decem primi*. **florentissimi:** cf. on §15 *gratia atque hospitiis florens*. *crudelissima*
receives emphasis by separation from *mors* as well as by final placement in
its clause. **cui de tanto . . . reliquisset:** Roman cult called for rites at the
tomb of the deceased a month after the death and then at yearly intervals
from the date of death; in addition, each May at the Rosalia the graves
of ancestors were adorned with roses; cf. Cumont 1922: 53; Toynbee 1971:
50–4; access is thus presupposed. A right of access (*iter*) to his father's tomb
would, however, impose a servitude (i.e. a right held by a non-owner) on
the property and so diminish its value; cf. Watson 1968: ch. 8; de Visscher
1963: 83–9; Helttula 1974; hence, apparently, its denial. For Magnus as a
praedo cf. §15 (*domestici praedones*) with n. The purchase (*emptio*), qualified as
flagitiosa ("shocking, disgraceful," perhaps related to *flagrum* ("lash, whip")
and punishment as a public spectacle; cf. *OLD* s.vv.), would have taken

place in the Roman forum (cf. *Off.* 2.83) out of sight of the Amerians (at §127 C. suspects that it never took place at all); what was visible was the *possessio* by Magnus in the name of Chrysogonus. The sentence concludes with keywords in asyndeton, giving the impression of an unbroken series of outrages. **furta, rapinae, donationes** refer back to the actions already described in §23 (*multa palam . . . donabat*). If, however, the *emptio* and *possessio* were legal, so was the disposition of the property by the new owner; so the claim of *furta* and *rapinae* depends upon the illegality of the sale (§21n.); C. is not claiming that Magnus acted without Chrysogonus' knowledge or approval.

nemo erat . . . dominantem T. Roscium: the two names form the opposite poles of this sentence, Sex. Roscius, the owner with his honorable epithets, contrasted with T. Roscius (Magnus), his rôle vividly described by participles; cf. Dyck on *Cat.* p. 19; for emphatic final placement of the name cf. §21n. For subj. in a relative clause with indefinite antecedent cf. G–L §631.2. **qui non ardere omnia mallet:** the attitude is inferred from the subsequent decree (§25). *illa* was inserted before *omnia* by the rhetorician Rufinus but is unnecessary; the drastic expression is apparently a colloquialism (cf. §26 *ut mori mallet* with n.). *iactare se* is to "flaunt oneself, show off": *OLD* s.v. *iacto* 12b; *dominor* to "be the master": *OLD* s.v. 1b.

25 itaque decurionum decretum . . . quaeso, cognoscite: the *decuriones* were town councillors in the *municipia* and colonies of Italy; they had charge of the community's finances and external relations; cf. *OCD*³ s.v. *decuriones*; the *decem primi* were presumably chosen from among their number. **decem primi:** sc. *ciuitatis*; cf. *Ver.* 2.4.15 *etenim est* [sc. Heius] *primus ciuitatis.* For *proficiscor* as setting out with a goal or on a mission cf. Fordyce on Catul. 46.10; *OLD* s.v. 1b. *doceo* ("inform") is used, as often, with acc. and indirect question: *OLD* s.v. 1b. The reputation (*fama*) of Roscius sen. is at issue insofar as it was claimed that he had been killed on the enemy side; cf. §§113 (*fama mortui*) and 125–6. Lintott 2008: 426 suggests that the embassy may also have been motivated by concern that other local property-owners might suffer a similar fate. **de istorum scelere et iniuriis:** *iste* is used contemptuously (cf. §17n.). The reference can only be to the two T. Roscii; yet Capito figures during the negotiations at Volaterrae as one of the *decem primi*, indeed the one whose one word is decisive; cf. Berger 1978: 39–40; our text is a sign of C.'s drive to demonize Capito even before he has profited from the death of Roscius sen.; cf. on §§26 and 108. **scelere et iniuriis** "wicked wrongs" by hendiadys. For the repeated references to Roscius jun. as *innocens* cf. §6n.

DECRETVM DECVRIONVM: in addition to summarizing the decree
C. has it read out, as he does occasionally elsewhere; cf. Wiesthaler 1956:
75. Such documents belong to the class of inartificial proofs (ἄτεχνοι πίστεις
Arist. *Rhet.* 1355b35), i.e. they are materials with which the orator has to work
but are not invented by him. Therefore, though read out in court, they were
not included in the published speeches; on rubrics marking abridgement in
the speeches (mostly inserted by C. himself) cf. Austin on *Cael.* 19. This is the
one concrete piece of evidence C. adduces in the case; he holds no witnesses
in prospect, merely (implicitly) blaming the prosecutor for failing to compel
the members of the embassy to testify (cf. §110 with n.) and Chrysogonus
for refusng to make the former slaves of Roscius sen. available for testimony
under torture (§§120–23).

legati in castra . . . et flagitia fieri: the narrative of the embassy, like
some other narratives (§84) and examples (§§56 and 82), begins in asyndeton.
The simple statement of the ambassadors' arrival is balanced by the simple
statement of their return after failing to accomplish their mission (*Ameriam re
inorata reuerterunt*: §26). C. immediately claims (as a kind of aside in asyndeton)
the fact that the ambassadors were blocked from seeing Sulla as support
for his previous assertion of Sulla's unawareness (§§21–2 with n. on *imprudens*
(§21)). It is also possible, however, that Sulla was fully aware of the fate of the
elder Roscius and his estate but that Chrysogonus nonetheless did not want
to risk a debate on the subject in front of him, for Sulla could change his
mind and blame his subordinates; cf. Dyck 2003: 240. **flagitia** "disgraceful
acts"; cf. §24n. *flagitiosa*.

nam statim Chrysogonus . . . esse facturum pollicerentur: *allego*
is to "send as an intermediary or representative": *OLD* s.v. 1; for the relative
clause with final force (*qui peterent*) cf. G–L §630; for secondary sequence
after the historical present ibid. 511 R.1. Kinsey 1980: 178 is skeptical: "What
is dubious is that these *nobiles* were sent by Chrysogonus . . . Members of
the *nobilitas* were hardly likely to tell Italian town councillors that they had
been sent by a Greek freedman." C. will have been told merely that the
decem primi first met with *homines nobiles*; the assumption that they were sent
by Chrysogonus obviates their having been sent by Sulla, whom C. must
separate as far as possible from the whole affair; cf. §21n.; Chrysogonus'
accompaniment in the forum by *magna caterua togatorum* (§135) might lend a
certain amount of credibility.

26 usque adeo autem . . . Sullam doceri: *pertimuerat*: the plupf. presents
this as background to the behavior just described. The drastic expression *mori malle*, attested in comedy (Pl. *Ba.* 519c, *Vid.* fr. xv, Ter. *Eun.* 66)

as well as in a letter (*Att.* 7.11.1–2), is probably colloquial; cf. §24 *qui non ardere omnia mallet* with n.; again Chrysogonus is given a comic attribute; cf. §6n.

homines antiqui . . . uacua filio traditurum: *antiquus* is "old-fashioned," often a term of praise in Latin; cf. Kinsey on *Quinct.* 59; *OLD* s.v. 9b. **qui . . . fingerent:** for the generic subj. see §1n. *fingo* is originally to "form, shape" (from wax, clay, or the like) but as early as Plautus is used to mean "form a mental picture of, visualize": *OLD* s.v. 1 and 8. The *decem primi* of Ameria are, however, unlikely to have been so easily gulled; cf. Stroh 1975: 58. Possibly they also received assurances that no other citizens of Ameria would be targeted; cf. Lintott 2008: 426. *ille* refers back to Chrysogonus (*OLD* s.v. 11). *eximo* is to "remove" from a class or category; *OLD* s.v. 3c. *uacuus* as applied to property means "not assigned to anyone, unoccupied": *OLD* s.v. 9a; Chrysogonus undertakes to return the farms in such condition that Roscius jun. will have a free hand to lease them or the like; for a different interpretation cf. Hinard and Benferhat 2006 *ad loc.*

cumque id ita . . . re inorata reuerterunt: Capito's intervention is decisive; why? If he were already in possession of three of the thirteen farms (§§17, 21), he surely would not have been appointed to an embassy the point of which was to restore his property to Roscius jun. This passage strongly suggests that Capito was, in fact, the *spiritus mouens* behind the embassy and that it was only in the course of the embassy that the deal was brokered (unknown to the other *legati*) assigning Capito three of the farms; cf. Alexander 2002: 155; §110 with n. *appromitto* occurs only here in classical Latin; it means "promise in addition" (sc. to Chrysogonus); cf. *OLD* s.v.; *TLL* s.v. *adpromitto*. **re inorata** "without pleading the case": *inoratus* is previously attested only at Enn. *trag.* 6 J.: *OLD* and *TLL* s.v.

ac primo rem differre . . . domino incolumi obtinere: the three stages are clearly marked with *primo . . . deinde . . . postremo. procrastinare* ("post-pone, delay" < *cras* "tomorrow") is first attested here; juxtaposition with its synonym *differre* obviates any misunderstanding; cf. *OLD* and *TLL* s.v. *procrastino*. For *isti* of those associated with the prosecution cf. §25n. Havet's deletion of *nihil* is attractive at first sight, but the set phrase should not be altered; cf. *OLD* s.v. *ago* 22b ("be idle, do nothing"); the narrative is also more pointed with *nihil*, their inactivity itself being slowed; for a different sense cf. §130n. *deludo* is to "deceive, dupe," a word C. appears to have taken over from comedy: *OLD* and *TLL* s.v. **id quod facile intellectum est** shows that C. has drawn an inference, evidently about the motive rather than the plots against his client's life. **insidias uitae . . . parare:** cf. Kinsey 1980: 179: "Cicero supplies suspiciously few details of this. He tells us that Roscius had

to be forcibly dispossessed (*per uim expulistis* in 32). We may wonder whether
he had tried to use force to return, been forcibly resisted and whether Cicero
was not making the most of some such incident." *Sex. Rosci* was deleted as
a gloss by du Rieu, perhaps rightly. **neque sese arbitrari . . . obtinere:**
the reasoning is repeated, in part with the same wording, from §6, where it
is assigned to Chrysogonus alone; for *incolumis* and *obtineo* see *ad loc.*

27 quod hic simul atque sensit . . . usus erat plurimum: born into
the most politically influential family of the time (cf. §15n.), with father,
grandfather, and brother all having served as consul, Caecilia Metella made
a good marriage with App. Claudius Pulcher (who would be consul for 79);
C.'s later enemy P. Clodius was their offspring. Her influence is shown by an
incident of 90 when her reported dream vision prompted the senate to restore
the cult of Juno Sospita; cf. *Div.* 1.4 and 99 with Pease *ad locos*; Kragelund 2001.
de amicorum . . . sententia: i.e. he convened a private *consilium* to advise
him; cf. Crook 1955: 4–7; thus Roscius' one narrated act is not even his own
decision; cf. Berger 1978: 40. **Romam confugit:** for the accusative of goal of
motion with the names of cities cf. G–L §337. **Nepotis sororem, Baliarici
filiam:** by inserting *sororem Baliarici* Garatoni restored the correct relations
from §147 (*Baliarici filia, Nepotis sorore*). Q. Caecilius Metellus Baliaricus, the
eldest son of Q. Caecilius Metellus Macedonicus (cos. 143), served as consul
for 123 and then conquered the Balearic islands (122) with resulting triumph
and cognomen; Q. Caecilius Metellus Nepos was consul in 98. Cf. Münzer,
RE III s.v. Caecilius nos. 82, 95, and 135. For C.'s emphasis on the social
standing of Roscius' supporters cf. §1n.; on the formula for polite naming cf.
§6n. **qua pater usus erat plurimum:** *familiariter*, though often added to
the phrase, is optional; cf. e.g. *Att.* 16.5.3 *Cn. Lucceius, qui multum utitur Bruto.*

  in qua muliere . . . uestigia antiqui offici remanent: *etiamnunc* is
the spelling in the five other occurrences in this speech, rather than *etiamnum*,
which Σ presents here; the meaning ("even now, still") is unaffected. C. often
states or implies that the observance of *officium* such as prevailed in former
times is fading from the world; cf. §26 (*homines antiqui*); Quinct. 59 *antiquam offici
rationem dilexit* [sc. P. Quinctius] *cuius splendor omnis his moribus obsoleuit.*

  ea Sex. Roscium . . . opitulata est: with *ea* C. takes up Caecilia
Metella as the new subject; cf. §6 (*is a uobis*) with n.; she and her action
enclose Roscius in the economy of this sentence just as she afforded him protection in life. *inops* ("resourceless, helpless") summarizes Roscius' position;
he was targeted in the first place, according to C., because of his *inopia* (§20);
his need is met by Caecilia's "providing aid" (*opitulor* + dat.). The following
participial qualifiers provide specifics: he is first the passive victim (*eiectum*

domo atque expulsum ex suis bonis), as described at §23, and then must act energetically to save his life (*fugientem latronum tela et minas*, an exploitation of the
verbal properties of the active participle rare in C.'s early work; cf. Laughton
1964: 45). For Roscius' dispossessors as *latrones* cf. §6n. *domum* is acc. of the
goal of motion; cf. G–L §337. Roscius jun. counts as her *hospes* on the basis of
the paternal connection (*qua pater usus erat plurimum*), such ties being heritable;
cf. §15n.

eius uirtute, fide, diligentia . . . in proscriptos referretur: Caecilia is again the focus of the sentence through her pronoun (*eius*). Of the
three qualities *uirtus* is the general one (on its application to her cf. §147n.);
fides ("loyalty"), in recognition of ties of *hospitium*, springs from it, and it is
expressed in action through her *diligentia*, the word first used here in the
speech (similarly §28 *init.*); at §75 it is a quality inculcated by the *uita rustica*;
C. claims at §148 that Roscius is being defended *diligenter*; and he attributes
diligentia to M. Valerius Messalla Niger at §149; he faults the prosecution for
not coming prepared carefully enough at §72 (*diligentius . . . uenisses*). *uiuus in
reos* and *occisus in proscriptos* form a striking contrast; the counterfactual supposition is that, as in the case of his father (§21; but cf. *ad loc.*), the name of
Roscius jun. would be added to the proscription list, his murder thus receiv-
ing *ex post facto* sanction. With the key word *reus* C. has brought his narrative
down to the present.

28 Nam postquam isti . . . tempore ipso pugnarent: an explanation
(*nam*) of how Roscius' status as a *reus* came about. Those behind the prosecution (*isti*; cf. §25n.) are now the agents; their recognition of Roscius' effective
protection forms the background (*postquam . . . intellexerunt*). *caedem facere* is a
fairly common paraphrase for *trucidare* or the like; cf. *OLD* s.v. *caedes* 1c. The
new aim is to fulfill the murder plan by other means; similarly already §8
nonne . . . ferro assequi consuerunt? C. thus assumes, as in §20, the rôle of omniscient narrator, reporting as facts what are in reality inferences; cf. Berger
1978: 40–1. *plenus* "full (of)" is often used in a non-material sense to characterize; cf. *OLD* s.v. 4a. *scelus* and *audax / -acia* have been associated with the
prosecution from early in the speech; cf. §§1, 7, and 12 with nn. The *consilium*
is defined by three *ut*-clauses, the last joined with *denique*. For *nomen deferre* cf.
§8n. For *parricidium* and the special penalty reserved for it cf. Introduction
sec. 1. For *accusator uetus* cf. §17n. (*uetus gladiator*). The prosecutor at Rome was
a private individual, not a state official, and the function was regarded as,
at best, a necessary evil; cf. C.'s remarks at §§55–7 and Alexander 2002: 7–8
and 13–14. *comparo* is "provide," sometimes with the implication of improper
purposes: *OLD* s.v. 3a and 5. For *de ea re . . . in qua re* and *crimen* and for *suspicio*

as the basis of prosecution cf. §8n. The *tempora* were said to inhibit potential
defenders (§1) and to favor *acria ac seuera iudicia* (§11); hence here *tempus ipsum*
is to be the prosecutor's chief weapon (*ipse* here is "on its own, apart from
other considerations": *TLL* s.v. 334.69); cf. *Clu.* 90 *uidetis igitur non in causa sed
in tempore ac potestate spem omnem accusatoris fuisse.*

   ita loqui homines ... ab nullo defensus esset: a *sermocinatio* or
invented speech; cf. Lausberg §820; other examples in this speech at §§32,
58, and 145. C. imagines these as the topics of deliberation among Roscius'
accusers, perhaps invoked to persuade Erucius to take on the case. This is
C.'s explanation of the prosecution's next move following the launching of
the *societas*, the dispossession of Roscius jun. and his flight to Rome. This matter is set off from the main narrative with *oratio obliqua*; cf. Wiesthaler 1956:
63–4 and 74n1; G–L §649 N.2. For the interval since the last regular trials
cf. §11n. **condemnari eum oportere ... adductus esset:** the logic is
debatable, perhaps invented to motivate Erucius' acceptance of a flimsy case;
cf. §11n. **huic autem ... defuturos:** cf. §58, reporting Erucius' (alleged)
thoughts: *unum illud spectaui quod Chrysogonus aiebat neminem isti patronum futurum.* **Chrysogoni gratiam:** not, of course, his popularity in general but
the favor he enjoys with Sulla. **de bonorum uenditione ... defensus
esset:** for the sale of the goods cf. §6; for C.'s picture of the *societas* cf.
§20n.; for *uerbum facere* §2n. For the force of *ipse* see the previous n.; for
nullo negotio §20n.; *defensus esset* stands for future perfect of the direct speech;
cf. G–L §516.

   29 hoc consilio ... uobis tradiderunt: C. commonly uses *hic* in transitions from reported speech to main narrative; cf. examples cited by Wiesthaler
1956: 99. In C.'s early speeches *atque adeo* sometimes (as here and §§100 and
113) is equivalent to *uel potius*, introducing a *correctio*; cf. Parzinger 1910: 110–11;
Lausberg §§784–6. He will take up the theme of *amentia* in §§33–4. *ipsi* "in
person" (cf. §1n.) as opposed to acting through (the jurors as) agents (for the
idea cf. §6). For the relative clause preceding its "antecedent" cf. §§6 and 8;
for *iugulo* cf. §13n. With *uobis* C. draws the jurors into the scenario he has
sketched and relates it to them personally; cf. §12 *ante tribunal tuum, M. Fanni,
ante pedes uestros, iudices*; Berger 1978: 41.

DIGRESSIO I (29–32)

These sections and their sequel (§§33–4) tend to be annexed either to the
preceding *narratio* (so Craig 1993: 33) or the following *partitio* (e.g. by Solmsen
1968: 232 and Berger 1978: 34). But adding no new facts, our passage should
probably be segregated from the *narratio*; and classifying our sections with

the *partitio* obscures rather than clarifies their function. Our passage takes the facts already disclosed and regards them from the standpoint of the defense counsel, inviting the reader/listener to share his feelings, first of despair, then of pity for a client faced with accumulated difficulties and repugnant alternatives, and finally of resolve to speak out in spite of all dangers. The passage concludes with pathetic appeals of client and *patronus* to the prosecutors, an example of "how easily the milder emotions of ethos are transformed into the vehement . . . emotions of pathos": May 1988: 24. For digressions in the speeches in general cf. Canter 1931.

29 Quid primum querar . . . fidem implorem?: the orator pretends to be overwhelmed, a reminiscence of the famous dilemma of C. Gracchus (*orat.* 48 no. 61 *quo me miser conferam?* etc.), closely imitated by C. at *Mur.* 88; cf. also *Ver.* 2.4.3 *unde igitur potius incipiam . . . ?*; Bonnet 1906. For complaint as the appropriate mode in this defense cf. §9 *his de rebus . . . me . . . neque satis grauiter conqueri . . . posse intellego.* For the deliberative subjunctive in rhetorical questions cf. G–L §§265 and 465–6. *auxilium* continues as the object until *uestram* signals the change; the postponement of *fidem* lends emphasis; for the jurors' *fides* cf. §10n.; for their *potestas* §154n. **hoc tempore** "at the present time" (for *hic* cf. §1n.), i.e. the time of the trial.

30 pater occisus nefarie . . . abesse uidetur?: the complaints pour out in a stream of short clauses in asyndeton (cf. Lausberg §939.2), made more abrupt by omission of the verb "to be," beginning and ending with the most drastic, the father's death and the danger to the son's life, with property matters inserted in the middle. For *nefarius/-e* cf. §6n. *obsideo* can mean "besiege" but also "occupy (a country) by force" (*OLD* s.v. 4a and c); here C. applies the latter sense metaphorically. **bona adempta, possessa, direpta** summarizes the stages described at §23. *infestus* is "exposed to danger, threatened" (*OLD* s.v. 5), clarified by the following description. Like *peto* (cf. §7n.), its compound *appeto* can mean "attack": *OLD* s.v. 7; for the claim cf. §26n.; the feminine participle secures the ditrochaic clausula. **quid . . . sceleris:** gen. of the rubric (cf. §8n.): "what within the realm of wickedness . . . ?" The separation of the pronoun from the limiting genitive serves emphasis; for *scelus* cf. §1n. The heroic clausula is avoided by C., but not absolutely, as our sentence shows; cf. Laurand 1911.

   tamen haec aliis . . . uitam amittere: *aliis nefariis*: sc. *maleficiis. cumulo* is "increase, augment," sometimes so used with the instrumental abl.; cf. *Cat.* 1.14 *alio incredibili scelere hoc scelus cumulauisti*; *OLD* s.v. 5. The addition of the synonym *adaugent* secures a clausula of trochee + spondee. *confingo* ("invent, fabricate": *OLD* s.v. 2a) varies *conflo* (§1); it recurs at §§47 and 76.

Capito is the only planned prosecution witness mentioned by C. (§§100–1). **in hunc . . . huiusce pecunia:** the polyptoton emphasizes the injustice; for *comparo* cf. §28n.; the point about the prosecutor is repeated at §55; see *ad loc.* The sentence concludes with a pathetic description of the dilemma which the defendant faces, comparable in some respects to the famous dilemma of C. Gracchus (see §29n.); cf. Craig 1993: 33 and n115. For *condicionem ferre* ("make a proposal") cf. Cael. *Fam.* 8.14.2 *fert illam tamen condicionem* [sc. Caesar], *ut ambo exercitus tradant. ceruix* ("the neck") is properly used in the pl. in early Latin; the transfer to the sg. is poetic (Enn. *An.* 483 Sk.) followed by Hortensius (Quint. 8.3.35) and later prose authors; cf. Löfstedt 1956: I 31; it figures in a number of contexts as the vulnerable part of the body; so here *ceruices dare* is "to offer up one's life," an expression evidently taken from gladiatorial combat; the *iunctura* recurs at *Sest.* 89; cf. *OLD* s.v. especially 2c–d (similarly §8 *quin illorum libidini Sex. Rosci uita dedatur*); Imholtz 1971–2: 230; for *iugulare* as the goal of Roscius' adversaries cf. §§13, 29, and 151. To be sewn into a sack (*insui in culleum*) was the traditional penalty for parricides; Roscius might have faced it if he confessed; cf. Introduction sec. 1; §5n. Lactantius twice alludes to our passage (*Inst.* 3.14.9 and 5.9.16).

  patronos huic defuturos . . . non deest profecto, iudices: the expectation of the prosecution was disappointed; hence *desunt*, transmitted after *putauerunt*, can hardly be right unless one were to insert e.g. *patronos* <*nobiles*>; that would accord with Erucius' visible relief when only C. rose to speak (§60). But at §58 the view is the same as in the text transmitted here: *Chrysogonus aiebat neminem isti patronum futurum.* In our passage the prosecution's expectation is met with *non deest profecto*; *desunt* must have been added by a reader who thought something missing; for an interpolation of similar type cf. *Off.* 3.29 with Dyck's n. For the sense of *libere dicere* and C.'s ability to do so in this case cf. §3 with n.; for the *fides* of the *patronus* cf. §10n. **id quod in hac causa satis est:** sc. because the rights and wrongs are so patent; cf. §34 *quid est in hac causa quod defensionis indigeat? qui locus ingenium patroni requirit* etc. *quoniam quidem suscepi*, transmitted before *non deest*, was rightly deleted by Heusinger as a repetition from the following chapter.

31 et forsitan . . . succurram ac subibo: *causam suscipere*, like *causam recipere* (§2n.), is used of an advocate's "taking on" a case: *OLD* s.v. *suscipio* 8c. C. described the factors that weighed with him in taking this case at §§2–5 (with no hint of the rashness now conceded; cf. on §2). *fecerim* is an example of the potential subj. used in modest assertions; cf. G–L §257; K–S I 176–8. The asyndeton before *quoniam* marks a sharp contrast (cf. §6n.) between his past decision and current resolve (for which cf. §10). *licet* before subj. develops into a conjunction ("although"): *OLD* s.v. 4. This is one of three occurrences of the colloquial interjection *hercules* in Ciceronian oratory; cf. *Man.* 54; *Phil.* 12.4 (for *hercule* cf. §50n.); it is a reduced form of *mehercules* (for which cf. §§58 and 141); cf. Hofmann 2003: 137–8. **omnes . . . omnia:** the careful chiasmus *omnes terrores . . . pericula . . . omnia* is disrupted by the change of *in me* (χψσ) to *minae* in most of the witnesses. Editors place a comma variously before or after *omnia*; it should follow the word for the sake of both the chiasmus and the cretic + dactyl. **ac subibo** (ΣΑπφ) effects trochee + spondee and so is preferable to the heroic clausula *atque subibo* presented by the other witnesses; cf. §30n.

   certum est deliberatumque . . . metus quam fides: *certum est* = "I am resolved": *OLD* s.v. *certus* 2b. **quae . . . omnia:** for relative clause preceding its "antecedent" cf. §6n. *audacter* alternates with *audaciter* (felt to be pedantic by Quint. 1.6.17) in MSS of C.'s speeches; in our speech the former is the reading of the medieval tradition (cf. §§104 and 118), albeit Priscian (*GL* 3.76.28) offers *audaciter* in §104, and this form has also been conjecturally restored in the other passages; cf. *OLD* s.v. *audacter.* **libenter . . . libereque:** *xyzque* appears to be the commonest way of organizing three items in Latin; cf. Pinkster 1969. *libere . . . dicere* is taken up from §§3 and 30; cf. on the former. *metus* varies the *terror et formido* that deterred the *homines nobiles* according to §5. C.'s *fides* stands expressively at the end of the sentence; cf. §10n.

32 etenim quis . . . neglegere possit?: for *etenim* introducing a rhetorical question cf. *OLD* s.v. b; Ramsey on *Phil.* 2.17.20. *dissolutus*, originally used with reference to clothing (Kinsey on *Quinct.* 38), is "lax, (morally) weak": *OLD* s.v. 2; for the relative consecutive clause with *qui* = *ut is* cf. *NLS* §230(3)(b). *haec* is the obj. of *tacere* (here trans.: "be silent about": *OLD* s.v. 4) and *neglegere* as well as *uideat.*

   'patrem meum . . . patrimonium meum possidetis': the complaints are restated in personal form from §30 with the proscription of the deceased added; for the *sermocinatio* cf. §28n.; May 1988: 24: "the sudden, impassioned outburst in first person causes the audience to forget momentarily that Roscius is not telling his own story and stirs feelings in them as no third-person narrative . . . could"; the device recurs at §145. **occisum in proscriptorum numerum rettulistis:** a *reduplicatio* by which the term *proscriptus* is repeated from the previous clause (cf. Lausberg §619); the idea of murder is also repeated but in different terms (*iugulastis, occisum*). C. assimilates this to the case of Q. Lucretius Ofella, whom Sulla had executed prior to his proscription; cf. Livy *ep.* 89; Münzer, *RE* XIII 2.1686.32 (Lucretius 25); cf. also Oros. 5.21.5 *alios autem postquam iugulauerant proscribebant*; but Roscius

sen. was not, in fact, included among the proscribed; cf. §21n. For *iugulo* cf.
§13n.; for the dispossession §23.

quid uultis amplius? . . . iuguletis Sex. Roscium?: what can go
beyond what Roscius' adversaries have already perpetrated? Surely C. imagines, as in §12, a killing in the courtroom itself (*ante pedes uestros . . . inter ipsa
subsellia*). The MSS offer *ut hic aut iuguletis aut condemnetis*, which on that supposition does not make sense; hence the reading adopted here; *condemnetis*
may have originated as a misguided gloss on *iuguletis*; cf. also §151. On final
placement for emphasis of the proper name cf. §21n. (*Chrysogonus*).

DIGRESSIO II (33–4)

These chapters form a second digression prior to the *partitio*. Though *amentia*
has been attributed to the prosecution (§29), the bearing of the *exemplum* of
Fimbria and Scaevola is not *prima facie* clear and has to be explained at §34:
Roscius' adversaries are like Fimbria in suing a man for refusing to die; cf.
Sest. 80 *et causam dicit Sestius de ui? quid ita? quia uiuit.* This digression, like
the preceding one, rouses pity (cf. Canter 1931: 359), but it is also an early
signal that C. feels no sympathy for the Marian side in the recent civil war;
it thus allays any suspicion that a political agenda underlies the case and
thus removes a potential impediment; cf. §§135–6 and 142; Dyck 2003: 243–
4; detailed analysis by Hutchinson 2005: 184–6. The *exemplum* was retailed
(from our passage) by V. Max. 9.11.2 under the rubric *dicta improba uel facta
scelerata*.

33 Hominem longe audacissimum . . . insanissimum: the political
adventurer C. Flavius Fimbria participated in the worst excesses that followed the capture of Rome by the Mariani, including the murders of P.
Licinius Crassus Dives and one of his sons and of C. and L. Caesar. Sent to
the Mithridatic War probably as quaestor to the consul L. Valerius Flaccus,
he undermined his commander and succeeded in ousting him. He made
progress against Mithridates until the aristocratic L. Lucullus refused naval
support. He committed suicide under siege by Sulla at Thyatira in the latter
part of 85; hence C.'s reference to him in the perfect tense (*nuper habuimus in
ciuitate*). He became a byword for *audacia* among later historians; cf. Wirszubski 1961: 20. Cf. in general Münzer, *RE* VI 2.2599.30 (Flavius 88); Badian
1962: 56–7. **inter eos qui ipsi quoque insaniunt:** i.e. among the members of the Marian faction. C. puns wittily on *insanus/insanire* in the usual
and the political sense (of those who desire revolution; cf. Achard 1981: 239);
insanus is varied below by *furiosus*; Fimbria is characterized in similar terms
at *Brut.* 233 *ita furebat tamen ut mirarere tam alias res agere populum ut esset insano*

inter disertos locus. ipsi quoque is used rather than *et ipsi* until Livy; cf. Bertocchi 1996: 541.

is cum curasset . . . eum posse uiuere: *is* takes up and focuses attention on Fimbria; cf. §6 (*is a uobis*) with n. *curo ut* is to "see that" something is done: *OLD* s.v. 6c; he did not do it himself; Marius' funeral took place in early 86. Q. Mucius Scaevola the Pontifex, one of his early teachers, was a noted expert in the law and much admired by C., as our passage shows; on him cf. Münzer, *RE* XVI 1.437.1 (Mucius 22). Scaevola was remotely connected by marriage to Marius; hence Gruen 1968: 235 finds it "no coincidence" that this attack "came immediately after the protective hand of Marius was removed." **uir sanctissimus:** the highly encomiastic description is used 11x elsewhere in C.'s speeches: Merguet 1877–84: IV 385–6; it applies with special force to Scaevola as pontifex maximus; cf. Szemler 1972: 124; Rüpke 2007: 168 and 2008: 115–17 and 805 (no. 2478). **neque hic locus est ut multa dicantur** "this is not the place for going on at length"; for the consecutive clause cf. G–L §552; but even the Roman *laudatio funebris* did not provide scope for extended literary treatment; cf. Kennedy 1972: 21–3; detailed study by Kierdorf 1980; there is another brief encomium of Scaevola at *Amic.* 1. **diem Scaeuolae dixit:** the insertion of the proper name focuses attention; cf. §21n. *diem dicere* is "to appoint a day, serve a summons" (to answer charges, in C. specifically before a *iudicium populi*); cf. *OLD* s.v. *dies* 7b; Lintott 1971: 696–7, who thus infers that Strabo 13.1.27 is probably right (against the other sources) to make Fimbria a quaestor in 85, since, apart from the *duumuiri perduellionis*, only tribunes, aediles, and quaestors had the power to convene such a court.

cum ab eo quaereretur . . . corpore recepisset: *quid tandem* "what on earth," with *tandem* showing impatience; cf. *OLD* s.v. 1b. **pro dignitate** "in view of his standing": *OLD* s.v. *pro* 16a. **ut erat furiosus** "madman that he was" provides parenthetical explanation: *OLD* s.v. *ut* 21a; Roby 1708(e); for *furiosus* cf. Opelt 1965: 140–1; Taldone 1993: 8–16. **quod non totum telum corpore recepisset:** Fimbria models the situation after that of a defeated gladiator; cf. *Sest.* 80 *num, ut gladiatoribus imperari solet, ferrum non recipit? totum telum*, with its alliteration and emphasis on the quantitative term, "would be a neat joke if it were not spoken by Fimbria in all earnestness" (Hutchinson 2005: 186). The subj. reports Fimbria's grounds; cf. G–L §541; V. Max. 9.11.2 paraphrases *quod parcius corpore telum recepisset*.

quo populus Romanus . . . ab iis ipsis interemptus est: after his recovery Scaevola lived for four more years only to be murdered at the end of March 82 on orders from the younger Marius, then consul, as part of a general liquidation of enemies shortly before his defeat by Sulla at Sacriportus: Münzer, *RE* xvi 1.440.51–441.7. Before *tantum potuit* the mss present *quae*; surely, however, the pronoun was originally *qui*, which was then carelessly assimilated to the gender of the immediately preceding word; this obviates an awkward change of subject in the following *ut*-clause. *possum* + internal acc. is "to have a specified power, influence" etc.: *OLD* s.v. 8. *compositio* is first used here in the sense "settlement of differences, agreement": *OLD* s.v. 7; *TLL* s.v. 2138.76–8; C. himself only took sides in the civil war after the attempt had failed (§136 *posteaquam . . . fieri non potuit ut componeretur*); see further Gabba 1976: 139–40. Similarly C. would seek, without success, to mediate in the civil war between Caesar and Pompey; cf. *Phil.* 2.24; Gelzer 1969: 243–54; Mitchell 1991: 243–52. Shackleton Bailey 1979: 237–8 wanted to eliminate *quia* and called attention to Ursinus' *qui quos* for *quos quia*. He takes *quos* as referring back to *omnes*, but surely its "antecedent" is found in *ab iis*, a common pattern in this speech; cf. §6n.; hence the pathos: his promotion of a peaceful solution made him suspect in the eyes of the Marians, whose lives he would have saved. *ab iis ipsis*, rather than the transmitted *ipse ab iis*, would seem to be required to underline the irony.

34 estne hoc illi dicto . . . passus non est: *hoc* is "the present matter," whereas the earlier incident is qualified with *ille*; the contrast *illud . . . hoc* continues below; cf. *OLD* s.v. *hic* 11 and *ille* 6. *quid ita?* ("how so?") is a formula eliciting more information: *OLD* s.v. *quis* 16. For *de manibus effugere* cf. §151; *Man.* 22; *Cael.* 65; *Mil.* 22.

illud, quia in Scaeuola . . . non est ferendum: *in Scaeuola*: *in* is "in the matter of (a person or thing)," almost equivalent to *de*; cf. *OLD* s.v. 42. In the earlier case judgment depends on the victim, in this case on the agent. Cf. *Ver.* 2.4.45 *superbum est et non ferendum*; *Phil.* 7.17; *Off.* 3.36 *potentiae non ferendae*. By now it is clear, if it was not before (cf. §6n.), why Chrysogonus is given such prominence in the speech: the Greek freedman makes an ideal target; at §§132–49 C. will mine this rich vein in earnest.

nam per deos . . . magno opere desiderat?: in the exclamation *per deos immortales* the epithet adds weight and sonority; found 50x in C., it will recur at §146 and twice in §153. **indigeat:** for subj. with indefinite antecedent cf. §24n. The denial that the case requires *ingenium* in the pleader contradicts the assumption of §1 that C. is less qualified than other possible advocates *inter alia* on grounds of *ingenium*; but cf. the assertion at §30 that the case merely requires someone who can speak freely and in good faith in the defendant's behalf. In general, §§30–4 show a marked gain in confidence compared with the beginning of the speech; cf. Offermann 1974: 73.

totam causam, iudices, . . . intellegetis: transition to the rest of the case; for the hortatory subjunctive (*explicemus . . . consideremus*) cf. G–L §263.1;

K–S I 180. For *ante oculos* cf. §13n. C. promises the jurors that they will understand three points: the motive behind the case (*contineo* here is "form the basis of": *OLD* s.v. 12a); the topics the defense has to handle (including sensitive issues of public policy, as hinted at §§2–4; see §35); and the basis on which the case should be judged (for the sense of *sequor* cf. §1n.).

PARTITIO (35–6)

Solmsen 1968: 232 and 237–8 rightly emphasizes just how unorthodox this *partitio* is from the standpoint of the rhetorical theory of Hermagoras of Temnos (*c.* 150 BC), which classified cases according to the points chiefly at issue (στάσεις = *constitutiones*). C. instead focuses on the different persons associated with the prosecution and their contributions, of which *audacia* and *potentia* had no counterpart in rhetorical theory; cf. Kennedy 1963: 303–21; Kroll, *RE* Suppl. VII 1090.20–96.48. C. adds (§36) that only the reply to Erucius' charges strictly belongs to his mandate; the other two aspects are the jurors' responsibility as officers of the state. The following *refutatio/argumentatio* follows precisely the scheme laid out in the *partitio*:

I   Reply to Erucius' charges (§§37–82)
II The *audacia* of Magnus and Capito (§§83–123)
III The *potentia* of Chrysogonus (§§124–49).

This organization of the material entails a certain amount of repetition (cf. §§77–8 and 119–23) but enables the speech to build to a climax of *indignatio*; cf. Offermann 1974: 70–3.

35 Tres sunt res . . . dicere oportere intellego: *obsto* is "be a hindrance to" in a general sense: *OLD* s.v. 3a; for the generic subj. cf. §1n. For *crimen* cf. §8n. *potentia* is unofficial power and thus differs from the *potestas* of the jurors (§154 with n.); cf. Ramsey on *Phil.* 1.29. For Chrysogonus and his (exaggerated) *potentia* cf. §6n. C. dilates on his rôle at §124. *confictio* is the "invention, fabrication" of the charge, used only here in classical Latin (cf. *OLD* and *TLL* s.v.), perhaps coined as the counterpart of *confingo* (§30). One expects proper names in each of the three categories; hence Richter's deletion of *accusator* (transmitted before *Erucius*) is more probable than Madvig's of *Erucius* and is adopted here; in addition, the prosecutor should be identified with *praenomen* on first mention, and *c* can easily have dropped out before *e*. *audacia* here stands for violence or the attitude that leads to it; cf. §§75, 78 and 122; Dyck on *Cat.* 2.10. *pars* is usually used, as here, in the pl. of a "part" one has to play, a "rôle," etc.: *OLD* s.v. 10; *posco* is to "demand, claim": *OLD* s.v. 1; cf. *Scaur.* 31 *qui has sibi partes depoposcit*; similarly §95. **qui plurimum potest,**

potentia pugnat: a good example of Ciceronian alliteration; similarly §133; cf. also *Var.* fr. 2 Crawford *studio, multitudine, pecunia, periurio pugnant*; Volkmann 1885: 516. **de hisce omnibus . . . dicere oportere intellego:** what appeared at first as the "obstacles" (*res . . . quae obstent*) to Roscius are now revealed to be the *diuisio* of the argumentative part of the speech; it is not merely a list of items but an interpretation of the case that has by now been carefully prepared; reduced to this compressed and powerful form, it will imprint itself on the jurors' memory; cf. Fuhrmann 1997: 54. The clear-cut *diuisio* is characteristic of the early C. (cf. *Quinct.* 36 with Kinsey's n.), perhaps under the influence of Hortensius (*diuidebat acute* according to *Brut.* 303). C. cross-refers to our passage at §122.

36 quid igitur est? . . . atque opprimere debetis: *quid igitur est?* calls for more information: "what is the case, then?": *OLD* s.v. *quis* 14a. **non eodem modo**: sc. *dicere oportet*. Here C. clarifies what he meant in calling for the jurors' collaboration at §10 (*hoc onus si uos aliqua ex parte alleuabitis . . .*). The division of labor he has in mind is clearly articulated by the initial pronouns *ego . . . uos*. On the charge of the *iudicia publica* to maintain public order at Rome cf. Riggsby 1999: ch. 6. *diluo* (literally "dissolve") is regularly used for "rebutting, refuting" charges: *OLD* s.v. 1 and 4. For *audacia* and *potentia* cf. the previous n. **intolerandam:** cf. §34 *quia fit a Chrysogono non est ferendum. primo quoque tempore* "at the earliest possible opportunity": cf. *OLD* s.v. *primus* 11b and *quisque* 5a; cf. e.g. *Ver.* 2.4.58.

REFVTATIO/ ARGVMENTATIO I: REPLY TO ERUCIUS
(37–82)

This is the part of C.'s speech that corresponds most closely to the teachings of the rhetorical handbooks. According to the theory of Hermagoras (cf. §§35–6n.) C. has chosen the line of defense called the *constitutio coniecturalis*, i.e. he denies that his client committed the crime; cf. Solmsen 1968: 234. C. divides the arguments into those *ex causa*, *ex persona*, and *ex facto ipso* (*Inv.* 2.16–51; cf. Craig 1993: 34). Of these, *causa* corresponds to IB in the following outline, *persona* to IA, and *factum ipsum* to V; these constitute the essence of C.'s *refutatio*, the other materials in this section being dilations or digressions.

I Parricide a monstrous crime requiring a high standard of proof unmet by prosecutor (37)

A   Roscius' character (39)
- (1)   Not a young man to be manipulated by criminals
- (2)   No previous criminal record
- (3)   Not given to luxurious living
  - (*a*)   No attendance at dinner parties
  - (*b*)   No debts
  - (*c*)   Lived a farmer's life

B   Motive: the father's alleged dislike (40)
- (1)   Grounds are unspecified
- (2)   Relegation to farm work adduced as proof (42)
  - (*a*)   But this is common policy for farmers of Sex. Roscius' region and class (43)
  - (*b*)   Roscius jun. was allowed to reap profit from some of the estates during his father's lifetime (44)
- (3)   Roscius sen. always kept his other son by him (45)
  - (*a*)   Counterexample from Caecilius: Eutychus no less loved than Chaerestratus (46)
  - (*b*)   Appropriateness of an example from poetry (47)
  - (*c*)   High prestige of agriculture (48)
    - (*i*)   Example of Atilius summoned to office from the plough (50)
    - (*ii*)   Devotion to agriculture made Rome great
- (4)   His father planned to disinherit him (52)
  - (*a*)   Charge of failure to socialize is insubstantial
  - (*b*)   Charge of parricide would require proof of many vices (53)
  - (*c*)   Bringing of such a charge without proof a mockery of the *lex Remmia* (53)

II   Digression: the usefulness of prosecutors in insuring conviction of the guilty (55)

A   Geese and dogs maintained on the Capitol (56)
- (1)   They make noise in case of a nighttime disturbance
- (2)   The dogs' legs are broken if they do so by day

B   Similarities to prosecutors (57)
- (1)   Some are harmless like geese, others can bite like dogs
- (2)   They are nurtured at public expense
- (3)   Their unseasonable barking will be punished with the letter *k* branded or tattooed on the forehead

III   Erucius, assuming a lack of defenders, has offered no substantiation for the alleged plan to disinherit (58)

A   This explanation is confirmed by his careless behavior at the trial (59)

B   The prosecution was thunderstruck by mention of Chrysogonus (60)

IV Motive has not been established in a parricide case (61)

   A   Even in trivial cases motive is a prime concern (62)

   B   Being contrary to nature, parricide imposes an especially heavy burden of proof (63)

     (1)   The sons of T. Cloelius accused of his murder (64)

     (2)   They were acquitted when it was shown that the door was open (65)

     (3)   Poetry depicts the hounding of those who have killed a parent (66)

     (4)   The Furies interpreted as psychological torment (67)

     (5)   Examples of the kinds of proof that would be required (68)

   C   The severity of the punishment accords with the high standard of proof (69)

     (1)   Solon provided no punishment for parricide so as not to suggest the idea (70)

     (2)   More wisely the Roman ancestors devised the unique punishment of the sack

       (*a*)   Deprives the criminal of the elements (71)

       (*b*)   Avoids polluting the world

   D   The subject matter of the case and quality of the jurors require a better effort from Erucius (72)

V Modality of the murder

   A   In person? But he was not in Rome (74)

   B   By agents

     (1)   Free men

       (*a*)   From Ameria? If so, who?

       (*b*)   From Rome?

         (*i*)   How did he know them?

         (*ii*)   How did he induce them?

         (*iii*)   If by pay, what was the amount and source?

         (*iv*)   Roscius' rustic way of life rules out this possibility (75)

         (*v*)   Who was summoned to the task and when? (76)

     (2)   Slaves (77)

       (*a*)   The prosecution controls Roscius' slaves and declines to make them available for questioning

       (*b*)   C. will return to this point later (78)

C   Summary of arguments under modality
VI For lack of arguments the prosecutor invokes the indiscriminate killing of that time (80)
  A   But the prosecutors themselves were among the ringleaders
  B   Roscius, on his farm at Ameria, was unaware of what was happening at Rome (81)
VII Erucius' charges have been refuted (82)
  A   What he said about Roscius' self-enrichment with public money is irrelevant and unsubstantiated
  B   If any point has been reserved for witnesses, we will be well prepared for that as well.

37 If C. has assumed a staggering burden of proof (§§8 and 18), he now begins to raise the requirements for the prosecution by invoking generally accepted principles of human psychology; similarly §§40 and 67; cf. Riggsby 1999: 56–7.

Occidisse patrem . . . complexa esse uideantur!: *occidisse patrem*, initially placed, foregrounds the shocking charge (cf. §18n.; §70 *insui uoluerunt in culleum uiuos*) and at the same time signals the new topic. *arguo* is "charge, accuse": *OLD* s.v. 4. C. uses *sceleratus* of persons, *scelestus* of things; cf. Reichenbecher 1913: 19–29. *facinus* is originally neutral ("a deed") and needs to be qualified (as here by *nefarium*), though through much use in such contexts it comes by itself to mean "crime, misdeed": *OLD* s.v. For the relative clause with consecutive force cf. §5n. The exclamation *di immortales!*, recurring at §77, sometimes preceded by *pro*, is found 123x in C.'s corpus; cf. also §34 (*per deos immortales!*) with n. **eiusmodi . . . uideantur:** cf. *Ver.* 2.2.82 *eiusmodi ut in uno omnia maleficia inesse uideantur*; for the contrast of *unus* and *omnia* cf. §§22 and 132.

etenim si . . . mortem obtulerit parenti: philosophers are referred to in the speeches non-technically as *sapientes*; cf. e.g. *Pis.* 70. The *uultus* is, as the ancients well knew, highly expressive; cf. Swain 2007, especially 180–1; for tiny details of behavior as indicative of mental states cf. *Off.* 1.146. *pietas* was originally the fulfillment of the duties imposed by the *di parentes* so as to insure the safety of the family from divine wrath; cf. Koch, *RE* xx 1.1221.58 (s.v.); besides the *parentes*, the *patria* and the *di* generally came to be included; cf. Fugier 1963: 381–5. The *a fortiori* argument is twisted into a rhetorical question; the underlying form would be "If a mere look can violate *pietas*, then murder of a parent . . . " For *acer* in this speech cf. §11n.; for *mortem offerre alicui* cf. *Sest.* 48 and *Vat.* 24; later C. prefers to use *offerre* with *morti* and the personal acc., e.g. *Mil.* 92 and 94.

pro quo mori ipsum... atque humana cogebant?: *ipsum* added to *mori* emphasizes the reversal of rôles, sharpening the antithesis to *(is) qui mortem obtulerit parenti. postularet* is past potential (cf. G–L §258); *cogebant* is indicative, as is regular in expressions of necessity, Latin expressing with indicative what it was incumbent on one to do in the past, whereas English focuses rather on the nonfulfillment (G–L §254 R.1). *iura diuina atque humana* recur (with reference to their violation by an act of parricide) at §65.

38 in hoc tanto... censes uti oportere?: parricide was indeed, so far as one can tell, rare at Rome; cf. Saller 1986: especially 9 and 19 and 1987: especially 21–2 and 34. For *atrox* cf. §9n. **portenti ac prodigi simile:** i.e. a bad omen for the entire state; for Roman methods of propitiation in such cases cf. Rosenberger 1998. **tandem** "may I ask" signals impatience; cf. §33n. R. Klotz's *tu* is needed for the transmitted *te*; in question at this stage are the general requirements of a prosecution under this charge; only at the end of the chapter does C. come to criticize Erucius' procedure in particular (*quorum tu nihil...*); scribes would naturally have tended to make the pronoun agree with *accusatorem*. The praenomen is included in this first address to Erucius but later dropped; cf. on §44; Dickey 2002: 51–2.

nonne et audaciam... profligata atque perdita?: *nonne* signals a question to which a positive response is expected (G–L §455). *qui in crimen uocetur* illustrates the use of subj. in a relative clause with indefinite antecedent: G–L §631.2. *singularem* is emphasized by its separation from *audaciam. censes oportere* is to be understood with *ostendere*. **mores feros:** in the course of his rebuttal C. cites Erucius' portrayal of Roscius' life this way: *hunc hominem ferum atque agrestem fuisse, numquam cum homine quoquam collocutum esse, numquam in oppido constitisse* (§74). For *immanis* ("savage, brutal") cf. *OLD* s.v. 1; the chiastic arrangement of nouns and epithets concentrates the savagery at the center. For *flagitium* cf. §25n. **denique omnia... perdita:** as usual, the final item in the series summarizes; for *ad perniciem profligata* = "reduced to ruin" cf. *OLD* s.v. *pernicies* 1b and *profligo* 1c.

quorum tu nihil... contulisti: *ne obiciendi quidem causa*: i.e. let alone providing the proof necessary for an accusation in court; *obicio* = "cast in one's teeth, lay to one's charge": *OLD* s.v. 10; cf. *Cael.* 6 *obiectum est de pudicitia... accusatio crimen desiderat, rem ut definiat, hominem notet, argumento probet, teste confirmet; maledictio autem nihil habet propositi praeter contumeliam. confero* is to "collect": *OLD* s.v. 8a.

39 A standard topic of criminal prosecution was the *probabile ex uita* or demonstration that the suspect's previous life foreshadowed the crime (cf. *Rhet. Her.* 2.5). This chapter accordingly raises and dismisses three theories by which Roscius' character could have led to parricide: a misdirected youth, a propensity to violence, or the need to support a luxurious lifestyle.

Patrem occidit . . . natus maior quadraginta: *qui homo?* "what kind of man is he?" (*OLD* s.v. *qui*[1] 2a). For the indeclinable adj. *nequam* ("worthless, depraved") cf. *OLD* s.v. 2. *natus* is used with the acc. of length of time; hence *quadraginta natus annos* (*Div.* 1.46) = "forty years of age": G–L §336.4; *maior* means "older" and is often used with *natu* (conjectured here by Gulielmius); cf. *OLD* s.v. 3a; with it one might have expected either *quam* or abl. *annis*, but the construction is well attested; the retention of the acc. may be colloquial; cf. K–S II 471–2 (to their examples add *Leg.* 3.9); von Albrecht, *RE* Suppl. XIII 1262.6.

uetus uidelicet sicarius . . . ne dici quidem audistis: for *uetus* cf. §17n. *uidelicet* ("doubtless, of course") often signals irony or disbelief; cf. *OLD* s.v. 3. For *sicarius* cf. §8n. *uersor* + *in* is "to be involved in"; cf. *OLD* s.v. *uerso* 12a; §98 *non uersatur ante oculos uobis in caede Glaucia?*

luxuries igitur . . . ad hoc scelus impulerunt?: lifestyle (*uictus*) was a common *topos* in arguments *e persona*; cf. *Inv.* 1.35. Like *uidelicet*, *nimirum* "without doubt, evidently" is also a common marker of irony: *OLD* s.v. *luxuries, aeris alieni magnitudo,* and *cupiditates* are personified as the subjects of *impulerunt*; though listed as items in series, they are interrelated, *cupiditates* leading to indulgence in *luxuries* and hence to debt, the Latin expression for which is characteristically concrete (*aes alienum,* literally "another's bronze"); cf. §75. For *indomitae cupiditates* cf. *Ver.* 2.1.62 *at, credo, in hisce solis rebus indomitas cupiditates atque effrenatas habebat.*

de luxuria purgauit . . . coniuncta est: what for Erucius had been proof that the defendant is *ferus* and *agrestis* (cf. §74) is turned to account by C. as proof that he did not indulge in luxurious living; similarly Erucius' point that Roscius remained in the country is used to show that the defendant developed no inordinate desires; in general, this is C.'s procedure in dealing with Roscius' character, an example of his technique of "appropriation and reversal" of the opponent's argument, on which cf. Riggsby 1995: especially 245–6. C. uses *luxuries* and *luxuria* about equally in the speeches, while using only the former in the *rhetorica* and only the latter in the *philosophica*; his inconsistency is especially marked in our passage and in §75, where the transmitted text shows the same alternation of nom. *luxuries* and abl. *luxuria*; cf. *ad loc.*; *TLL* s.v. *luxuria* 1919.70–2 and 75–7. From "free from impurities" and "clear (space) of obstacles" *purgo* goes on to be used of religious purification and then (as here) of "absolving, exonerating" from charges; cf. *OLD* s.v. Certainly the *conuiuium* was a major vehicle for displaying or indulging in luxury (cf. Edwards 1993: 186–8 and 199–204) but by no means the only one, so C.'s proof is at best incomplete. C. follows this with the brief assertion *nihil umquam debuit* and then the point that *cupiditates* are unlikely to arise in a rural context, the beginning of a lengthy argument (through §51) based on stereotypes of city vs. country; cf. Vasaly 1993: 157–92. But desires of various kinds could arise in the country no less than the city, though the objects might be different. The charge of *peculatus* (self-enrichment with public funds) levelled against Roscius, for which C. offers no adequate reply (§82), would, if true, argue that his desires exceeded his means. The chiastic arrangement of participles and prepositional phrases may perhaps mirror the farmer's well-ordered life. For *cupiditas* and *officium* in opposition cf. *Inv.* 2.35 *si nihil deliquisse, nulla cupiditate impeditum ab officio recessisse.* The idea that agricultural work teaches virtue can be found in Gk texts such as Xen. *Oec.* 5.12 (translated by C.) and was adopted by Cat. *Agr.* 1.4 *at ex agricolis et uiri fortissimi et milites strenuissimi gignuntur maximeque pius quaestus . . . consequitur minimeque inuidiosus, minimeque male cogitantes sunt qui in eo studio occupati sunt*; see further Diederich 2007: 272–97; Kenney on *Moretum* xxxviii–xl.

40 Quae res igitur . . . et perspicuam fuisse: *furor* is *par excellence* the quality of the parricide; cf. §§66–7; in this context the reader/listener will be reminded of Fimbria, whom C. has compared to the prosecutors (§§33–4). *obicio* here is "bring (misfortune or the like) upon, produce for": *OLD* s.v. 3a (cf. the different sense at §38 *fin.*). **'patri . . . placebat?:** C. imitates the style of the *altercatio*; similarly §54 *'cogitabat.' cogitabat?*; cf. also §§92, 94, 96, and 120. For such repetition in dialogue between two speakers cf. examples from comedy cited by Wills 1996: 342. **necesse est . . . perspicuam fuisse:** C. once again raises the standard of proof the prosecution must meet; cf. §37n. Just as C. has promised to make his case *perspicuum* at §18 (and claims to have succeeded at §§82, 86, and 98), so he demands the same of the prosecution here; in §41 he will twice claim that it is *perspicuum* that the prosecutor's position is unsupported. He introduces his own inferences with *nonne perspicuum est . . . ?* at §§105 and 108.

nam ut illud . . . magnis et necessariis: it might be objected that hatred and murder are rather different things; nonetheless C. places the two on a similar level of probability. *odio* is an "object of loathing": for the predicative dative, after C. tending to be replaced by nominative, cf. G–L §356.3; H–S 99–100.

41 This chapter poses a dilemma to the prosecution: the described relationship of father and son implies a defect either in the son or the father; C. contradicts both possibilities (*at . . . at*).

rursus igitur eodem . . . nullum fuisse: for the hortatory subjunctives cf. §34n. *eodem* "to the same place" (*OLD* s.v.), i.e. the question of the defendant's possible *uitia*, raised in §39. *in unico filio* applies only to the most recent period, as is clarified in the following section. For C.'s claims of perspicuous argument cf. §18n.

pater igitur amens . . . fuit omnium constantissimus: characteristic of C.'s early speeches, *amens* alternates about equally with *demens* in speeches from the 50s on; cf. von Albrecht 2003: 29. *qui odisset* has causal force; cf. G–L §633. *quidem*, adhering, as often, to a pronoun, lends emphasis without a following contrast; cf. Solodow 1978: 94–6. For the *constantia* of the elder Roscius cf. the political posture described at §16.

ergo illud iam . . . sceleris filio fuisse: *illud* "the following" (defined by the acc. + inf.); cf. *OLD* s.v. *ille* 12b. *perditus* is "morally depraved": *OLD* s.v. 4a (a different sense at §23).

42 **'Nescio' inquit . . . in praedia rustica relegauit':** unable to name a motive, Erucius is represented as falling back on a *signum* or *indicium* that the relation was as he claims, i.e. "something serving as . . . presumptive evidence in support of a charge": *OLD* s.v. *signum* 4c; Lausberg §358. Benferhat 2003–4: 266–7 sees a careful strategy by which the elder Roscius hoped for one son to go into politics at Rome, the other to sustain the family's fortune in its native place. *relego* and *relegatio* are legal terms for banishment to a certain (specified) distance from Rome; the punishment plays a large rôle from Sulla onward; cf. *OLD* s.vv.; Mommsen 1899: 964–80. Here *relego* is non-technical: "remove from the scene, dismiss to an obscure or less desirable place": *OLD* s.v. 2. *relegauit* may either point to an act on a particular (past) occasion or describe an existing state of affairs; was there perhaps some offense that precipitated the "banishment"? In any case C. chooses to focus attention on whether *relegatio* is the right description, rather than what might have led to this state of affairs.

quod Erucio accidebat . . . reperire non possum: *usu uenire* ("to occur in one's experience": *OLD* s.v. *usus* 8) varies *accidere. commenticius* is "fabricated, fictitious" (ibid. s.v. 2); it recurs at §82; cf. also §35 (*confictio criminis*). *confirmare* and *infirmare* are the opposed tasks of prosecution and defense; the alleged weakness of the charge has led to the described impasse; for the prosecution's dealing in *leuia* cf. §52. For *diluo* cf. §36n.

43 quid ais, Eruci? . . . ac tuenda tradiderat?: *quid ais?*: the tone is
incredulous and leads to a further question, as often in comedy: "look here,
I say"; cf. *OLD* s.v. *aio* 6. For the value, number, and location of the farms
cf. §§6 and 20. *fructuosus* is "abounding in produce," hence "valuable": *OLD*
s.v. 1–2; C. explains in §44 that Roscius jun. was allowed to derive a living
from some of the farms. For *relegatio* cf. the n. before last. In spite of C.'s
incredulity, it was in his day possible to interpret such an assignment as a
mark of disapproval, since estate management was commonly the work of
a slave (*uilicus*); cf. Cato *Agr.* 5; Wiedemann 1981: 141–53; moreover. C.'s one
named Roman example, C. Atilius Serranus, is from a much earlier age; see
on §50.

  quid? hoc patres . . . studique consumere?: *quid?* is transitional,
indicating that the questioning introduced by *quid ais?* continues; similarly in
§44; cf. *OLD* s.v. *quis* 12b. *hoc* is the subj. of *esse*; its content is defined by the
following acc. + inf.: *OLD* s.v. *hic* 12b. Our passage and §120 are the only occurrences of *pater/patres familiae* in C., who usually prefers the archaic *familias*;
cf. Leumann 1977: 409–10; Hellmuth 1877: 107–8. **praesertim homines
illius ordinis ex municipiis rusticanis:** Vasaly 1993: 159 finds a "thinly
veiled note of condescension" here (see on §47); the qualification was needed,
however, since such views and values were not necessarily those prevailing
in Rome of the day; cf. the previous n.; Lo Cascio 2006: 56–9. *res familiaris* in
this context should be taken in the literal sense "family property"; cf. *OLD*
s.v. *familiaris* 1c and 3.

44 an amandarat hunc . . . amandatio appellabitur?: *amando* is
"send away, relegate"; the related noun *amandatio*, used only here in classical Latin, was perhaps coined *ad hoc*; cf. *OLD* s.vv. and *TLL* s.vv. *amendo*,
amendatio; the pairing with *relegatio* clarifies the unusual word. *ad uillam* is an
archaism found in the early speeches for *in uilla*; cf. *Tull.* 20 *seruus respondit . . . dominum esse ad uillam*; *OLD* s.v. *ad* c.13; von Albrecht, *RE* Suppl. 13
1303.5–9. The terms on which Roscius jun. lived are important for assessing
his life in the country; he was, C. claims, not supported at a mere subsistence
level but enjoyed the fruits of designated farms during his father's lifetime.
But this leaves unanswered the question whether the son perceived the living
thus provided as adequate for his needs.

  uides, Eruci, . . . atque a ueritate: in light of the preceding, one
might have thought that Erucius' argument merely diverged from the facts
of this case; but C. will go on to claim that Erucius' position is at odds with
Roman practice generally. For the address to Erucius without praenomen cf.
§38n. and Adams 1978: 145–6, who refers such single naming of adversaries
at the bar to "a sort of camaraderie among advocates."

quod consuetudine patres . . . fecisse dicis: C. represents Erucius as perversely distorting reality, having confused custom with innovation (for *nouus* cf. §1n.), kindness with hatred, honor with punishment; he couches all three points in the strictly parallel *quod . . . id* structure (for the relative preceding its "antecedent" cf. §6n.).

45 neque haec tu . . . contraque opiniones omnium: here C. makes the benevolent assumption that his adversary really knows better but is driven to this expedient by the poverty of his case; he is less kind at §46. The two negatives (*neque . . . non*) cancel each other out; cf. §8 (*nonnihil*) with n. For *arguo* cf. §37n. That Erucius must speak against C. (*nos*) is inevitable in an adversarial judicial system, but he has imprudently set himself against three powerful entities besides. **contra rerum naturam** "at odds with the course of nature": *OLD* s.v. *natura* 6a; cf. also *Phil.* 5.49 with Manuwald's n.

45–7 'At enim cum . . . uitae cotidianae uideremus: this argument discredits the psychological theory underpinning Erucius' prosecution in an unorthodox way, namely by citing the behavior of characters known from Roman comedy. C. includes subsidiary arguments explaining Erucius' apparent failure to understand the underlying psychological mechanisms and establishing the suitability of such material as proof in court; see further Harries 2007: 135–6.

45 'At enim cum . . . ruri esse patiebatur': *at enim* poses an objection with an explanation: "but here's the rub"; cf. Dyck on *Off.* 3.79. This rejoinder merely restates the point made at §42.

quaeso, Eruci, . . . commonendi gratia dicam: *hoc* "what I am going to say." *in bonam partem accipere* is to "take in good part," i.e. not be offended; cf. *OLD* s.v. *pars* 14b. There may be various motives for criticism; C. claims that his remarks here are meant to improve Erucius; similar the case of those *qui admonent amice* at *N.D.* 1.5. But he will, in fact, be speaking *exprobrandi causa* ("by way of reproach": *OLD* s.v. *exprobro*). *gratia* here merely varies *causa* (for a different view cf. Rankin 1961).

46 si tibi fortuna . . . alienus esses: the implications are clear: slaves were not technically permitted to marry, and so the son of a slave woman could not be said to have been born *patre certo*; cf. Ulp. fr. 4.2 *qui matre quidem certa, patre autem incerto nati sunt spurii appellantur*; Westermann 1955: 81n84–6; Bradley 1984: 50–1. Social background, including the parents' status, was a standard topic of invective; cf. Nisbet on *Pis.* p. 194. For *animus patrius* cf.

e.g. *Sest.* 81; *Phil.* 3.29. **non parum** "an adequate amount, a sufficiency," by
litotes: *OLD* s.v. *parum* 1. *humanitas* here is "human feeling": *OLD* s.v. 3; cf. §154;
Phil. 2.7 *homo et humanitatis expers et uitae communis ignarus.* For the sense of *accedo*
cf. §4n. Erucius' alleged *studium doctrinae* and in particular his acquaintance
with *litterae* ("literature"; cf. Goldberg 2005: 90–1n7) clears the way for the
following example.

 ecquid tandem tibi . . . supplici causa relegasse?: *ecquid* is sometimes used, as here, "in surprised questions where a negative answer is
expected" ("surely you do not suppose . . . "); cf. *OLD* s.v. 1a. **ut ad fabulas ueniamus** is a bit abrupt, albeit prepared somewhat by the previous
reference to Erucius' education; C. would later learn to manage such transitions much more skillfully (cf. *Mur.* 61; *Arch.* 1–3). On the generally broad
range of *exempla* in this speech cf. Riggsby 1999: 61–2. For *fabula* = "play" cf.
OLD s.v. 6. Caecilius Statius was an Insubrian Gaul who made a fine career
as a Roman comic playwright during the second century; see further Dyck
on *N.D.* 1.13; Blänsdorf in Suerbaum 2002: 229–31. C. refers to characters
from the *Hypobolimaeus*, based on an original by Menander; cf. *com.* 75–91;
Men. frr. 372–93 K.–A.; Webster 1960: 100–1 reconstructs the plot along the
lines of Terence's *Adelphi* as a contrast of two sons, one (the supposititious son
of the title) raised in the city, the other in the country; for its later reception
cf. Goldberg 2005: 91n8. **minoris facere** ("to attach lesser value to") is an
example of the gen. with verbs of rating; cf. G–L §379–80. **nam . . . hoc
nomine est:** C. feigns uncertainty because the advocate must not appear
too learned in literature, art, or the law; cf. §125 *ipsa lege . . . siue Valeria est siue
Cornelia —non enim noui nec scio*; *Ver.* 2.4.5 *Canephoroe ipsae uocabantur; sed earum
artificem — quem? quemnam? recte admones — Polyclitum esse dicebant* with Baldo's
n. on 2.4.4 (*nimirum didici . . . nomina*); *Sest.* 48; similar scruples apply in the
senate (*Phil.* 13.49 *ait poeta nescio quis*). The play must somehow have made it
clear that the ascribed motives (*honoris causa . . . supplici causa*) are absurd; but
the relegation of a son to work on the farm is a fairly common comic motif
and tends to be viewed by the son as unwelcome; cf. examples cited by Dyck
on *Off.* p. 637.

47 C. confronts the obvious objection that such a literary example is merely
fiction and thus lacks any probative force. "Marcus" uses similar arguments
to discredit the examples of divination adduced by "Quintus" in *Div.* (2.22,
27, 80, 113, 136); cf. Krostenko 2000: 367. Here C. justifies his procedure on
grounds that comedy is true to life and it would be odious to name individuals.
 'quid ad istas . . . assiduos esse cupiunt: for *iste* conveying a note
of contempt cf. §17n.; for *ineptiae* = "follies, frivolities" cf. *OLD* s.v. *ineptia*
b. **quamuis multos** "as many as you like": *OLD* s.v. *quamuis* 1. *profero* is

COMMENTARY: 47–8   117

"adduce" (*OLD* s.v. 5b), *tribulis* a "fellow-tribesman" (*OLD* s.v. a). For *plurimi facere* see §46n.

uerum homines notos . . . ex agro Veiente nominem: *sumo* is to "adopt" as suitable to one's purpose: *OLD* s.v. 10a; cf. §97 *unum hoc sumo*. The reluctance to name individuals suggests that they might have thought themselves held up to ridicule if C. had done so; cf. Moreau 2006: 297. For the possibility of condescension in his mention of *homines illius ordinis ex municipiis rusticanis* (§43) see *ad loc.* **futurus sit** "is likely to be," a "prophetic" future; cf. Kenney on Ov. *Her.* 16.136. **utrum hunc ego comicum:** the insertion of *ego* serves euphony but also, if used, is expected in this position with the demonstrative as host; cf. Adams 1994b: 122–4. **ex agro Veiente:** Veii was an Etruscan city about 12 miles north of Rome; the *ager Veiens* may have been chosen at random, but it will later figure as the site of a new villa of Chrysogonus (cf. §132). The MSS VA present *Veientem*, the apparent reading of the archetype, corrupted to *uenientem* in the other witnesses but corrected by Ψ² to *Veiente*; this is the easiest correction; some adopt Fleckeisen's *Veienti* in view of Livy 5.52.9 (*affectae Veienti bello rei publicae*).

etenim haec conficta . . . uitae cotidianae uideremus: for *confingo* cf. §30n.; *effingo* is originally to "shape, fashion" and hence metaphorically "portray": *OLD* s.v. 1–2; for the pun (*conficta — effictos*) cf. Holst 1925: 64. *exprimo* is "reproduce, copy": *OLD* s.v. 6. For comedy as an *imago uitae* cf. *Hort.* fr. 10 G.; the *topos* can be traced back to the scholars of Alexandria; cf. Pfeiffer 1968: 190–1; for C.'s references to comedy in general cf. Wright 1931: 61–72.

48 age nunc . . . et culpae dedisse: *age* ("come") is a colloquial marker for a command or exhortation used independently of number; cf. Hofmann 2003: 149; cf. §§93 and 105. *sis*, the spoken form of *si uis* (ibid. 288), is added for politeness' sake. *ad ueritatem*, i.e. as opposed to the example cited from comedy. The reference of *in his* is unclear; one expects a movement from narrower to broader, which could be effected e.g. by *in omnibus. dare* is one of the small group of verbs often used with the double dative construction; G–L §356 and R.2; H–S 99. Here C. summarizes the argument of §§42–5.

ac non modo . . . suauissimam esse arbitrantur: *hoc . . . faciunt*: another verb in the vicinity often lends content to *facio* (cf. Pinkster 1990: 11–12), but here the whole context provides the idea *agros colunt*. For adjs. and advs. with the *per-* prefix (like *permultos*) cf. §20n. **nisi me fallit animus:** this is the full expression, found in earlier and archaizing authors; elsewhere C. prefers the urbanely elliptical *nisi me fallit*; cf. Landgraf 1878: 41. **unus quisque uestrum:** sc. *nouit. incensi* is "inspired, fired": *OLD* s.v. *incendo* 4. *probro et crimini* "a cause for blame and accusation" (*OLD* s.vv.); for the construction cf. §40n. C. would later place a warm encomium of the *uoluptates agricolarum* in the mouth of Cato at *Sen.* 51–9.

49   quid censes . . . quam hic in suo: *intellegentia* ("understanding in a special field, discernment": *OLD* s.v. 2b) is more at home in C.'s theoretical writings than his oratory; cf. Manuwald on *Phil.* 9.10. Little has been said of Roscius' living relations apart from their advice to seek refuge in Rome (§27); there must have been many of them (cf. §96 *tot propinqui cognatique*). The pronoun (*hic*; cf. §1n.) suggests that they are supporting the defendant at the trial; in his later speeches C. would use such support to good effect (cf. Winterbottom 2004: 221); one of them, Magnus, is, however, conspicuously seated on the prosecution side (§§17, 84 and 95). *artificium* is a "profession, trade": *OLD* s.v. 2. The mention of Erucius' profession (*artificium accusatorium*), harmless enough here, prepares the way for the criticism at §§54–7. Roscius' devotion to agriculture is one side of the coin of his character as a *rusticus*; the other will be his lack of experience in the city, the chief pillar in the proof of his innocence; cf. §§74 and 79.

uerum, ut opinor, . . . famam potest obtinere: the emphasis is once again on Chrysogonus; cf. §§6, 7, 20, 25 etc.; for his purchase of the farms and dispossession of the defendant cf. §§6 and 23. **aequo animo** "with calmness" or "patience": *OLD* s.v. *aequus* 8a. Similarly the address to Chrysogonus at §145 *praedia mea tu possides, ego aliena misericordia uiuo; concedo, et quod animus aequus est et quia necesse est.* For the sense of *obtineo* cf. §6n. For retaining his life as the purpose of Roscius jun. cf. §5n.

hoc uero est . . . crimini fuerit: for *uero* adding focus cf. Kroon 1995: 319–25. **quod ferri non potest:** cf. §34 *hoc, quia fit a Chrysogono, non est ferendum. fraus* is "detriment, harm, danger": *OLD* s.v. 1; for the double dative cf. §48n. **ut parum miseriae . . . crimini fuerit** "it is bad enough for him to have cultivated his farms for others rather than for himself, without also being put on trial for having cultivated them in the first place" (tr. Berry). *aliis colere* will refer to the fact that Chrysogonus and Capito are now in possession of his farms (§§6 and 17) and thus reaping the benefit of Roscius' work (*quoniam ita Chrysogono uidetur* serves to remind the reader/listener of that point), rather than the fact that his father reaped the profit from most of them during his lifetime (cf. §44).

50   Ne tu, Eruci, . . . qui consules fierent: the counterfactual form concedes that the kind of enthusiasm for agriculture C. has described is, in fact, now rare among the Roman elite. *ne* is the affirmative particle ("truly, indeed"), regularly followed, as here, by a pronoun; cf. *OLD* s.v. *ne²*; Hofmann

2003: 135–6. *illis temporibus* "in those times," an abl. of time when, indicating remoteness; cf. *OLD* s.v. *ille* 7; G–L §393. **adcesso* becomes *arcesso* ("summon") by regular sound change; cf. *OLD* s.v. *arcesso*; Leumann 1977: 155. With the imperfect C. suggests that this was a regular occurrence, though he cites only one example; for the relative clause with final force cf. §25n.

etenim qui praeesse . . . atque inhonestissimum iudicares: C. cites this Atilius as "that famous" (*ille: OLD* s.v. 4b); he is mentioned here for the first time in extant Latin; cf. also the brief allusion at *Sest.* 72 (*non ille Serranus ab aratro*). V. Max 4.4.5 (under *de paupertate*) adds that he celebrated a triumph but does not specify the enemy. Clearly the anecdote is meant to explain the cognomen *Serranus / Saranus* borne by a branch of the Atilii. *Saranus* appears to be the older form; the later spelling may rest on a popular etymology (< *sero*, paraphrased by C. with *spargo*) assimilating the ancestor to L. Quinctius Cincinnatus (dict. 458), subject of a similar anecdote. Given the absence of historical context in our sources, it is hard to say which of the consular Atilii is in question; cf. *MRR* 1 208n1; Klebs, *RE* II 2.2094.57 (s.v. Atilius 57–71).

qui missi erant is vague; one assumes that they have come to notify him of his election to the consulate (cf. *qui consules fierent*); V. Max. *loc. cit.* says *qui ad eum arcessendum a senatu missi erant ad imperium populi Romani suscipiendum,* also ambiguous; but the situation more plausibly fits appointment as dictator than election as consul. *conuenio* is sometimes used transitively to mean "visit, meet": *OLD* s.v. 2. **turpissimum atque inhonestissimum:** for the *turpe* and *honestum* in binary opposition; cf. *Cat.* 2.21 with Dyck's n.; at §68 C. wants to make a *turpis adulescentia* prerequisite to parricide.

at hercule maiores . . . nobis reliquerunt: here C. contrives to allow some of the ethos of early Rome to rub off on his client. The interjection *hercule* (for *hercules* cf. §31n.), apparently the latinized vocative of Gk *ʽΗρακλος, occurs in all periods of Ciceronian oratory but especially in the early period (7x in *Quinct.*, 5x in the *Verrines*); it recurs at §89; an appeal to Hercules for help, it was ordinarily used only by males; cf. *OLD* s.v. *hercle, hercule.* The *maiores*, memorialized by upper-class Romans with busts displayed in the atrium of the house (cf. Flower 1996: ch. 7), were the standard by which Romans judged themselves and their achievements; the appeal to them here and in §§51, 69–70 and 102 shows that C., though a *municipalis* without a personal or family record in politics, has, unlike Erucius, assimilated Roman ideals. He may be thinking of Cat. *Agr.* 1.4 (cited on §39). **et de illo et de ceteris talibus uiris** neatly makes Atilius representative of an entire class, rather than an isolated case; cf. *Cael.* 39 *ex hoc genere illos fuisse arbitror Camillos, Fabricios, Curios omnesque eos qui haec ex minimis tanta fecerunt.* As Vasaly 1993: 162 notes, "few cultures have guarded the memory of their simple beginnings as fiercely as did Rome"; similarly Sal. *Cat.* 52.19 (Cato's speech) and Suet. *Aug.* 31.5; for Romans' views of their *imperium* cf. in general Brunt 1990: 433–80.

suos enim agros ... nomen auxerunt: *suos ... agros ... non alienos* stand in emphatic contrast and remind one of Chrysogonus' assault *in alienam pecuniam* (§6). *appeto* here is "seek to obtain, strive after" (*OLD* s.v. *appeto*[1] 5a; for another sense cf. §30n.); *cupide* ("zealously": *OLD* s.v. 1) balances *studiose* and reinforces the idea of immoderate behavior. **quibus rebus:** rather vague; C. evidently means the discipline that comes with successful application to agriculture; the following ablatives are the items by which Rome was increased; they themselves grow in number of syllables and in the size of what they describe in parallel with the growth of Rome. **populi Romani nomen** is the Roman nation or race: *OLD* s.v. *nomen* 19a.

51 neque ego haec ... honestius facere posset: *eo* ("to that end") ... *quo* ("that") with following final clause, the usual conjunction after a negative; cf. G–L §545.1–2; for *profero* cf. §47n.; cf. §125 (with reference to Roscius sen.) *non fuit tantus homo Sex. Roscius in ciuitate ut de eo potissimum conqueramur.* In spite of his denial, C. is suggesting just that; cf. Vasaly 1993: 162. For the epithets *summi* and *clarissimi* often found together in C. and reserved for those who have held high office cf. Berry on *Sul.* 3.4 and 4.10. **omni tempore** is used 5x in this speech but only 3x in all C.'s subsequent oratory; cf. Landgraf *ad loc. gubernaculum*, literally the "steering oar of a ship," often appears metaphorically of the "helm of the 'ship of state'"; it is sometimes treated, as here, as a *plurale tantum*; cf. *OLD* s.v. Since *ignosco* is used with the dat. of the person, it is impersonal in the passive (with the same construction). **qui ... fateatur** is a hypothetical category; hence the generic subj.; cf. §1n. Roscius' activity is found in the end to satisfy three criteria: the most important for a young man under *patria potestas* is that it is *patri gratum* (cf. §18n.); he also takes pleasure in it himself (*sibi iucundum*); and in general it is *honestum*, i.e. socially reputable (§7n.).

52 Odium igitur acerrimum ... ruri esse patiebatur: C.'s refutation of this point began at §40; by now the ironic summary (signalled by *opinor*) can serve as a dismissal.

numquid est aliud? ... ad rem pertineat: *numquid* raises a question anticipating a negative response ("there is nothing else, is there?": *OLD* s.v.); cf. §107 *numquisnam praeterea?* Comic parallels suggest a colloquialism; cf. Landgraf 1878: 23. *immo uero* enters a contradiction, *immo* ("rather") correcting and *uero* signaling the reaction; cf. Kroon 1995: 295. As on C.'s lips the defendant is *hic* ("my man"; cf. §6n.), so in arguments attributed to the prosecutor he is *iste* ("your man"; cf. *OLD* s.v. B5b). *exheredare* ("to disinherit") is a large step, a sign of hatred (cf. *Clu.* 135 *cum eum filium* [sc. Cn. Egnatius] *exheredaret quem oderat*) and a possible motive for (preemptive) murder. C.'s response *audio* "very well then" (*OLD* s.v. 12, a colloquialism with parallels in comedy) acknowledges the relevance. **pertineat:** for the generic subj. cf. §1n.

nam illa, opinor, . . . nisi perraro ueniret: for trivial matters (*res . . . leues*) allegedly raised by the prosecution cf. §42. C.'s characteriza-tion, brisk pace, and insertion of these matters between the announcement of another topic and its execution show him eager to sweep them aside; but they point to character, and C. has no really satisfactory response; see below. The defendant's failure to attend *conuiuia* with his father was evidently cited by the prosecution as evidence of the defendant's anti-social character; at §39 C. had deployed it to clear his client of any suspicion of *luxuries*. C. counters one fact with another but does not offer any underlying rationale. An optional marker of causal relative clauses, *quippe* signals sarcasm; cf. §41n (*qui odisset*). *oppidum* here evidently refers to Ameria (hence *ne . . . quidem*) as opposed to the *urbs* (i.e. Rome); cf. §74. For the adv. compounded with *per-* cf. §20n.

'domum suam istum . . . neque reuocaturus esset: the previous response was that Roscius seldom came *in oppidum*, here that he did not live *in urbe*. But could he not have cultivated friendships in Ameria, especially since he had so many relations there (§96)?

53 uerum haec tu . . . nullo modo potest: for the prosecutor's "under-standing" (*intellegis*) cf. the things the presiding magistrate is said to "under-stand" at §11 or what Caesar "understands" according to *Cat.* 4.9. After adversative asyndeton, *illud* (opposed to *haec*) resumes the previous topic, namely the contemplated disinheritance. For the emphatic colloquial nega-tion *nullo modo* cf. Hofmann 2003: 209.

'exheredare pater filium . . . potuisse non arbitror: the assertion is repeated from §52 with *cogitabat* varying *in animo habebat*. *mitto* = "forbear" (for *omitto*, cf. *OLD* s.v. *mitto* 4b) is a poetic usage found in the early speeches; cf. Landgraf 1878: 40–1. C. presumably takes this tack because of Erucius' inability to supply a motive for the father's dislike (§§40–1). *qui* is adverbial: "how" (*OLD* s.v. *qui²* 1a); for *tametsi* cf. §3n. For indicative *oportebat* ("you ought to have") cf. §37n. *certus accusator* is the "true" or "dependable prosecutor"; cf. *OLD* s.v. *certus* 8a. **qui . . . argueret:** for the generic subj. cf. §1n.; for the genitive with judicial verbs G–L §378; for *arguo* §37n. C.'s previous survey

(§§39–41) failed to disclose such *uitia ac peccata*. *incensus* here is "provoked, stirred up": *OLD* s.v. *incendo* 5 (for a different sense cf. on §48). *eicio* ("throw out") is a violent verb, previously used of Roscius' ejection from his property (§23); C. will hesitate to apply it to his treatment of Catiline (*Cat.* 2.1). For *huiusce* cf. §6n. *-isse non arbitror* forms a fine double cretic.

54 uerum concedo tibi . . . planum facere debes: *uerum* is the adversative conjunction, in contrast to *uere* below ("truly"). The two poles of the sentence are C.'s *concedo*, matched by Erucius' *concedis*. **cum taces . . . concedis:** *cum* is explicative, virtually equivalent to *quod*: "in that"; cf. G–L §582. For silence as an implicit admission cf. Otto 1890: 339. *nulla* varies *leuia*, *inepta*, and *nugatoria* of §§42 and 52; cf. *OLD* s.v. *nullus* 4d. The asyndeton marks a sharp contrast. *illud* is emphasized by *quidem* (without a following contrast; cf. §41n.) and defined by the following acc. + inf.; *certe* adds restrictive force: "at all events, if nothing else": *OLD* s.v. 2a. *planum facere* is often used by C. of the task of the prosecutor or advocate: "make clear"; see below and §65 (of his own prospective argument at §101); *Clu.* 97, 98, 99, etc.; *OLD* s.v. *planus* 7; it is varied with *ostendere* (§69) and *probare* (§72).

   quid ergo affers . . . dignitati illudere: *affero* varies *profero*; cf. §47n. *fingo* is equivalent to *confingo* (§30); for a different sense cf. §26n. *saltem* ("at least": *OLD* s.v. 1) presents this as a last resort. For C.'s own worries about being able to speak *commode* cf. §9. For Roscius as *miser* cf. §23n. *hi uiri tales* are the senatorial jurors (cf. §72 *probare . . . talibus uiris*); hence their *dignitas*, also referred to at §9. *illudo* sometimes + dat., as here, is "to make sport of, mock": *OLD* s.v. 1a. Here C. adroitly links his client with the jurors as joint victims of the prosecution; similarly *Cael.* 1.

   'exheredare filium . . . 'nemini': C. represents a rapid-fire *altercatio* between prosecution and defense. As in the case of the father's dislike, the motive (*causa*) eludes the prosecution (cf. §§40–2). The exchange illustrates the difference between perfect and imperfect: C. keeps probing to find a completed past act (*exheredauitne? . . . quis prohibuit? . . . cui dixit?*), whereas the prosecution claims that the disinheritance was merely something the father was contemplating (*cogitabat*) without definite outcome.

   quid est aliud . . . ne coneris quidem?: *maiestas* varies the preceding *dignitas* (cf. *OLD* s.v. 1b: "the dignity of a god or exalted personage"). **ad quaestum:** an oblique reference to the *lex Cincia* of 204 forbidding payment for advocacy in court, widely flouted; cf. Rotondi 1912: 261–3; *RS* §47; Berry on *Sul.* p. 40; Alexander 2002: 178; see the next section. **ad libidinem** "arbitrarily" (*OLD* s.v. *libido* 2c). For *obicio* cf. §38n.; for *planum facere* see above. **possis . . . coneris:** subj. in relative clause with indefinite antecedent; cf. G–L §631.2; Erucius continues as subject.

55 nemo nostrum est . . . aliquid ualere oportere: *nemo nostrum est . . . quin sciat* ("there is none of us but that he knows," i.e. we all know) illustrates the origin of *quin* in *qui ne* (cf. *OLD* s.v.) as well as its use in sentences of character after a negative: G–L §632; *NLS* §185; similarly §154 *nemo est quin intellegat*. *inimicitias . . . nullas esse* is colloquial for *non esse*; cf. §128 *haec bona . . . nulla redierunt*: Hofmann 2003: 208–9; H–S 205; *OLD* s.v. *nullus* 6. *inimicus* "as an enemy" is commonly used with the dat. (*huic*, a certain correction for transmitted *huc*). At Athens the prosecutor regularly tried to establish a basis for his case in personal enmity so as to avert the suspicion of being a malicious informer (συκοφάντης); cf. e.g. [Dem.] 59.1. **sciunt . . . adductum esse:** the claim appeared in a more general form at §30 (*testes in hunc et accusatores huiusce pecunia comparant*). *tamen* i.e. in spite of having received payment; for *oportebat* cf. §37n.; it is followed by a consecutive clause with limiting force (on which cf. *NLS* §167; K–S II 249–51): "however eager you may have been for financial gain, you should nevertheless have reflected that the view this jury will take of you and the Remmian law ought to have some weight" (Berry's translation, slightly modified). To knowingly launch an unfounded criminal prosecution fell under *calumnia*, itself a criminal offense; it was regulated by the *lex Remmia*, which specified that the charge of *calumnia* be tried before the same tribunal that handled the original case; conviction entailed branding or tattooing on the forehead with a *k* (for *kalumniator*; cf. §57) and *infamia*; cf. Rotondi 1912: 363–4; Mommsen 1899: 491–8; Greenidge 1901: 468–70; Levy 1933: 151–77; Jones 1987: 153; Camiñas 1990; Alexander 2002: 7; Berger s.v. *calumnia*.

55–7 Accusatores multos . . . accusare possitis: a digression introduced to ridicule prosecutors generally; for such "digressions of ridicule" cf. Manuwald on *Phil.* 3.21.

55 Accusatores multos esse . . . illudamur ab accusatoribus: *audacia*, the quality associated with Roscius' accusers (cf. on §§7, 12, and 35), is here set into a larger context of civil society. C. offers further reflection on the deterrence of crime at *Leg.* 1.40–1. For the consecutive clause with limiting force see the n. before last; for *illudo* on §54.

innocens est quispiam . . . aliquomodo ignoscere: the hypothesis is not stated with *fac* (cf. *OLD* s.v. *facio* 20) or the like but simply as a fact. The expression is clumsy, however, with an unnecessary doubling of the idea of innocence (*innocens est quispiam . . . quamquam abest a culpa*) and an overdetermination of adversative relations (*uerum tamen . . . tamen . . . tametsi . . . tamen*).

tametsi miserum est: sc. *reo*; Roscius as *miser* is a leitmotiv of this speech; cf. §23n. **qui . . . accuset:** for the subj. in a relative clause with indef.

antecedent cf. §38n. **possim . . . ignoscere:** the subj. is potential: G–L §257. C. at least has not lost the *ignoscendi ratio* (cf. §3). The following explains (*enim*) C.'s reason.

cum enim aliquid . . . sciens non uideatur: cf. §8 *quodsi aut causa criminis aut facti suspicio aut quaelibet denique uel minima res reperietur quamobrem uideantur illi nonnihil tamen in deferendo nomine secuti . . . ludificor* varies the preceding *illudo*; for *calumnia* see above; for the potential subj. (*uideatur*) see the previous n. *uideatur* here is not "to seem" but "to be seen to."

56 quare facile omnes . . . causam non dicere: as early as Plautus, *facile patior* is "tolerate, be content": *OLD* s.v. 4c. *nocens* and *innocens* are in binary opposition here; interestingly, *innocens* is attested much earlier (Naev. *trag.* 9), whereas *nocens* apparently developed as its antonym only in C.'s time; cf. *OLD* s.vv.; *TLL* s.v. *innocens*; cf. also Holst 1925: 71. In the court *de repetundis* (and probably generally in the *quaestiones perpetuae*) the jurors submitted wax voting tablets marked *a* or *c* for *absoluo* or *condemno*; cf. Mommsen 1899: 179n4 and 445n7. **utilius est:** sc. *rei publicae*, a frequent criterion in C.'s writings; cf. Gaudemet 1951: 467–8.

anseribus cibaria publice . . . quae est cautior: the example is introduced in asyndeton, as is fairly common; cf. Dyck on *Off.* 1.36; the connection is at first unexplained (similarly §33); it will prove to be an analogue to prosecutors (§57). *cibaria* denotes "food supplied to animals": *OLD* s.v. 1b; *publice* "at public expense": *OLD* s.v. 1b; *loco* is "to contract for having (a thing) done": *OLD* s.v. 5a. Romans would think of the rôle of the geese in raising the alarm as the Gauls were on the point of invading the Capitol in 390; cf. Livy 5.47.1–8; D.S. 14.116.6; D.H. 13.7.3; Plut. *Cam.* 27.2–5; for further sources see Fluss, *RE* xiv 1.1170.35–60 (Manlius 50), though in our passage *fures* replace *hostes* as the perceived danger. *significo* is intransitive here: "signal, give indication": *OLD* s.v. 3. *noctu* appears to be the abl. of an otherwise lost 4th declension fem. *noctus*, driven out by *nox*, frozen as an adv.; cf. *diu* and *OLD* s.vv.; Leumann (1977) 357. The function of signalling what is suspect (*suspiciosum*) is what connects this example with the behavior of prosecutors (§55 *suspicione tamen non caret . . . suspiciose dicere*). The concessive idea (*tametsi bestiae sunt, tamen*) is somewhat clumsily added; hence Krueger's (too radical) deletion of *tametsi . . . tamen*; his transposition of *et* so that it precedes *tametsi* rather than *quia* is needed, however. C. seems to mean that they show greater rationality than might have been attributed to animals; cf. *Off.* 1.11 with Dyck's n. For *in eam partem* with defining relative clause cf. *OLD* s.v. *pars* 2c: "on the side of greater caution" or the like.

quodsi luce quoque . . . suspicio nulla sit: an ideal conditional with pres. subj. in both clauses; cf. G–L §596.1. *luce* is "in the daytime": *OLD* s.v *lux* 4b. *salutatum* is acc. of the supine (indicating goal of motion; cf. H–S 380–1) of *saluto* and governs *deos*. *suffringo* is "break the lower part of" or here "break from under (them)": *OLD* s.v.; the punishment will correspond in the analogue to that for *calumnia* mentioned in §57; cf. David 1992: 303. *opinor* is parenthetical, as often ("I think, I suppose"), here without irony (contrast §52): *OLD* s.v. 1e. *quod acres sint* gives the grounds of those who inflict the punishment; cf. G–L §541. **tum cum suspicio nulla sit:** though the indicative would have been expected in a purely temporal *cum*-clause (cf. G–L §580), it is attracted to the mood of the verb on which it depends (ibid. §508.4).

57 simillima est . . . et mordere possunt: from this point to the end of the paragraph C. addresses prosecutors in general (2nd person plural), although he has molded his remarks to fit the particular situation of Erucius (*sin autem sic agetis ut arguatis aliquem patrem occidisse . . .*). Since Latin is not rich in special words for animal sounds, *clamo* is applied to the noise made by various birds and beasts, including the honking of geese: *OLD* s.v. 1b; *latro*, the specific word for a dog's barking, is an exception, however. The distinction between making noise and biting is not pursued in the sequel; hence Spengel wanted to delete *alii uestrum anseres . . . mordere possunt.* The analogy of prosecutors to dogs appears to have been traditional; cf. the attribution of the phrase *caninum . . . studium* to the ancients at Col. 1 *praef.* 9. Another aspect of the dog, namely fawning on those in power, might apply to Erucius vis-à-vis Chrysogonus; cf. the words attributed to Verres at *Ver.* 2.3.28 *horum canum quos tribunal meum uides lambere.*

cibaria uobis . . . populo gratissimum est: prosecutors' rewards (referred to by C., in line with the preceding analogy, as *cibaria*; cf. §56n.) were at this period primarily in the political realm, e.g. a lower ranking senator could take the place of another whom he successfully prosecuted; monetary rewards were used only in certain rare cases under the Republic; cf. in general Mommsen 1899: 504–11; Alexander 1985; David 1992: 570–1 (list of probable rewards during the Republic). *impetum facere* ("attack") appears in a literal sense at §21 (*in reliquas omnes fortunas iste T. Roscius . . . impetum facit*). **hoc populo gratissimum est:** cf. *Div. Caec.* 7 (of the prosecution of Verres) *quid est quod . . . populo Romano gratius esse debeat . . .?*; sim. *Ver.* 2.1.14.

deinde, si uoletis, . . . id quoque concedi potest: for the intransitive use of *committo* ("commit an offence, break the law") cf. *OLD* s.v. 17; Hotoman's insertion of *aliquid* after *aliquem* is thus unnecessary. *in suspicione* "in suspicious circumstances": *OLD* s.v. *in* 40 ("expressing conditions under which an action occurs"); cf. §56 *quia id est suspiciosum* of the dogs' licit barking. This is the first appearance of *latro* as a metaphor for human speech: *OLD* s.v. 3a; *TLL* s.v. 1. *latro* 1014.8–12; for the "future" imperative cf. §18n.

sin autem sic . . . accusare possitis: for *sin* cf. §8n. *aut quomodo* forestalls the argument at §§73–80. *tantummodo* is "merely"; cf. *Pis.* 8 *cumque is* [sc. Metellus Nepos on C.'s laying down of the consulship] *mihi tantummodo ut iurarem permitteret; OLD* s.v. *tantus* 9a. *quidem* introduces the first half of a contrast (cf. Solodow 1978: 30 and 123). C. again uses *hic* with reference to the jurors; cf. §54n. Only *kalendae* and the derived word *kalendarium* were regularly spelled with *k* in C.'s time, and *k* could be an abbreviation for the former; cf. *OLD* s.vv. For the punishment cf. §55n. The period concludes with a pun on the two main meanings of *accuso*: "charge (someone) with a crime" and "find fault with": *OLD* s.v.; Holst 1925: 55.

58 Quid mihi . . . ad suspicandum?: the irony of the address *bonus accusator* is no less palpable than the description of Magnus as *uir optimus* at §23. *hisce* are again the jurors; see §54n. *ad suspicandum* connects the present case with the justification of prosecution *in suspicione* as argued at §§55–7.

'ne exheredaretur . . . in mentem uenerit: with these words C. returns to the point at §§52–4 from which he had digressed. For *audio* cf. §52n. At §54 his response was *certe tu planum facere debes*, restated here as a command. **nihil est** "there is no proof" (tr. Freeze). For archaic *quicum*, preferred by C. to *quocum*, see G–L § 105N3. *certiorem facere* is to "inform" a person: *OLD* s.v. *certus* 12b. *uobis* associates Erucius with others; cf. §35; possibly Magnus was formally a member of the prosecution team (*subscriptor*); so *TLRR* no. 128; cf. Alexander 2002: 152; on §§94 and 104. *in mentem uenire* is "to come to (one's) mind, occur (to one)," regularly, as here, with the personal dative: *OLD* s.v. *uenio* 12a.

cum hoc modo accusas . . . auderet hoc tempore': for the address to Erucius with a single name cf. §44n. A *sermocinatio* is attributed to Erucius; cf. §28n. *quid acceperim*: the *lex Cincia* is assumed to have been flouted; cf. §54n. For the verbal play *scio . . . nescio* cf. Holst 1925: 71. For Chrysogonus' initiation of the case and its (supposed) motive cf. §§6 and 132; the impf. *aiebat* suggests reiteration of the point in the process of persuading Erucius to participate. The point about the lack of a *patronus* was forestalled at §30; for *iste* used of the defendant from the prosecutor's standpoint cf. §52n. The sale of the goods was, in fact, one of C.'s first points (§6); at §60 he describes the surprised reaction on the prosecution side. For the *societas* cf. §20n.; for *uerbum facere* §2n. With final placement of *hoc tempore* C. once again emphasizes the times as a major factor in the prosecution's plan; cf. §28 (*ut . . . tempore ipso pugnarent*).

haec te opinio . . . quemquam responsurum putasses: for the word order by which the emphatic demonstrative serves as host to the enclitic pronoun cf. §47n. C. traces a gradation of increasingly sinister motives on the side of the prosecution and its allies: from *opinio falsa* (Erucius) to *auaritia* (Capito, Magnus) to *auaritia + crudelitas* (Chrysogonus); cf. §§146 and 150. *fraus* here is "deception, fraud," in this case the putting forward of a claim without proof; for another sense cf. §49n. *mehercules* was the form of the oath prevalent in C.'s youth, though *mehercle* appears in his late work; it is short for *(ita) me Hercules (iuuet ut)*; cf. §50n.; Hofmann 2003:137–8. The final assertion is hyperbolic; it cannot be literally true, as even the following *digressio* (§§59–61) implicitly admits.

59 Operae pretium erat . . . in accusando considerare: *operae pretium esse* + inf. is colloquial in the sense "be worthwhile" (to do something): *OLD* s.vv. *opera* 3b, *pretium* 2b. C. has already criticized the *neglegentia* of the prosecutor's argument; in the sequel he focuses on his behavior in court.

credo, cum uidisset . . . nullam dixerim: *credo* shows that this is simply C.'s presumption (as below *ut . . . puerum uocaret, credo cui cenam imperaret . . . credo qui Chrysogono nuntiarent*). For the *subsellia* cf. §12n.; with *hisce* C. indicates the ones nearer himself, i.e. on the defense side. *ille* is the vague identifier in Latin: "so-and-so or such-and-such": *OLD* s.v. 15. **defensurus esset:** the periphrastic substitute for the missing future subj. in secondary sequence, substituting for *defendet* of the direct question; cf. G–L §515. For *causam publicam nullam dixerim* instead of *non dixerim* cf. §55n. C. had appeared in a private case in spring 81 when he substituted in the last session for M. Junius, who was called away by other duties (*Quinct.* 3 and 34), in the defense of P. Quinctius, his first published speech but not his first case; cf. **Quinct.** 4.

posteaquam inuenit neminem . . . pro summa solitudine abuteretur: *neminem eorum qui possunt et solent* contradicts §1 (*tot summi oratores*). For *in mentem uenire* cf. §58n. From 11.3.61 to the end of the Book Quintilian discusses appropriate delivery; the faults he criticizes at 11.3.156–60 are subtler than the ones C. describes here. C. was in general an astute observer of opposing counsel and deploys this power to advantage especially in *Cael.*; cf. Gotoff 1986. *seruus* is used to indicate servile status in formal contexts, whereas *puer* is used informally with reference to a specific person's slave(s); cf. Adams 2003: 564–5. **cui cenam imperaret:** for the final force of the subj. cf. §25n. *prorsus* is a formula introducing the summarizing consecutive clause: "all in all"; cf. *OLD* s.v. 4a. *consessus* ("gathering, assembly") is often used of jurors in court: *OLD* s.v. 1. *abutor* ("misuse") is often combined with *pro* + abl.: "misuse as if it were" will give the sense: *OLD* s.v. *abutor* 4a.

60 perorauit aliquando, assedit . . . non alius potius diceret: the
short clauses here and in the next several lemmata serve to make the *narratio
aperta* and hence *probabilis* (cf. Lausberg §§315–25). *peroro* is to deliver the final
part of the speech (the *peroratio*) and hence "wind up the case, conclude" (*OLD*
s.v. 2a); cf. Hortensius' complaint *priore patrono causam defendente numquam perorari
potuisse* (*Quinct.* 34). *respiro* is literally "recover one's breath" but metaphorically
"recover from anxiety or alarm" (*OLD* s.v. 1), though, in view of his previous
deportment, the anxiety must have been rather mild! *quod . . . diceret* gives
Erucius' (supposed) reasoning; cf. on §§2 and 33.

coepi dicere . . . quid eum pepugisset: the first mention of Chrysogonus marks the turning point in Erucius' behavior. Only here does C. follow
the anticipatory formula *usque eo* with *antequam*. *simul atque . . . statim* emphasizes the instantaneous response. *attingo* can be used of "mentioning briefly,
touching on" a topic: *OLD* s.v. 9a. **mirari uisus est:** he thus shares, for a
different reason, the jurors' reaction to the beginning of C.'s speech (§1). For
pungo cf. §6n.

iterum ac tertio . . . dicere auderet: Quintilian cites this passage
both as a narrative about the present (4.2.3) and as a *ficta narratio* intended
to arouse the jurors (4.2.19). *curso* is itself frequentative ("rush constantly
about": *OLD* s.v.), but the picture of ceaselessly frenzied activity is reinforced
by *ultro et citro non destiterunt. qui Chrysogono nuntiarent* is another relative clause
with final force (§25n.). *esse* in emphatic position is veridical or assertive;
cf. Adams 1994a: 69–75. For the subjunctive with indefinite antecedent
(*aliquem . . . qui . . . auderet*) cf. §24n. Here for once the boldness (*audere*) is on
C.'s side; contrast §2, where he denies being *audacissimus . . . ex omnibus*; §7n.

aliter causam agi . . . rem indignam uideri: C.'s own summary of
the reaction to his speech in *oratio obliqua* as a report brought to Chrysogonus;
cf. Wiesthaler 1956: 25. With advs. expressing dissimilarity *atque* = "than":
OLD s.v. 13b. At §58 C. offered a reconstruction of how Chrysogonus thought
the case would proceed. For the *societas* cf. §§20 and 35; for Chrysogonus'
gratia cf. §28n. **iudices diligenter attendere:** cf. *Arch.* 17 *me in hoc nouo
genere dicendi tam diligenter attenditis*; this is a bad sign for the other side; cf. *Clu.*
93 *quid ergo est causae quod nunc nostra defensio audiatur tanto silentio . . . ?*; *Cael.* 25
with Gotoff 1986: 127–31. **populo rem indignam uideri** is inferred from
the reactions of the spectators (*corona*).

61 quae quoniam te . . . non iudicium futurum: *quae* summarizes the
developments just described. *uerto* here is "reverse, change to the contrary":
OLD s.v. 7a. For C.'s doubts about his ability to plead the case *satis commode*
cf. §9; for *libere dicere* cf. §3n.; by now it is clear that this phrase refers to

the discussion of Chrysogonus' rôle. With their similar sound *dedi* and *defendi* form a neat contrasting pair; cf. *Ver.* 2.4.10 *ereptionem esse, non emptionem*; Holst 1925: 85. **quos tradituros sperabas:** for the jurors as the presumptive agents or helpers of those behind the prosecution cf. §§6, 8, 32, 101, 151. **ea spe . . . quod:** the demonstrative prompts a following defining clause, as often; cf. K–S II 270–1. C. has shown how shallow the prosecution case really is; Erucius can respond in either of two ways, by resuming his former cleverness and practical understanding (i.e. prior to this case, which he was duped into taking on: §58) or openly confessing his expectations; Hotoman's insertion of *aut*, here adopted, restores this relation of ideas; it can easily have dropped out after *-am*. For denial of the character of a *iudicium* cf. *Clu.* 92, 96, 103 etc. To make the court proceeding into a *latrocinium* would be to complete the work of Roscius' adversaries; cf. §6n. Our passage was echoed by Pope Leo I when, writing to Pulcheria (*Ep.* 95.2), he described the Council held at Ephesus in 449: *nec opus est epistolari pagina comprehendi quidquid in illo Ephesino non iudicio sed latrocinio potuit perpetrari.*

De parricidio . . . filius occiderit: restatement of the conclusion reached at §54 prior to the digressions; the point is all the more powerful for being put simply and starkly; asyndeton is the strongest adversative marker. As Quintilian remarks, though the horror of parricide is manifest, C. contrives to amplify even this (9.2.53).

62 quod in minimis noxiis . . . non putat oportere: the relative clause precedes its "antecedent" once again; cf. §6n. An *a fortiori* argument with *in minimis noxiis* and *in his leuioribus peccatis* introduced as a foil for *in parricidio. noxia* is an offense, often, as here, as a basis for accusation; cf. *OLD* s.v. 1b. On the importance of establishing motive cf. *Inv.* 2.19.

in quo scelere . . . ingenio res iudicatur: *multae causae* contrasts with the case of Erucius, who has not produced a single credible motive. **conuenisse . . . congruere:** the chiastic arrangement of verbs and prepositional phrases concentrates the latter in the center and thus seems to mirror the described convergence. Since *credo* is intransitive in the sense "believe" (*OLD* s.v. 4), *creditur* must be impersonal passive (cf. *ignosco* §51n.). For the prosecution's arguments characterized as *leues/leuia* cf. §§42 and 52. In its earliest usage *coniectura* is the "interpretation (of dreams)," then the "inference of one fact from another," hence, as here, "guesswork, conjecture"; *OLD* s.v.; Zellmer 1976: 180–2. *pendo* here is "weigh, evaluate": *OLD* s.v. 6a. **testis incertus:** witnesses were, of course, a standing feature of litigation; accordingly the rhetorical schools taught a number of ways to lend weight to or denigrate their testimony; cf. e.g. Quint. 5.7; with the *testis incertus* contrast

the *certus accusator* held up as an ideal at §53. The *ingenium* of the counsel on
either side was often, as it is now, a factor in the outcome of a case; at §1 C.
has denied that his *ingenium* is equal to that of some others on the defense
side; but here he wants to rule out that a parricide case is judged merely as
a rhetorical duel. For C.'s laying down of "judging paradigms" for the jurors
cf. in general Riggsby 1999: 17–20 and *passim*.

cum multa antea . . . furor atque amentia: the bar for the prosecution case is raised once again; cf. §40n. Ordinarily one finds clauses balanced
with the simple *cum . . . tum* (cf. *OLD* s.v. *cum* 14), but here the prior clause
is doubled (and the *tum* clause also expanded): "both . . . and . . . and." For
perditus cf. §41n. **summus furor atque amentia:** the phrase recurs at §66;
amentia is the permanent state, whereas *furor* may come in fits; cf. Dyck on
Cat. 1.25.

haec cum sint omnia . . . credi non potest: *expressus* is literally
"pressed out," hence "clearly defined, distinct": *OLD* s.vv. *exprimo, expressus. uestigia* are "footprints, tracks," a metaphor from hunting; cf. §74; *OLD*
s.v. *uestigium* 1 and 7b. *per quos* "with what agents"; *OLD* s.v. *per* 15a. *admitto*
(sometimes with *in me*) is fairly frequent in the sense "commit, perpetrate"
(a crime); *OLD* s.v. 13a. *manifesta* varies the preceding *expressa. profecto* is per-
suasive: "surely" (*OLD* s.v. 1). For *scelus/scelestus* cf. on §§1 and 37; for *atrox*
§9n.; for *nefarius* §6n. *-faria credi* forms a hexameter ending, redeemed by the
addition of the emphatic cretic *non potest*; the result is the equivalent of C.'s
second-favorite clausula (with the first long resolved); see Appendix.

63 magna est enim . . . natura ipsa conciliet: for *humanitas* cf. §46n.
For the force of *communio sanguinis* cf. *Off.* 1.55 *magnum est enim eadem habere
monumenta maiorum, isdem uti sacris, sepulcra habere communia. reclamito*, apparently
used only here in classical Latin, is to "cry out against" (+ dat.): *OLD* s.v.
For *portentum* cf. §38n.; here *monstrum*, rather than *prodigium*, appears as its
synonym; it is an unnatural thing that points to (*monstrare*) trouble in the
future: *OLD* s.v. At *Rep.* 2.48 (in speaking of the tyrant) C. formulates similarly:
qui quamquam figura est hominis, morum tamen immanitate uastissimas uincit beluas;
similarly also *Off.* 3.32. For *immanitas* ("savagery, cruelty") cf. *TLL* s.v.; Berry
on *Sul.* 7.10; the word recurs at § 150. *atque* binds together *partus* and *educatio* as
parts of a single process; this is followed by the generalizing *natura ipsa*. The
appeal to the behavior of animals was a commonplace, albeit sometimes at
variance with the facts; cf. Juv. 15.159–64 with Mayer's n.

64 Non ita multis . . . mane iugulatum: this case is the one historical
parallel C. cites (for the rarity of parricide cf. §38n.). For Cloelius, not Caelius

or Clodius, as the form of the name cf. Wiseman 1967; Shackleton Bailey 1992: 14. The anecdote also appears at V. Max. 8.1 absol. 13, who adds the detail that the victim's brothers conducted the prosecution; cf. Münzer, *RE* III 1.1256.8 (Caelius 15). *quendam* shows that C. does not expect the jurors to know the name. **hominem non obscurum:** V. Max. is more fulsome: *Cloelii . . . splendido Tarracinae loco nati*; the epithet suggests equestrian status; cf. Nicolet 1966–74: II 838–9. For the supine *cubitum* cf. §56n. *conclaue* is a room in a house: *OLD* s.v. **iugulatum:** the significant fact is reserved for the very end; following *mane* C.'s seventh favorite clausula is effected (see Appendix); for *iugulo* cf. §13n.

cum neque seruus . . . de parricidio delata sunt: *ea suspicio*: i.e. *suspicio eius facti*. Suspicion would fall in the first instance on any household slave or free person with access; only when these have been excluded is action taken against the sons. The colloquial *id aetatis* ("at that time") is used adverbially; cf. *OLD* s.v. *aetas* 2b; H–S 47 and 52; G–L 336.4 N.2. *propter* is the adv. rather than the preposition ("nearby"), a usage that dies out after C.; cf. *OLD* s.v. A1. For *nomen deferre* cf. §8n.

quid poterat . . . ea suspicio conueniret: *poterat . . . esse* "could be," the imperfect indicative as present unreal; cf. G–L §§254 R.2; Lebreton 1901: 280–1. *suspicio* is what triggers a prosecutor's intervention; cf. §8n. After *suspiciosum* the archetype presents *autem*; Busche's *aut tam inauditum* is usually adopted. **neutrumne sensisse?:** the infinitive is used colloquially to express indignation or wonderment, especially in comedy and in C.'s early speeches and letters; cf. H–S 366; Hofmann 2003: 166–7. *committere se* is "to venture" (to or into): *OLD* s.v. *committo* 10b. *potissimum* lays emphasis: "especially, above all": *OLD* s.v. 1. *conuenio in* (+ acc.) is to "be consistent with, fit": *OLD* s.v. 6a.

65 tamen, cum planum . . . suspicione omni liberati sunt: for *planum facere* cf. §54n. *ostium* is the door, especially the front door of a building: *OLD* s.v. 1a; that they were sleeping *aperto ostio* was decisive: anyone could have gained access and without the noise of breaking down the door. For *absoluo* and *condemno* as the judicial alternatives cf. §56n.; Mommsen 1899: 3n3 suggests that *absoluo* ("set free from bonds, release") is based on the assumption that the defendant is kept in custody.

nemo enim putabat . . . sine metu possunt: for "divine and human laws" cf. §37; similarly §63 *natura ipsa. polluo* ("defile, make ceremonially impure": *OLD* s.v. 2) recurs at §71. *somnum capere* ("fall asleep") is a common *iunctura*; cf. e.g. *Tusc.* 4.44; *Att.* 8.1.4. An *a fortiori* argument about the behavior of parricides; the sequel explains why they cannot *spirare . . . sine metu*.

66 Videtisne quos nobis . . . sine scelere esse potuerunt?: *poetae* is deliberately vague, to avoid an appearance of learning before the jurors; cf. §46n. *supplicium sumere de aliquo* is to "exact punishment from someone," often, as here, "put to death": *OLD* s.vv. *supplicium* 4b, *sumo* 6b. *cum praesertim* "even though" correlates with *tamen*: *OLD* s.v. *praesertim* 2b. **iussis atque oraculis** can be taken by hendiadys as "oracular commands." *ut* ("how") introduces the indirect question following *uidetis*. C.'s description applies to the sagas of both Alcmaeon and Orestes, who were *pii* in avenging their fathers and obeying oracular commands but had nonetheless to atone for the murder of their mothers; the next section clarifies that he has in mind figures from plays (*fabulae*). Alcmaeon was the subject of plays by Ennius and Accius (*trag.* vv. 16–31 J. and *trag.* pp. 165–6 respectively). Aeschylus inherited a version of Orestes' saga in which Apollo commanded or consented to the matricide; cf. Sommerstein on *Eum.* pp. 1–2; that is the version followed by Aeschylus (*Ch.* 269), Sophocles (*El.* 35) and Euripides (*Or.* 280); the theme is not known to have been dramatized at Rome prior to the date of the trial. The saga was also a popular subject for depiction on vases and other media; cf. Sarian, *LIMC* s.v. Erinys especially nos. 37–80. For C.'s later treatments of the saga see §67n. *agito* "harry, chase, pursue vexatiously" is often used of the action of the Furies: *OLD* s.v. 3b; *consisto* is to "be at rest": *OLD* s.v. 5a.

   sic se res habet . . . paternus maternusque sanguis: anaphora and use of synonyms drive home the point; cf. §63 (*communio sanguinis*) with n. Our passage illustrates the oldest sense of *religio*: "a supernatural feeling of constraint having the force of a prohibition"; cf. *OLD* s.v. 1. *maternusque* is added in light of the examples just cited.

   ex quo si qua . . . atque amentia consequatur: *ex quo* (sc. *sanguine*). *macula* is a "stain" or "spot"; like *polluo* above, it is used of ritual pollution; cf. §113, where both terms appear with reference to moral stain. *eluo*, literally "remove by washing," is often used figuratively of "purging" guilt or the like; cf. *Leg.* 2.24 *animi labes nec diuturnitate euanescere, nec amnibus ullis elui potest*; *OLD* s.v. 2a. *permano* is "flow through": *OLD* s.v. This verb effects the transition by which the shed blood, endowed with religious power, becomes the catalyst of madness; cf. Hutchinson 2005: 187. For *summus furor atque amentia* cf. §62n.

67 nolite enim putare . . . Furiarum taedis ardentibus: a passage adapted from Aeschines' speech *Against Timarchus* 190–1, the wording influenced by Enn. *trag.* 27 J. (*circumstant cum ardentibus taedis*); the content is rewritten in C.'s later style at *Pis.* 46; cf. also *Leg.* 1.40; Weische 1972: 24–5. In Rome, a slave-owning society, a prohibition was usually softened for politeness' sake to the imperative of *nolo* + inf.; cf. G–L 270 R.2; *OLD* s.v. *nolo* 4. For *quemadmodum* cf. §5n. C. is careful to maintain contact with the experience of the jurors, who may not have read deeply in the poets but can be assumed to have attended plays; see §66n. *numero* adds weight to *saepe* without change of meaning; cf. *De orat.* 1.1 *cogitanti mihi saepenumero . . .*; it recurs at §119. For *agito* cf. on §66. **taedis ardentibus:** for the source see above. *taeda* ("a pine-torch") was possibly a sacral term; cf. *OLD* s.v. 2; Jocelyn on Enn. *trag.* 27. The final placement of the participle secures C.'s second-favorite clausula; see Appendix.

   sua quemque fraus . . . a consceleratissimis filiis repetant: C. reinterprets the actions depicted in the plays as psychological processes; the point is driven home by the anaphora of the reflexive possessive (*sua . . . suus . . . suum . . . suae*) as well as by assonance (*agitat amentiaque afficit*). *fraus* here is "crime" in general (*OLD* s.v. 3), varied in the sequel by *scelus*; *uexat* varies *agitat*, which recurs in the next clause. *amentia* was the punishment the Furies inflicted on Orestes and Alcmaeon. *conscientia*, originally with the gen. *animi* or *mentis*, later without limitation, is the "inward perception of the rectitude or otherwise of one's actions, moral sense, conscience": *OLD* s.v. 3a; the pl. matches *cogitationes*; for C.'s use of pl. abstracts cf. §14n. *domesticus* varies the reflexive possessive: "personal, one's own": *OLD* s.v. 4. For *dies noctesque* cf. §6n. *parentium poenas* "their parents' penalties," i.e. the ones exacted by their parents (for the subjective gen. cf. G–L §363.1); Aeschylus' *Eumenides* shows clearly that the Furies were conceived as the agents of the murdered parent. This is the first occurrence of *consceleratus* ("wicked, depraved"), perhaps coined as an alternative when the much-used *sceleratus* had come to seem too weak; cf. *OLD* and *TLL* s.v.; Fraenkel 1968: 52. *poenas repetere* is to "demand satisfaction": *OLD* s.v. *repeto* 8b.

68   In this chapter C. continues to raise the bar of proof needed for a successful prosecution; cf. §§37, 40, 62.

   haec magnitudo malefici . . . abhorreat ab insania: *manifestus* is "detected in the act, flagrant": *OLD* s.v. 2; the following *nisi* clauses (and the next sentence) can be seen as an *enumeratio* (cf. Lausberg §§669–71) of the requirements established by the first; hence the punctuation with a colon (Weidner, however, wanted to replace the first *nisi* with *si*; *etsi* would also be conceivable). For *turpis* cf. §50n.; for *flagitium* §25n. *inquino* is literally "to stain" and hence metaphorically "to pollute (a person) with crime or immorality": *OLD* s.v. 1 and 3; for *effundo* cf. §6n. *probrum* ("disgrace, ignominy, shame":

OLD s.v. 2) is more or less synonymous with *dedecus. prorumpo* is ordinarily to "burst forth" from restraining barriers; cf. §12; our passage shows a rare transitive use: "give vent to": *OLD* s.v. 4c (Heerdegen wanted to smooth over the unusual construction by reading *prompta*).

accedat huc oportet . . . credituri sunt: through *amici improbi* C. continues enumeration of elements that fall under the *probabile ex uita*; next follow the specific steps leading to the execution of the crime, then the vivid, climactic *respersas manus sanguine paterno.* The chiastically arranged *odium parentis* and *animaduersionis paternae metus* have been claimed by the prosecution (§§40 and 53), albeit, according to C., with insufficient evidence. *conscius* is "privy to the plot," sometimes implying "accessory to the crime": *OLD* s.v. 2. For *tempus* cf. §22n. *capio* here is "choose, select": *OLD* s.v. 9a. **respersas manus sanguine paterno:** these words would perhaps have been accompanied by an expressive gesture (so Falco 1982: 225). For *sanguine respersus* cf. *De orat.* 3.10 *neque collegae sui, pontificis maximi, sanguine simulacrum Vestae respersum esse uidit*; *Phil.* 3.4 *quorum ante pedes eius morientium sanguine os uxoris respersum esse constabat.* For *immanis* cf. §38n. *si . . . credituri sunt* "if they are going to believe" or "are likely to believe"; for the periphrastic future participle expressing capability or tendency cf. G–L §247.

69 Quare hoc quo minus . . . singulare supplicium inuenerunt: a transition to the next topic: the harshness of the punishment correlates with (and, we are told at §72, demands) the high standard of proof just described. *conuincere* is to "prove" a person's guilt: *OLD* s.v. *conuinco* 4a. The praise of the *maiores* continues and builds upon what was said in §50 (implicitly about their superiority *armis*); they were known for imposing severe punishments; cf. §§111 and 116; Roloff 1938: 104. For *cum . . . tum* cf. §8n.; for *plus possum* §33n. *in impios* substitutes for *in parricidas*; cf. §37n.

qua in re . . . considerate: C. takes the opportunity to insert a comparison (σύγκρισις); this was one of the *progymnasmata*, rhetorical exercises in which C. was probably trained in his youth; cf. Frazel 2009: ch.1. *prudentia* is "practical understanding," the quality *par excellence* of the lawgiver; cf. *OLD* s.v. 1. *praesto* ("be superior to") is regularly combined with the dat.: ibid. s.v. *praesto*[2] 2a; similarly *De orat.* 1.197 *quantum praestiterint nostri maiores prudentia ceteris gentibus tum facile intellegetis si cum illorum Lycurgo et Dracone et Solone nostras leges conferre uolueritis.* **qui apud ceteros sapientissimi fuisse dicuntur:** the Greeks had a canon of seven wise men; cf. Barkowski, *RE* IIA 2.2242.37 (s.v. Sieben Weise); C. will offer a comparison with only one of them, Solon. By postponing the imperative C. achieves his fourth favorite clausula; see Appendix.

70 prudentissima ciuitas Atheniensium...scripserit: *prudens*
takes up the point about *prudentia* while varying *sapiens*. *dum ea rerum potita
est* "while it was master of the world": *OLD* s.v. *potior*[1] 5a. C. tends to assign
exemplary value to hegemonial states as plausible parallels to Rome; cf. *Fam.*
5.17.3 *cogitaresque et in nostra ciuitate et in ceteris quae rerum potitae sunt multis fortis-
simis atque optimis uiris iniustis iudiciis tales casus incidisse.* C. reports, rather than
espousing, these views (*traditur...dicunt fuisse*); he will temper them in the
sequel. For Solon as *sapiens* cf. *ad Brut.* 23.3 *Solonis dictum...qui et sapiens unus
fuit ex septem et legum scriptor solus ex septem*; *Sen.* 73. **qui leges...scripserit:**
the senatorial jury will be inclined to respect such ancient laws (cf. *Phil.*
5.14 *an Atheniensium antiquissimas leges negleget?*), albeit the claim is not altogether true: although Athens was a *libera ciuitas* under Roman rule, some of
Solon's laws had been superseded, as C. himself acknowledges at *Leg.* 2.64–6
apropos restrictions on expenditure for tombs. He shows a similar tendency
to privilege the Twelve Tables over later Roman legislation; cf. Dyck on *Leg.*
2.54–68. Here C. lends weight to Solon in the eyes of his audience by giving
him a place-value at Athens corresponding to that of the *maiores* at Rome.

is cum interrogaretur...quam admonere uideretur: *is* refers
back to Solon and signals that he is the new subject; cf. §6 (*is a uobis*) with n.
supplicium constituere is "to fix a penalty": *OLD* s.v. *constituo* 7a. The anecdote
(= Solon test. 406b Martina; similarly D.L. 1.59) was probably invented to
account for what was later perceived as a gap in Solon's code; similarly
Hdt. 1.137.2 reports that the Persians believed parricide impossible. In early
societies families handled such matters without state intervention. **sapienter**
is emphatic, vindicating Solon's claim to the title *sapientissimus*; C. evidently
knows the story from an Athenian source; again he distances himself (*dicitur*).
nihil sancire is to "ordain nothing, enact no law": *OLD* s.v. *sancio* 2–3; for the
semantic development cf. Fugier 1963: 118–25. Sen. *Cl.* 1.23 ratifies Solon's
approach *multo minus audebant liberi nefas ultimum admittere quam diu sine lege crimen
fuit...itaque parricidae cum lege coeperunt, et illis facinus poena monstrauit.*

quanto nostri maiores...a maleficio summouerentur: *nostri* is
emphasized, for contrast with the Athenian example just cited; cf. §69 *maiores
nostros.* Cato claimed superiority for the Roman constitution precisely because
it was the product of a collective (the *maiores*) as opposed to a single lawgiver
as in the Greek city-states (*Rep.* 2.2). For the implied argument cf. Riggsby
1999: 62: "Roman law is superior...because it recognizes the possibility
of parricide (as distinct from ordinary murder) and so better protects ties
of blood." **quod non aliquando uiolaret audacia:** relative clause with
consecutive force (*quod = ut id*); cf. §5n. *audacia*, here personified, has been
identified as the quality of the parricide *par excellence*; cf. §§38, 62, 68; it is

the quality of lawbreakers generally (§55) and the source of all criminality (§75); it is often attributed to some or all of Roscius' adversaries (§§12,
14, 17, 28, 35, 36). **supplicium . . . singulare** is repeated from §69; the
hyperbaton creates slight suspense and thus adds emphasis. **natura ipsa**
is "nature herself," "unaided nature"; for the use of *ipse* cf. §28n.; at §§53
and 63 C. has spoken of parricide as an act contrary to nature. *ii* was conjectured for *in* (Σ) by Naugerius in line with the general tendency for the
"antecedent" pronoun to follow when the relative clause precedes (cf. §§6,
8, 29, 33, 44, 62; §71 is a counterexample but involves no change of case); it
could easily have been skipped before the following *m. summoueo* is the act of
moving aside (e.g. of a crowd by the lictors when a magistrate is approach-
ing), hence used here metaphorically of "restraining, deterring": *OLD* s.v.
submoueo 1 and 5d. C. reflects on the deterrent value of *natura* and *poena* at
Leg. 1.40.

    Insui . . . in culleum uiuos . . . in flumen deici: a chiastic arrange-
ment of acts and places with the referent for the parricides placed squarely in
the middle. **uoluerunt** "they determined": *OLD* s.v. *uolo*[1] 13. **ita** "like that":
OLD s.v. 5–6. On the punishment see the Introduction sec. 1.

71 o singularem sapientiam . . . nata esse dicuntur?: the *singularis
sapientia* of the ancestors is matched to their *supplicium . . . singulare* (§70); cf.
Hartung 1974: 563. For the force of *nonne* cf. §38n. *uidentur* is literal: "can they
not be seen to have removed . . . ?" In C.'s interpretation the *maiores* have
put in place a carefully calibrated system of retributive justice. *rerum natura* is
"the natural order": *OLD* s.v. *natura* 14b; by *enumeratio* the collective term is
then broken down into the four elements with *caelum* representing air and *sol*
fire. *eum . . . unde ipse natus esset* substitutes for *parentem* for parallelism with the
following cosmic entities. **ex quibus omnia nata esse dicuntur:** C. discusses cosmogonic theories in *N.D.* 1, Thales tracing the world back to water,
Anaximenes to air, Empedocles seeing the four elements as fundamental
(§§25–6 and 29); he omits Heraclitus, who gave primacy to fire.

    noluerunt feris corpus obicere . . . immanioribus uteremur:
the asyndeton is explicative (cf. §6n.): C. now elucidates the general point
by dividing it into its components (*diuisio*, διαίρεσις). Exposure to wild animals was not a regular punishment in the Roman Republic but is known
from some early societies; cf. cases cited by Radin 1919: 122. *quoque* marks an
extreme case: "even, actually" (*OLD* s.v. 4a), since beasts were expected to
be *immanes* (cf. §38n.). *attingo* is "touch, come into contact with": *OLD* s.v. 1;
utor + pred. adj. (usually of persons) is to "find to be (such and such)":
OLD s.v. 10.

non sic nudos . . . partem ullam reliquerint: *non* [sc. *uoluerunt*] takes up the preceding *noluerunt. sic* implies ease of execution: "without further ado"; cf. Livy 2.10.11 *Horatius sic armatus in Tiberim desiluit*; *OLD* s.v. 11b. *ipse* sets the sea apart as the chief agent of purification, its own pollution correspondingly grave; cf. *TLL* s.v. 345.6; Eur. *IT* 1193 θάλασσα κλύζει πάντα τἀνθρώπων κακά ("the sea purifies all human ills"); Parker 1983: 226-7 and n108. C. has dealt with two of the four elements, earth and water; instead of continuing through the list, he summarizes *denique . . . reliquerint*. The relative clause has consecutive force *(cuius = ut eius)*; cf. §5n.; for the content cf. on §72.

72 etenim quid tam est . . . mortui conquiescant: the most famous passage of the speech, later cited by C. himself *(Orat.* 107) and Quint. 12.6.4 (the first sentence only) as an example of youthful promise. The parricide's punishment is now described in different terms, no longer as a deprivation of the four elements (though three of the four recur here) but of what is common to human beings in certain conditions. For *spiritus uiuis* cf. *Cat.* 1.15 *potestne tibi haec lux, Catilina aut huius caeli spiritus esse iucundus . . . ? uiuus* and *mortuus* appear frequently in polar opposition. *fluctuo* is "to be tossed or driven by waves," first attested here in this sense; hence the following paraphrase *iactantur fluctibus*: *OLD* s.v. 2a; the substantivization of the participle is likewise bold; cf. *TLL* s.v. 944.29-33; *eicio* ("cast out") would be ambiguous but for the context. C. proceeds to explain the deprivation at each of the four points. *ducere animam* paraphrases *spiritus* without resorting to *spirare* (which occurred in §65). **ut eorum ossa terra non tangat:** they are thus deprived of the oldest form of burial as described at *Leg.* 2.56 with citation of Xen. *Cyr.* 8.7.25. *fluctibus* is to be taken both with *iactantur* and *alluantur*, the latter = "touch, wet, lap": *OLD* s.v. *alluo* 2; they are thus deprived of water's purificatory powers; see on §71. **ne ad saxa quidem:** this is perhaps what C. meant when he said *nihil tam uile neque tam uulgare est cuius partem ullam reliquerint* (§71).

    tanti malefici crimen . . . protuleris?: for the sense of *crimen* and the repetition of the antecedent within the relative clause cf. §8n.; for the correlation between the stiff penalty and a high standard of proof cf. §69 with n. **talibus uiris:** i.e. the senatorial jurors; cf. §§8 and 54. For Erucius' inability to identify a plausible motive *(causa)* for the crime cf. §§40-54.

    si hunc apud . . . paratiusque uenisses: the *bonorum emptores* are those who bought the goods of the proscribed at auction; it was a badge of honor to have abstained; cf. *Phil.* 13.8; Nep. *Att.* 6.3 *ad hastam publicam numquam accessit*. At §133 Chrysogonus is portrayed as heavily involved; hence his "presidency" *(praeesset)* of C.'s imaginary tribunal; cf. the hypothesis of a council of *latrones* enacting laws at *Leg.* 1.13. *uenisses* "you should have come," an example of the past jussive; cf. G–L §272.3; K–S I 187.

73 utrum quid agatur . . . sine causa admittere: C. poses a dilemma for Erucius: he has mistaken either the nature of the charge or of the jurors. In each alternative *ago* appears in a different sense: *quid agatur* "what is at issue, at stake" (*OLD* s.v. 38b); *apud quos agatur* "before whom the case is being argued" (ibid. s.v. 40a). At §62 C. already made the point that *parricidium* requires a showing of many motives; for *suscipio* cf. §31n. **neminem ne minimum quidem maleficium . . . admittere:** after another negative *ne . . . quidem* lends emphasis but does not cancel out: "no one commits even the slightest crime"; cf. H–S 803. For *admitto* cf. §62n.

   Esto, causam proferre . . . fretus huius innocentia: *esto* grants a concession: "so be it." **statim uicisse debeo:** the jurors may not have agreed if it is true that establishing an alternative suspect was virtually *de rigueur* for a successful defense on charges of murder; cf. §12n. C.'s *de meo iure decedam* ("I shall step back from my rights") makes a show of generosity; cf. Brut. and Cass. *Fam.* 11.3.3 *de suo iure decedere*; the advice at *Off.* 2.64 *conueniet . . . esse . . . aequum facilem, multa multis de suo iure cedentem.* The point argued so keenly since §40 (with some digressions) is thus dropped; in C.'s argumentative writing generally the concession often functions as a transition to a new point; cf. Dyck on *N.D.* 1.80. *fretus* "relying on" (+ abl.) remains etymologically obscure; cf. Ernout and Meillet s.v. *ferrumen. innocentia* is emphasized by final placement; Roscius as *innocens* has been a motif from early in the speech, well before any effort was made to prove it; cf. §6n.

   non quaero abs te . . . si quid uoles, interrogandi: the modality (*quomodo*) is to be the new focus. **C. Eruci:** the address with praenomen shows greater than usual formality and thus serves to call attention; cf. Dyck on *N.D.* 1.66. *facio potestatem* + gen. of the action is to give someone the right or opportunity to do something: *OLD* s.v. *potestas* 5c. For a similar offer cf. *Clu.* 67 *audete negare ab Oppianico Staieno iudici pecuniam datam, negate, negate, inquam, meo loco*; similarly Demosthenes offers Aeschines the opportunity to reply "on my water" (ἐν τῶι ἐμῶι ὕδατι), time being measured by the water clock (κλέψυδρα); cf. 18.139 (with Wankel's n.), 19.57. So confident is C. that Erucius has nothing to offer in this area that he pretends that the *altercatio*, which follows the set speeches of prosecution and defense, can already begin. This ostensible courtesy proves to be the prelude to a storm of questions, a standard Ciceronian tactic for befuddling the opposition; cf. Classen 1982: 168–9n6.

74 This passage illustrates C.'s point *fateor me oratorem . . . non ex rhetorum offici-nis, sed ex Academiae spatiis exstitisse* (*Orat.* 12), for he uses the method of division (διαίρεσις) taught in the Academy. He first divides the agents into Roscius himself or others, then the others into slave and free, the free persons into residents of Ameria or Rome; then he assumes that the murderer was hired and distinguishes between hiring in person or through agents as well as the source and the amount paid. He thus emphasizes the many ramifica-tions of Erucius' claim and how woefully short the prosecution's case has fallen.

quomodo occidit? . . . quaero: quos?: the first of a series of alter-natives posed to Erucius. Only the first one (*ipse percussit*) is shown to be impossible; the rest might be called pseudo-dilemmas, creating the appear-ance of rigor; cf. Alexander 2002: 160: "instead of presenting his opponent with several choices and showing that each one is impossible, he presents a number of options, each of which is quite possible, and then attacks the prosecution for its inability to specify which option it has selected"; cf. also Craig 1993: 35–6 on "unsubstantiated" sliding into "impossible." Any action can be divided between personal agency and action through others. For *ipse* "in person" cf. §1n. *percutio* is to "strike dead," possibly originally from sacral language; cf. *OLD* s.v. 2a. **Romae non fuit:** C. was careful to place his client at Ameria when he first narrated the murder in §18.

seruosne an liberos? . . . quomodo persuasit?: *indidem* is "from the same origin" with the source then specified: *OLD* s.v. 3; it occurs only here in C.'s speeches; for the plain abl. of origin for the names of towns cf. G–L §395 N.2. Since the trial is held at Rome, the local cutthroats (*sicarii*; for the term cf. §8n.) are referred to with a form of *hic* (strengthened by *-ce*; see §6n.); but one expects a different pronoun to refer to those from Ameria; hence Havet's *ii* for *hi* is adopted here. **qui Romam multis annis non uenit:** an interesting but unexplained detail; was it because of his *relegatio* to the family farms (§§42–51), his own anti-social nature (§§39 and 52), or some combination of the two? *triduum* is "a period of three days": *OLD* s.v. a. For *conuenio* cf. §50n. *qui* is the adv.: "in what way? how": *OLD* s.v. *qui*² 1a.

'pretium dedit' . . . perueniri solet?: the obvious means, a contract killing, is assumed. The answer to *cui dedit?* could be but is not necessarily the same as to the preceding *quos?* **per quem dedit?:** C. takes a shortcut rather than asking whether Roscius gave the payment himself or through an agent (as he had in the case of the killing; see above). *unde* = *a quo*; the answer to the question *unde . . . dedit?* could have important consequences, as in the *Caeliana*, where Clodia's supplying of gold to the defendant becomes an issue (§§30,

33, 51–3 with Craig 1993: 113–16). For *uestigia* cf. §62n. *caput* is the "source, origin": *OLD* s.v. 12.

et simul tibi . . . in oppido constitisse: the "future" imperative *facito* has greater weight than *fac*; cf. §18n.; the imperative of this verb is used with subj. (with or without *ut*) as an emphatic colloquial command: "see that, be sure to"; cf. *OLD* s.v. *facio* 16a; Risselada 1993: 267–9. For *in mentem uenire alicui* cf. §58n.; an indirect question is, as often, the subject: *OLD* s.v. *uenio* 12a; cf. *Ver.* 1.51 *fac tibi . . . ueniat in mentem*. For *quemadmodum* cf. §5n. *depingo* evolves from "depict (in painting)" to "describe, represent (in words)": *OLD* s.v. 1 and 4. **hominem ferum atque agrestem:** *agrestis* is *per se* "connected with the fields, rural" (*OLD* s.v. 1–2); but Erucius seems to have used it as a pejorative equivalent of *rusticus* (§75 *fin.*); here *ferus* ("wild, uncivilized") gives it a certain direction, emphasizing the remoteness from civilization; cf. Vitr. 2.1.6 *ex fabricationibus aedificiorum gradatim progressi ad ceteras artes et disciplinas, e fera agrestique uita ad mansuetam perduxerunt humanitatem.* **numquam . . . constitisse** is hyperbolic; Erucius evidently claimed that Roscius jun. never went to parties, rarely appeared in town, and never invited anyone to his home (cf. §§39 and 52). *consisto* here is "to reside, live" in a place: *OLD* s.v. 9a; cf. *Ver.* 2.1.101 *Romae post quaesturam illam nefariam uix triduum constitisset.*

75 **qua in re . . . gigni non solere:** the *praeteritio* (ostensible omission of a topic that is nonetheless sketched in outline; cf. Lausberg §§882–6) enables C. to continue the show of benevolence begun in §73. For the double dative (*mihi maximo argumento*) cf. G–L §356. For *poterat esse* cf. §64n. **in rusticis moribus . . . non solere:** the argument was rehearsed at §39 *fin. uictus* goes from "means of bodily sustenance" to "way of life" in general (*OLD* s.v.); *aridus*, literally "dry," is a metaphor for the "mean, frugal, austere": *OLD* s.v. 1, 7; cf. C.'s characterization of his client at *Quinct.* 93 *uitam omnino semper horridam atque aridam cordi fuisse.* **istiusmodi maleficia** "crimes of the kind you allege": *OLD* s.v. *iste* 2. C. offers a kind of theory of the genesis of crime; cf. Marchetti 1986: 111; the agricultural metaphor implicit in *gigni* ("be produced") becomes explicit in the sequel: *OLD* s.v. *gigno* 5a.

ut non omnem . . . in omni uita nascitur: for the original sense of *facinus* seen here cf. §37n. *uita* is "way of life": *OLD* s.v. 7. *nasci* varies the preceding *gigni*.

in urbe luxuries . . . iustitiae magistra est: for *luxuries* and *luxuria* alternating in C.'s corpus cf. §39n. C. offers a loose Latin rendering of a commonplace of early Gk moralizing in the form of a *gradatio* (figure of thought in which a part of the prior member is repeated in the following one, and a part of the second in the third: x, x-y, y-z); cf. Lausberg §623; Solon 6.3–4 W. (repeated with minor variations at Thgn. 153–4 W.): (τίκτει γὰρ κόρος ὕβριν, ὅταν πολὺς ὄλβος ἕπηται| ἀνθρώποις ὁπόσοις μὴ νόος ἄρτιος ἧι ("satiety breeds arrogance, whenever much wealth attends men lacking sound judgment"). *luxuries* could stand for κόρος ("satiety") and *audacia* for ὕβρις ("arrogance"), but the Gk model has no equivalent for C.'s *auaritia*, prominent in moralizing authors of his time and later; cf. e.g. Sal. *Cat.* 10.3–5. *creatur* is a simple act; *exsistat necesse est* introduces constraint, which is then intensified in *erumpat* [sc. *necesse est*] ("break out" of confinement) implying violence: *OLD* s.v. *erumpo* 6. For *agrestis*, not necessarily pejorative, though so used by Erucius, cf. §74n. **uita autem haec . . . magistra est:** for *diligentia* and *parsimonia* juxtaposed cf. *Ver.* 2.2.7; *Off.* 1.92 and 2.87; for the idea cf. Cat. *Agr.* 1.4 (cited on §39).

76 Verum haec missa . . . conficere potuerit: *haec* are "the points just mentioned"; *illud*, defined by the following indirect question, is the new focus. *missum facere* is "disregard, pay no heed to": *OLD* s.v. *mitto* 5. **qui . . . numquam inter homines fuerit:** cf. §74n. **per quos homines . . . potuerit:** the idea is repeated from §74. *facinus* clearly has its pejorative sense here; cf. §37n. The large scale (*tantum*) of the deed, its covert nature (*occultum*), and the fact that he controlled it without being on the scene (*absens*) point to special mastery, C. suggests.

   multa sunt falsa . . . culpam inesse concedam: *arguo* here is "allege, assert": *OLD* s.v. 2 (for a different sense cf. §37n.); *suspiciose* is "in a manner designed to awaken suspicion": *OLD* s.v. The asyndeton is strongly adversative. A similar claim was made at §§8 and 18.

76–7 Romae Sex. Roscius . . . per seruos id admiserit: refutation of a complex argument by successive elimination of its components; cf. Quint. *Inst.* 5.10.66; cf. the similar pattern at *Quinct.* 86–7 and *Q. Rosc.* 13 and 43–5; Platschek 2005: 182–6.

76 Romae Sex. Roscius . . . Romae nouerat neminem: the point about the scene of the murder and the whereabouts of Roscius jun. at the time are repeated from §18. A letter (*litterae*) would be the obvious means of communicating over a distance; for *sicarius* cf. §8n. For the depreciatory implications of *aliquis* cf. Kinsey on *Quinct.* 72. The younger Roscius' lack of acquaintance in Rome is inferred from his long absence from the city (§§74 and 79). The reasoning is, as Craig 1993: 36 points out, disingenuous: "A man who would come to Rome and stay in the house of Caecilia, a woman

related to both of the consuls-elect, would not be completely ignorant of how
events might be made to happen in the City."

arcessiuit aliquem . . . de parricidio dicitur: again C. harps on the
lack of specifics undergirding the prosecution's case. *pretium*, *gratia*, and *spes*
appear in various combinations in lists of means of procuring an outcome;
cf. e.g. *Caec.* 16 *deterrentur emptores multi partim gratia . . . , partim etiam pretio*; *Off.*
2.21–2, where *pretium* and *spes* are among the factors that cause one person
to lend support to another; *promissis* concretizes *spe*. For *nihil . . . ne . . . quidem*
cf. §73n., for *confingo* cf. §30n., for *criminis confictio* as Erucius' charge §35.
For the higher standard of proof required for a charge of *parricidium*
cf. §§61–8.

77–8 C. diverts attention from the possibility that the defendant suborned
slaves to kill his father by quickly shifting to the question of examination
under torture of two slaves formerly belonging to the elder Roscius. Such
a quick change of subject is symptomatic of a weak case; cf. *Cael.* 58–60,
where C. diverts attention from the prosecution's claim that Caelius actually
tried out the poison on a slave bought just for this purpose by shifting to the
sudden death of Metellus Celer, Clodia's husband, with the implication that
he was the victim of poisoning at her hand; cf. Alexander 2002: 240–1; Craig
1993: 35.

77 Reliquum est ut . . . facere non licet?: C. reverts to his basic division of agents into slave and free (§74); having found the prosecution unable
to provide details supporting the latter hypothesis, he moves on to the former. For *per* and *admitto* cf. §62n.; for *di immortales!* §37n. **rem miseram
et calamitosam** is the exclamatory accusative; cf. G–L §343.1. *quod* is the
relative pronoun, preceding its "antecedent" *id*, as often (cf. §6n.). For the
double dative (*innocenti saluti*) cf. §75n. *quaestio* is "interrogation" (*OLD* s.v. 2),
in the case of slaves necessarily involving the use of torture; cf. Mommsen
1899: 412–18, 432, 439 and n3; Greenidge 1901: 491–3; Wiedemann 1981: 9
and 168–71; Robinson 1981: 223–7; C. narrates, for instance, several brutal inquisitions presided over by Sassia at *Clu.* 176–87. For *facere non licet*
cf. §34n.

uos qui hunc accusatis . . . relictus non est: under *uos qui hunc
accusatis*, C. understands above all Chrysogonus, as the sequel shows. The
asyndeton is explicative; cf. §6n. *unus puer* contrasts with *tanta familia*; a person
of standing might have expected to retain at least one body-servant (*uictus
cotidiani administer*; for the sense of *uictus* cf. §75); cf. Plin. *Ep.* 3.16.8 (narrating
Arria's argument for being allowed to sail with her captive husband back to

Rome) *'nempe enim' inquit 'daturi estis consulari uiro seruolos aliquos, quorum e manu cibum capiat, a quibus uestiatur, a quibus calcietur; omnia sola praestabo.'*

te nunc appello . . . T. Roscium recusare?: here we discover the names of two of the *homines nobilissimi* who have come to court to show support for the defendant without, however, themselves taking on his defense (cf. §1). The Scipio mentioned here may be P. Cornelius Scipio Nasica, who served as praetor and governor of Further Spain in 93; one of his sons was adopted by the Caecilii Metelli, an indicator of strong ties between the families; cf. Münzer, *RE* IV 1.1497.22 (Cornelius 351). If the praenomen is correctly restored, our Metellus is the same man who was elected praetor for 69 and drew the court *de repetundis*; Verres hoped in vain to be tried with him presiding. He was evidently the son of C. Metellus Caprarius, who was in turn the youngest son of Q. Metellus Macedonicus; he was thus a cousin of Roscius' protector Caecilia, daughter of Macedonicus' eldest son, Baliaricus (§27). Cf. Münzer, *RE* III 1.1206.5 (Caecilius 78). When C. reverts to the matter at §119, *aliquotiens* becomes *saepenumero*, and the two agents are qualified as *homines nobilissimi atque integerrimi nostrae ciuitatis*. For the connotations of *postulo* cf. §6n. T. Roscius is Magnus, acting as agent for Chrysogonus (§23), as the sequel clarifies. These two slaves were evidently known to have been with Roscius sen. on the fatal night; Kinsey 1985: 191 suggests that, though C. says nothing of this, the son must have questioned them immediately after the fact, while they were still in his possession.

quid? ii serui . . . orat atque obsecrat: *sector* is to "wait upon, attend": *OLD* s.v. 5. Here C. plants the idea that these slaves enjoy high honor and esteem with Chrysogonus (*apud eum sunt in honore et in pretio*); only at §120 does he spin dark suspicions from that fact (*necesse est sciant aliquid quod, si dixerint, perniciosum uobis futurum sit*). C. goes on to represent the slaves as (like his client) rustics from Ameria and Chrysogonus' refusal to provide them for judicial inquiry as inexplicable (unless he has something to hide). The verbs associated with *ego* and *hic* differ in intensity insofar as the stakes for the latter are higher; for **postulo** cf. §6n., for **orat atque obsecrat** §9n.

78 quid facitis? . . . ex caede uiunt: the command *dubitate*, emphatically placed, challenges the jurors; the argument is framed less pointedly at §88 *restat, iudices, ut hoc dubitemus, uter potius Sex. Roscium occiderit . . . etiamnunc* implies a certain impatience; cf. its use just above (§77 *etiamnunc . . . postulo*); §105 *quaeritur etiamnunc quis eum nuntium miserit?* The alternative answers to *a quo sit Sex. Roscius occisus* are provided with descriptions, not names; the points poverty/wealth and request for/denial of judicial examination of the slave-witnesses are chiastically arranged. The invocation of Roscius' poverty and his accusers' wealth adumbrates the *cui bono?* argument developed at §84, as though the self-aggrandizement and the murder could not have been separate. *patris potestas permittitur* is another example of Ciceronian alliteration; cf. §35n. **in caede atque ex caede uiuunt** has not been shown in spite of C.'s insinuations at §17; but the repetition of *caedes* with two different prepositions is meant to drive home its connection with the accusers: it is both their way of life and source of livelihood.

omnia, iudices, in hac causa . . . filio non licet!: *omnia . . . misera* might almost be the theme of the speech; cf. §23n. *hoc*, the abl. of measure of difference (cf. §2n.), is emphatically placed since it is destined for elaboration. *acerbus* is "grievous, bitter, distressing": *OLD* s.v. 7; *acerbius* and *iniquius* consider the matter both subjectively and objectively. The polyptoton (*paternae . . . paternis*) underlines the irony; similarly §30n.

ne tamdiu quidem . . . de patris morte quaeratur?: on the possibility that he did, in fact, do so cf. §77n.

ueniam, neque ita multo post, . . . cum Eruci crimina diluissem: C. reminds the reader/listener that he still must conclude the first item of the tripartite *diuisio*, on which and the consequent separation of naturally coherent matter cf. §§35–6n. *neque ita multo post* aims to secure patience with the intervening matter; cf. *Off.* 2.19 *quibus autem rationibus hanc facultatem assequi possimus . . . dicemus, neque ita multo post, sed pauca ante dicenda sunt.* The matter pertains rather to Chrysogonus as the current owner of the slaves than to the Roscii, of whom Magnus merely acted as Chrysogonus' agent in the matter. For *diluo* cf. §36n.

79 Nunc, Eruci, ad te uenio . . . potes ostendere: a fresh onset after the reminder of the plan of the speech, *ad te* contrasting with the foregoing *ad Roscios*; similar transitional formula at §83 in moving from the first to the second point of the *argumentatio/refutatio*. C. has, of course, been dealing with Erucius and his charges since §37. There is a mild pun on *uenio* ("come") and *conuenio* ("agree": *OLD* s.v. 6a); for the following transitive use of *conuenio* cf. §50n. C. takes up the division of possibilities from §74 except that here the first (*ipsum sua manu fecisse*) is ruled out in view of the impossibility of tying the defendant to the murder scene (§§18 and 76). For *per quos* cf. §62n. *spes* and *pretium* are among the inducements named at §76; see *ad loc.*

ego contra ostendo . . . temere discesserit: *ego contra* sets C.'s position in stark opposition, as in §7 *ego contra brevem postulationem affero*. *quod* + subj. is expected in indirect discourse; cf. G–L §541. The long absence from Rome is repeated from §74. C. construes his client's staying at home as prudent: *neque . . . temere discesserit.*

restare tibi uidebatur . . . recidere intellegas: C. takes up from §77 the point *reliquum est ut per seruos id admiserit* and interprets it from the standpoint of the prosecution's strategy. *seruorum nomen* is "the category of slaves": *OLD* s.v. *nomen* 24. *reiectus* is to be taken closely with *a ceteris suspicionibus*, *in portum* with *confugere*; *quasi* apologizes for the bold nautical metaphor, which continues with *scopulus* ("a projecting rock in the sea": *OLD* s.v. 1), by which he presumably means the prosecution's refusal to make the slaves available to testify; similarly *Tull.* 33 *scopulo atque saxis pro portu stationeque utuntur*. *hic* is used to refer to the just mentioned *scopulus*; for *crimen* cf. §8n. *resilio* is to "rebound" (*OLD* s.v. 3); similarly *recido* is "to fall back, rebound (on to its author)": *OLD* s.v. 2. Here, as in §18, C. makes it clear that he is following a strategy of *anticategoria*, i.e. of turning the tables so as to claim that the accusers were themselves behind the murder; cf. §§83–123n.

80 quid ergo est . . . facere potuisti': *quid* initiates a series of aggressive questions in dialogue with the prosecutor continued with *quid ais . . . nonne cogitas . . . quid postea.?* Cf. e.g. *Ver.* 2.4.135. *inopia argumentorum* is abl. of attendant circumstances: *NLS* 43(5)(ii); K–S 1 408–12; cf. §42. The license to kill applied only to those proscribed; cf. the Introduction sec. 3; for *sicarius* §8n.; for *nullo negotio* §20n.

interdum mihi uideris . . . a quibus mercedem accepisti: *merces* refers to Erucius' presumed violation of the *lex Cincia*; cf. §§54 (with n.) and 58. *una mercede duas res assequi uelle* embodies the proverbial notion of gaining two at the price of one; cf. Pl. *Am.* 488 *uno ut labore absoluat aerumnas duas*; *Cas.* 476 *uno in saltu . . . apros capiam duos*. **iudicio perfundere** is a bold metaphor, perhaps still under the influence of the preceding nautical images: "to flood with litigation" or the like; cf. *OLD* s.v. *perfundo* 2.

quid ais? . . . collorum et bonorum?: C. has raised similar questions about the prosecutors' attempt to tie his client to the crime (§§74, 76); now he connects them with the general situation that prevailed at the time of the murder. **a sectoribus:** a *sector* is "one who buys captured or confiscated property at public auction": *OLD* s.v. 2; the process itself is called the *sectio bonorum*: ibid. s.v. *sectio* 2; on entailed legal issues cf. Scherillo 1953. The legal terms probably refer to the division of the auctioned property into smaller lots for resale (< *seco* "cut"); cf. Ramsey on *Phil.* 2.39.35. Actually only one person, Chrysogonus, is shown to be a *sector* (cf. §§6 and 133 but also §88 (claim about Magnus)). C. puns on the literal and legal senses of the agent noun with the two obj. genitives *collorum* and *bonorum*: "cutthroats and cutpurses"; cf. *OLD* s.v. 1a and 2; Holst 1925: 51. Lintott 2008: 426 is skeptical: "That there were connections between some members of each class, the *sicarii* and *sectores*, is highly plausible, but a universal link is unlikely."

81 ii denique qui . . . huic crimini putabunt fore?: *tum*, like the preceding *per ista tempora*, conjures the time of the proscriptions; cf. the following *temporis illius*. The operative word, *armati*, is placed to the front for emphasis. For *dies noctesque* cf. §6n. *qui Romae erant assidui* is a feature shared with the elder Roscius; cf. §16n. *praeda* has been associated with the prosecution side since §6; cf. §8 and the characterization as *praedones* at §15. For *in . . . sanguine uersari* cf. §78 *in caede . . . uiuunt* and §98 and for the sense of *uersor* §39n. **in qua ipsi duces ac principes erant:** quasi-military language, as in §17 *qui . . . ante hanc pugnam tiro esset*, though supporting evidence is so far lacking (cf., however, §100). For the double dative construction (*huic crimini*) cf. §75n. Placement of the infinitive after the finite verb yields a fine cretic plus dactyl (*-i putabunt fore*).

   qui non modo . . . tute confiteris, fuit: the other side of the coin of Roscius' claimed skill in farming (§49) — and the point of the argument — is his ignorance of urban matters; he is thus assimilated to the stereotype of the *rusticus bonus*; cf. Vasaly 1993: 161; for his constant presence in the country cf. §18; for the concomitant absence from Rome §§74 and 79; for the implausibility of the construction cf. Craig quoted on §76. Madvig's *nesciuit* (for transmitted *nesciret*) seems to be needed to match the preceding *fuit*; a careless scribe can easily have assimilated the verb to the mood of the preceding *ageretur*. Erucius' "confession" follows from the argument *hunc in praedia rustica relegauit* (§42).

82 Vereor ne aut . . . diutius disseram: *molestus esse* is colloquial for "to be tiresome"; cf. *OLD* s.v. *molestus* 1b; *TLL* s.v. 1351.47–50. For *perspicuus* used of C.'s case cf. §18n.

   Eruci criminatio tota . . . ac noua obiecit: the explicative asyndeton (cf. H–S 830) provides greater energy than a connection with *nam* or *enim*; cf. von Albrecht 1989: 81 and 83 (on the effect in Sallust). The prominent invocation of the prosecutor's name helps to mark this as the conclusion of the first part of the threefold *argumentatio/refutatio* (cf. §35 *criminis confictionem Erucius suscepit*). *criminatio* ("making of charges") varies *crimen* (§81) with an added verbal force (< *criminari*); cf. *OLD* s.v. For *diluo* cf. §36n.; *dissoluo* varies it. *peculatus* is the "embezzlement of public money or property" (*OLD* s.v.; cf. the detailed study of Gnoli 1979) and could apply to Roscius jun. if he withheld part of the property following his father's death (cf. Landgraf *ad loc.*; von der Mühll, *RE* IA 1.1117.34–6; Alexander 2002: 159), albeit C. claims that his client surrendered everything (§144). The incident, if it occurred at an earlier stage, suggests that Roscius jun. found the means at his disposal inadequate (cf. §44). For *commenticius* cf. §42n.

quae mihi iste . . . uerbo satis est negare: C. accuses Erucius of simply lifting a passage from a previous speech, a damning criticism; to do so must have tempted young advocates; hence *Rhet. Her.* 2.43 warns against falling into irrelevancies; cf. Stroh 2003: 8–9. *declamo* ("declaim") may also suggest that Erucius (like C.) is a young advocate barely finished with his training. *commentor* is often used of a speech in the sense "practice, prepare": *OLD* s.v. 2b. *peculatus* could, however, be relevant to parricide if it points to motive; see the previous n. The repetition of *uerbo* presents C.'s response as an appropriate act of balancing. The contemptuous dismissal may conceal a weakness in C.'s case, however; cf. Quint. 5.13.22.

si quid est quod . . . quam putabat: in contrast to Erucius, criticized for inadequate preparation (especially §72 *fin. diligentius paratiusque uenisses*); for the confounding of Erucius' expectations cf. §§58 and 60. For more specific threats directed at a prosecution witness (Capito) cf. §100.

REFVTATIO/ARGVMENTATIO II: ANTICATEGORIA OF MAGNUS AND CAPITO (83–123)

An alternative suspect was a virtual requirement of a successful defense on murder charges (cf. §12n.). C. turns the tables and claims those behind the prosecution as the murderers, an example of counteraccusation (*anticategoria*); cf. Quint. 3.10.4 and 7.2.9; Lausberg §153. Similarly in the defense of Varenus C. would claim (without success) that the crime was committed by the prosecutor's slaves; cf. Crawford 1994: 7–18. So as not to provoke a vendetta, it is framed by an elaborate *apologia* (§§83 and 123). Already at *Inv.* 2.16 C. had treated the topics *ex causa*, *ex persona*, and *ex facto ipso* as belonging to both the prosecution and defense of a *constitutio coniecturalis*; hence it is no surprise to see them occur not only when he defends his client against Erucius' charges (cf. §§37–82n.) but also in the counteraccusation. Thus in the accusation of Magnus IIA, B, and F in the following outline correspond to the three categories *ex causa*, *ex persona*, and *ex facto ipso*; for Capito he includes the first two (IIIA and B) but not the third since he was in Ameria at the time of the murder. The denunciation of Capito's treachery during the embassy is spun out to great length (§§109–17), a sign not only of C.'s eagerness to blacken his reputation prior to his testimony but also of the paucity of materials at C.'s disposal (the treatment of Capito's *uita ante acta* (§100) is also

notably thin and nonspecific). For the function of the digression at §§89–91
see *ad loc.*

I   *praemunitio*: the following motivated purely by C.'s obligation to his
    client (83)
    A   C. has no desire to rise by ruining others
    B   He will pursue the matter only so far as his client's safety requires
II T. Roscius Magnus, a prime suspect (84)
    A   Motive
        (1)   L. Cassius always raised the question "who profited?"
        (2)   In this case the answer is clear (86)
    B   *probabile ex uita*
        (1)   Previously poor
        (2)   Greedy
        (3)   Bold
        (4)   An enemy of the deceased
    C   Proof
        (1)   Poverty cannot be hidden
        (2)   Avarice shown by his joining the *societas* (87)
        (3)   Boldness shown by his presence on the prosecutor's side of
              court
        (4)   Enmity with Roscius sen. sprang from property disputes
    D   Comparison of Magnus and Roscius jun. as suspects (88)
    E   Digression: If Erucius had a case like this . . . (89)
        (1)   He owes his current standing to the recent bloodbath among
              prosecutors
        (2)   This occurred while the supreme commander was preoc-
              cupied (91)
        (3)   But the perpetrators lived in such a way that there will always
              be matter for accusation
        (4)   C. will deal with the matter lightly as demanded by his duty to
              his client
    F   Means of committing the crime (92)
        (1)   Murder occurred in Rome, where Magnus was at the time
        (2)   Two types of assassin (93)
              (a)   Those who profit directly
              (b)   Those who work for hire
        (3)   Magnus profited directly from the death of Roscius sen.
        (4)   Hired assassins were clients of one of the members of the *societas*
        (5)   Comparison with the defendant (94)

G   Immediate aftermath of the murder (95)
   (1)   Magnus' client Mallius Glaucia reports the news in Ameria (96)
   (2)   First announcement made to Capito
   (3)   Where or how did Glaucia hear of it? (97)
   (4)   Why did he make the journey so quickly?
H   A vivid portrait of the murder and its immediate sequel (98)
III Capito's rôle (99)
A   The fact that he was the first notified of the death is connected with his gaining possession of three farms
B   His *uita ante acta* (100)
   (1)   Skilled in all methods of murder
   (2)   He once threw a man off a bridge into the Tiber
C   He will testify from a script prepared by Erucius (101)
   (1)   Magnus' sending of the swift messenger has foiled all hopes of concealment (102)
   (2)   Ancestral custom forbids testimony on matters affecting one's own interests
D   Digression: address to Magnus (104)
E   Next phase (105)
   (1)   The news reaches Sulla's camp at Volaterrae
   (2)   Chrysogonus organizes the sale of the estates of Roscius sen.
   (3)   Surely he must have been informed of them by the T. Roscii, with whom he shared the profits (106)
   (4)   But their services went beyond merely providing information, or they would not have been so handsomely rewarded
F   Capito's treachery during the embassy (109)
   (1)   He hinders a meeting with Sulla (110)
   (2)   He betrays the legates' policies to Chrysogonus
   (3)   He bargains with Chrysogonus for a share of the profits
   (4)   He fobs off the other legates with false promises, and they leave
   (5)   Even careless handling of a private mandate was punished by the ancestors with *infamia* (111)
   (6)   Much worse the present case, a public mandate, in which the reputation of a dead man and the fortunes of a living man are at stake (113)
   (7)   The consequences if Sex. Roscius had commissioned Capito privately (114)
   (8)   But what Capito has done is far worse (115)

(9)   Deception of a partner a serious crime punished by the ances-
      tors with *infamia* (116)

(10) Capito deceived not just a single partner but his nine fellow
      legates (117)

(11) Then he joined in partnership with their adversaries

(12) Now he is threatening us

(13) The perpetrator of the crime at issue in this trial will be found
      to have such a character

IV Magnus' refusal to allow the slaves to testify (119)

 A   No possible reason applies

  (1)   Those making the request were worthy

  (2)   The man for whom they were requested deserved pity

  (3)   The cause was just (120)

 B   The refusal suggests the fear that their testimony will be damning

 C   The argument that slaves should not be made to testify against their
     masters does not apply

 D   Objection that the slaves are with Chrysogonus is implausible

  (1)   They are rustic slaves not equal to the refinement of his own
        slaves (121)

  (2)   Something is being hidden (122)

  (3)   No intent to implicate Chrysogonus in the murder itself

V These matters are being pursued no further than necessary (123)

83 This chapter forms the transition from the first to the second part of C.'s
argumentatio / refutatio; cf. §35. Since this section comprises his *anticategoria* (cf. the
headnote to the commentary and the previous n.), he begins with a *praemunitio*
(cf. Lausberg §854) justifying his procedure in advance and claiming that he
will take the matter no further than his case requires. He also insists on his
own superior prosecutorial evidence and technique; cf. Riggsby 1999: 58.

Venio nunc eo ... dum utrumuis licebit: a standard transitional
formula (cf. §79 *nunc, Eruci, ad te uenio*) varied by the emphasis on C.'s motive,
viz. his pledge (*fides*) to his client; cf. §10n. C.'s attitude toward prosecution
remained fairly constant throughout his life; cf. *Off.* 2.47, 49 and 50 with
Dyck *ad locos*. He made an exception only of Verres, clearly a man *ex quo
crescere posset*, and Clodius' follower T. Munatius Plancus Bursa. For the use
of *cresco* of "advancing in standing" or the like cf. *OLD* s.v. 7a; for *certum est*
cf. §31n.

is enim mihi uidetur ... incommodum et calamitatem: C.'s
explanation (*enim*) of the foregoing resolution. *amplus* of persons is

"distinguished, great": *OLD* s.v. 8; similarly *amplitudo* (cf. §2n.). **ascendo** "attain a more distinguished position, rise" (**OLD** s.v. 7) varies **cresco**.

desinamus aliquando . . . unumquidque tangam: *aliquando* ("at length, at long last": *OLD* s.v. 5) introduces a note of impatience. For the inanity of Erucius' case cf. §42 *crimen commenticium . . . res tam leues*; §48 *inopia criminum*; §54 *finge aliquid saltem commode*; §58 *planum fac; nihil est . . . non mehercules uerbum fecisses, si tibi quemquam responsurum putasses*; §73 *esto, causam proferre non potes*. The clear marking of units with initial correlatives (*ibi . . . ubi et . . . et*) suggests a systematic approach that has been lacking in the prosecution case. **certum crimen:** the phrase is topicalized by placement in front of the conjunction *quam*; cf. Devine and Stephens 2006: 291 and 585; for the sense of *certus* cf. on §53 (*certus accusator*); for the required convergence of many indices of guilt cf. §68. *coarguo* is to "prove a charge or allegation": *OLD* s.v. 2. *tametsi* appears this time without *tamen*, as in §3 (contrast §49). *neque . . . et* substitutes for *et . . . et* when the prior clause is negativized. Used of discourse, *tango* is to "make a (slight) mention of, touch on" (*OLD* s.v. 10a), here further attenuated by *leuiter* ("slightly": *OLD* s.v. 3).

neque enim id facerem . . . mea fides postulabit: *id erit signi*: genitive of the rubric; cf. §8n. As often, the pronoun is defined by a following *quod*-clause ("the fact that"); cf. *OLD* s.v. *quod* 2a. For *signum* cf. §42n. **salus huius et mea fides:** the chiastic arrangement brings together the words referring to client and patron. C. speaks throughout of his client's life being at stake; cf. §5n.; for C.'s *fides* see above.

84 The justification complete, C. launches in on the new argument. As early as §6 C. had highlighted Chrysogonus' possession of Roscius' patrimony, at §17 that Capito was now owner of three of the farms; here it becomes clear that these facts constitute the centerpiece of C.'s *anticategoria*.

Causam tu nullam . . . aduersarium esse profiteris: the direct address to Erucius resumes from §83; he was notably unsuccessful in assigning a motive for his father's hatred of Roscius jun. or for the murder (cf. §§42 and 61–3) in spite of its importance in cases of this type (cf. *Inv.* 2.19). *at ego* creates a sharp contrast (like *ego contra* at §§7 and 79). C. pretends that T. Roscius Magnus' presence in the *subsellia* on the prosecution's side of the court (*istic*) is a provocation; the point is amplified at §87; for the possibility that he was a *subscriptor* cf. §58n.

de Capitone post uiderimus . . . ne audisse quidem suspicatur: the attempt to intimidate witnesses on the opposing side was apparently standard courtroom practice; *Cael.* offers striking examples at §§19–22, 31–8 and 66–7; cf. Schmitz 1985: 124–7. *post uiderimus* "we shall deal with Capito

presently"; the fut. pf. can connote certainty; cf. G–L §244.4N1; Apul. *Met.*
5.24.5 with Kenney's n. **paratum esse audio:** the nature of the "preparation" is explained at §101 *explicet suum uolumen illud quod ei planum facere possum
Erucium conscripsisse.* C. reverts to the ironic imagery of gladiatorial victory
previously associated with Capito (cf. §17 *plurimarum palmarum uetus ac nobilis
gladiator*). **de quibus me ne audisse quidem suspicatur:** the theme of
C.'s being better prepared than the opposition anticipates (cf. §82 *fin.*) is taken
up with a menacing tone.

   L. Cassius ille . . . atque emolumento accedere: asyndeton marks
the onset of a narrative (cf. §25n.) serving as background to the following
assertion *facile me paterer . . . illo ipso . . . quaerente . . . pro Sex. Roscio dicere* (§85). *ille*
marks this bearer of the name (as usual with the Romans there were many
homonyms) as "the famous": *OLD* s.v. 4b. L. Cassius Longinus Ravilla (cons.
127, cens. 125) was known for his severity as a judge, with the result that
he was appointed extraordinary judge after the Vestals accused of *incestum*
in 113 had been acquitted; cf. *TLRR* no. 43; Cornell 1981. He is favorably
viewed in this speech, where C. is calling for severity (cf. §§11–12), much less
so apropos his law providing the secret ballot for the people's courts except
for cases of *perduellio*; cf. *Leg.* 3.35 with Dyck's n.; cf. in general Münzer, *RE* III
2.1742.11 (Cassius 72). **cui bono** "for whose benefit"; for the double dative
cf. G–L §356; cf. also *Phil.* 2.35 *illud Cassianum 'cui bono fuerit'.* **spe atque
emolumento** "the hope of gain" by hendiadys; *emolumentum* was probably
originally "the output from a mill" (< *emolo* "grind out"); the Latin word (=
"benefit, advantage") is broader than the Engl. derivative, which has become
specialized as "pay"; cf. *OLD* s.vv.

85 hunc quaesitorem ac iudicem . . . ad seueritatem uidebatur:
quaesitor here is a "member of an extraordinary commission to investigate
a particular case" (*OLD* s.v. 1) and suggests that C. is thinking above all
of the case of the Vestals. **quibus periculum creabatur:** i.e. defendants,
periculum being applied sometimes specifically to the position of the defendant
on trial; cf. §§110, 148 and 152; *OLD* s.v. 3. For *tametsi . . . tamen* cf. §49. *applicatus*
"devoted (to)" varies *propensus* "having a disposition (to)."

   ego, quamquam praeest . . . pro Sex. Roscio dicere: for the pres-
ident of the tribunal, M. Fannius, cf. §11n.; for *audacia* cf. §35n. *ab* here is
"as regards, as to": *OLD* s.v. 25a; for *clemens/clementia* cf. Konstan 2005. For
facile patior cf. §56n. *Cassiani iudices* "judges like Cassius" were proverbially
severe; cf. *Ver.* 2.3.137 *quem tu in cohorte tua Cassianum iudicem habebas . . . Papirium
Potamonem*; similarly ibid. 146; cf. Otto 1890: 77. *nomen ipsum* "the mere name,"
to say nothing of the reality; cf. *TLL* s.v. *ipse* 334.69. *reformido* is to "shrink
from (in fear)": *OLD* s.v. 1a.

COMMENTARY: 86–7 153

86 in hac enim causa . . . quam ad egestatem: *hic* is, as usual, the defendant; cf. §6n.; he is opposed to *illi*; C. must pluralize at this point since Magnus alone is not in possession of any of Roscius' property; he is merely Chrysogonus' estate manager (§23); §87 clarifies that he is speaking of the *societas* as previously described (§20). *mendicitas* is the "condition of beggary" (*OLD* s.v. 1), varied in the sequel by *tenuitas*. Contrasting *quidem* often adheres to *ille*; cf. Solodow 1978: 38–9. **eo perspicuo** "since it is obvious"; for the abl. absolute cf. §6n.; the trademark question would thus be elided.

quid si accedit . . . qui occisus est inimicissimus?: here the sg. returns, for the implied character sketch pertains to Magnus alone. For *tenuis* in such contexts cf. §19n.; the point is forestalled at §23 (*qui in sua re fuisset egentissimus*). Magnus' *audacia*, if it existed, evidently had not been manifested in deeds given C.'s admission that he was *ante hanc pugnam tiro* (§17). Hostile relations with the deceased were previously claimed for Capito and Magnus (§17). C. will offer proof for these points at §§87–8 except for *tenuitas*, which he claims requires none.

num quaerenda causa . . . quo magis occultatur: for "railroading" *num* implying that a negative answer should follow cf. *OLD* s.v. 3. For the paradox cf. §121 *est quiddam quod occultatur; quod quo studiosius ab istis opprimitur et absconditur, eo magis eminet et apparet.*

87 auaritiam praefers . . . cum alienissimo: for the *iunctura coire societatem* cf. §20n.; for the relative clause with causal force §41n. The *societas* of §20 is assumed as a fact (though it was a mere inference on C.'s part; see *ad loc.*) and is the basis for an inference about Magnus' character; see Berger 1978: 36–7. *alienissimus* refers, of course, to Chrysogonus. *cognati* is C.'s one clear indication that Magnus was related to his client; see §17n.

quam sis audax . . . concedas necesse est: *obliuiscor* can mean "to put out of mind deliberately," in which sense it can govern either gen. or acc.: *OLD* s.v. 4. For the *societas* cf. on §§20 and 96. For *sicarius* cf. §8n. For Magnus' place in court treated as a provocation cf. §84n.; for the generic subj. cf. §1n. Beginning with comedy, *os* often appears as a metaphor for shamelessness; cf. *OLD* s.v. 8b; Corbeill 1996: 102; at §95 *impudentia* varies *os*. The distinction between *os ostendere* and *os offerre* appears to be that between "putting it forward" and "letting it be seen"; cf. *TLL* s.v. *offero* 499.58–9; the assonance of *o* is striking. **magnas rei familiarias controuersias:** this is C.'s sole explanation for bad feeling among the Roscii; one wonders if it applies also to the enmity between Capito and Roscius sen. (§§17 and 19); if so, it may help to explain the division of spoils at §110; see *ad loc.*

88 restat, iudices, . . . inimicus potius an filius: a comparison (cf. §69n.), adumbrated at §18, between Roscius jun. and Magnus as potential murderers of Roscius sen. To the modern reader it may seem surprising for the decision in a murder trial to hinge on relative probability rather than facts; cf. Riggsby 1999: 64; but with a weak police and prosecutorial apparatus (cf. Nippel 1995: 27–30 and on §28), at Rome even murder trials tended to become rhetorical duels. *dubito* is "consider": *OLD* s.v. 4; cf. the similar structure following *dubitate* at §78. C. presents five disjunctive pairs beginning with the financial position in the aftermath of the murder (repeated for emphasis), the character issues *auaritia* and *audacia* and their opposite traits, and finally the relation to the deceased (*inimicus potius an filius*), whereby the last item is highlighted as particularly germane (*id quod ad rem mea sententia maxime pertinet*). In framing the matter this way, C. presents the jurors with a kind of dilemma without having established that these two candidates exhaust the possibilities; cf. Riggsby 1999: 63. The rôle reversal was already depicted at §23, where Magnus is described as previously *egentissimus*; it was not, however, the murder itself but the *ex post facto* assimilation of Roscius sen. to those *in aduersariorum praesidiis occisi* (§§126–7) that had these consequences, which could not necessarily have been predicted at the time of the deed, a fact that C. never mentions. C. sometimes uses *flagrans* or *ardens* with a noun in the abl. for vivid (and usually negative) characterization; cf. *Sest.* 134; *Phil.* 2.45, 4.4, and 5.42; *Att.* 13.21a.2; *auaritia* is applied to Magnus here on the same basis as in the previous section; for *ardens auaritia* cf. *Fin.* 3.36 *quis umquam fuit aut auaritia tam ardenti*. C.'s distinction between *quaestus* and *fructus* seems based on the application of the latter to agricultural produce (*OLD* s.v. 3; cf. §44 *certis fundis patre uiuo frui solitum esse*), whereas *quaestus* is "profit" in a broader sense that can include trade (*OLD* s.v.). For *sector* cf. §80n.; the picture of Magnus as *omnium sectorum audacissimus* agrees with his depiction as most audacious of the *societas* (§87). For the portrait of Roscius' *insolentia* in urban affairs cf. §§79 and 81 with nn.; in claiming *urbem ipsam reformidet*, C. now goes still further; for *reformido* cf. §85n.

89–91 The point of this digression is not *prima facie* clear. Here C. alludes to the proscriptions and the interruption of judicial business in a manner clearly exculpating Sulla. One suspects that the young advocate is feeling his way with the jury to see how they will react and to prepare the ground for the fuller and more pointed discussion of such topics in the *peroratio*.

89 Haec tu, Eruci, . . . possis consumere: Magnus, C. suggests, would make a prime target for prosecution. *iacto* used reflexively is to "flaunt oneself, show off"; cf. §24n. For *hercule* cf. §50n. For time failing the orator engaged on a choice topic cf. *Cael.* 29 *facile est accusare luxuriem. dies iam me deficiat, si quae dici in eam sententiam possunt coner expromere*; cf. also *Ver.* 2.4.59 with Baldo's n. The *singulae res* are presumably his *auaritia, audacia*, previous poverty, enmity with the elder Roscius, etc.

neque ego non possum ... posse dicere: C. puns on the antithetical terms *derogo* and *arrogo*, respectively "take away, subtract" and "make undue claims, be conceited" (with neuter acc. pronoun); cf. *OLD* s.vv. 2 and 3c; Holst 1925: 64. Possessing *copia dicendi* enabled one to expatiate on a topic; it was much admired and sometimes stands for eloquence itself; cf. *Inv.* 1.1.

uerum ego forsitan ... ad Seruilium uidimus: C. claims merely a position *in grege*, i.e. as a common soldier (*gregarius miles*) in the ranks of advocates; cf. *Brut.* 332 *numerari in uulgo patronorum*. The *pugna Cannensis* (end of June, 216) was the proverbial bloodbath of Roman history; cf. Otto 1890: 72–3, citing *Ver.* 2.5.28 and later echoes of our passage. The shift to another disaster of the Hannibalic War, *Trasimenus lacus* (21 June 217 by the Roman calendar), enables a pun on the *Seruilius lacus*, a cistern near the forum where the heads of the proscribed senators were displayed (presumably after they became too numerous for display in Sulla's house; see the Introduction sec. 3); cf. Richardson s.v. Lacus Servilius; Sen. *Dial.* 1.37–8; on the fate of the corpses of the proscribed in general cf. Hinard 1985a: 45–9. An *accusator sat bonus* is an "adequate prosecutor," *sat* having depreciatory force here; cf. *OLD* s.v. *satis* 9b; Landgraf 1878: 38.

90 Lintott 2008: 427 is rightly critical: "His flippant attitude in the speech to the killing of the Marian accusers ... is a somewhat distasteful Sullan posture."

'quis ibi non est uulneratus ferro Phrygio?': a quotation from a tragedy of Ennius (*trag.* 312 J. (inc.)). Schol. Gronov. *ad loc.* refers the words to Ulysses when asked by Ajax why he has run from battle.

non necesse est ... leges pugnare prohibebant: on the implications of this passage for the chronology of Roman forensic activity cf. §11n. **Curtios, Marios** "men like Curtius and Marius"; for the generalizing pl. cf. K–S 1 72.3 with many examples from C. The professional prosecutors mentioned as victims of the Sullan proscriptions are not certainly identifiable. Our Curtius may have been the father of the C. Curtius recommended by C. in 45 (*Fam.* 13.5.2); cf. Hinard 1985a 347–8; David 1992: 725. Any Marius would have been vulnerable following Sulla's victory; Münzer, *RE* XIV 2.1810.27–31 (Marius 2) suggested a reference to M. Marius Gratidianus, C.'s

relative murdered by Catiline (cf. Dyck on *Off.* 3.80); but he is not known
to have prosecuted; cf. Hinard 1985a: 374–5; Ursinus restored *Memmios*, the
name of known prosecutors of the period (cf. *Brut.* 136), for the transmitted
Mammeos; for identifications suggested for Antistius cf. Hinard 1985a: 330–1.
Priamum ipsum senem may be another allusion to tragedy, albeit it is unclear
whether or how these words might have found a place in Ulysses' speech; see
Ribbeck on *trag.* 311 and the previous n. "The laws" is a vague reference to
the *lex Remmia*, on which cf. §55n.

   iam quos nemo . . . seruanda sunt: for *sescenti* of an indefinitely large
number cf. *OLD* s.v. 2. **inter sicarios et de ueneficiis:** i.e. in the current court; cf. §11 (*iudicium inter sicarios*) and Introduction sec. 2. The imperfect *accusabant* refers to the time before the recent lawlessness when the
courts were suspended; cf. §11; Berry 2004: 82–3. **quod ad me attinet**
differentiates C.'s case from Erucius' (§89 *te pugna Cannensis accusatorem sat
bonum fecit*). **nihil . . . mali:** for the gen. of the rubric cf. §8n. The dog as
a metaphor for the prosecutor continues the imagery of §§56–7. There is
a slight play on the identical verb stem of *obseruandi* and *seruanda*; cf. Holst
1925: 71.

91 uerum, ut fit, . . . ac turba molitur: with *imprudens* C. chooses the
same adj. he had applied to Sulla at §21; cf. *ad loc.* C. personifies *uis belli ac
turba* as subject of *molior* (cf. §22n.), agreeing, as usual, with the nearer subject;
cf. G–L §211 R.1; in addition to the inevitable *belli . . . turba* were the actions
of those who *omnia . . . miscebant*, as the sequel shows.

   dum is in aliis rebus . . . et iudices sustulerunt: Sulla is referred
to this time (in contrast to §§6 and 21) by rôle (*qui summam rerum administrabat*)
rather than name. **occupatus** "busy, occupied, engaged," is often used with
in + abl., as here: *OLD* s.v.; cf. §22 *cum . . . tam multi occupationem eius obseruent.
summa rerum* is "the fortunes or interests of the whole body, the state": *OLD* s.v.
summa 6b; cf. §22 *cum . . . unus omnia gubernet. offundo* ("pour over") is often used
of darkness or the like; cf. Quint. 2.17.21 (C. on *Clu.*) *se tenebras offudisse iudicibus
gloriatus est; OLD* s.v. 1b. C. appears to be the first to use *tenebrae* of a "gloomy
state of affairs": *OLD* s.v. 5; *nox* is similarly used; cf. *Har.* 11 *in illa tempestate ac
nocte rei publicae.* The burning of the *subsellia* symbolizes the utter destruction
of the courts, just as C. tries to make the burning of the curia during Clodius'
obsequies symbolic of the program of that adventurer (*Mil.*13, 33, 61, 90–1);
for the defiling of the courtroom cf. also §§12 and 32. For the elimination of
the courts cf. §11n.

   hoc commodi est . . . iudicia fient: *hoc commodi* is another example
of the gen. of the rubric; cf. §8n. *ita uixerunt,* i.e. so brazenly, given the

described consequences. **si cuperent . . . non possent** "even if they had wished . . . they could not have"; on the impf. for plupf. cf. Blase 1903: 134. **qui accuset:** for the relative clause with final force cf. §25n. C. tends to use *ciuitas* to designate the state as comprised by laws and institutions such as the courts; cf. Wood 1988: 126 with 242n23. **erit . . . non deerit:** the point is underlined by the homoeoteleuton and play on words; cf. Holst 1925: 71.

uerum, ut coepi dicere, . . . sed officio defendere: C. first cross-refers to (and partially repeats) §89, from which he has digressed on the fate of an earlier generation of prosecutors and the recent disorders; his second cross-reference is to §83 (*leuiter unumquidque tangam*). *perstringo* is "to glance along the edge of" and hence "touch on, glance at (a subject)": *OLD* s.v. 2a and 3b; cf. *Ver.* 2.4.105; *Phil.* 2.47. *studium* and *officium* are two of the qualities of an orator; cf. *Brut.* 245 (of T. Torquatus T. filius) *studio huic non satisfecit, officio uero nec in suorum necessariorum causis nec in sententia senatoria defuit*; the lack of *studium* varies the earlier claim *me inuitum facere* (§83); cf. also §94 *te ipsum non libenter accuso*.

92 Video igitur causas esse . . . suscipiendi malefici fuerit: *igitur* ("well then") resumes after the digression; cf. *OLD* s.v. 5. For the generic subj. (*quae . . . impellerent* "the kind which would drive him") cf. §1n. C.'s case against Magnus follows the same order as his refutation of the charges against his client: first the motive (§§37–54, 58, 61–3) and then the means (§§73–81). In *ecquis* the prefix lends a certain emphasis to the interrogative ("whether there was any . . . "); cf. *OLD* 1b. The *iunctura maleficium suscipere* will recur at §94; cf. also *Inv.* 1.45.

ubi occisus est . . . et alii multi': a more extensive imitation of the style of *altercatio* than in §§40 and 54; the technique recurs at §§94 and 96. Magnus responds energetically, dispensing with verbs. The repetition of the single-word sentence *Romae* at the beginning of his answers is telling. **et alii multi:** for *et* = "also" cf. *OLD* s.v. 5; K–S II 8–10; similarly §94 *fateor me sectorem esse, uerum et alii multi*.

quasi nunc id agatur . . . omnino non accesserit: "*quis ex tanta multitudine* . . . strengthens Magnus' point, but mocks his mockery" (Hutchinson 2005: 189). The choice is thus narrowed to the two suspects who were already compared from this standpoint at §18 and the question to one of relative probability; cf. §88n. **assiduus . . . Romae** varies *frequens Romae* (§18). For Roscius' absence from Rome for many years cf. §§74 and 79. The strengthened negation *omnino non* recurs at §§94 and 95 but not otherwise in this speech (cf., however, *omnino numquam* at §105); after C.'s exile the combination occurs 12x in the essays but is virtually banned from the speeches (2x).

93 age nunc ceteras . . . homines impune occidebantur: for *age* cf. §48n.; for the order of topics cf. §92n. C. has already quoted Erucius' observation (§80).

   quid? ea multitudo . . . ut aliquem occiderent: C. now takes up and dissects the prosecutor's point, the *multitudo sicariorum*, another example of the division (διαίρεσις) of a topic; cf. §74n. *occupati*, meaning "busy, occupied, engaged" (cf. §91n.), is transmitted. Shackleton Bailey 1979: 238 objects: "But why talk of these assassins . . . as *busy* with other men's goods, when the only relevant fact is that they had got possession of them?" Hence he proposed *occupatis*. But surely C. means to refer again, as in §81, to those *qui . . . in praeda et in sanguine uersabantur.* C. again frames the matter so as to place financial interests in the foreground (cf. §§84–8).

   si eos putas . . . cum tua conferetur: C. proceeds to examine the two alternatives and to conclude that in either case Magnus is the likelier suspect; for *si . . . sin* cf. §8n. For Magnus' self-enrichment at Roscius' expense cf. §23; for his *auaritia* §87. But Chrysogonus and Capito were actually the primary beneficiaries of the death of Roscius sen., Magnus merely the *procurator Chrysogoni* (§23); he is, however, the "softer target" and hence the first object of C.'s attack. *percussor* is a prose word first attested here; as our passage shows, it was felt to be a euphemism for *sicarius* (cf. Adams 1973: 290n69 "presumably because it designated a person who struck someone without necessarily inflicting death") and largely supplanted *sicarius* during the Empire except as a legal term; cf. *TLL* s.v. especially 1236.11 and 33–4. **in cuius fide** "under whose protection"; cf. *TLL* s.v. *fides* 663.83. For the *societas* cf. §20n.; for the "future" imperative §18n.

94 dices: 'quid postea . . . ab eiusmodi crimine': this fictive *altercatio* captures the salient differences between the two suspects; cf. §40n. As Kinsey 1975: 97 remarks apropos our passage, "C. will put answers to his charges in an opponent's mouth if they allow him a crushing retort." Thus he has Magnus successively admit to having been habitually at Rome, a *sector*, and one of the *sicarii*. For *omnino non* cf. §92n.; the argument is overstated; Roscius jun. had been to Rome, albeit not for many years (§§74 and 79). **ut tute arguis** assimilates Magnus to the prosecutor and suggests that he might be a *subscriptor*; cf. §58n.; for the prosecution's attempt to paint Roscius as an anti-social rustic cf. §§39, 52, 74, and 76. Magnus' next point focuses on C.'s claim that the *sicarii/percussores* were under the protection of one of the members of the *societas* (i.e. Chrysogonus) (§93); he counters that it cannot be inferred that he himself is a *sicarius*. But again Roscius is further from suspicion; C. has argued the impossibility of Roscius' arranging a contract killing at §79.

permulta sunt quae . . . oratio mea pertinere uideatur: *permulta*: for C.'s fondness for adjs./advs. compounded with *per-* cf. §20n. For *maleficium suscipere* §92n.; for *te ipsum non libenter accuso* cf. §91n. **ista eadem ratione qua Sex. Roscius occisus est:** i.e. fraudulently. This sentence, with its suggestion that such abuses were spread more widely, is perhaps the boldest in the speech and might well, if pursued, have forced the conclusion that more people, including Sulla, were implicated.

95 Videamus nunc strictim . . . inuitus ea dicam: cf. the similar transition at §105 *age nunc illa uideamus . . . quae statim consecuta sunt*. *strictim* is "cursorily, summarily": *OLD* s.v. 2; cf. §83 *leuiter . . . tangam*. This is a bit misleading; apart from the imaginary scene conjured at §98, C. will be describing the actions of Glaucia and Capito. **medius fidius** "I call heaven to witness" or "so help me God," an oath by Fidius, the avenger of violated oaths; *fidius* began as an epithet of *Iuppiter* and then, like Fides, developed an independent cult; cf. *OLD* s.vv. *medius²*, *Fidius*; Hofmann 2003: 139; Wissowa 1912: 118. The pretence of unwillingness recalls §83 (*me inuitum facere*).

uereor enim . . . non pepercerim: this is one of fourteen Ciceronian occurrences of *cuicuimodi* ("no matter of what kind"), based on an archaic gen. *cui/quoi*; cf. *OLD* s.v. *modus* 12b and *quisquis init.*; Leumann 1977: 479. For *omnino non* cf. §92n.

cum hoc uereor . . . oris tui: for C.'s *fides* cf. §10n. For *in mentem uenire* here used, as other expressions of remembering, with gen. cf. §58n. For Magnus' "face" (in several senses) cf. §87n.

tene, cum ceteri . . . sederes cum accusatore?: the acc. + inf. (*te . . . depoposcisse*) is often used in emotional exclamations, whereby *-ne* appended to the emphatic word suggests doubt that the phenomenon could occur at all; cf. *Phil.* 14.14 *quemquamne fuisse tam sceleratum qui . . .* and other examples cited at K–S I 720–1. **cum ceteri socii tui fugerent ac se occultarent:** Chrysogonus was not present in court (cf. §60), but the motive assigned here for his absence and that of Capito is clearly a *color*; cf. Lausberg §§329 and 1061. This sentence encapsulates C.'s reframing of the issue as *de illorum praeda*, rather than *de huius maleficio*. *deposco* is to demand a certain task or, as here, rôle (*partes*); cf. *OLD* s.v. *deposco* 1b; for *iste* prompting a following consecutive clause cf. K–S II 248–9.

qua in re ... et impudentia: *assequor* is "to achieve" a result: *OLD* s.v. 4a. For *omnes mortales* cf. §11n.; for *audacia* §12n.; for *impudentia* varying *os* cf. §87n.

96 occiso Sex. Roscio ... minime omnium pertinebat?: Mallius Glaucia was first mentioned at §19, where he received the same description as the *cliens et familiaris* of Magnus, the only point linking Magnus to the scene of the murder. C. at once tries to spin dark suspicions of an already existing *societas* out of the circumstances in which word of the murder first reached Ameria, but this would have been sensational news there, and the first bearer could have reckoned with a reward; this might have been motive enough for a *homo tenuis* (§19) to have undertaken the all-night journey; C., however, chooses to assume that Glaucia acted on Magnus' prompting; cf. §98. *consilium inire* is to "form a plan or plot": *OLD* s.v. *ineo* 7b; *societas* ("partnership") is used in a wide variety of spheres as is shown by the genitives *sceleris* and *praemi*; cf. *OLD* s.v. *societas* 4b. *ad te minime omnium pertinebat* is inferred from their status as enemies; cf. §§17 and 87. At §20 C. dates the formation of the *societas* to the arrival at Volaterrae of the news of the death of Roscius sen. and thus exonerates Chrysogonus of involvement in the murder; here he speaks of the *societas* as existing before the death of Roscius sen., a significant difference.

'sua sponte Mallius ... ut nihil diuinatione opus sit: for the *altercatio* cf. §40n. Certainly it will not have been by chance (*casu*), but the man's financial exigency provides sufficient motive; see the previous n. *eo rem ... adducam ut* "I shall bring the matter to (such) a point that ... "; the demonstrative adv. *eo* is among the locutions commonly prompting a consecutive clause; cf. K–S II 248–9.

qua ratione ... potissimum nuntiaret?: the pl. *liberi* suggests the possibility that Roscius sen. had more than one surviving child (if so, a daughter, rather than a son; cf. §42), though *liberi* is sometimes used of a single son even by C.; cf. Landgraf *ad loc.*; Ramsey on *Phil.* 1.2.15. **tot propinqui cognatique optime conuenientes** "so many relations and kin on excellent terms"; cf. *OLD* s.v. *conuenio* 4b. C. mentions them only here and none by name; if any of them appeared in court to support him, C. fails to exploit the fact; cf. §49n. **sceleris tui nuntius** makes explicit what C. has implicitly claimed since the first mention of the murder at §18. *primo* suggests that Capito was merely the first in a series of stops that morning; cf. Kinsey 1980: 176; if so, the fact that Capito was first seems less significant and might have to do with accidents of geography.

97 occisus est . . . festinatioque significat?: similarly in the first narrative §18 *occiditur . . . rediens a cena Sex. Roscius*. In our passage the detail *a cena rediens* is a chronological pointer and is combined with the pre-dawn arrival of the news to yield a picture of an *incredibilis cursus*; §19 offers precise details of the time and distance travelled.

non quaero . . . non laboro: a series of emphatic denials with *nihil* varying *non* in the strong initial position. The act is referred to (twice) with the euphemistic *percutio*, rather than more graphic equivalents such as *caedo*; cf. §93n. (*percussores*). The words *nihil est, Glaucia, quod metuas* will hardly reassure the addressee: the agent acting on orders could be prosecuted to create a *praeiudicium* against the mastermind, as in Cluentius' prosecution of Scamander, who was represented by C. in 74; cf. *Clu.* 50–5. There is a mild play on *percutio* and *excutio*, which literally means "shake out" but is here used for "examining" a person: *OLD* s.v. 9a; it is varied by *scrutor* "search" for concealed weapons or the like: *OLD* s.v. 1b; for a different sense cf. §128n. **quid . . . ferri:** for the gen. of the rubric cf. §8n. This was already narrated at §19 *peruolauit . . . ut . . . telum . . . paulo ante e corpore extractum ostenderet*. **consilio . . . manu:** similar contrast at *N.D.* 1.115 (of Epicurus) *eum qui . . . nec manibus ut Xerses sed rationibus deorum immortalium templa et aras euerterit.* **inuenio . . . non laboro:** *inuenio* is conative (cf. §1n.); *non laboro* ("I am not worried, concerned") is followed by indirect question; cf. *Mil.* 98 *ubi corpus hoc sit non . . . laboro*; *OLD* s.v. 7.

unum hoc sumo . . . partem noctis requiesceret?: for *sumo* cf. §47n. *tuum scelus* is openly claimed since §96; cf. §98 *sui sceleris . . . nuntium*; §102 *suum scelus*. For the adverbial *qui* ("how?") cf. §53n. *facio* here is "suppose (for the purposes of an argument), imagine": *OLD* s.v. 20b. **nocte una** (for the abl. of time within which cf. G–L §393) is highlighted by juxtaposition with *tantum itineris*. *contendo* (here used with internal acc.) is "to hasten, press forward": *OLD* s.v. 5a. *necessitas* and especially *tanta* receive emphasis by their separation (hyperbaton); their enclosure of Glaucia's pronoun mirrors the sense. *iter facere* is a common expression for "making a journey": *OLD* s.v. *iter* 1b. *id temporis* ("at that time") functions as a quasi-adverb in colloquial Latin; cf. §64 (*id aetatis*) with n.

98 Etiamne in tam perspicuis . . . oculis uidemini, iudices?: the eyes are proverbially more powerful than the ears; cf. Otto 1890: 251. If the jurors do not already perceive with their eyes (*cernere oculis*) the events of the fatal night, C. will help them in the sequel, an exercise in *descriptio*; cf. §12n.; for the underlying theory cf. *De orat.* 3.202. Similarly at *Phil.* 11.7 after a sober narration of the facts C. conjures up a vivid picture of the crime. For the claimed perspicuity of C.'s case cf. §§18n., 41, 101, and 105; cf. also §34 *quid est in hac causa quod defensionis indigeat? qui locus ingenium patroni requirit aut oratoris eloquentiam magnopere desiderat?*; similarly *Ver.* 2.2.102 and 2.4.11. For *coniectura* cf. §62n.

non illum miserum . . . in caede Glaucia?: here the circumstance that Roscius sen. was returning from dinner has a different function from §97: it shows that he was the unsuspecting victim of foul play and therefore, like his son (cf. §23n.), *miser*; cf. §18n. For *in caede uersari* cf. §39 (with n.) *uetus uidelicet sicarius . . . saepe in caede uersatus*; *Cat.* 4.11 *uersatur mihi ante oculos aspectus Cethegi et furor in uestra caede bacchantis.* Glaucia's rôle is inferred not only from his immediate knowledge but also from his display of the victim's gore and of the murder weapon (cf. §19). In the sequel the anaphora of *non* with immediately following verb recurs, emphasizing the actions: *non uersatur . . . non adest . . . non orat.*

non adest iste . . . quam primum nuntiet?: Glaucia's journey is C.'s sole evidence for placing Magnus at the scene of the murder, the assumption being that he must have been acting on orders from his patron; but there are other possibilities; cf. §96n. Automedon was Achilles' charioteer and hence a byword for speed; cf. Juv. 1.60–1 *peruolat axe citato | Flaminiam puer Automedon*; the allusion also has the effect, as often in Juvenal, of emphasizing the chasm between heroic saga and sordid reality; cf. Schmitz 2000: 248–55. For *sui sceleris* cf. §97n.; for *nefarius* §6n. **ut Capitoni quam primum nuntiet:** C. claims that the initial report to Capito was the goal, not a contingent fact; cf. §96n.

99 quid erat quod . . . eum uideo possidere: C.'s construction of the immediate aftermath of the murder depends upon his assumption of a preexisting *societas* among Magnus, Capito, and Chrysogonus (but cf. §96n.), but this is most unlikely in view of the manner in which Capito acquired his three farms; cf. §110n.; his property interest was emphasized already when he was first named at §17; the total number of farms was already indicated at §20.

100 audio praeterea . . . Roma ei deferatur: *hanc suspicionem* is the suspicion of involvement in murder, as the sequel clarifies. *conferre suspicionem* is "to cast suspicion"; cf. *OLD* s.v. *confero* 3b; there is a slight play on the two compounds of *fero, conferri* and *deferatur*. The gladiatorial imagery continues from the first discussion of Capito at §17 (*plurimarum palmarum uetus ac nobilis gladiator*); cf. *ad loc.* A *lemniscata* [sc. *palma*] is one "adorned with ribbons" as a mark of special distinction; cf. *OLD* s.v. *lemniscatus*. If this was, as C. implies, Capito's first murder carried out at Rome, similar arguments might apply to the ones C. used on behalf of his client at §74.

nullum modum esse . . . in Tiberim deiecerit: *ferrum* and *uenenum* were for the Romans the two means of murder *par excellence*, a distinction captured in the name of the relevant law, the *lex Cornelia de sicariis et ueneficiis*; cf. Introduction sec. 2. For *habeo . . . dicere* cf. Dyck on *N.D.* 1.63. C. complains with tongue in cheek that Capito could not even commit murder in a properly Roman fashion! He alludes to the obscure proverbial expression *sexagenarios de ponte*; for the testimonies cf. Otto 1890: 320–1. It has been variously connected with *pontes* in the sense "gangways leading to the voting booths" (Var. *VPR* fr. 71), on the grounds that the *iuniores* sought to exclude sixty-year-olds from voting since they could no longer hold office, or the rite by which on the Ides of May the Vestal Virgins cast puppets called the *Argei* from the Pons Sublicius into the Tiber; cf. Var. *Men.* 494; Ov. *Fast.* 6.621–34; Lact. *Inst.* 1.21.6–9; Fowler 1911: 321–2; Wissowa 1912: 27 and 420; Néraudau 1978; Suder 1995: especially 405–9; Parkin 2003: 266 and 434n133.

100–1 quae, si prodierit . . . esse dicturum: C.'s blatant attempt to intimidate this prosecution witness (cf. Schmitz 1985: 36) is somewhat mitigated by Capito's own attempt to intimidate Roscius. For *atque adeo* cf. §29n.; for *planum facere* §54n. The prosecutor was expected to rehearse his witnesses at home so as to avoid inconsistencies and the like (cf. Quint. 5.7.11); but for the prosecutor to have written out the witness's testimony for him, as C. claims Erucius has done (*uolumen illud quod . . . Erucium conscripsisse*), was, of course, improper. *illum* is Capito, not the more recently mentioned Erucius; cf. *OLD* s.v. *ille* 6. *intento* is to "hold out towards" (in a threatening manner; the verb is often used of weapons): *OLD* s.v. 1.

101 o praeclarum testem . . . iusiurandum accommodetis!: for similar mockery of prospective witnesses cf. *Cael.* 63 '*in balneis delituerunt.' testes egregios! 'dein temere prosiluerunt.' homines temperantes!* For *honestus* cf. §7n.; for the jurors' oath §8n.; for the prosecution's attempt to instrumentalize the jurors cf. §61n.

profecto non tam perspicue . . . auaritia et audacia: for the claim of perspicuity cf. §98n. **ipsos** "the men themselves" as opposed to their *maleficia*; cf. *OLD* s.v. *ipse* 5. C. often connects *cupiditas* with blindness; cf. *Inv.* 1.2, *Quinct.* 83, *Sul.* 91, *Dom.* 60, *Pis.* 58; in Seneca *caeca* is virtually its standing epithet. **cupiditas et auaritia et audacia:** for a similar unholy trinity cf. §12 *cupiditatem et scelus et audaciam* and for *cupiditas* §8 (*quibus nihil satis est*) with n. C. claims a genetic relation between the latter two at §75.

102 alter ex ipsa caede . . . ante omnium oculos poneret: the asyndeton is explicative of the preceding *nisi ipsos caecos redderet . . . audacia*; cf. H–S 830. The assumption once again is that Magnus was at the scene of the murder and gave instructions for Glaucia's journey; cf. §98 with n. *ipse* is sometimes used, as here, to define circumstances in a narrative ("out of the very midst of the slaughter"): *TLL* s.v. 334.45–6. *uolucer* (literally, "able to fly") is often used metaphorically as "rapid, swift": *OLD* s.v. 1 and 2b. C.'s claim that Magnus and Capito are *socii* is clear, but when was the *societas* formed? For C.'s self-contradiction here cf. §96n. Capito and Magnus are clearly depicted as senior and junior partners respectively at §17 (similarly §119); hence A. Klotz's *administrum* ("helper, assistant") for transmitted *ad magistrum* will hardly be right; likewise Eberhard's restoration of the corrective *atque adeo* (§29n.) seems wrong, the designation *socius* requiring no correction; better simply to assume, with Havet, that *ad* has been carelessly repeated, the scribe's eye having skipped from *socium* back to *Ameriam*. **si dissimulare omnes cuperent . . . pertineret:** such a conspiracy of silence among "all" seems most unlikely, but C., apparently unable to produce any witnesses of his own, is driven to this assumption; even the *decem primi* of Ameria will testify only if compelled by the prosecutor (§110). **ut . . . ipse apertum suum scelus . . . poneret:** this is represented, in line with previous criticisms of his *os* (§87) and *audacia* and *impudentia* (§95), as Magnus' perverse purpose, frustrating all attempts at concealment; *ipse* contrasts with *omnes*, singling him out from the mass; cf. *TLL* s.v. 335.37. For *suum scelus* cf. §97n. For *ante oculos* cf. §13n.

   alter, si dis . . . uindicandum sit: for Capito's threatened testimony cf. §§100–1. *si dis placet* signals a shocking or unexpected fact: "if you please!" or "would you believe it?": *OLD* s.v. *placeo* 4d. For *uero* calling attention to a critical point cf. Kroon 1995: 319–25. Capito sees the proceedings as a test of his credibility (*utrum . . . credendum* [sc. *necne*]); hence he has fortified himself with the *uolumen* prepared by Erucius (§101); C. dismisses that view and speaks once again as if Capito were on trial and he himself the prosecutor; cf. §12 *petimus . . . ut quam acerrime maleficia uindicetis.*

102–3 itaque more maiorum . . . non crederetur: *comparo* "to provide" (cf. §28n.) can be used of laws, customs and the like; cf. *OLD* s.v. 7. For *amplus* of persons cf. §83n. The reference is to the younger Africanus, i.e. P. Cornelius Scipio Aemilianus, taken as a model of probity; on him cf. Astin 1967. The supposition is purely hypothetical, as the subjunctives (*ageretur . . . diceret*) indicate. The threefold division of the world into Europe, Asia and Africa (or Libya) established by Hecataeus of Miletus (*c.* 500 BC) continues to dominate geographical thinking throughout antiquity; cf. e.g. the epigrams at *AL* 396–9 S.B. associating Pompey's triumphs and his own death or that of one of his sons with each of the three continents. *illud* refers to the following counterfactual supposition; cf. *OLD* s.v. *ille* 13. For the legal position cf. Greenidge 1901: 482 and n5.

103 uidete nunc . . . de cuius morte quaeritur: the present is, typically, represented as a decline from the standards set by the *maiores*, conceived as at least two generations remote; cf. Roloff 1938: 131; on §§50 and 69. **sector . . . et sicarius:** the assonance reinforces the identification; cf. §151 *sectores ac sicarii*; §152 *ex altera parte sectorem*, *inimicum*, *sicarium*, as well as the pun on *sector* at §80. **illorum ipsorum bonorum de quibus agitur emptor:** in fact, the trial is about murder, not about property issues, and the status of the property will not have been altered by Roscius' acquittal; cf. Harris 1971: 265 and 274; the point is given prominence because it is easy to show that Capito was a *bonorum . . . possessor*, much less clear that he was connected with the murder. *curo* is "undertake, see to," often, as here, with the acc. + gerundive: *OLD* s.v. 6b; for a different construction cf. §33n.

104 Quid? tu, uir optime, . . . res permagna agitur: C. now turns back to Magnus; for the ironic *uir optime* cf. §23n. For *ecquis* cf. §92n. *ausculto* "listen to" is used only here in C.'s speeches; predominantly attested in comedy, it has a colloquial coloring and is continued by It. *ascoltare*; cf. *OLD* s.v. 1a; Hofmann 2003: 281; von Albrecht, *RE* Suppl. 13 1303.9–11. For the *per-* compound cf. §20n.

multa scelerate . . . de accusatoris subsellio surgit: the anaphora of *multa* is for contrast with *unum*. For *audacter* vs. *audaciter* cf. §31n. C. assumes that Erucius, as a professional (cf. on §§49, 54 and 58), will have avoided this elementary error. **istic** "over there," i.e. on the prosecution side; C. thus concludes his treatment of Magnus with the point with which he began it (§84 *istic sedes*). Since the prosecution speaks before the defense and Magnus has not spoken, he is, if a member of the prosecution team (cf. §58n.), an *accusator mutus*. If he is a witness, his credibility is compromised by his association with the prosecution; cf. e.g. Hortensius' complaint that the witness Artemo of Centuripae was in league with the prosecution (*Ver.* 2.2.156); cf. on §§102–3.

huc accedit quod . . . facere uideamini?: the second reason (*huc accedit*) why Magnus' seating was stupid. For *tamen* cf. §8n. For Magnus' making

a display instead of concealing cf. §102; for the *cupiditas* of the opposing side
cf. §101n. *nunc*, as often, signals the return to reality following a counterfactual
proposition; cf. *OLD* s.v. 11a. *ea dedita opera a nobis* is abl. abs.: "though that
task [i.e. the defense] was provided by us." For Magnus' self-incrimination
cf. §102 (*ut . . . poneret*); similarly, Erucius is said to have partially accused his
mandants (§80).

105 Age nunc illa uideamus . . . Chrysogono nuntiatur: for *age* cf.
§48n.; similar transitions at §§95 and 108. For Sulla's camp at Volaterrae
and the time claimed for the news to arrive there cf. §20n. As Kinsey 1980:
178 remarks, "it was in Cicero's interest to stress the speed with which the
news was taken to Volaterrae since it gave the appearance of premeditation";
similarly Berger 1978: 37. C. cannot have known who was the first recipient
of the news; that it was Chrysogonus is inferred from his purchase of the
property; the supposition also fits with C.'s second picture of the *societas*; cf.
§96n.

  quaeritur etiamnunc . . . eundem qui Ameriam?: i.e. Magnus (cf.
§98), but the point is, *pace* C., not obvious; Sulla must have had a regular
messenger service between Volaterrae and other parts of Italy. In §20 the pl.
verb *demonstrant* is left without subject, but the conclusion *societas coitur* suggests
that Magnus and Capito are meant, i.e. that they themselves brought word
to Volaterrae. For C.'s claims of perspicuity cf. §18n.

  curat Chrysogonus . . . omnino numquam uiderat?: again action
is attributed to Chrysogonus based on his later purchase; cf. the n. before
last; for *curo ut* cf. §33n. For adverbial *qui* cf. §53n. At §133 C. claims that
Chrysogonus plundered *multae splendidaeque familiae*; most or all of the owners
will have been unknown to him personally. He may have had a considerable
network of informants; his interest in the farms of Sex. Roscius suggests
some local knowledge but not necessarily contact with the T. Roscii. For an
emphatic negation preceded by *omnino* cf. §92n.

105–6 soletis, cum aliquid . . . me ponere hoc putetis: the fellow-
townsman or neighbor (*municipem aut uicinum*) can supply the local knowledge
Chrysogonus lacks. But this line of approach will not lead him specifically to
the T. Roscii, and so C. breaks it off and takes the argument in a different
direction. *prodo*, as often, is "betray": *OLD* s.v. 7. For *hic* = "in this context" cf.
Berry on *Sul.* 50.6. The transmitted *suspicionem hoc putetis* is clearly impossible.
The best solution so far proposed is Sydow's *suspicione me ponere hoc putetis*,
whereby -*m* would be the remnant of *me* and *ponere* would have been omitted
by haplography; for *pono* "state, specify" cf. *OLD* s.v. 18.

106 non enim ego . . . et clientelam contulerunt': certainly Chrysogonus gathered a considerable entourage (cf. §135); but C. lumps Magnus
and Capito together here, implausibly. A prior *amicitia* between Chrysogonus
and Capito is unlikely in view of their contact during the embassy of the *decem
primi*; see on §110; Capito's lack of activity at Rome also weighs against the
possibility (cf. §100n.). Magnus, on the other hand, was frequently at Rome
(§§18, 94) and so is more likely to have been in contact with Chrysogonus
or his agents. A possible preexisting link between Magnus and Chrysogonus
puts the murder in a different light; cf. the Introduction sec. 5. On the heritability of patron-client relations cf. §15n. The disordered 80s must have
been a time of many realignments of such relations, as claimed by C. in this
passage; cf. Badian (1958) 250–1; but one wonders whether he is painting an
accurate or merely a plausible picture; Stroh 1975: 58n14 is skeptical.

107 haec possum omnia . . . accessisse impulso suo: for *coniectura
nihil opus est* cf. §96 *eo rem iam adducam ut nihil diuinatione opus sit*; for the semantic
development of *coniectura* cf. §62n.; for *certo scio* cf. §21. Here C. seeks to shore
up his construction of a *societas* among Magnus, Capito, and Chrysogonus
prior to the purchase of the farms (§20), but C.'s claim is suspect: if the T.
Roscii pointed Chrysogonus to Sex. Roscius' farms in the first place, why did
Capito only manage to extract a share under the pressure of the embassy of
the *decem primi* (§110)?

si eum qui . . . qui indicarit?: *indiciua* is a substantivized fem. adj., a
legal term meaning "reward for information given"; cf. *OLD* s.v.; translate:
"he who accepted a share as a finder's fee"; on the text cf. Shackleton Bailey
1979: 238–9.

qui sunt igitur . . . partem praedae tulerunt?: C.'s answer *duo
Roscii* conceals an important difference (as does his narrative of the dispossession at §23): Capito has apparently been given outright the *tres nobilissimos fundos* of §99 (where *possidere* is used; similarly §17), whereas Magnus is
merely acting as Chrysogonus' agent (§23 *procurator Chrysogoni*). There may
have been a difference of motive corresponding to this different treatment.
The upgrading of Magnus continues in §108, where it is claimed *quae reliqua sunt iste . . . omnia cum Chrysogono communiter possidet*; but it is most unlikely
that Chrysogonus gave him joint title to the properties rather than merely
employing him as his agent. The reason is that Magnus, as the one who
was in Rome at the time, can more plausibly be linked to the murder than
Capito; hence the emphasis on him as C. claims that rewards were given
for services *in ista pugna* (§108). Kinsey 1980: 177 pertinently asks "why should
Chrysogonus have rewarded Magnus and Capito at all for a murder he is

supposed to have had no hand in . . . ?" **numquisnam praeterea?** "surely no one besides?", a colloquialism; cf. *Agr.* 1.11; *Phil.* 6.12; *De orat.* 2.13; *Fam.* 11.27.1; von Albrecht, *RE* Suppl. XIII 1302. 56–8; *OLD* s.v. *num* and *quis²*. For the verbal play *obtulerint . . . tulerunt* cf. Holst 1925: 71.

108 Age nunc ex ipsius . . . tantis praemiis donabantur?: for the transitional formula *age nunc* cf. §105n. For the murder of Sex. Roscius sen. as a *pugna* cf. §17; for *operae pretium* cf. §59n. But if he gave rewards for the murder, Chrysogonus was surely party to the planning of the murder in the first place; if the murder had taken place without his involvement (as C. claims at §20), he could have arranged for the sale of the property at auction without rewarding the murderers; see previous n.

    si nihil aliud fecerunt . . . honoris aliquid haberi?: *defero* appears here in the general sense "report" (*OLD* s.v. 8), not the legal sense (cf. §8n.); the "matter" (*rem*) will, of course, be the death of Roscius sen. and his possession of the farms. For C.'s fondness for such *per-* compounds as *perliberaliter* cf. §20n. *honor* here is a concrete mark of honor, i.e. a reward or tip; cf. *OLD* s.v. *honor* 2c.

    cur tria praedia . . . re cognita concessisse?: *tantae pecuniae* "of such value"; for *pecunia* cf. §6n.; for the gen. of quality cf. §17n. *statim* is contradicted by §110 (*cum illo partem suam depecisci*), from which it is clear that Chrysogonus yielded the three farms to Capito only under the pressure of the embassy of the *decem primi*, not immediately upon purchase of the thirteen, as C. claims here; for Capito's premature demonization cf. also §25n. The claim that Magnus was joint owner with Chrysogonus of the other ten is also contradicted by other indications in the speech; cf. §107n. Finally, there would have been no reason for Chrysogonus to reward the murderers after the fact; see the n. before last. **manubias:** the imagery of spoils continues from §8 (*ut spoliis ex hoc iudicio ornati auctique discedant*), but *manubiae* are specifically "a general's share of booty" (*OLD* s.v. 1), which he could distribute at his discretion to his troops; cf. Bona 1960; Shatzman 1972; Churchill 1999; Chrysogonus is thus figured as a general and Capito and Magnus as under his command.

109 Venit in decem primis . . . ex ipsa legatione cognoscite: for the embassy of the *decem primi* sent to Sulla by decree of the *decuriones* of Ameria cf. §25. Capito's inclusion among the legates, mentioned already at §26, shows that he was a man of standing in the community and also that no one in Ameria connected him with the murder. His special influence over the other ambassadors (§26 *cumque id ita futurum T. Roscius Capito . . . appromitteret,* *crediderunt*) suggests that he was the sole representative of the family of the deceased and perhaps indeed the *spiritus mouens* behind the embassy. If so, and if property issues were at the heart of his enmity with Roscius sen. (cf. §§17 and 19), as was the case with Magnus (§87), he may have seen the embassy as the only means of asserting his rights. C.'s following criticism of his performance on the embassy is designed both to undermine his credibility as a witness (cf. §§100–1) and to make his connection with the murder plausible (*probabile ex uita*).

nisi intellexeritis . . . eum iudicatote: C. begins the attack by setting himself a characteristically heavy burden of proof; cf. §8 with n. For the relative clause with consecutive force (*quod = ut id*) cf. §5n. *uir optimus* is a conventional formula of commendation; cf. §104. For *iudicatote* cf. §18n.

110   impedimento est . . . Chrysogono enuntiat: *impedimento est*: sc. *Capito*. But this is only likely to have been the case after he struck a deal with Chrysogonus; before that point he presumably had as much interest as the other delegates in appealing to Sulla over Chrysogonus' head. The real impediment will have been Chrysogonus himself; see the next n. Capito was evidently allowed (as *de facto* head of the embassy? cf. the n. before last) to meet privately with Chrysogonus to explain the purpose of the mission; there was not necessarily any treachery in his so doing.

monet ut prouideat . . . capitis periculum aditurum: Chrysogonus did not need these supposed warnings. He knew presumably better than anyone the danger of an open debate in front of Sulla, who, whatever his involvement may have been, could always repudiate the seizure and sale of the property as the unauthorized work of his freedman; nor did Chrysogonus need to be reminded what was at stake in the repeal of the sale. By referring to his own danger of criminal prosecution (*sese capitis periculum aditurum*) Capito would be placing himself in Chrysogonus' power, not gaining leverage. C. has framed this fictive conversation so as to give Capito the initiative; but the construction is implausible, the initiative much more likely to have lain with Chrysogonus.

illum acuere . . . aditus ad Sullam intercludere: at this point C. adds vividness by changing from finite verbs to historical infinitives for the series of unfolding actions; for the effect cf. von Albrecht 1989: 71–2. *acuo* (literally "sharpen") is often used metaphorically for "rouse, incite": *OLD* s.v. 3; for the content see the previous two notes. *hi* are the other delegates, so referred to as both associated with Capito and present in Volaterrae (cf. on §§1 and 6), *ille* Chrysogonus. For *consilium inire* cf. §96n. *depeciscor* is "bargain for": *OLD* s.v. b; it describes Capito's action again at §115. What was Capito's bargaining chip? Hardly his strategy for handling the other ambassadors. Perhaps he had a claim on three of the farms dating back before the elder Roscius' death (and the source of enmity between the two); by ceding the three farms, Chrysogonus would have satisfied his claim and won his cooperation in frustrating the embassy. Or did Capito have a still more potent card to play in the form of knowledge of Chrysogonus' rôle in arranging the murder (through Magnus)?

postremo isto hortatore . . . spem falsam domum rettulerunt: *postremo* "in the end" hints at a lengthy process of chicanery. In spite the leading rôle assigned to Capito here (*isto hortatore, auctore, intercessore*), it was Chrysogonus who could block access to Sulla; Capito's rôle was more probably that of fobbing off the delegates with assurances, as narrated at §26. For the play on *fides/perfidia* cf. §10n. While it is true that only the prosecutor could compel the testimony of witnesses (cf. Mommsen 1899: 403–5; Greenidge 1901: 485–6), friendly witnesses were free to offer their testimony to the defense. Stroh 1975: 60 suspects that the other legates would testify that Capito's cooperation was bought by Chrysogonus during the course of the embassy and that would be fatal to C.'s picture of Capito as mastermind of the murder.

111 in priuatis rebus . . . admisisse dedecus existimabant: this will prove to be an *a fortiori* argument from a private to a public charge (§113). *mandatum* is "a consensual contract by which a person assumed the duty to conclude a legal transaction or to perform a service gratuitously in the interest of the mandator or of a third person" (Berger s.v.). This is the fourth invocation of the *maiores* in this speech; cf. §§50, 69–70, and 100, with notes. C. evidently infers the severity of the *maiores* from the fact that Roman law allowed a *bona fide* action against the person charged with the mandate with *infamia* as the penalty (ibid. and s.v. *bona fides*).

itaque mandati constitutum est . . . disturbat uitae soci-etatem: *itaque* is used, unusually, in conjunction with the following *propterea quod*; cf. *Balb.* 19 *itaque . . . idcirco*; in general *TLL* s.v. 530.17. Certainly *furtum* was regarded as discreditable (though the thief was not subject to *infamia* but to other penalties; cf. Berger s.v. *furtum*); C. is at pains to create a conceptual link between *furtum* and betrayal of a *mandatum*. **quibus in rebus ipsi interesse non possumus** "in matters in which we cannot be personally involved": *OLD* s.v. *ipse* 4. **uicaria . . . supponitur** "is put in place of," whereby the predicative *uicarius* is pleonastic; cf. *OLD* s.vv. *uicarius* 1 and *suppono* 6; *Ver.* 2.3.120; ibid. 2.4.81 *succedam ego uicarius tuo muneri.* **commune praesidium** would be vague if it were not clarified by the sequel; cf. *Ver.*

2.1.153 *communi praesidio talis improbitas tamquam aliquod incendium restinguendum est*. **quantum in ipso est** "as far as in him lies": *ipse* substitutes for the reflexive pronoun and adds emphasis; cf. *OLD* s.v. 10b. The *uitae societas*, varied by *hominum societas* and the like, is a major criterion of action in *Off*. (cf. e.g. 1.12, 15, and 45); its preservation is sought (cf. 1.15 and 17), its disruption to be avoided (3.22 and 28).

non enim possumus . . . mutuis officiis gubernetur: this is the kind of thinking that led to the development of specialized professions, a marked feature of the ancient world from Hellenistic times onward; cf. Schneider 1967–9: II 70–1. At the same time the "service economy" was relatively undeveloped so that such instrumental friendships remained a feature of life throughout antiquity; cf. *Off*. 1.56 with Dyck's n.

112 quid recipis mandatum . . . officis et obstas?: with the second-person address C. adopts the diatribe-style he often uses to lend vividness to his arguments; cf. Dyck 1998: 231 and n54. *recipio* is to "take upon oneself, undertake": *OLD* s.v. 10. As usual, the future participle + *esse* expresses purpose; cf. Roby §1494; G–L §247; the two possible forms of malfeasance are repeated from §111. The *ob-* prefix (or its assimilated version) dominates the second sentence, first in a seemingly helpful gesture (*te offers*) but then with the idea of blockage, including the pun *officio . . . officis*.

recede de medio . . . ipsi leues sunt: (*d*)*e medio* is "from the scene": *OLD* s.v. *medium* 3b; for *per* + acc. of person cf. §62n. *suscipis onus . . . posse* evidently describes a situation in which withdrawal would be appropriate; hence Kayser's *non posse* is adopted (for transmitted *posse*). For taking on an *onus offici* and the difficulties entailed cf. §10 *plus oneris sustuli quam ferre me posse intellego* etc. The terms *grauis* and *leuis* are, as often, opposed here; either H. J. Müller's change of transmitted *graue* to *leue* (here adopted) or Dobree's of *minime* to *maxime* seems required; in either case those who possess *grauitas* will take such obligations very seriously indeed.

ergo idcirco turpis . . . nisi credidisset: this failing is disgraceful because if it is proven *infamia* is the consequence; cf. §111n. For *fides* as *sancta* cf. Catul. 76.3. For the sense of *perditus* cf. §41n.; on the need for caution in dissolving friendship cf. *Off*. 1.120.

113 itane est? . . . inter uiuos numerabitur?: *in minimis rebus . . . condemnetur necesse est* rephrases *in priuatis rebus . . . dedecus existimabant* (§111) and provides an *a fortiori* contrast to the present case through a description of what is at stake; see *ad loc*. For the elder Roscius' reputation being at issue cf. §25n.
commendatae . . . atque concreditae: an alliterative pair dropped in

C.'s later speeches; see above p. 14n.46. After *mortuum* one expects a reference to the consequences for the living Sex. Roscius to balance *ignominia
mortuum*, just as the stakes for the living and dead are contrasted in the previous clause; either *egestate uiuum* (Jannoctius) or *inopia uiuum* (Havet), here
adopted, would serve. For *honestus* cf. §7n.; for *atque adeo* §29n.; *inter uiuos*
implies that Capito's behavior on the embassy should be a capital offense;
if he had his way C. would have enacted severer penalties in this and other
matters; cf. e.g. *Leg.* 2.21 (disobeying an augur to be a capital offense); *Phil.*
13.17 *unum ob hoc factum* [sc. offering Caesar the crown] *dignum illum omni poena
putarem.*

in minimis . . . quo iudicio damnabitur?: another contrast for the
sake of *a fortiori* argument, here emphasizing the public dimension of Capito's
allegedly subverted mission and that malicious intent (*perfidia*), not mere
neglegentia, was at the root of it. For the *crimen mandati* and the penalty for
violation cf. §111n. Though first attested in C. (*Inv.* 2.66 and 161), *caerimonia*
("holiness") seems likely to be an old word; its origin remains obscure, an
Etruscan source being sometimes claimed; cf. Roloff 1953; the use of this
word and of the quasi-synonymous *polluo* and *macula afficio* (cf. §66n.) elevate
Capito's offense into the religious sphere; the rhetorical question hints that
no human court or penalty could provide sufficient justice.

114 si hanc ei rem . . . honestatem omnem amitteret?: the demonstrative is host for another pronoun and split from its referent, a common
pattern; cf. examples in Adams 1994b: 134 and 144. C. puts forward a thought-
experiment: suppose his client had privately commissioned Capito to nego-
tiate with Chrysogonus . . . *transigo* is often used in business contexts with
reference to "settling matters": *OLD* s.v. 3b; similarly *decido* is to "reach a settlement, come to terms": ibid. s.v. 6a. **inque eam rem:** C. seldom attaches
-que to a monosyllabic preposition unless it is followed, as here, by a demonstrative; similarly e.g. *Phil.* 1.10 *exque eo. interponere fidem* is to "pledge one's
word": *OLD* s.v. *interpono* 6b. **illeque:** C. rarely adds *-que* to a final open
-e; cf. Powell on *Sen.* 16 (p. 138). For *recipio* cf. §112n.; for the force of *nonne*
§38n. *tantulum* "ever so little": the adj. of size, when diminutivized, emphasizes the smallness (*paululum* corresponds in §115); cf. Hanssen 1951: 18, 52–3,
55, 151–2. An *arbiter* was either appointed by agreement of the two parties
(*ex compromisso*) or assigned (*datus*) by a judge if the case required specialized
knowledge; cf. Berger s.vv. *arbiter, arbiter datus, arbiter ex compromisso*; M. Wlas-
sak, *RE* II 1.408.34. **honestatem omnem amitteret:** *honestas* is "title to
respect, honorable status" (cf. *OLD* s.v. 1), i.e. he would suffer *infamia* with
entailed disabilities; cf. Berger s.v.

115 nunc non hanc ... fidem suam fecit: for *nunc* signalling a return to reality cf. §104n. *ipse* is emphatic: "Sex. Roscius himself," not just his appurtenances; cf. §101n. *a decurionibus publice* contrasts with the hypothetical act of Sex. Roscius *priuatim* (§114). Such is the fondness of colloquial Latin for diminutives that the word for small itself can be diminutivized: *paululum nescioquid* "a trifle": *OLD* s.v. *paululus* 1b; the adj. occurs only here in C.'s speeches. For *ipse* heading an emphatic contrast cf. §23. **tria praedia sibi depectus est:** cf. §110 *cum illo partem suam depecisci* with n. **tantidem quanti** "just as much value as," i.e. as little as; for the gen. with verbs of rating cf. §46n.

116 Videte iam porro ... sese non contaminarit: transitional formula; the topic proves to be, however, not really "other matters" (*cetera*) but rather the same action considered from another point of view, *viz.* as a betrayal of the other ambassadors. For *fingo* cf. §26n. At §§92 and 94 C. argued that Magnus had better opportunity than his client to undertake the crime (*maleficium suscipere*), i.e. to murder Roscius sen.; but now he makes a much broader claim for Capito's involvement in *maleficia*. *contamino* varies *polluo* (cf. §113) as a term for polluting morally; cf. *OLD* s.v. 5; for the generic subj. cf. §1n.

in rebus minoribus ... rem communicauit: *in rebus minoribus* prepares the listener/reader for another *a fortiori* argument. **socium fallere turpissimum est:** a *bonae fidei actio* was available for violation of *societas*; conviction resulted in *infamia*; cf. Watson 1967: 140–1. With adjs. or advs. expressing similarity *atque* = "as": *OLD* s.v. 13b. Violation of a *mandatum* was likewise punished with *infamia*; cf. §111n. For *neque iniuria* cf. §17n. For *auxilium adiungere* cf. *Cat.* 3.12 (Lentulus to Catiline) *cura ut omnium tibi auxilia adiungas, etiam infimorum.* **qui cum altero rem communicauit** is a paraphrase for *socius*; cf. *Ver.* 2.3.50; §20n.

ad cuius igitur fidem ... cui se commiserit?: for *ad* (or *in*) *alicuius fidem confugere* ("take refuge in someone's protection") cf. *Quinct.* 10; *Off.* 1.35 with Dyck's n. **per ... fidem** "by (misplaced) trust in, reliance on" (+ gen.); cf. *OLD* s.v. *per* 14b.

atque ea sunt ... praecauentur: C. lays down a legal principle, evidently inferred from existing Roman legislation, about the relation of crime and punishment; cf. §69 *init.* Since Plautus *praecaueo* varies *caueo* in the sense "be on one's guard": *OLD* s.vv.

tecti esse ... qui possumus?: C. opposes the concepts *tectus* and *apertus*, the former used of persons to mean "guarded, secretive": *OLD* s.v. 2b. *intimus* "inmost" comes to be used of one's "closest" friends; the masc. appears here as a substantive for the first time; cf. *TLL* s.v. *interior, intimus* 2212.53–5. For the adv. *qui* cf. §53n.

   quem etiam si . . . haberi oportere: for *ius offici* cf. *Flac.* 57 *ut . . . iura omnia offici humanitatisque violarent.* Once again current law at Rome is the achievement of the *maiores*; cf. §§69–71, 111. Status among the *uiri boni* was, of course, removed by *infamia*, the punishment for breach of *societas*; see above.

117 at uero T. Roscius . . . et perfidia fefellit: *at uero* provides contrast and focus (cf. §49n.). The conclusion of the *a fortiori* argument: Capito's deception was not practiced on a single individual in a private matter but upon nine men on a public mission. **posse ferri uidetur:** cf. §§34 and 49. For *honestissimus* cf. §16n. The series *munus, officium, mandatum* proceeds from general to specific; for the former two cf. Dyck on *Off.* p. 6n13. *legationis*, transmitted after *muneris*, was rightly deleted as a gloss by Fleckeisen. **induxit . . . fefellit:** by the law of increasing members we find units of 3, 3, 4, 8, and 16 syllables each. The combination *offici socius*, occurs twice in our passage but nowhere else in C.

   qui de eius scelere . . . orationi uanae crediderunt: *non debuerunt*: §116 established the obligation to trust a partner (*quem etiam si metuimus, ius offici laedimus*). *malitia* is "wickedness" in a general sense: *OLD* s.v. 1. **orationi uanae** "false words": *OLD* s.v. *uanus* 3. Details were supplied at §26: *cum ille* [sc. Chrysogonus] *confirmaret sese nomen Sex. Rosci de tabulis exempturum . . . cumque id ita futurum T. Roscius Capito . . . appromitteret, crediderunt.*

   itaque nunc illi . . . prouidique fuisse: if their reputations had really suffered so much, would they not have been sufficiently indignant to testify for the defense in this case? Cf. §110 n. C. could, however, argue that they were deterred by Chrysogonus' influence; cf. *Font.* 3 *si qua gratia testes deterrentur . . .*

   iste, qui initio . . . hoc est praemiis sceleris, ornatus: the adversative asyndeton provides for emphatic contrast; cf. §6n. C. describes (twice) two stages of Capito's behavior, first as a betrayer of confidences (*proditor*), then as a deserter (*perfuga*). **cum ipsis aduersariis:** *ipse* here is both anaphoric and intensive, calling attention to the irony; cf. on §120. Though *coiit* is weakly attested (σχ), the perfect is required within this narrative (and there is clear evidence for *coiit* but not *coit* as a Ciceronian perfect; cf. *TLL* s.v. *coeo* 1415.25–30); for the combination *societatem coire* cf. §20n. **terret etiam nos ac minatur:** cf. §101 *quod* [sc. *uolumen*] *aiunt illum Sex. Roscio intentasse et minitatum esse* etc. **tribus praediis . . . ornatus:** cf. §8 *ut spoliis ex hoc iudicio ornati . . . discedant.*

   In eiusmodi uita . . . reperietis: with these words C. effects a transition from Capito's alleged betrayal of the embassy to the murder currently on trial (*hoc maleficium de quo iudicium est*). He has already argued that the *probabile ex uita* tells against his client's participation (§§39, 75–9); he will now assess Capito from this angle. For *flagitium* cf. §25n.

118 etenim quaerere ita . . . putatote: another charge to the jurors (cf. §§6–7). *quaero* is to "hold judicial inquiry": *OLD* s.v. 10b. Fourfold anaphora of *multa* with following adv. creates the impression of an overwhelming number of instances, though, apart from his behavior on the embassy, C. has adduced only one crime committed by Capito and that with few specifics (§100). The *ubi . . . ibi* structure facilitates the correlation of general findings with a particular case; cf. examples at *OLD* s.v. *ibi* 3b. For *audacter* cf. §31n., for *scelus* §1n.; for the "future" imperative *putatote* §18n.

    tametsi hoc quidem . . . conuincatur: for *tametsi* adding a correction cf. §3. *hoc* [sc. *scelus*]; for *quidem* following a pronoun for emphasis but not contrast cf. §41n. The correction is prompted by the verb *latere*: the standard description of a crime does not apply; rather, the participles of two verbs compounded with *pro-*, denoting the idea of "bringing out into the open" (*OLD* s.v.), are deployed (*promptum*, *propositum*). The consecutive clause is built on the opposition of Capito's (alleged) past crimes (*illa maleficia*) and the present case (*hoc* [sc. *maleficium*]): our case is so clear that his former crimes can be proven (*OLD* s.v. *conuinco* 4) from it, rather than vice versa, a reversal of the usual *probabile ex uita* argument (cf. §39n.). Anastrophe (postponement) of *de* is common in C.

    quid tandem, quaeso, . . . gemina audacia: for Capito as the *lanista* and Magnus as his *discipulus* cf. §17 with n. For the force of *num* cf. §86n. *hic discipulus* of the scholia (for *is discipulus* of the mss) seems likely in view of Magnus' presence in court (cf. on §§1 and 84). For *tantulum* cf. §114n. The comparison shows pupil and teacher well matched in four respects, three corresponding to Capito's *flagitia* listed above, the fourth, Magnus' characteristic *impudentia* (§95; cf. *os tuum* (§87)), replacing *perfidia*, which describes Capito's behavior on the embassy (§§110, 113, 117).

119 Etenim, quoniam . . . discipuli aequitatem: transition to the next point, the refusal to allow the slaves to testify. The chiastic arrangement *fidem magistri . . . discipuli aequitatem* continues the presentation of Capito and Magnus as a balanced pair. In fact, the real obstacle is not Magnus but Chrysogonus, whose agent he was (just as the real obstacle to the embassy's meeting with Sulla was Chrysogonus, not Capito: §110n.); see §120n. Thus §§119–23 form a transition to the third and last member of the *societas* to be targeted (cf. §35).

dixi iam antea ... T. Rosci, recusasti: for *saepenumero* cf. §67n. The matter was discussed at §§77–8. T. Roscius refers to the *discipulus*, Magnus, who is now the focus. For the implications of *postulo* cf. §6n. **recusasti:** syncopated 2nd person plpf. is found in poets but also in C.; cf. Neue and Wagener 1892–1905: III 500–5.

quaero abs te ... tibi iniqua uidebatur?': the question was already posed at §78 (*cur recusatis?*). C. offers three possible explanations for Magnus' refusal, each destined for refutation; but the truly relevant point is that the owner, Chrysogonus, refuses; see the n. before last. For *indignus qui* followed by a consecutive clause cf. G–L §552 R.2; for the absolute use of *impetro* ("have one's request granted") cf. *OLD* s.v. 1c. *res ipsa*, i.e. the demand, *res* typically taking its color from the context.

postulabant homines nobilissimi ... non aequum putaret: the verb is emphatically placed and repeated at the head of the next sentence; it is postponed and changed to passive for variety in the sentence after next; the imperfects suggest the application of pressure over time (cf. *saepenumero* above). For *homines nobiles* in C.'s usage cf. §1n. C. refers to P. Scipio and M. Metellus, who acted as agents for Caecilia Metella in the matter (cf. §77n.); the attitude of the Roman people is inferred from Scipio's election to office. For subj. in the relative clause following *nemo* cf. §24n.

postulabant autem pro homine ... de patris morte quaerere-tur: for the defendant as *miser* cf. §23n. *uel* is of the type "introducing what might be thought an extreme or unlikely possibility": "even, one might go so far as to say" (*OLD* s.v. 5a). C. has already suggested that his client is uninterested in property issues (§7), but here he constructs Roscius as utterly pathetic and servile; for Roscius' humility as related to his characterization as a rustic cf. Vasaly 1993: 166.

120 res porro abs te ... de maleficio confiterere: this refers to C.'s third suggested reason for refusal (*res ipsa tibi iniqua uidebatur*: §119). He wants to convince not Magnus but the jurors that refusal was tantamount to a confession of guilt. For the disjunctive question after *interesse* cf. §47 *nihil intersit utrum hunc ego comicum adulescentem an aliquem ex agro Veiente nominem.*

quae cum ita sint ... recusaris: having disposed of the three possible explanations he had proposed (§119), he puts the question again.

cum occiditur Sex. Roscius ... neque purgo: *ibidem* is the strength-ened local adv.: "on the spot"; cf. §13n. **seruos ipsos:** *ipse* is used to call attention to a major point: *TLL* s.v. 316.3–8. In dealing with Mallius Glaucia (§97), C. professed to be concerned only with the mastermind, not the agent who committed the crime; here he adopts a neutral attitude toward the slaves' possible culpability (*neque arguo neque purgo*); for *purgo* cf. §39n.

quod a uobis . . . uobis futurum sit: from "attack (a fortified position)" *oppugno* goes on to "attack" in a broad sense: *OLD* s.v. **ne in quaestionem dentur:** for torture as the implication cf. §77n. To decline to subject slaves to judicial investigation suggests that they were deemed too valuable to be risked; hence C. speaks of their being *in honore tanto*, a point on which he ironically dilates in the sequel.

'in dominos quaeri . . . dominos esse dicitis: a return to an *altercatio* with the other side; cf. §40n. Tac. *An.* 2.30.3 declares that the prohibition rested on a *senatus consultum*, not simple equity (*iniquum est*); in any case, the principle was well established (*Mil.* 59, *Deiot.* 3, *Part.* 118). C. makes it appear that it is settled that judicial inquiry against a former master is licit, but under the Empire Paulus held the opposite (*Dig.* 38.18.18.6), and it is possible that that opinion goes back to C.'s time; cf. Alexander 2002: 306n33. Another possible argument would have been that the testimony of the prosecutor's slaves (and C. treats Chrysogonus as the *de facto* prosecutor throughout) is without legal force: *Dig.* 48.18.3; Lincke 1890: 197. The transmitted text has had to be altered in three places: *non* (Büchner) for transmitted *ne*; deletion of *enim* (Plasberg) transmitted after *neque*; insertion of *in dominos quaeritur* (Halm).

'cum Chrysogono sunt' . . . . patris familiae rusticani: Chrysogonus is the current owner, and his slaves cannot be subjected to judicial inquiry, which must include torture, against his will: *Dig.* 47.15.34; Lincke 1890: 197. He has plundered not only slaves but also much other property from wealthy opponents of Sulla, as C. details at §133: *tantum scilicet quantum e multis splendidisque familiis in turba et rapinis coaceruari una in domo potuit. puerulus* is the recomposed diminutive of *puer* (cf. the earlier *puellus*); the diminutive reflects Chrysogonus' fondness; cf. Hanssen 1951: 114; for use of *puer* (as opposed to *seruus*) cf. also §59n. **homines paene operarios . . . rusticani:** another application of the country–city dichotomy to mislead. Similar contrast of a lettered ex-slave with another called an *operarius* ("a mere mechanic" tr. Shackleton Bailey) at *Att.* 7.2(125).8. But Roscius sen. clearly had a house with staff in the city and was hardly planning, on the fatal night, to make his way back to his bed in Ameria; his city slaves are unlikely to have fallen below general standards of urban refinement; cf. Alexander 2002: 306n33. For *pater familiae* cf. §43n.

121 non ita est . . . et fidem: a series of denials, highlighted by anaphora of *non*. When negativized *uerisimile* is regularly followed by *ut* + subj., rather than acc. + inf.; cf. Berry on *Sul.* 57.10. *amo* is augmented by the intensive prefix *ad-* to create *adamo* "to come to love or admire greatly"; our passage is its first attestation; cf. *OLD* s.v. 1b; *TLL* s.v. *humanitas* here is "culture": *OLD* s.v. 2; for a different sense cf. §46. *fides* and *diligentia* are often juxtaposed; cf. e.g. §27.

est quiddam quod . . . eminet et apparet: similarly with reference to poverty §86 *tenuitas hominis eiusmodi est ut dissimulari non queat atque eo magis eluceat quo magis occultatur.* The refusal to subject the slaves to judicial inquiry shows that the prosecution did not expect the results to help its case or not enough to warrant the sacrifice; cf. Lincke 1890: 197; it is possible, but not certain, that the results could have benefited the defense, as C. wants to suggest.

122 quid igitur? . . . arbitror omnia conuenire: C. now hastens to dispel the suspicion that Chrysogonus is concealing his own crime (*suum maleficium*); he will instead reassert the claim that the freedman's contribution lay in exerting influence after the fact (cf. §35). For *minime* amounting to a negative in reply to a question cf. *OLD* s.v. 2b. For *conuenio in* + acc. cf. §64n.; similarly *Inv.* 2.16 *non omnes in omnem causam conuenire*; C. alludes to a proverbial expression; cf. Otto 1890: 106.

ego in Chrysogono . . . Rosciorum esse debebit: *quod ad me attinet* emphasizes again (cf. §120) that this is C.'s individual view (while suggesting that another view may be possible). For *in mentem uenire* cf. §58n. *meministis . . . causam* cross-refers to §35. *in crimen cuius* [sc. *causae*]; for *partes* = "rôle, part" cf. §35n. **quicquid malefici . . . esse debebit** spells out more explicitly than he had in §35 what C. understands under *audacia*; for the gen. of the rubric cf. §8n.

nimiam gratiam potentiamque . . . uindicari oportere: for Chrysogonus' *gratia* [sc. with Sulla] cf. §28 with n.; for his *potentia* §6n.; for the sense of *obstare* §35n. **perferre nullo modo posse:** cf. §34 *quia fit a Chrysogono, non est ferendum*; *Phil.* 7.17 *quis huius* [sc. *L. Antoni*] *potentiam poterit sustinere?*; for *nullo modo* cf. §53n. **quoniam potestas . . . uindicari oportere:** for the distinction between *potentia* and *potestas* cf. §35n. The jurors' *potestas* derives, of course, from their constituting the jury in the homicide court; cf. §29 *uestramne, qui summam potestatem habetis hoc tempore, fidem implorem?*; *Mur.* 83 *huiusce rei potestas omnis in uobis sita est.* C. once again speaks in the manner of a prosecutor (cf. §§12 and 102), but only his client's punishment is at issue in this court; a lessening of Chrysogonus' authority (*infirmari*; cf. *OLD* s.v. *infirmo* 3a) is a more accurate description of the effect of an acquittal than his punishment (*uindicari*).

123 ego sic existimo . . . de maleficio suo confiteri: arguments for
and against the reliability of testimony obtained from slaves under torture
(cf. §77n.) were offered by teachers of rhetoric from early times; cf. Arist. *Rhet.*
1376b31–77a7; Quint. 3.5.10 gives *an tormentis credendum?* as a general question
that may arise in a conjectural case. With *qui recuset . . . de maleficio suo confiteri*
C. repeats the second horn of the dilemma of §120 *init. maleficium* continues
to be qualified as *suum* in this general formulation in spite of C.'s denial that
this applies to Chrysogonus (§122).

    Dixi initio, iudices, . . . coniecturaeque committo: C. cross-refers
to §83; once again he emphasizes his moderate handling of matters that
could be pursued at length (cf. §83 *fin. non persequar longius quam salus huius et
mea fides postulabit*). Lambinus' *de unaquaque* is more elegant but not absolutely
necessary since *dico* can be used, even by C., transitively ("speak of, mention");
cf. *OLD* s.v. 7a. *necessario* "of necessity" has been treated as an adv. in Latin
prose since Cato; cf. *OLD* s.v. 1. Once again the colloquial *nullo modo* is the
emphatic negation; cf. §122. For *suspicio* as the prosecutor's guidepost cf. §8n.;
for *coniectura* §62n.

REFVTATIO / ARGVMENTATIO III: CHRYSOGONUS
(124–42)

C. has been careful to separate Chrysogonus from the murder charge proper
and present him merely as an accessory after the fact (§§20, 35 and 122). But
why? If *cui bono?* is a pointer to the murderer of Roscius sen. (§§84–6), then
the major beneficiary, Chrysogonus, should be the prime suspect. It is he,
after all, who now owns ten of the thirteen farms that once belonged to the
deceased (§§6, 17, 99, 108). C. obfuscates this point, never stating in so many
words that Chrysogonus now owns ten of the farms; at §23 he speaks as if
Magnus, though merely the *procurator Chrysogoni*, were the new owner; and
at §108 he says of Magnus *quae reliqua sunt . . . omnia cum Chrysogono communiter
possidet.* He also wants to bring Capito into the picture as early as possible,
claiming that the *societas* among him, Magnus and Chrysogonus was formed
when news of the murder first reached Volaterrae (§20). But, in fact, Capito's
participation in the spoils was not arranged until the embassy of the *decem
primi* (§110 *cum illo partem suam depecisci*). The first beneficiary was Chrysogonus.
The torments Chrysogonus is depicted as suffering and that have led him to
instigate the prosecution (§§6 and 132) fit the man behind the murder, not
a mere beneficiary after the fact. See further Fuhrmann 1997: 56–7. It is by
shielding Chrysogonus from the murder charge itself that C. is able to get
away with this devastating portrait. At the same time he is careful to isolate

his target from the cause of the nobility in the recent civil war generally and Sulla in particular (V and VIIID and F on the following outline).

I   *praemunitio*: this is no attack on the *sectores* in general (124)
II   Chrysogonus' purchase of Sex. Roscius' property (125)
   A   How could it be sold under the law?
      (1)   The law allows for sale of goods of
         (*a*)   The proscribed
         (*b*)   Those killed in enemy fortifications (126)
      (2)   Neither of these applies
   B   Chrysogonus was responsible (127)
      (1)   He pretended that Sex. Roscius was killed among the enemy
      (2)   He hindered Sulla from meeting with the legates from Ameria
   C   1 June was the statutory deadline for proscriptions and sales (128)
      (1)   Sex. Roscius was not killed until some months later
      (2)   Either there was no entry made in the public records or they were corrupted
III   The following will be partly on Roscius' behalf, partly on C.'s own (129)
IV   Questions for Chrysogonus (130)
   A   Why were goods of a citizen sold who was neither proscribed nor killed among the enemy?
   B   Why were they sold after the deadline?
   C   Why were they sold for so low a price?
V   These things were done behind the back of Sulla (131)
VI   This is clear from the following events
   A   The present trial, which Chrysogonus instigated (132)
   B   His hasty removal of Roscius' property (lacuna in the text)
VII   Chrysogonus' lifestyle (133)
   A   His house on the Palatine
   B   His country estate
   C   His collection of Corinthian and Delian vases
   D   His *authepsa*, bought for a vast sum
   E   Embossed silver, coverlets, paintings, statues
   F   Source: the plundering of distinguished families
   G   Large number of slaves equipped with many skills, including musicians whose din fills the neighborhood during his nightly parties (134)
   H   He is seen flitting through the forum with an entourage of *togati* (135)
   I   He despises everybody else

VIII C. has license to criticize
  A After abandoning hope of peaceful resolution, C. supported Sulla's
     cause (136)
  B Resisting the prosecutors in this case will enhance the cause of the
     nobility (138)
  C The ruling class must meet ethical qualifications (139)
  D People should not regard an attack on Chrysogonus as an attack
     on themselves (140)
  E His power should not be allowed to extend to the courtroom (141)
  F He who considers criticism of Chrysogonus criticism of him-
     self . . . (142).

124 Venio nunc . . . laesos sese putent: transition to the third and
final part of the *argumentatio/refutatio* (cf. §35). *ille* "that famous"; cf. §50n.
Chrysogonus is a *nomen aureum* because derived from Gk χρυσός "gold";
moreover, the *nomen* is an *omen*, suggestive of his wealth; cf. Holst 1925: 47–
8; Corbeill 1996: 88n95. *Chrysogoni* transmitted following *aureum* was rightly
deleted as a gloss by Weidner; similarly *Phil.* 12.8 *illud pulcherrimum [Mar-
tium] nomen amittet*, where *Martium* was deleted by Manutius; cf. also Baldo
on *Ver.* 2.4.111. **sub quo . . . tota societas latuit:** a *nomen* can be "a name
used to disguise the true nature of a person or thing" (*OLD* s.v. 15a), and
here the *nomen aureum* begins to look like such a façade. For the construction *nomen . . . sub quo nomine* cf. §8n.; for the *societas* §20n. For the prosecution's expectation that the *societas* would remain hidden and Chrysogonus
go unmentioned by C. cf. §60. **neque quomodo dicam . . . possum:** at
§29 C. faced the general dilemma of the defense (*quid primum querar* etc.),
whereas here it is the specific problem of dealing with Chrysogonus. **si
enim taceo . . . relinquo:** he would largely have to abandon the *cui bono?*
argument (§§84–6), but, more than that, he would be unable to canalize the
jurors' anger and resentment over the proscriptions at such a convenient
target (§§133–5). **id quod ad me nihil attinet:** C. is evidently unafraid
of offending Chrysogonus; it is wider implications that could be worrisome.
Detaching Chrysogonus from these "others" will be C.'s project in §§140
and 142. Stephanus' *laesos sese putent* effects C.'s second favorite clausula (see
Appendix) and so deserves preference over the unrhythmical *laesos se esse
putent*.
    tametsi ita se res . . . singularis est: for the term *sector* cf. §80n.; for
profecto §62n. **nihil magnopere** "nothing particularly, nothing very much";
cf. *OLD* s.v. *magnopere* 3; Livy 42.26.1 *nihil magnopere, quod memorari attineat, rei
publicae eo anno consules gesserant*; similarly with adv. *nihil* ibid. 3.65.2 and 37.60.5.
There is a tension between C.'s emphasis on the uniqueness of the case here

and the attempt to establish wider implications at §§7 (*periculum quod in omnes intenditur*) and 150–4; and his warning against a new set of proscriptions (§153) is indeed directed *in communem causam sectorum*, contrary to his claim in our passage.

125 bonorum Sex. Rosci emptor est Chrysogonus: the point was first mentioned as Chrysogonus' assertion (§6 *bona patris huiusce Sex. Rosci . . . sese dicit emisse . . . Chrysogonus*) but here is restated dogmatically; the problems emerge in the sequel. For the emphatic final placement of the proper name cf. §21n.

   primum hoc uideamus . . . uenire qui potuerunt?: C. begins his discussion of the sale by clearing away a possible misunderstanding: he is not going to claim that it is outrageous (*indignum*) for Roscius in particular to have been targeted; his problem is whether the action is according to the law, provisions of which he quotes in the next section. For *libere dicere* cf. §3n.; for *potissimum* §1n. **ista ipsa lege:** for *ipse* used, as here, of the measure by which a thing is judged (and which is exceeded) cf. *TLL* 348.56–7 and 73–5. C. is vague about which law is actually in question (*siue Valeria est siue Cornelia*); similar perhaps is his reluctance to appear too learned in literary matters at §46. In addition, C.'s hesitancy is explicable if the proscriptions actually began before the passage of the *lex Valeria* by which in 82 Sulla was created dictator *legibus scribendis et rei publicae constituendae* (Rotondi 1912: 348–9) but it included a clause ratifying his previous *acta* (App. *BC* 1.97; cf. Mommsen 1887–8: II 736 and n5) and there was also a *lex Cornelia* (quoted below) regulating the scope and legal consequences of the proscriptions (Rotondi 1912: 349; *RS* §49). Butler (2002) 17 thinks that the relevant law was unavailable for consultation, but C. does not raise that claim, and *leges* were deposited in the *aerarium*, albeit not easy to consult; cf. Culham (1989); cf. also Hinard and Benferhat *ad loc.* **uenire:** *uēnire*, not *uĕnire*.

126 scriptum enim ita . . . Romae occisus est: citing relevant provisions (= *RS* §49), C. is at pains to establish that Roscius sen. belonged to neither category of persons whose goods were to be sold according to the law. He offers a simple denial that he was proscribed (for the possible basis see §128n.). **in aduersariorum praesidiis:** *aduersarius* is not a legal term (cf. *OLD* s.v.); cf. *Phil.* 12.17 *ego semper illum appellaui hostem, cum alii aduersarium*; it was perhaps chosen in lieu of *hostis* since the senate had declined to declare Sulla's enemies *hostes*; cf. §153 with Hinard 1985a: 108–9. As proof that he was not "in enemy fortifications" the circumstances of his death are now reported for the fourth time (cf. §§18, 97, 98), each report having a different purpose.

One can imagine C. repeating the information here with his lips curled into a sardonic smile. Clark rightly supplied *omnes* as subject of *recesserunt*; it can easily have dropped out after *armis*. **in summo otio:** *summus* denotes the maximum degree of all manner of things; cf. *OLD* s.v. 8; the combination recurs in the speeches at *Ver.* 2.1.63 and 5.8; *Balb.* 15.

si lege . . . qua lege uenierint quaero: C. will not impugn the quality of the law if the goods can be shown to have been sold *lege*; for *sin* cf. §8n. *mos* is the appropriate alternative to *ius* or *lex* as a justification here (for *ius*, *mos* and *lex* as the relevant criteria cf. §143); hence the adoption of Ernesti's *quo more* for transmitted *quo modo*.

127 In quem hoc dicam . . . omni tempore purgauit: for C.'s care in clearing Sulla of any involvement in wrongdoing cf. §§6, 21–2, 91 and 130–1; for *purgo* cf. §39n.

ego haec omnia . . . passus non sit: for a form of *hic* + substantive followed by an epexegetic *ut*-clause cf. *OLD* s.v. *ut* 39 ("namely that," "that"); the past sequence follows *fecisse*; cf. G–L §518. *ut ementiretur* and *ut malum ciuem Roscium fuisse fingeret* both evidently refer to the same act, an example of the *iuuenilis abundantia* of this speech (cf. Quint. 12.1.20); Pluygers, however, wanted to delete the former phrase. Chrysogonus need only have claimed that Roscius was a "bad citizen" (i.e. an opponent of Sulla) or that he had died "in enemy fortifications" to justify the sale of his goods, not both. From §26 it appears that the deception of the Amerian delegates was the joint work of Capito and Chrysogonus; just as, when denouncing Capito (§117), C. leaves Chrysogonus' rôle unmentioned, so here in the section on Chrysogonus he omits Capito.

denique etiam illud suspicor . . . aperietur: for *illud* defined by acc. + inf. cf. §41n. C. sometimes speaks as though there had been no sale (cf. §21n.; §23) and gives the non-sale of the property as an alternative possibility at §128. The topic will be dealt with *postea* because it is among the property issues that C. raises on his own at §§130–42. Evidently the supporting argument has been lost in the lacuna at §132 (see *ad loc.*).

128 opinor enim esse . . . kalendas Iunias: was 1 June [sc. 81] the deadline for both proscriptions and sales or for proscriptions only? Kinsey 1988b argues convincingly that the law, in fact, only governed the proscriptions and that, inasmuch as military action was ongoing, the sales of property of those *apud aduersarios occisi* were free to continue. *dies* is feminine in the sense of a day appointed as a deadline; cf. *OLD* s.v. *init.* and 7.

aliquot post menses . . . non potuisse constat: this is the one, rather vague, indication of the date of the death of Roscius sen., not included in the first narrative at §18. With *bona uenisse dicuntur* C. reverts to the reporting of §6 (*quae . . . sese dicit emisse*) as opposed to the bold assertion of §125; see *ad loc.* For *nullus* as an emphatic negation instead of *non* cf. §55n. *nebulo* "a scoundrel, trifler," first attested at Ter. *Eun.* 269, is among the comic/satiric words adopted by C.; cf. *OLD* s.v. C. has evidently checked the public records and found no entry for the elder Roscius' goods (*pace* Kinsey 1988a: 78n2); possibly it is on this basis that he infers that Roscius was not proscribed (§126). Such a transaction would have been recorded in the magistrate's (i.e. Sulla's) day books (*commentarii*), which could be referred to as *tabulae publicae*, though they sometimes remained in his custody; cf. Mommsen 1887–8: III 1016 with n6. Sedgwick 1934 believes that Roscius' name was removed from the proscription list (and presumably the record of the sale deleted at the same time) in response to the embassy of the *decem primi* (§26) and that this is why Chrysogonus felt the need to initiate the prosecution to secure his property rights (§6). For "adversative *quidem*," contrasting with what precedes cf. Solodow 1978: 75–81; *bona* is acc. pl., not abl. sg. The assertion rests on what was established at §§125–6.

intellego me ante tempus . . . reduuiam curem: as in §127, C. reins himself in from discussing the sale of the property *ante tempus*; cf. *ad loc.* and Kinsey 1988a: 78. *scrutor* is to "inquire into, investigate": *OLD* s.v. 2; for a different sense cf. §97n. For the causal relative clause cf. §41n. C. puns on *caput*, the "life" of Roscius at issue in this trial (cf. §5n.) but also literally his "head." Here *reduuia* "hangnail" makes its first appearance in extant Latin; cf. *OLD* s.v.; *reduuiam curare* appears to be proverbial for "attend to minor matters"; cf. Otto 1890: 295.

non enim laborat . . . crimine liberatus sit: for Roscius' alleged unconcern about his property cf. §5n.; for *laboro* cf. §97n. **ficto crimine:** here *fingo* is equivalent to *confingo*, as in §54; cf. §30n.

129 uerum quaeso a uobis . . . pro Sex. Roscio: cf. *Clu.* 143–60, where C. introduces "on his own account" (cf. §130 *mea sponte*) the argument that Cluentius should be acquitted because the law against judicial murder applies to senators only, not to *equites*, with Alexander 2002: 185–6. At §143 *init.* C. signals that the intervening material has been *oratio . . . mea.* The peroration (§§150–4) will combine defense of his client with C.'s concerns about the state. **haec pauca quae restant:** to hold attention toward the end of a lengthy presentation C. often assures his audience that the end is in sight; cf. *Ver.* 2.2.118 *nos modum aliquem et finem orationi nostrae criminibusque faciamus, pauca* *ex aliis generibus sumemus*; ibid. 2.3.163 *de quo dum certa et pauca et magna dicam breviter, attendite*; *Tull.* 55 *ut rem perspicuam quam paucissimis verbis agam*; *Sest.* 96 *de qua pauca, iudices, dicam*; *Vat.* 40 *concludam iam interrogationem meam teque in extremo pauca de ipsa causa rogabo.*

quae enim mihi . . . iudices, audietis: *mihi* and *pro me ipso* emphasize that these are C.'s personal opinions; as such they are, as he has pointed out (§§2–3), much less weighty than they would be on the lips of a more senior figure. **ad omnes . . . arbitror pertinere:** cf. §7 *periculum quod in omnes intenditur*; at §§150–4 C. dilates on the general danger he foresees. **ex animi mei sensu ac dolore** plays upon and varies the Roman oath formula *ex animi mei sententia*; cf. *Luc.* 146 *quam rationem maiorum etiam comprobat diligentia, qui primum iurare ex sui animi sententia quemque uoluerunt, deinde ita teneri si sciens falleret.* **ad huius uitam causamque:** transmitted is *ad huius uitae casum causamque*; *casus* "(mis)fortune" seems out of place, however, and the two genitives are confusing; hence Richter's change of *uitae* to *uitam* and deletion of *casum*, here adopted; the former change assumes an assimilation to the case of the preceding word, the latter that *casum* and *causam* are variant readings that came to stand side by side in the text. **quid hic pro se dici uelit . . . audietis:** sc. §§143–5.

130 Ego haec a Chrysogono . . . cur tantulo uenierint: his client is thoroughly dissociated from this line of inquiry (*mea sponte remoto Sex. Roscio*); for the strategy cf. Alexander 2000: 67–8. The various points are marked *primum . . . deinde . . . deinde . . . deinde . . .* C. usually contents himself with the simple opposition *primum . . . deinde*; but *deinde* is repeated at *Ver.* 2.2.44 and 143 and *Agr.* 2.93. Later he comes to prefer the more differentiated *primum . . . deinde . . . postremo* (first at *Ver.* 2.3.165) or *primum . . . deinde . . . tum* (first at *Man.* 6) or for a series of four items, as in our passage, *primum . . . deinde . . . tum . . . postremo* (*Cat.* 4.5). For *optimus* referring to an *eques* cf. Hellegouarc'h 1963: 499; *ciuis optimus* has political connotations; cf. Achard 1981: 369–70; cf. §16. **neque proscriptus** was rightly added by Hotoman to restore the other provision of the law cited at §§125–6; the words will have fallen out by a scribe's eye having skipped from the first to the second *neque*. **post eam diem . . . quae dies:** for the gender of *dies* cf. §128n.; for the construction cf. §8n. *praefinio* is "prescribe, determine": *OLD* s.v. 1b. For *tantulus* cf. §114n.; for the purchase price contrasted with the actual value cf. §6. C. does not mind repeating *uenierint* in each of the questions.

quae omnia si . . . imprudente L. Sulla commisisse: as in §22 C. places the full onus on Chrysogonus, classed as a *libertus nequam et improbus*, and exculpates Sulla. For *nequam* cf. §39n. *confero* is "lay to one's charge, put (blame) on": *OLD* s.v. 5c. *nihil ago* is "accomplish nothing, labor in vain," or the like; cf. Prop. 2.32.19 *nihil agis, insidias in me componis inanes*; Hofmann 2003: 354; for a different sense cf. §26n. **qui nesciat:** for the syntax cf. §24n. The transmitted *partim imprudente* implies a complementary term with another *partim*; Clark's *partim improbante* is adopted here; the scribe's eye will have skipped from one *partim* to the next. That Sulla was *imprudens* was already asserted at §21 *fin.* and §25, that "many" had an eye out for his moments of distraction at §22. The repetition of *multus* in various forms is common; cf. e.g. *Phil.* 1.17 *ut multis multa promissa non fecit.*

131 placet igitur ... sed necesse est: though the argument that Chrysogonus acted *imprudente L. Sulla* was already put forward at §§21–2, only here does C. raise the question whether such a state of affairs is to be condoned. The necessity to which C. appeals (*necesse est*) proves to be a necessity built into human nature; it is argued *a fortiori* from the divine nature.

etenim si Iuppiter ... animaduertere non potuisse?: here, as in §22, the exculpation of Sulla takes the form of a long, involved period. C. tacitly appropriates a Stoic argument in extenuation of divine providence; it is quoted (for refutation) at *N.D.* 3.86 *at enim minora di neglegunt neque agellos singulorum nec uiticulas persequuntur, nec si uredo aut grando cuipiam nocuit, id Ioui animaduertendum fuit*; similarly Sen. *Nat.* 2.46, adapting popular arguments; cf. Hine *ad loc. optimus maximus* is the official cult title of Capitoline Jupiter; it designates him as the greatest and best of all Jupiters; cf. Wissowa 1912: 125–9; Thulin, *RE* x 1.1135.35; Pease on *N.D.* 2.64. For *nutu et arbitrio* cf. *Ver.* 2.5.34 *quin sciret iura omnia praetoris urbani nutu atque arbitrio Chelidonis meretriculae gubernari*; *Orat.* 24 *ad eorum* [sc. *qui audiunt*] *arbitrium et nutum totos se fingunt et accommodant.*

saepe ... fruges perdidit: Berry 2000: 8 classes our passage with §22 as containing "praise of Sulla [that] seems insincere and double-edged"; similarly, Gabba 1976: 138 finds sarcasm here. Berry 2004: 84 elaborates: this description of Jupiter's destructiveness goes on too long and implies that Jupiter's counterpart, Sulla, "has destroyed the cities of Italy and ruined Italian agriculture"; he thus sees this as a passage added to the speech by C. after his return from Greece (and after Sulla's death). On the other hand, Offermann 1974: 68 believes this picture of what Jupiter is or is not held responsible for has been contrived *ad hoc*; but what, then, would be the probative value? *Iuppiter* is, in fact, used in two senses in Latin, as the anthropomorphic god and by metonymy as "the heavens, sky," etc. that were his special province; cf. *OLD* s.v. 1–2. The weather has certain undeniable effects, but one does not attribute these, C. claims, to the "divine plan" of the anthropomorphic deity (who is Sulla's counterpart in the comparison);

the anthropomorphic god operates at one remove, creating the physical principles governing the formation of clouds, etc., but is not the proximate cause. On the underlying strategy of elevating Sulla so high that it seems absurd to associate him with Chrysogonus' misdeeds cf. Berger 1978: 38. The alliterating puffs of breath in *uentis uehementioribus* seem to mirror the phenomenon described. **nihil . . . diuino consilio:** Roman cult recognized, however, such negative deities as Febris and Mala Fortuna; cf. *Leg.* 2.28. The archaic gen. *pernicii* is restored from the indirect tradition; the form is also attested for Sisenna (*hist.* fr. 128 = Gel. 9.14.12). **lucemque qua fruimur:** possibly a poetic allusion; cf. Verg. *Aen.* 4.618–19 *cum . . . regno aut optata luce fruatur*; German. *Ar.* 661 *nil Pristis luce fruetur*; Sen. *Oed.* 854 *non potuit ille luce, non caelo frui*. **spiritumque quem ducimus:** cf. §72 *quid tam est commune quam spiritus uiuis . . . ita uiuunt ut ducere animam de caelo non queant.* **cum solus . . . gubernaret:** this makes him the earthly counterpart of Jupiter *cuius nutu et arbitrio caelum terra mariaque reguntur.* The point was forestalled at §22 *cum et pacis constituendae rationem et belli gerendi potestatem solus habeat, cum . . . unus omnia gubernet.* **tum legibus confirmaret** is an oblique allusion to Sulla's official title *dictator legibus scribendis et rei publicae constituendae*; cf. §22n. For *aliqua animaduertere non potuisse* cf. §22 *si aliquid non animaduertat.*

  nisi hoc mirum . . . adepta non sit: for the relative clause preceding its "antecedent" cf. §6n. C. thus spells out the underlying *a fortiori* argument: if even the god Jupiter does not attain total control of outcomes (see previous n.), it is hardly surprising that a human being like Sulla cannot. It might be objected, however, that C.'s analogy is flawed: Jupiter does not intervene because he sees no need to, not because he lacks the power to do so.

132 uerum ut haec . . . unum esse Chrysogonum?: *missum facere* is to "set aside, drop": *OLD* s.v. *mitto* 4a. *cum maxime* "at this very moment": *OLD* s.v. *maxime* 6b; with *ea quae nunc cum maxime fiunt* C. refers to the current trial, as the sequel makes clear. The Gk loan-word *architectus* has been used metaphorically since Pl. *Mil.* 1139–40: Milphidippa: *quid agis, noster architecte?* Palaestrio: *egone architectus? . . . non sum dignus prae te palum ut figam in parietem. machinator* (literally "one who devises or constructs machines") is likewise metaphorical here ("a contriver of plots or other events"); cf. *OLD* s.vv. For contrast of *unus* and *omnia* cf. §22; the point is even more striking when, as here, the one is identified as the source of "all"; cf. e.g. *Quinct.* 85 *ex quo uno* [sc. *iudicio*] *haec omnia nata et profecta esse concedit.* Chrysogonus' name is reserved for emphasis to the final position; cf. §21n.

  qui Sex. Rosci nomen . . . se dixit Erucius: this accounts for C.'s imaginative reconstruction of the conversation between Erucius and

Chrysogonus when the former was engaged to take the case (§58); it is striking that, in spite of his own mention of Chrysogonus, Erucius did not expect
the defense to do so (§60). Kinsey 1980: 184n14 and 1988a: 79 points to the
prosecution's concealment (§5) and tries, accordingly, to explain away our
passage ("Cicero must mean that something Erucius had said was equivalent
to an admission that he was speaking on behalf of Chrysogonus" etc.). But
§§5–6 suggest that what was hushed up was not Chrysogonus' involvement in
the case but rather that his property interests were at stake. For *nomen deferre*
cf. §8n.; for *curo* + acc. with gerundive cf. §103n. The words *hoc iudicium*,
transmitted after *curauit*, were rightly expelled by Madvig; they do not fit
syntactically: *iudicium* can hardly be the antecedent of *cuius*, which, as the
parallels suggest, should be a person (cf. Merguet 1877–84: II 506b).

A lacuna was marked at this point in some derivatives of the famous lost
Cluny MS (and in the Cluniacensis itself according to F. Barbarus). Some
phrases are cited in the Scholia Gronoviana D (here printed in boldface, the
words of the scholiast in bold italic), so a general reconstruction is possible,
though the extent of the loss remains in doubt. The passage seems to have
dealt primarily with Roscius' estate and Chrysogonus' title to it. The last
moves of Roscius sen. were his dining **in uico Pallacinae** (this was evidently
located in the Campus Martius; cf. Richardson s.v.) followed by his death
ad balneas Pallacinas (§18), hardly *in aduersariorum praesidiis* as required by the
law for the sale of goods (§126). From the swift removal of goods from the
property (§23) C. evidently inferred that Chrysogonus was afraid that Sulla
would rescind his ownership (**maxime metuit *Sullam scilicet***); cf. §26 *ut
mori mallet quam de his rebus Sullam doceri*. If C. returned to the non-sale of the
property here (a point denied by Kinsey 1988a: 79), he will have "concluded
from this dispersal that it had not been sold at all" (so Freeze *ad loc.*). C.
goes on to represent Chrysogonus as claiming that the goods were needed to
furnish a new mansion that he had under construction in the district of Veii
(**deriuat tamen et ait se** with following explanation by the scholiast); one
suspects the scene was described similarly to Antony's pillaging of Caesar's
property: *quid hic uictor non audebit, qui . . . refertam eius domum exhauserit, hortos
compilauerit, ad se ex eis omnia ornamenta transtulerit* (*Phil.* 3.30). **manupretia**
("rewards") is Orelli's conjecture for transmitted *manu praedia*, incoherently
explained in the scholia; the bearing on the argument remains unclear. **hic
ego audire istos cupio:** as elsewhere, *audire cupio* is no doubt part of a
provocative challenge to the other side; cf. *Caec.* 33; *Flac.* 55; *Vat.* 37; *Phil.* 2.84.
The scholiast claims that C. found space in this chapter for an enumeration
of Chrysogonus' pleasures and his possessions acquired by pillage; these
are, however, also the subject of §§133–5; it is hard to see how they could

have been broached in the lacuna if §132 *fin.* connects with §133 *init.*; see below.

. . . aptam et ratione . . . audire nuntium possunt: when continuous text resumes, C. appears to be contrasting the taste of some other(s) who prefer estates so remote that they scarcely receive word (from Rome) three times per year (*unde uix ter in anno audire nuntium possunt*). The lost fem. substantive will presumably be *uillam*. The Sallentini were a people of Illyrian origin who lived in southern Calabria. The Bruttii, of Oscan stock, lived in mountainous southwestern Italy; though allied with Rome from 270, the region was still subject to brigandage; an area where Sulla's followers amassed large estates (cf. Seager, *CAH* IX 204), it was later exploited by Spartacus.

133   alter   tibi   descendit . . . praeclarum   et   propinquum: *alter . . . alter* is a pattern for highlighting a contrast, as in §102; cf. *OLD* s.v. *alter* 5a; in view of the preceding lacuna it remains unclear what person(s) were contrasted with Chrysogonus. *tibi* is the ethic dative used in lively and ironic statements: "there you have," "there you see" or the like; cf. Roby §1150; G–L §351; §4n. **animi causa** appears elsewhere in the sense of *animi relaxandi causa* ("to relieve the tension of the mind": *OLD* s.v. *relaxo* 2b), which is the reading of ψ alone; cf. §134 *animi et aurium causa*; *Phil.* 7.18 *et qui illud animi causa fecerit, hunc praedae causa quid facturum putatis?* *rus* appears as early as Pl. *Cas.* 485 in the sense "a country estate"; cf. *OLD* s.v. 2. **plura praeterea praedia . . . praeclarum et propinquum:** for the alliteration cf. §35n. *suburbanus* "close to the city" (*OLD* s.v. 1a) is the operative word from Chrysogonus' point of view, reinforced by *propinquum* in final position; cf. §132n.

domus referta uasis . . . putatis esse?: Verres had similar tastes: *illud quidem statim curatur, ut quicquid caelati argenti fuit . . . ad istum deferatur, quicquid Corinthiorum uasorum, stragulae uestis* (*Ver.* 2.2.46); for links between Verres and Chrysogonus see further Buchheit 1975a: 207n74 and 208n76. Corinthian bronzes were prized in antiquity; hence Trimalchio's claim to be the only possessor of genuine ones and his account of their origin (Petr. *Sat.* 50); see further Baroin 2005. No less sought after by Verres (cf. *Ver.* 2.2.83–4) and still more ancient (Plin. *Nat.* 34.9) were Delian bronzes. An *authepsa* was a cooker containing its own heating element, the Romans, as often, having borrowed the name along with the object from the Greeks; our passage is the word's first and only attestation; cf. *OLD* and *TLL* s.v. Seneca seems to have it in mind when he excoriates luxuries at *Ep.* 78.23 *cocorum . . . ipsos cum opsoniis focos transferentium . . . ne quis intepescat cibus* etc. *numero* is "to count out" in this case the money to be paid; cf. *OLD* s.v. *quid*, transmitted before *praeconem*, was rightly deleted by A. Klotz (an anticipatory error before *quid praeterea*). **quid praeterea caelati argenti** etc.: for the "genitive of the rubric" cf. §8n. *quid signorum* pushes *quid marmoris* in the direction of "marble (as the material of sculptures)": *OLD* s.v. *marmor* 1a.

   tantum scilicet ... una in domo potuit: for the phrasing cf. *Ver.* 2.4.7 *tot domus locupletissimas domus istius una capiet?*; *Phil.* 5.12 *tanta pecunia una in domo coaceruata est ut* ... The preceding looked at first sight like a rhetorical question, but supplying the answer enables C. to indicate the source of this wealth, a further goad toward resentment; for envy attaching to *nouveaux riches* cf. Arist. *Rhet.* 1387a6 especially 22. For *splendidus* as a typical epithet for an *eques* cf. §20n. **turba et rapinis** may be taken together by hendiadys: "disorderly acts of pillage" such as Roscius suffered (cf. §23).

   familiam uero quantam ... quid ego dicam?: this time the question is allowed to stand as rhetorical. The *familia* is "the slaves of the household" (*OLD* s.v. 2); C. painted a picture of Chrysogonus' refined slaves for contrast with Roscius' (presumed) rustic ones at §120 *fin.* Not only the number but also the skill of the slaves will, of course, determine their value; cf. Plin. *Nat.* 7.39 = Wiedemann 1981: 104 (§99).

134   mitto hasce artes ... tota uicinitas personet: *mitto* is to "pass over, say nothing of": *OLD* s.v. 5; similarly *missum facere* (§132); for the *praeteritio* cf. §75n. The representatives of the "vulgar arts" are loosely placed in apposition to the arts themselves, whereby the *musici* are set apart for extended treatment. For *animi ... causa* cf. §133n. With voice, string, and flute C. lists the major types of civilian music-making; polysyndeton here varies the asyndeton of the previous list. The adjs. *cotidianus* and *nocturnus* denote these as regular occurrences and correspondingly irritating; similarly Trimalchio surrounded himself and his guests with music in and out of season; cf. Petr. 28.5 and 31.4. The *conuiuia*, notoriously offering opportunity for the display of Roman luxury (cf. Edwards 1993: 186–8 and 202–4), are emphasized. Used of a place, *persono* is "to be filled with noise": *OLD* s.v. 1b.

   in hac uita ... deuersorium flagitiorum omnium: expenditures (*sumptus*) were regulated by law at Rome, and violations were punished by the censors; cf. Sauerwein 1970; Bonamente 1980; Clemente 1981; Baltrusch 1989; La Penna 1990. The point is sharpened to *effusio* "lavish expenditure" (of money): *OLD* s.v. 4. *conuiuia* is repeated from the previous sentence, this time for elaboration in final position. For *honestus* cf. §7n.; for the ironic use of *credo* ("doubtless, I suppose") cf. *OLD* s.v. 8c. For *haberi potius quam* cf. *Div.* 1.112 *ne Pherecydes quidem ... potius diuinus habebitur quam physicus. officina* is a "place where something is made, workshop": *OLD* s.v. 1; *deuersorium* is a "stopping place" (during a journey), sometimes, as here, with gen. of purpose: *OLD* s.v.; such places may have been perceived as louche; similarly Tac. *An.* 13.25 *Nero . . . et lupanaria et deuerticula . . . pererrabat*; elsewhere in the speeches only at *Phil.* 2.104 (apropos Varro's estate occupied by Antony) *studiorum enim suorum M. Varro uoluit illud, non libidinum deuersorium.*

135 ipse uero quemadmodum . . . solum potentem putet: this portrait, moving from the physical to the psychological, is not far from the rhetorical schools; its ancestor is Demosthenes' picture of Aeschines striding through the *agora*, puffed up by Philip's friendship (19.314); cf. Weische 1972: 28–9; cf. also the example cited at *Rhet. Her.* 4.62 *iste qui cotidie per forum medium tamquam draco serpit . . . ipse* "the man himself" (as opposed to his house); cf. §101 with n.; *uero* lends focus to the new topic; cf. §49n. *componere capillum* is "to arrange the hair properly," so first at Pl. *Mo.* 254; cf. *OLD* s.v. *compono* 5c; it is a detail added to the description of the tyrannical Gabinius at *Red. sen.* 13; cf. also Gel. 3.5.2. In the MSS here and elsewhere *delibutus* alternates with *dilibutus* without any apparent semantic distinction, the latter form showing the expected regressive assimilation of vowels; cf. Leumann 1977: 101. It is the participle of an otherwise lost verb (probably in turn from a lost *u*-stem noun: ibid. 543) and means "thickly smeared"; cf. *OLD* s.v. a. *uolito* is first used here by C. Literally "go to and fro", it perhaps has a connotation similar to "gad about": *OLD* s.v. 3a; cf. *Phil.* 11.6 (of Dolabella) *uolitat ut rex. caterua* is a "band" without order or regular formation sometimes opposed to Roman troops; cf. *OLD*, *TLL*, and Ernout and Meillet s.v. His followers are characterized by their dress as Roman citizens; cf. *OLD* s.v. *togatus*, the word apparently used here for the first time as a substantive. Unlike the bully Midias, who strides through the *agora* with his retinue (presumably of slaves) clearing others out of the way (Dem. 21.158), Chrysogonus is more absurd than frightening; cf. Weische 1972: 29. **ut omnes despiciat . . . solum potentem putet:** *potentia* is the asset Chrysogonus brought to the *societas* according to §35; at §6 C. recognized his *potentia* but with a significant restriction: *adulescens uel potentissimus hoc tempore nostrae ciuitatis* (see *ad loc.*); his *potentia* is clearly related to his *gratia* (sc. with Sulla; cf. §28 with n.; §60 *gratiam potentiamque eius neglegi*; §122 *nimiam gratiam potentiamque Chrysogoni*). Here C. claims that Chrysogonus mistakes his relative *potentia* for something greater (*se . . . solum potentem putet*) – a symptom of a tyrant's megalomania; cf. Buchheit 1975a: especially 200–1.

Quae uero efficiat . . . a causa nobilitatis existimet: *imperitus* ("inexperienced") is often used as a mildly negative characterization of those holding points of view C. does not subscribe to; cf. Dyck on *Leg.* 1.4. As in §§16, 126, 136, and 142 C. speaks of the victory as already accomplished even though military action was ongoing. C. adopts the Sullan propaganda according to which he stood for the *causa nobilitatis*; cf. Paterson 2004: 86; for *tametsi* §3n. For *pars* used of a political faction cf. §16n. C. expresses himself confident of his optimate credentials even though he did not participate in the civil war (see the next n.); the anecdote of Fimbria and Scaevola (§§33–4) was perhaps inserted in part as an early signal of his sympathies to the jurors; see *ad loc.*

136 sciunt ii qui . . . qui uicerunt: *pro sua parte* is "for one's own part" or "as far as in one lies": *OLD* s.v. *pars* 8c–d; the modifiers *tenui infirmaque* continue C.'s self-deprecation from §§1–3. **fieri non potuit, ut componeretur:** *compono* is "to settle (differences)" (*OLD* s.v. 15a), here in the impersonal passive. Like his teacher Scaevola, C. would have preferred a peaceful solution; cf. §33 *quos . . . seruare per compositionem uolebat* [sc. Scaevola]. The decision will have followed Sulla's rejection of the senate's embassy in 84; cf. Lintott 2008: 427. C. would take a similar stance in early 49 as civil war was brewing between Caesar and Pompey; cf. Gelzer 1969: 243–54; Mitchell 1991: 243–52; cf. also *Phil.* 7.7 *ego ille qui semper pacis auctor fui.* **id maxime defendisse:** sc. *uerbis, oratione*, or the like; he took no part in the fighting, as he clarifies later (§142 *inermis*); cf. Paterson 2004: 88. **qui uicerunt:** i.e. the Sullan faction, whose victory is treated as a *fait accompli*; cf. §135n.

   quis enim erat . . . de amplitudine contendere?: C. appeals to the general perception as justification (*enim*) for his stance. *humilitas* and *dignitas* are collective terms for social class: "men of low rank" and "men of rank" respectively; cf. Hellegouarc'h 1963: 515 and n11 and Achard 1981: 48n74; for *amplitudo* cf. §2n.; similarly *Phil.* 8.7. Hartman (1911) proposed *cum amplitudine de dignitate*, which is possible but unnecessary.

   quo in certamine . . . foris auctoritas retineretur: for *perditus* cf. §41n.; for *incolumis* §6n. The contrast *domi . . . foris* recurs in the speeches at *Arch.* 16 and *Phil.* 2.69 and 78.

   quae perfecta esse . . . gesta esse intellego: for *suum cuique tribuere* as a description of just dealing cf. Dyck on *Off.* 1.21. *gradus* here is "a stage in the scale of dignity, rank, or fortune": *OLD* s.v. 8. With elisions assumed, the three units from *deorum uoluntate* through *felicitate L. Sullae* account respectively for seven, nine and eighteen syllables, the implication being that Sulla deserves the lion's share of the credit. Here and elsewhere C. speaks as one who knows the *deorum uoluntas*; cf. *Phil.* 4.10 *quid est quod de uoluntate caelestium dubitare possimus?* For *consilium et imperium* cf. *Rab. perd.* 3 *summum in consulibus* *imperium, summum in senatu consilium putare*; *Phil.* 14.37 *eorum . . . uirtute impe-rio consilio . . . felicitate populum Romanum . . . seruitute liberatum*; for Sulla as *felix* cf. §22n.

137 quod animaduersum est . . . laudo: a carefully balanced pair of assertions each led by a *quod*-clause serving as obj. ("the fact that": *OLD* s.v. *quod* 4). *animaduerto* is "to inflict (capital) punishment on," here used, as often, impersonally with *in* + acc.: *OLD* s.v. 8b. *omni ratione* "by any (available) means," i.e. with no holds barred; cf. *OLD* s.v. *ratio* 14a. *honos habitus est* "honor was bestowed": *OLD* s.v. *habeo* 19d.

   quae ut fierent . . . fuisse confiteor: C. does not doubt, or so he claims, the purity of the motives underlying the war, i.e. that it was fought to achieve the stated results (*quae ut fierent*) and not for other reasons (such those set out in the next sentence). His personal commitment is restated from the previous section; for the sense of *pars* cf. §16n.

   sin autem id . . . populus Romanus est: with *sin* (cf. §8n.) C. raises a darker alternative possibility only to dismiss it in the sequel. *postremus* "last" is used here of moral character: "worst, lowest"; cf. *OLD* s.v. 5b. *locuples* (< *locus*) is literally "rich in lands," i.e. wealthy; hence the derived verb *locupleto* "enrich": *OLD* s.vv. The described behavior is imputed to Chrysogonus and his confederates: for the seizure of *pecunia aliena* cf. §6 with n.; for *in fortunas impetum facere* cf. §21 *in reliquas omnes fortunas iste T. Roscius . . . impetum facit*. C. would later speak of Sulla's misuse of his victory (*Off.* 2.27) and see his sale of confiscated property as an incentive for further civil wars (ibid. 2.29) and Antony as *auidum in pecuniis locupletium* (*Phil.* 5.22). An intensification is often added with *et is*; cf. K–S I 619. *re . . . uerbis* ("in fact . . . in words") often forms an antithetical structure as in Gk ἔργωι . . . λόγωι; cf. *OLD* s.v. *uerbum* 12. For *uero* cf. §49n. *recreo* is to "re-establish (after adversity), restore, revive": *OLD* s.v. 3; elsewhere the process is described by *restituo* alone (§§139 and 149); here the double predicate matches the following *subactus oppressusque*.

138 Verum longe aliter . . . uerum etiam ornabitur: for *uerum* cf. on §§5 and 54. C. raises the spectre of unscrupulous motives underlying the civil war only to dismiss it; later it became a truism that the victory was sullied by its ruthless exploitation; cf. *Off.* 2.27; Sal. *Cat.* 11.4. C. returns to the starting point of this digression, namely possible damage to the *causa nobilitatis* in the event of an acquittal (§135). *isti homines* are those behind the prosecution with *iste* conveying, as often, a note of contempt; cf. §17n.

   etenim qui haec . . . non esse commemorant: *haec* are "the present proceedings"; cf. §1n.; for *tantum posse* §33n.; for Chrysogonus' *potentia* (*tantum* *posse*) §6n. **concessum ei non esse:** sc. by Sulla, according to C.'s argument at §§21–2 and 131.

ac iam nihil est . . . et ordine iudicaris: *nihil est quod quisquam . . . sit* "there is no reason for anyone to be"; cf. G–L §541 N.2. **tam stultus . . . qui dicat:** for the relative clause with consecutive force cf. §5n. The person who takes the contrary view is now more harshly characterized, no longer merely *imperitior*, as at §135. Each counterfactual by the intimidated juror is met with an empowering reply. Coupled with *recte, ordine* is quasi-adverbial: "properly": cf. *Phil.* 10.5 *litteras . . . recte et ordine scriptas*; *OLD* s.v. *ordo* 14.

139 dum necesse erat . . . auctoritasque est restituta: for the contrast of *unus* and *omnia* cf. §§22 and 132; *omnia posse* intensifies the *tantum posse* attributed to Chrysogonus (§138). *creare magistratus* is to "appoint magistrates"; cf. *OLD* s.v. *creo* 5a; the idea is expressed abstractly at *Leg.* 3.10 (*creatio magistratuum*). For Sulla's appointment as *dictator legibus scribendis et rei publicae constituendae* cf. on §§22 and 125. *procuratio* is "responsibility," often used of public matters; cf. *OLD* s.v. 2; the implication is that the restored courts are now autonomous; cf. §11. Our passage in combination with Plut. *Sull.* 6.5 and 34.3 is the foundation for the case of Badian 1970: 8–14 that Sulla yielded power in stages, first the dictatorship by the date of our speech, then by the beginning of 79 the consulship (*aliter* App. *BC* 1.103–4, perhaps under the influence of accumulation of offices by the emperors).

quam si retinere . . . concedant necesse est: for Romans' oft expressed concern about their ability to retain the courts and other institutions of their state cf. *Off.* 3.44 with Dyck's n. *obtineo* here = "maintain": *OLD* s.v. 2. *sin* introduces the alternative possibility; cf. §8n.; *ii qui reciperarunt* continues as the subject: all depends upon the attitude of citizens like the jurors. **has caedes et rapinas et hos . . . sumptus**, i.e. the ones C. has just described, as indicated by *hic*, used of what is currently at hand (cf. §1n.). C. breaks off rather than rehearse the dire consequences; cf. Lausberg §§887–8 (*aposiopesis* or *reticentia*); C. follows an opposite strategy of spelling out the (hoped for) consequences at *Cat.* 1.33 *hisce ominibus . . .* The postponement of the pronoun emphasizes *unum*; cf. H–S 407. For C.'s usage of *nobiles* cf. §1n. Later, when he has held office himself, C. speaks of the threat to *noster ordo* if it is thought incapable of properly managing the courts; cf. *Ver.* 2.3.225 *perniciosum nostro ordini populum Romanum existimare non posse eos homines qui ipsi legibus teneantur leges in iudicando religiose defendere. ornamentum* is a badge or other outward mark of rank or office: *OLD* s.v. 3. Of the qualities C. wants to see in the nobles the chief is that they be *misericordes*; cf. §3 (*ignoscendi ratio*). For the leading group giving way to others cf. *Cat.* 2.19, where C. asks of one sub-group of the Catilinarian conspirators: *non uident id se cupere quod, si adepti sint, fugitiuo alicui aut gladiatori concedi sit necesse?*

140–2 These chapters comprise C.'s plea to the jurors not to close ranks behind Chrysogonus. The cause of the nobles might be shared by others, like C. himself, an *eques*, if its values are pure, and it is strengthened, rather than weakened, by a repudiation of Chrysogonus' behavior. Boren 1964: 59 sees here an adumbration of C.'s later policy of *concordia ordinum*.

140 quapropter desinant aliquando . . . ferre posse: anaphora of *desinant* lends strong emphasis; *nostri isti nobiles* continue as the subject. *aliquando* is often used in exhortations in the sense "now at last, before it is too late": *OLD* s.v. 5. *male* is to be taken with *locutum esse*, not *dicere*; *male loqui* is colloquial for "speak ill of, abuse, insult": *OLD* s.v. *male* 2c. For *suam causam . . . communicare* cf. *Ver.* 2.4.24 *quibuscum omnia scelera sua ac latrocinia communicauit. ille* is the just mentioned Chrysogonus. **de se aliquid detractum:** i.e. the *causa nobilitatis* in general is not thereby damaged, as C. has argued since §135. The *turpe* is again the criterion; cf. §§50, 112, and 116. **qui equestrem splendorem pati non potuerunt:** for *splendor / splendidus* applied to *equites* cf. §20n. This group comprises "the more conservative and reactionary elements of the oligarchy" (Gabba 1976: 139). **serui . . . ferre posse:** the point is adumbrated at §§6 (*adulescens*), 22 (*nemo potest esse . . . qui neminem neque seruum neque libertum improbum habeat*), 34 (*quia fit a Chrysogono, non est ferendum*), and 130 (*quemadmodum solent liberti nequam et improbi facere*); but now the term *libertus* is dropped, and Chrysogonus becomes merely a *seruus*. For *nequissimus* cf. §39n. (*nequam*). *dominatio* (the abstract noun is first attested here) is the position of power exercised by the *dominus* over his household, including his slaves; it is a paradox for such authority to be exercised by a slave; when used with reference to the state it is usually vituperative; cf. *OLD* and *TLL* s.v. especially 1878.34–5; Buchheit 1975a: 202–3.
    quae quidem dominatio . . . sincerum sanctumque restat: for repetition of the antecedent within the relative clause (*dominationem . . . quae dominatio*) cf. §6n. For contrasting *quidem* cf. §57n.; for *uero* calling attention cf. §49n. **quam uiam . . . affectet:** these words may comprise an embedded verse from drama; inserting *illa* after *munitet* (Gruter's conjecture) or a proper name of equivalent metrical shape would yield a trochaic octonarius; cf. Fleckeisen 1892. The frequentative *munito* ("busy oneself with building") occurs only here in classical Latin; cf. *OLD* and *TLL* s.v. *iter* or *uiam affectare* is "to set out on a journey"; cf. *Agr.* 1.5 *uidete nunc quo affectent iter apertius quam antea*; *OLD* s.v. *affecto* 1. **ad fidem . . . iudicia uestra:** i.e. C. sees the

fundamenta rei publicae endangered; cf. Buchheit 1975a: 205. For the jurors' oath
and the prosecution's designs on it cf. §8 with n. **sincerum sanctumque:**
for the alliterative pair cf. *Quinct.* 5 *profecto nihil est iam sanctum atque sincerum
in ciuitate*; Sen. *Ben.* 1.3.5 *incorrupta sunt* [sc. *beneficia*] *et sincera et omnibus sancta*;
Wölfflin 1933: 275.

141 hicne etiam sese . . . id ipsum queror: *hic . . . hic* sharply focuses
attention on the place, i.e. the courtroom, and the inappropriateness of
Chrysogonus' effort to exert *potentia* here; cf. C.'s humorous dismissal of the
prosecution's witnesses as out of place in the courtroom at *Cael.* 67 *quam
uolent in conuiuiis faceti, dicaces, non numquam etiam ad uinum diserti sint, alia fori
uis est, alia triclini, alia subselliorum ratio, alia lectorum; non idem iudicum comissato-
rumque conspectus . . .* For *aliquid posse* cf. §138 *tantum posse.* The postponement of
Chrysogonus' name lends emphasis; cf. §21n.; for the exclamatory accusative
cf. §77n. For *acerbus* cf. §78n.; for a different sense §150n. For *mehercules* cf. §58n.
indigne fero is "to be indignant at, take ill": *OLD* s.v. *indigne* 3. *uerear* is subj. since
this is a rejected reason; cf. G–L §541; the true reason has the indic. (*quod
ausus est* etc.). For *quid* substituting for *aliquid* (used above and below) after *ne*
ibid. §107.1 R. **tales uiros:** i.e. the jurors; cf. §8 *qui ex ciuitate in senatum propter
dignitatem, ex senatu in hoc consilium delecti estis propter seueritatem*; §151 *arbitrantur
isti . . . uos hic, tales uiros, sedere . . .* For the repeated references to his client as
innocens cf. §6n. *id ipsum* specifies and emphasizes: "this very point (and no
other)": *OLD* s.v. *ipse* 8; *TLL* s.v. 335.37.

  idcircone spectata nobilitas . . . uexare possent?: Landgraf's *spectata* ("distinguished": *OLD* s.v. *spectatus* 2) is surely needed for transmitted
exspectata. C. speaks respectfully but not uncritically of the *nobilitas* in this
speech; cf. §§1, 139–40, and 142 with the picture of the behavior of the ideal
noble at §149; Gabba 1976: 138–9. C. later shows awareness that Sulla's
rem publicam reciperare was a double-edged sword; cf. *Har.* 55 *idem iterum Sulla
superauit; tum sine dubio habuit regalem potestatem, quamquam rem publicam reciperarat*;
the phrase recurs during the struggle following Caesar's assassination: *Phil.*
3.7 (*ad rem publicam reciperandam*) and 5.11 (*in spem rei publicae reciperandae*). The
diminutive *seruuli* expresses contempt ("mere slaves"), as often; cf. Hanssen
1951: 12; though this is phrased generally, as in §140 (*serui nequissimi dominationem*), Chrysogonus is clearly the target; cf. Kinsey 1980: 188. For the x, y,
z*que* organization of items cf. §31n. C. gives his account of the true motive for
the war at §149 *fin.*

142 si id actum est . . . iudices, sensi: the alternatives are framed in
the *si . . . sin* structure so often used in this speech; cf. §8n. The apodoses are

similarly structured, each led by emphatic *fateor*; for such anaphora cf. *Caec.*
66 *fateor me homines coegisse, fateor armasse, fateor tibi mortem esse minitatum, fateor*
hoc interdicto praetoris uindicari; then follows indirect statement, then a causal
qui-clause (cf. §41n.); the self-condemnation intensifies from *errasse* to *insanisse*;
for a case of political "insanity" cf. §33. In a polarized situation *sentire cum*
aliquo is to "side with someone": *OLD* s.v. *sentio* 8b. *tametsi* appears this time
without a correlative *tamen* (cf. §3n.). **inermis:** Plut. *Cic.* 3.3 emphasizes that
at this period C. devoted himself to studies and Greek masters.

    sin autem uictoria . . . gratissimam esse oportet: for the victory
presented as already complete cf. §135n.; for the double dative construction
§48n. For *emolumentum* cf. §84n. *optimus quisque* may be rendered "every good
man"; similarly below *nequissimus quisque* is "each wicked man": G–L §318.2.
mea oratio = "my words," as often: *OLD* s.v. *oratio* 5a.

    quod si quis . . . separatur: this is the real point of the argument, to
separate criticism of Chrysogonus from that of the *causa nobilitatis* generally.
For the sense of *ignoro* cf. §5n. "Knowing oneself" is a philosophical project, as
C. well knew from his studies in Academic philosophy (cf. *Leg.* 1.58–62 with
Dyck *ad loc.*). One either knows oneself or does not; hence Madvig's *probe*
("properly") is adopted for transmitted *prope*. Far from suffering damage,
the cause will grow more lustrous (*splendidior*) if it has not merely military
might but moral worth. The asyndeton between *resistetur* and *ille* is strongly
adversative; cf. §6n. C. defines the person who is damaged (*laeditur*) by his
critique of Chrysogonus in such a way (*ille improbissimus Chrysogoni fautor*) that
the jurors will shrink from that position; for *fautor* cf. §16n.; for Chrysogonus
as (implicitly) *improbus* cf. §130. *ratio* appears here as a synonym of *causa* as
in the phrase *ratio popularis*; cf. *OLD* s.v. 11c; cf. §140 *desinant suam causam cum*
Chrysogono communicare.

PERORATIO (§§143–54)

At *Inv.* 1.98 C. distinguished three components of the final segment of a
speech (which he there calls the *conclusio*): *enumeratio, indignatio,* and *conquestio.*
In accord with his dismissal of the prosecution's case as insubstantial (§§42–
58, 79–82), he does not offer a formal *enumeratio* of his counterarguments. The
closest approach to a summary of the case is the comparison of the two he
presents as alternative suspects, Magnus and his client, elaborated from §18
(§152). The emphasis is rather on *indignatio* in the portrayal of Chrysogonus'
motives (§§145–9); Solmsen 1968: 239 refers to "the terrific crescendo of the
epilogue where Cicero fans the indignation of the audience to a white heat."
The speech concludes with a *conquestio,* not so much over the individual

fate of Roscius (cf. §125 apropos the father *non fuit tantus homo Sex. Roscius in ciuitate ut de eo potissimum conqueramur*), as the condition of the *res publica* in the event of Roscius' conviction: this would be a symptom of hardened *crudelitas* and would foreshadow the doom of the children of the proscribed (§§150–4). A standard feature of the *peroratio*, namely the parade of the defendant and his relatives dressed in sordid raiment (*sordes*) so as to move the jurors' pity is omitted here, perhaps for lack of support by his relatives, none of whom is individually identified as present in court (cf., however, §49n.) except for Magnus, who is prominently seated on the prosecution side (§§17, 84, and 95).

I   The foregoing argument belongs to C., not Roscius (143)
II Roscius appeals to Chrysogonus for his life (144)
III Possible motives for Chrysogonus' pursuit of the defendant (145)
  A   Spoils
  B   Personal enmity
  C   Fear
  D   Digresssion on Chrysogonus' cruelty
  E   Outrage that Roscius has been clothed; rôle of Caecilia (147)
  F   Outrage that Roscius is being defended with care (148)
    (1) Messalla's rôle (149)
    (2) An example to the nobility
IV If his appeal to Chrysogonus fails, Roscius' one last hope is the jurors' pity (150)
  A   No hope if they have been infected by the general cruelty
  B   The prosecution's goals:
    (1) For the jury to intercept those who have escaped their hands (151)
    (2) General elimination of the children of the proscribed (153)
  C   Call for the jurors to remedy the situation (154)

143 Verum haec omnis ... de suo patrimonio queritur: C. thus signals the end of *mea oratio*, i.e. the argument offered since §130 on his own account in defense of Roscius' claim to his property and against the self-aggrandizement of Chrysogonus; he cross-refers to §129, where see n. *res publica*, *dolor meus* and *istorum iniuria* are personified as the subject of *coegit* (the verb agreeing with the nearest; cf. §91n.). *isti* refers to those behind the prosecution, not without contempt; cf. §17n. The negatives *nihil ... neminem ... nihil* are likewise emphatic. For his client's alleged unconcern with property issues cf. §5n.

143–4 putat homo imperitus . . . omnibus commodis dicit: C. has
claimed Roscius as an enthusiastic and skilled *agricola* (§49); the prosecution
called him *agrestis*, a pejorative equivalent of *rusticus* (§74). The other side of
the coin is his lack of familiarity with the city and its ways (§§74 and 79),
which, C. has argued, make him unlikely to have masterminded a murder
committed in the city. Now a further consequence is that he is *imperitus morum*
generally (cf. §26 of the Amerian legates: *homines antiqui qui ex sua natura ceteros
fingerent*) and thus accepting of the claim of the other side that the loss of his
property is legally binding. **quae uos per Sullam gesta esse dicitis:**
Sulla's involvement is again treated as an allegation of the other side; cf. §6
bona patris huiusce . . . quae de . . . Lucio Sulla . . . sese dicit emisse . . . Chrysogonus with
n. The *ius gentium* governed relations of Romans with foreigners; such cases
were handled at a court presided over by the *praetor peregrinus*. Since Ameria
was an Italian *municipium*, its inhabitants enjoyed Roman citizenship by 90
at the latest (the *lex Iulia*); cf. E. Kornemann, *RE* XVI 1.587.21–590.10 (s.v.
municipium). Chrysogonus, though, as his name indicates, of Greek origin,
was a Roman citizen, since freed slaves automatically became such at this
period. The relevance of the *ius gentium* is thus unclear; either C. cites it as
a default criterion that would apply even in wartime when other laws are
suspended, or *gentium* should be deleted as a gloss. **culpa liberatus . . . a
uobis discedere:** for a similar statement of the defendant's goal cf. §7. C.
plays on two different senses of *careo* "to be free of (blame or the like)" and
to "go without" or "lose": *OLD* s.v. 3b vs. 4–5; cf. Holst 1925: 59. The goal of
the other side is less modest: *ut spoliis ex hoc iudicio ornati auctique discedant* (§8).

144 rogat oratque . . . in egestate degere: both here and in §146 C.
apostrophizes the absent Chrysogonus (cf. §60). Skillfully turning the prosecution into a persecution of his client, C. offers an elaborated version of the
postulatio he presented to Chrysogonus on his own at §7. *rogare* is combined
with *orare* 5x in the *Verrines* and once each in *Div. Caec.* and *Agr.* but in no
speech thereafter. The five protases all restate the same idea, the last two
with concrete and pathetic embellishment, the aim being to arouse pity for
his client and revulsion at Chrysogonus' cruelty; he continues to ratchet up
the pressure on Chrysogonus in §146. For the value of the elder Roscius'
estate cf. §6. *in suam rem conuertere* is to "direct toward one's own purposes": cf.
OLD s.v. *conuerto* 6a. In spite of C.'s insistence that his client held back none of
his father's property, the charge of *peculatus* mentioned but quickly dismissed
at §82 might be relevant here; see *ad loc.* The distinction between *annumerare* and *appendere* (the latter attested here for the first time) is that between
counting and weighing out; cf. *Opt. Gen.* 14 *in quibus* [sc. the translations of

Aeschines and Demosthenes] *non uerbum pro uerbo necesse habui reddere, sed genus omne uerborum uimque seruaui. non enim ea me annumerare lectori putaui oportere, sed tamquam appendere.* For Roscius' destitution following his eviction cf. §23 *nudum eicit domo.* The ring (*anulus*) was a very personal possession of Romans (the point is emphasized by the hyperbaton *anulum . . . suum*), often decorated with an ancestral device or portrait, and used to seal documents; cf. *OCD³* s.v. ring; hence the emphasis on Roscius' surrender even of this. For Roscius as *innocens* cf. §6n. *amicorum opibus* will refer above all to the aid given by Caecilia Metella; cf. §§27 and 147.

145 'praedia mea . . . et ferendum puto: C. places on his client's lips (*sermocinatio*; cf. §28n. and §§32 and 58) descriptions of three aspects of his present plight, each followed by his acquiescence. The chiastic arrangement of nouns, possessives, and pronouns effects a stark contrast: *praedia mea tu . . . ego aliena misericordia.* For his forced abandonment of agriculture cf. §49. **mea domus . . . mihi clausa est:** *mea* is placed first both for variety after *praedia mea* and for emphasis. Indeed, not only was his home blocked to him, but Roscius was denied right of passage (*iter*) to his father's grave; cf. §24. The point that Roscius is bereft of slaves is repeated from §77 (*unus puer . . . relictus non est*). For emphatic *nullus* cf. §55n. With *ferendum puto* contrast §34 (spoken in C.'s own person) *quia fit a Chrysogono, non est ferendum.*

quid uis amplius? . . . quid tibi obsto?': here begins a series of questions that continues to the end of this section as C. seeks to show that Chrysogonus has no motive for pursuing Roscius in the courts. The *sermocinatio* should continue through *obsto*, the last first-person verb, not *puto* (as in Kasten's edn.). *insequor* is "pursue" but also "persecute, hound": *OLD* s.v. 1 and 4; for *oppugno* cf. §120n. *officio* and *obsto* already appeared as synonyms at §112.

si spoliorum causa . . . propulsare non posse?: three motives are invoked and then refuted. For *spolia* as the issue in this trial cf. §8 *ut spoliis ex hoc iudicio ornati auctique discedant.* Personal enmity played a large rôle in Roman life and politics (cf. Epstein 1987) but is not applicable here, C. remarks, in view of the fact that the two principals had not even met before the property changed hands. *ipse* is "the man himself," contrasted with his farms; similarly §115, where see n. **ipsum ab se:** *ipse* is added to lend emphasis to the reflexive pronoun, as often; cf. *OLD* s.v. 2. *atrox* is "shocking"; see §9n.

sin, quod bona . . . bona patria reddantur?: Naugerius' insertion of *quod* after *sin* is needed for coordination with following *idcirco*; for the force of *nonne* cf. §38n. **praeter ceteros** "you of all men" (tr. Freese). **tu metuere non debeas:** sc. because he enjoys the favor of Sulla; cf. §28n. For *quando* substituting for *aliquando* after *ne* cf. §141n. (*ne quid*). A general restoration of the children of the proscribed at some future date would be Chrysogonus' sole legitimate worry; for C.'s effort to link this case with that group cf. §152 with n.

146 facis iniuriam, Chrysogone, . . . quas L. Sulla gessit: for the apostrophe cf. §144n. Since *iniuria* has no cognate verb, the paraphrase *facere iniuriam* must serve; cf. e.g. *Quinct.* 31 *iniuriam facere fortissime perseuerat*; *Caec.* 101 *eos . . . quibus Sulla uoluit iniuriam facere*; *OLD* s.v. *facio* 23a. For *spes* with the object of one's hope expressed in the gen. cf. *OLD* s.v. 1b. *emptio* concedes that the property was purchased, as Chrysogonus claimed (§6), in spite of the doubts raised at §§127–8. For a form of *is* with following determinative relative clause cf. K–S I 618. *res gerere* is "to perform exploits," whence *res gestae* "exploits"; cf. *OLD* s.v. *gero* 9b.

   quod si tibi . . . immanisque natura?: C. now argues that Chrysogonus is indulging in gratuitous cruelty; the charge is repeated at §150 (*nisi etiam crudelitati sanguis praebitus sit*) with the even more disturbing notion that it prevails in the Roman state (*ea crudelitas quae hoc tempore in re publica uersata est*); cf. Marchetti 1986: 109. *nullus* is again emphatic (§55n.). For the portrayal of Roscius as *miser* cf. §23n.; for his complete surrender of his property cf. §144. **ne monumenti quidem causa** "not even as a keepsake"; cf. *OLD* s.v. *monumentum* 3. For the exclamation *per deos immortales!* cf. §34n. For *immanitas* cf. §63n.; the shift to *immanis natura* (rather than continuing with *immanitas* as parallel to *crudelitas*) is simply for variety.

   quis umquam praedo . . . spolia detrahere mallet?: C. has already referred to those behind the prosecution as *praedones* or *latrones* and the elder Sex. Roscius' estate as their *praeda*; cf. §6n.; but the Gk-derived *pirata* is attested here for the first time; cf. *OLD* and *TLL* s.v. *barbarus* is frequent in invective; cf. *Dom.* 140 *nemo umquam praedo tam barbarus . . . fuit*; Opelt 1965: index s.v. The prosecution's goal was described as to depart from court *spoliis . . . ornati auctique* (§8); here the goal is the more sinister *cruenta spolia*.

147 scis hunc nihil . . . ei detrahere possis?: the fourfold anaphora of *nihil* strongly denies any threat emanating from his client; cf. the emphatic denials (partly with *nihil*) at §§97 and 143. *et* conveys indignation and leads "an indignant exclamation usually in the form of an ironical question"; translate: "and after all that . . . ?": *OLD* s.v. *et* 15a. For *oppugno* cf. §120n. **quem neque metuere potes nec odisse debes:** C. rules out both attitudes; he alludes to the notorious words of Accius' Atreus: *oderint dum* *metuant* (*trag.* 203). **quicquam . . . reliqui:** for the "gen. of the rubric" cf. §8n.

nisi hoc indignum . . . nudum expulisti: again C. speaks as if Chrysogonus were present in court (*uides*); cf. §144n. C. was fond of using *naufragium/-gus* figuratively; cf. e.g. *Rab. perd.* 25 *scopulos . . . in quibus C. Deciani naufragium fortunarum uideres*; *Cat.* 1.30 *eodem ceteros undique collectos naufragos aggregarit*; *Sul.* 41 *patrimoni naufragus*. Roscius was depicted as *nudus* at §§23 and 144; his condition is thus well matched to the simile of the shipwreck.

quasi uero nescias . . . ex sua laude redderet: the specific reference to Caecilia was prepared by the mention of *amicorum opibus* (§144) and *aliena misericordia* (§145). C. presents her to the senatorial jurors as an implicit foil for the *ignobilitas* of Chrysogonus and thus reinforces their prejudice. For her father and brother cf. §27n. Her three paternal uncles (*patruos*) were likewise distinguished: L. Caecilius Metellus Diadematus (cos. 117); M. Caecilius Metellus (cos. 115); and C. Caecilius Metellus Caprarius (cos. 113); cf. Münzer, *RE* s.v. Caecilius 93, 77, and 84 respectively. For the sense of *spectatus* cf. §141n. **cum esset mulier, uirtute perfecit:** the *cum*-clause is adversative, playing on the etymology of *uirtus* from *uir* (cf. *Tusc.* 2.43). C. imagines a reciprocal process by which Caecilia, rather than resting on her inherited rank (*dignitas*), from her own virtue (*laus*: *OLD* s.v. 3) pays back *non minora ornamenta* to her relations; the litotes (*non minora*) is a strong affirmation; cf. Lausberg §§586–7.

148 An, quod diligenter . . . non liceret: for *diligentia* in this speech cf. §27n.; for the semantics of *facinus* (here evidently pejorative) cf. §37n. Once again C. balances the alternatives by means of the *si . . . sin* structure; cf. §8n.; within each category action is conceived "in proportion to" (*OLD* s.v. *pro* 12a) certain facts. That the elder Roscius was *hospitiis florens hominum nobilissimorum* was established already at §15. *adsum* + dat. is "to give support by one's presence in court (to), be an advocate (for)": *OLD* s.v. 12. **et auderent libere defendere** is the sticking point; cf. §§1–3. C. already raised the claim that larger interests are at stake at §7 (*periculum quod in omnes intenditur*); at §145 he began to connect the case to the plight of the *proscriptorum liberi* in general. **summa res publica** is "the welfare of the state": *OLD* s.v. *summus* 16b; for *periculum* of the defendant's position cf. §85n.; *tempto* is to "make an assault upon": *OLD* s.v. 9d. *consisto* is "to appear as in court" or "as a litigant": *OLD* s.v. 6c. For *mehercule* cf. §58n.

nunc ita defenditur . . . superari putent: *sane* sometimes adheres to negatives; it apologizes slightly without lessening the force of the denial (translate "actually"); cf. *Leg.* 2.41 with Dyck's n. *moleste ferre* is colloquial for "be annoyed at": *OLD* s.v. *moleste* b; C. thus counters the supposition mentioned at the beginning of this section. C. himself may not bring *potentia* to bear, but some of his client's supporters certainly do; nonetheless C. depicts the *potentia* as on the other side; cf. §35 *Chrysogonus . . . potentia pugnat* and the later claim that the speech was a blow struck *contra L. Sullae dominantis opes* (*Off.* 2.51); cf. Kinsey 1980: 183 and 1985: 189; §6n.

149 quae domi gerenda . . . pro Sex. Roscio diceret: *domi* contrasts with *fori iudicique ratio* as the two relevant spheres of operation with the woman assigned to the domestic sphere. For Caecilia cf. §27n. The reference appears to be to M. Valerius Messalla Niger who served as consul of 61; he would thus have been two or at most four years younger than C. (four years if the theory of Badian 1964 is correct that patricians were allowed to present themselves as candidates two years early); he helped persuade C. to defend P. Sulla (*Sul.* 20), served as censor (55–4), and was a member, with C. and others, of Scaurus' defense team **de repetundis** in 54; he was dead by 46, when he was praised by C. for his diligence and care in oratory (*Brut.* 246); cf. F. Münzer, *RE* 8A 1.162.48 (s.v. Valerius 266). Since Messalla was not below the minimum age for litigation (seventeen, according to Ulpian, *Dig.* 3.1.1.3), he must have declined to defend for other reasons: Münzer loc.cit. 163.27–31 suspects that he wanted to avoid offending Sulla, to whom the family had close ties, whereas Kinsey 1980: 186 thinks the case was too unimportant for the nobles to take on themselves; cf. also Alexander 2002: 157. The alternative candidate is Messalla's cousin, M. Valerius Messalla Rufus, who was two years younger still and served as consul of 53; on him cf. R. Hanslik, *RE* 8A1.166.61 (Valerius 268). **ut uidetis** shows that Messalla was present in court as an *aduocatus* for Roscius albeit not a *subscriptor* since he is not going to speak. **ipse** "in person"; cf. §1n.

  quoniam ad dicendum . . . sententiis iudicum permitteretur: C. has spoken of his own *pudor* at §9; for such feelings as an ornament of youth cf. *Off.* 2.46 *prima igitur commendatio proficiscitur a modestia.* For *aetas* and *pudor* as an obstacle cf. Kaster 2005: 166n48. C. again plays on different senses of *causa* (cf. §5), here "case" and "for his sake" (*sua causa*); cf. Holst 1925: 56. For the sense in which C. was "under obligation" (*debere*) to take the case cf. §4. For *ipse* used for emphasis and contrast cf. §13n. For Roscius' adversaries as *sectores* cf. §§80–1, 88, 94, and 103; the theme recurs at §§151–2; for the defendant's life being at stake cf. §5n. At all periods C. uses *eripi de* (or, more commonly, *e*) *manibus* of a sudden rescue; cf. e.g. *Ver.* 2.1.9 *istum ex manibus populi Romani eripi nullo modo posse*; *Vat.* 34 *accusatores esse tuos de tuis tuorumque manibus ereptos*; *Phil.* 13.25 *non hic parens uerior a quo certe uitam habemus e tuis facinerosissimis manibus ereptam?*; similarly §151 *qui de suis manibus effugerint.*

nimirum, iudices, . . . ex inuidia minus laborarent: contrast the rejected motive for the war given at §141. **pro hac nobilitate:** i.e. of the type represented by the just mentioned Caecilia and Messalla. **ut ii nobiles restituerentur in ciuitatem:** many fled in the wake of the taking of Rome by Cinna in 87 and the subsequent purges; Sulla reentered Italy in the spring of 83 and fought his way back into Rome; for an overview of the history of the period cf. R. Seager, *CAH* ix ch. 6. For a form of *is* followed by determinative relative clause cf. §146n. With anaphora of *qui* C. details characteristics of the "true noble" as opposed to the behavior described at §139; for the subj. in a relative clause of characteristic cf. A–G §535. **qui quantum . . . mallent ostendere:** such considerations led C., following the Verrine prosecution, to devote himself almost exclusively to defense; cf. Dyck on *Off.* 2.50. *loco natus* ("born in (a specified) position in society") is a set phrase without preposition; cf. G–L §385 n.1; *OLD* s.v. *locus* 17; Caes. *Gal.* 5.25.1 *erat in Carnutibus summo loco natus Tasgetius. laboro* is "to be distressed" or "in difficulties" from physical but also non-physical causes: *OLD* s.v. 3–4; cf. *Inv.* 2.5 *quod si in ceteris quoque studiis a multis eligere homines commodissimum quodque quam sese uni alicui certe uellent addicere . . . aliquanto leuius ex inscitia laborarent. inuidia* is mentioned as the motor that drove the revolution against the nobles; cf. Hellegouarc'h 1963 195–8; at *Leg.* 3.25–6 "Marcus" considers whether *inuidia* had a rôle in precipitating his own exile.

150 Verum si a Chrysogono . . . bonitas et misericordia: *uerum si . . . uitam ne petat* restates the *postulatio* of §7. For Chrysogonus' thorough pillaging of the defendant (*cum ademerit nobis omnia . . . propria*) cf. §§23, 144, and 146. **ne lucem . . . eripere cupiat:** cf. §71 *cui repente caelum, solem, aquam terramque ademerint.* **si non satis habet . . . explere:** cf. §8 (*quibus satis nihil est*) with n. For Chrysogonus' (alleged) *crudelitas* cf. §146. *perfugium* ("refuge") was a favorite word of C.'s that tends to be replaced after him by *refugium*; cf. *OLD* s.v. 1; for the jurors conceived as such cf. *Clu.* 7; *Mur.* 87. **una spes . . . quae rei publicae:** Roscius' *spes* is very different from the *spes emptionis suae* that drives, according to C., Chrysogonus' pursuit of his client (§146). The separation of *una spes* from *eadem* serves emphasis. For the attempt to connect Roscius' case with problems of state cf. §§7 (*periculum quod in omnes intenditur*) and 148 (*quod summa res publica in huius periculo temptatur*). *pristinus*, like *priscus*, connotes "good old-fashioned"; cf. *OLD* s.vv. **bonitas et misericordia:** cf. *Lig.* 37 *nihil est tam populare quam bonitas, nulla de uirtutibus tuis plurimis nec admirabilior nec gratior misericordia est.* At §3 C. laments the loss of the *ignoscendi ratio*; at §139 he desiderates nobles who are *misericordes.* For Sulla as the *punitor misericordiae* cf. V. Max. 9.2.1, citing the execution of M. Plaetorius for fainting at the grisly murder of the praetor M. Marius.

quae si manet . . . in hac tanta immanitate uersari: C. raises two alternative possibilities (for *sin* cf. §8n.), the latter being, as usual, destined for elaboration. For the issue as Roscius' *salus* or his being *incolumis* cf. §§6 and 26. For the second alternative cf. *Rab. Post.* 46 *si iam obliuisci uestrae mansuetudinis uolueritis. crudelitas* is personified as the subject of *uersor* "to be abroad, subsist (in a place)": *OLD* s.v. *uerso* 11a; see below and for a different sense §39n. Instead of using a counterfactual form, C. inserts the aside *id quod . . . non potest. acerbus* is "cruel, harsh": *OLD* s.v. 3a; for a different sense cf. §78n.; for the comparative without explicit standard of reference cf. §3n. **actum est** "it is over with", emphasizing completion; cf. *OLD* s.v. *ago* 21c. After the elaborate protasis *sin . . . reddit*, this two-word apodosis cuts off the sentence, just as the jurors' harshness would cut off Roscius' hopes. **inter feras . . . uersari:** cf. Cael. *Fam.* 8.17.1 *perire satius est quam hos uidere.* For the attribution to Chrysogonus of a *fera immanisque natura* cf. §146; cf. also §154 *fin.*

151 ad eamne rem . . . iugulare non potuissent?: cf. §8 *nonne . . . hoc uel indignissimum est, uos idoneos habitos per quorum sententias iusque iurandum id assequantur quod antea ipsi scelere et ferro assequi consuerunt?* The selection of the jurors was presented in far different terms ibid.: *qui ex ciuitate in senatum propter dignitatem, ex senatu in hoc consilium delecti estis propter seueritatem.* **sectores ac sicarii:** the equation of the two began punningly at §80 (*eosdem fere sectores fuisse collorum et bonorum*); see *ad loc.*; then Capito was called *et sector et sicarius* at §103; in the next section both terms are included among Chrysogonus' attributes. For *iugulo* cf. §13n.; for the relative clause of characteristic cf. §149n.

solent hoc boni . . . de improuiso incidant: for a form of *hic* followed by a defining *ut*-clause cf. §127n. Landgraf *ad loc.* suspects that *boni imperatores* has been chosen for similarity to *bonorum emptores* (§72 and below). *quo fugam hostium fore arbitrentur* is attracted to the subj. since the clause depends on *collocent* and forms an integral part of the thought; cf. G–L §§507.4 and 629. **in quos . . . incidant** is a relative clause with final force; cf. §25n. This seems like a reasonable stratagem but is not, in fact, among those listed at Fron. *Str.* 2.5, the attempt usually being to lure the enemy into reckless pursuit; but that, of course, would not fit Roscius' situation. The closest parallel is perhaps Scipio's igniting of a fire in combustible material in Syphax's camp with the plan to cut down his men as they fled (ibid. 2.5.29).

nimirum similiter arbitrantur . . . effugerint: for *tales uiros* cf.
§141n.; for *qui excipiatis* cf. the previous n.; for *qui de suis manibus effugerint*
cf. §34n.; cf. the similar *de manibus eripi* at §149.

di prohibeant . . . praesidium sectorum existimetur!: for the
pious formula *di prohibeant* cf. Ter. *An.* 568, Pollio *Fam.* 10.33.4, Tac. *Hist.*
4.74.3. The construction with *ut* rather than *ne* (conjectured here by Whitte)
was defended by Draeger 1866: 587 with reference to *SHA* Iul. Cap. *Maxim.*
28.7 (*dii prohibeant ut quisquam ingenuorum pedibus meis osculum figat*). For the jury
as a *consilium* (*publicum*) cf. §8n. For *praesidium* of a (private) bodyguard cf. §13n.

152 an uero, iudices, . . . in Sex. Rosci periculo quaeri?: proceeding along lines adumbrated at §145 (*nequando liberis proscriptorum bona patria
reddantur*), C. seeks to widen the implications of this case. The children and
grandchildren of the proscribed had lost not only their property but also
the right to stand for political office; such punishment was unprecedented
and perceived as particularly cruel; cf. Sal. *Hist.* 1.55.6 (speech of Lepidus)
quin solus omnium post memoriam humani generis supplicia in post futuros [sc. *Sulla*]
composuit etc.; Mommsen 1899: 593 and 986n1; see further §153n. For the
sense of *agi* cf. §8n.; for *ratio* §137n. For the jurors' oath and the prosecution's designs on it cf. §§8 with n., 101, and 140; for the defendant's *periculum*
cf. §85n.

dubium est ad quem . . . patris bona uenierunt?: a question without an interrogative particle or pronoun is unusual in C., and when it occurs,
it usually contains an expression of doubt (as here) or possibility; cf. K–S II
501–2. In surveying some Ciceronian recapitulations Winterbottom 2004: 219
remarks: "The rhetorical question of *Rosc. Am.* 152, comparing the accuser
and the defendant, in no way grates; but it deftly summarizes a main con-
tention of the speech." As when he first described the murder in §18 C.
confronts the jurors with a dilemma by suggesting that a simple comparison
of the characteristics of two suspects will lead to the murderer; cf. §88n.
For the terms *sector* and *sicarius* applied to those behind the prosecution cf.
§151n. For *inimicitiae* between the victim and his son and the T. Roscii cf.
§§17, 19, 30, 86–8. A form of *idem* is often attached with *atque* or *-que* to stress
identity: "the same the accuser"; cf. K–S I 627. **probatum suis filium:**
such approval can be a linchpin of the defense; this includes a freedman in
relation to his *patronus*, as at *Clu.* 52 *cum illa defensione usus essem . . . Scamandrum
patrono esse probatum* or a citizen in relation to his fellow townsmen, as at *Cael.*
5 *nam quod est obiectum municipibus esse adulescentem non probatum suis . . .* C. has
adduced little evidence in support of this assertion, only the argument that
relegatio to work on the farms did not show the father's dislike (§§42–51) or

that his relatives approved of his fleeing to Rome for protection (§27). For the
absence of specific mention of supporting relatives at the trial cf. §49n. *culpa
nulla* chimes in with the repeated reference to his client as *innocens* (cf. §6n.).
consisto is "find a home, settle"; cf. *OLD* s.v. 7a. *numquid* anticipates a negative
response ("surely . . . not"); cf. *OLD* s.v.; for *obsto* cf. §35n. For the sale of the
goods but survival of the heir bringing a tormenting *scrupulus* to the mind of
Chrysogonus and thus motivating the trial cf. §6.

153 Quodsi id uos suscipitis . . . instaurata esse uideatur: *quodsi id
uos . . . profitemini*: i.e. they will aid the prosecution, not the defense, as C. had
hoped (§10). Since Tac. *Dial.* 23.1 and Quint. *Inst.* 9.4.73 *esse uideatur* has been
regarded as C.'s trademark, but at 4.7 per cent frequency the type was only his
seventh-favorite clausula (see Appendix). **ut ad uos adducantur . . . bona
uenierunt:** i.e. he conceives this as merely the first in a series of such trials.
Hinard and Benferhat *ad loc.* argue that the children of the proscribed had
been exiled and were partially restored only in 70; they therefore argue
that this material was added to the speech when it was published in 70
or later; Berry (2004) 84–5 argues similarly but places publication in 77;
he notes (correctly) that the argument contradicts C.'s point about Roscius
sen. not having been properly proscribed (§§125–8), but that is hardly the
central argument of the speech. C. has hinted from the beginning that larger
public issues will be broached (§2 *si uerbum de re publica fecisset, id quod in
hac causa fieri necesse est*; §7 *periculum quod in omnes intenditur*; §129 *quaeque ad
omnes, nisi prouidemus, arbitror pertinere*); our passage redeems these pledges.
Furthermore the rhetoric is designed to create pity (*ad infantium puerorum
incunabula*), a requisite of the peroration (cf. Winterbottom 2004: 226), whereas
it is hard to see why C. should have added the topic to a version of the speech
published later. Finally the young C. is unlikely to have held back this speech,
a striking recommendation of his talent, for so long a time. The exclamation
per deos immortales, previously met at §§34 (see *ad loc.*) and 146, recurs twice
in this section, each time following an imperative, a symptom of heightened
emotion. The separation of *proscriptio* from its epithets provides suspense and
emphasis; for the sense cf. §21n. *instauro* was originally a religious term for
"repeating" a ritual that had been performed defectively; here it is used in a
broader sense of "resuming" or "renewing"; cf. *OLD* s.v. 1–2.

illam priorem . . . peruenturam putetis!: *illam priorem*: sc. *proscrip-
tionem. eos qui arma capere potuerunt* proves to have been formulated (instead
of simply *eos qui arma ceperunt*) for the sake of contrast to the fate of *infantes
pueri*. **senatus suscipere noluit:** the senate declined to pass an enabling
law; Sulla acted simply under his authority as dictator, established by the *lex*

Valeria (see §125n.); nor did Sulla communicate with any magistrate before publishing the first proscription list; cf. Plut. *Sull.* 31; Hinard 1985a: 71–2; §125n. **ne quid acrius . . . factum uideretur:** for *acer* cf. §11n.; for the *maiores* as a standard §50n. The senate, like the jury (§§8 and 151), was a *publicum consilium*. For *uero* adding focus to the contrasting point cf. §49n. *eorum* refers back to *qui arma capere potuerunt. pueri* varies *liberi* ("children"), as often: *OLD* s.v. *puer* 4a. *incunabula*, a *plurale tantum*, is literally a "cradle" and hence here and elsewhere a symbol of infancy: *OLD* s.v. 1; he thus adds a pathetic touch to the peroration without displaying his client or his client's relatives dressed in mourning clothes (*sordes*), as was usual; cf. on §§143–54.
rem publicam peruenturam putetis: *res publica peruentura sit* would have been possible but unrhythmical; as it is, C. has secured his fourth favorite *clausula* (see Appendix), reinforced by alliteration, on C.'s use of which cf. §35n.

154 The proposal to remedy a general ailment of the state by action in a specific case is less striking in a Roman court than it would be in a modern one given that "the *iudicia publica* were simultaneously about specific offenses and the general political order" (Riggsby 1999: 162); cf. in general ibid. 157–63.
homines sapientes . . . maxime mederi conuenit: for the *sapientia* of the jurors cf. §10; in this they are similar to the *maiores* (cf. §§69–71); L. Cassius, the *sapientissimus iudex*, was an implicit model (§84). For *iste* of something well known without implying contempt cf. §5n.; similarly *Mur.* 13 *cum ista sis auctoritate, non debes, M. Cato, arripere maledictum ex triuio.* The jurors' *auctoritas* is implied at §8 *qui ex ciuitate in senatum propter dignitatem, ex senatu in hoc consilium delecti estis propter seueritatem*; cf. also *Sest.* 2 *hos uestra auctoritate . . . se oppressuros arbitrantur*; for their *potestas* cf. §122n. For the relative clause preceding its "antecedent" cf. §6n.; *res publica* is personified as the subj. of *laboro*, for the sense of which cf. §149n. *medeor* + dat. continues the medical imagery: "to cure": *OLD* s.v. 1a.
uestrum nemo est . . . domestica crudelitate laborare: for the sentence structure cf. §55 with n. **in hostes lenissimus:** C. offers a (not very convincing) proof from the word *hostis* itself at *Off.* 1.37; he evidently has in mind such examples as the wars fought *de imperio* listed ibid. 1.38. *domesticus* here is "civil, against citizens" as opposed to the treatment of foreign enemies implied by the words *in hostes*; cf. *OLD* s.v. *domesticus* 3 and *hostis* 1–2; Jal 1963. At §150 *crudelitas* was attributed *ex hypothesi* to Chrysogonus but also said to be more widespread (*in re publica uersata est*), a point combined here with a call for remedy.

hanc tollite . . . in hac re publica uersari: with emphatic anaphora (*hanc . . . hanc*) C. puts his finger on what ails the state and needs to be removed. This sentence illustrates that commands may be expressed straightforwardly with the imperative whereas prohibitions use the imperative of *nolo* + inf.; cf. §67n. For *uersor* cf. §150n.

quae non modo . . . consuetudine incommodorum: *id . . . mali*: for the gen. of the rubric cf. §8n.; for the hyperbaton §30 *quid . . . sceleris*. For the hope for an end to the bloodletting cf. §11. **tot ciues:** various figures are given for those slain, whereby civil war and proscription victims are sometimes combined; cf. p. 4 and on the whole problem Hinard 1985a: 116–20. For *atrox* cf. §9n.; C. sees the only remaining hope in the jurors' *bonitas et misericordia* (§150 with n.); Roscius is currently living *aliena misericordia* (§145) thanks to the intervention of Caecilia Metella. **consuetudine incommodorum** is reserved for last as the point to be developed in the sequel, the euphemistic *incommodum* ("disadvantage, misfortune") varying *malum*; cf. *OLD* s.v. 2a.

nam cum omnibus horis . . . ex animis amittimus: *omnibus horis* is still more exaggerated than the *cotidiano . . . sanguine* of §11. Since for the ancients, as for us, seeing was proverbially more powerful than hearing (cf. §98n.), *etiam* should be taken with what follows it. *molestia* ("annoyance") is another euphemism; its rich attestation in comedy, C.'s essays and letters etc. and absence from the high genres suggests a colloquialism; cf. *OLD* s.v. 1a. For the sense of *humanitas* cf. §46n.; cf. §150 *inter feras satius est aetatem degere quam in hac tanta immanitate uersari.* **amittimus:** this is represented as an ongoing process that must be broken off before it is complete (present tense). Konstan 2001: 100 contrasts our passage with *ad Brut.* 1.2.3, 1.2a.2, and 2.5.3–5, where C. advises against clemency to Antony and his partisans on the grounds that clemency would merely prolong the civil war; Konstan concludes that C. "had learned a lesson from Caesar's fate."

APPENDIX: PROSE RHYTHM

One characteristic feature of Ciceronian prose is the preference for certain rhythmical shapes, especially at the close of sentences,[1] but also marking smaller units.[2] This mannerism was so firmly rooted in C. that it appears even in hastily written letters.[3] The basic unit is the cretic ($-\smile-$), varied with trochee ($-\smile$) and iamb ($\smile-$); the last syllable is anceps ($\times$), i.e. it may be either short or long; and a long may be resolved into two shorts. The following are C.'s favorite shapes in order of preference:

1   $-\smile--\times$ (cretic + trochee)
2   $----\smile\times$ (molossus + cretic)
3   $-\smile--\smile\times$ (double cretic)
4   $----\smile-\times$ (molossus + double trochee)
5   $-\smile--\smile-\times$ (cretic + double trochee)
6   $-\smile-\times$ (cretic + iamb)
7   $-\smile\smile\smile-\times$ (first paeon + trochee).[4]

Pro Sexto Roscio provides many examples of such rhythms before a pause.[5] C. also has certain aversions, in particular the hexameter ending, though the avoidance is not so thoroughgoing as in his later speeches.[6]

One phenomenon that can serve as a stylistic marker is the use of *atque* before a consonant. The Roman elegists are fairly strict in avoiding this,[7] whereas Cato and older prose generally shows no such inhibition.[8] C. used *atque* before consonants more freely in the early speeches,[9] elsewhere for archaic *color* and rhythmic effect, especially in prayers or passages in exalted style.[10] Apart from occurrences before the aspirate, our speech shows 17 of 85 instances of *atque* before consonant or a frequency of 20%. Two parasynonyms joined by *atque* can create a sonorous phrase suitable for ending a colon or sentence,[11] e.g. the double cretic or equivalent at §113 *commendatae sunt atque*

---

[1] The fundamental insight was that of Zielinski 1904.
[2] The point is emphasized by Nisbet 1990.
[3] Cf. Fraenkel 1968: 164–9; for prose rhythm in the letters see further Hutchinson 1998: 9–12.
[4] Cf. Wilkinson 1963: 156.
[5] Cf. General Index s.v. *clausula(e)*.
[6] Cf. Laurand 1911: 78 and 84–5.
[7] Nisbet 1990: 355.
[8] Cf. Fraenkel 1968: 130 and 162–3.
[9] Nisbet 1990: 357.
[10] Cf. Hutchinson 1995: 486–90.
[11] Similarly in the poets, e.g. Virg. *A.* 6.622 *fixit leges pretio atque refixit*.

concreditae and §114 *transigeret atque decideret*; or C.'s third-favorite clausula at §6 *effundere atque consumere.*

Close attention to rhythm enables one to appreciate the decisions that lie behind the text. Thus in §8 the addition of *atque horrere* after *metuere* and prior to *debent* changes an unrhythmical close into trochee + spondee; that same rhythm is the result of addition of the synonym *adaugent* in §30. Changes in the expected word order can also be rhythmically motivated, as e.g. the postponement of the imperative to follow the indirect question effects C.'s fourth favorite clausula (§69); similarly at §81 reversal of the expected order of infinitive and finite verb produces his second favorite type; again at §153 C. could have written *res publica peruentura sit*, but the change to *rem publicam peruenturam putetis* secures his fourth favorite pattern.

Since the understanding of these patterns was lost between the end of antiquity and their rediscovery by Zielinski, they are an invaluable aid to restoring the original text. Thus at §31 the tradition is divided between *atque subibo* and *ac subibo*; but the latter is much more likely since it effects trochee + spondee rather than the heroic clausula. The rhythm promotes Stephanus' conjecture *laesos sese putent* (§124: C.'s second favorite clausula) for the unrhythmical transmitted *laesos se esse putent*. On the other hand, the rhythm argues against Ernesti's *consueuerant*, which destroys the transmitted trochee + spondee (§5).

REFERENCES

Standard commentaries on other texts are cited by the name of the commentator (e.g. "Berry on *Sul.*") and are omitted from this list.

Achard, G. 1981. *Pratique rhétorique et idéologie politique dans les discours "optimates" de Cicéron.* Mnemosyne Suppl. 68. Leiden

Adams, J. N. 1973. "Two Latin words for 'kill'," *Glotta* 51: 280–92

 1978. "Conventions of naming in Cicero," *Classical Quarterly* 72: 145–66

 1994a. *Wackernagel's law and the placement of the copula esse in Classical Latin.* Proceedings of the Cambridge Philological Society Suppl. 18. Cambridge

 1994b. "Wackernagel's law and the position of unstressed personal pronouns in Classical Latin," *Transactions of the Philological Society* 92: 103–78

 2003. "The new Vindolanda writing-tablets," *Classical Quarterly* 53: 530–75

Afzelius, A. 1942. "Zwei Episoden aus dem Leben Ciceros," *Classica & Mediaevalia* 5: 209–17

Albrecht, M. von 1989. *Masters of Roman prose from Cato to Apuleius.* Tr. N. Adkin. Leeds

 2003. *Cicero's style.* Leiden and Boston

Alexander, M. C. 1985. "*praemia* in the *quaestiones* of the late Republic," *Classical Philology* 80: 20–32

 2000. "The repudiated technicality in Roman forensic oratory" in M. Hoeflich, ed., *Lex et Romanitas: essays for Alan Watson* (Berkeley) 59–72

 2002. *The case for the prosecution in the Ciceronian era.* Ann Arbor

Amacker, R. 2002. "Conditions contextuelles et pragmatiques sur l'emploi de la polysyndète chez Cicéron, César et Varron" in A. M. Bolkestein et al., eds., *Theory and description in Latin linguistics* (Amsterdam) 27–42

André, J. 1951. "Les adjectifs et adverbes à valeur intensive en *per-* et *prae-*," *Revue des études Latines* 29: 121–54

Astin, A. E. 1967. *Scipio Aemilianus.* Oxford

Bablitz, L. 2007. *Actors and audience in the Roman courtroom.* London and New York

Badian, E. 1958. *Foreign clientelae (264–70 BC).* Oxford

 1962. "Waiting for Sulla," *Journal of Roman Studies* 52: 47–61

 1964. "Caesar's *cursus* and the intervals between offices," *Studies in Greek and Roman history* (New York) 140–56

 1970. "Additional notes on Roman magistrates," *Athenaeum* 58: 3–14

Baltrusch, E. 1989. *Regimen morum. Die Reglementierung des Privatlebens der Senatoren und Ritter in der römischen Republik und frühen Kaiserzeit.* Munich

Baroin, C. 2005. "'Les candélabres corinthiens n'existent pas'. Comment les Romains ont inventé un art grec à usage romain" in F. Dupont and E. Valette-Cagnac, eds., *Façons de parler grec à Rome* (Paris) 103–34

Bauman, R. 1996. *Crime and punishment in ancient Rome.* London

Belayche, N. 1995. "La neuvaine funéraire à Rome ou 'la mort impossible'" in
F. Hinard and M.-F. Lambert, eds., *La mort au quotidien dans le monde romain* (Paris)
155–69

Benferhat, Y. 2003–4. "*Vita rustica*: un idéal politique et moral? Réflexions sur le *Pro
Roscio Amerino*" in R. Bedon and N. Dupré, eds., *Rus amoenum. Les agréments de la
vie rurale en Gaule romaine et dans les régions voisines* (Limoges) 259–87

Berger, D. 1978. *Cicero als Erzähler. Forensische und literarische Strategien in den Gerichtsreden.*
Frankfurt a.M.

Bernardo, Y. L. 2000. *Severitas: a study of a Roman virtue in Cicero.* Diss. University of
North Carolina. Chapel Hill

Berry, D. H., ed. and tr. 2000. *Cicero: Defence speeches.* Oxford
  2004. "The publication of Cicero's *Pro Roscio Amerino*," *Mnemosyne* 57: 80–7

Bertocchi, A. 1996. "Some properties of *ipse*" in H. Rosén, ed., *Aspects of Latin: papers
from the Seventh International Colloquium on Latin Linguistics* (Innsbruck) 539–52

Blase, H. 1903. "Tempora und Modi" in G. Landgraf, ed., *Historische Grammatik der
lateinischen Sprache.* III: *Syntax des einfachen Satzes.* Leipzig

Bona, F. 1960. "Sul concetto di *manubiae* e sulla responsabilità del magistrato in ordine
alla *praeda*," *Studia et Documenta Historiae et Iuris* 26: 106–75

Bonamente, M. 1980. "Leggi suntuarie e loro motivazioni" in *Tra Grecia e Roma: temi
antichi e metodologie moderne* (Rome) 67–91

Bonnet, M. 1906. "Le dilemme de C. Gracchus", *Revue des études anciennes* 8: 40–6

Boren, H. C. 1964. "Cicero's *concordia* in historical perspective" in M. F. Gyles and
E. W. Davis, eds., *Laudatores temporis acti: studies in memory of W. E. Caldwell* (Chapel
Hill) 51–62

Bradley, K. R. 1984. *Slaves and masters in the Roman Empire.* New York and Oxford

Briquel, D. 1980. "Sur le mode d'exécution en cas de parricide et en cas de *perduellio*"
Mélanges de l'Ecole Française de Rome. Antiquité 92: 87–107
  1984. "Formes de mise à mort dans la Rome primitive. Quelques remarques sur
une approche comparative du problème" in *Du châtiment dans la cité. Supplices
corporels et peine de mort dans le monde antique* (Rome) 225–36

Brunt, P. A. 1990. *Roman imperial themes.* Oxford

Buchheit, V. 1975a. "Chrysogonus als Tyrann in Ciceros Rede für Roscius aus Ameria," *Chiron* 5: 193–211
  1975b. "Ciceros Kritik an Sulla in der Rede für Roscius aus Ameria," *Historia* 4:
570–91

Burian, J. 1984. "Latrones. Ein Begriff in römischen literarischen und juristischen
Quellen," *Eirene* 21: 17–23

Butler, S. 2002. *The hand of Cicero.* London

Camiñas, J. G. 1990. "Le *crimen calumniae* dans la *lex Remmia de calumniatoribus*," *Revue
internationale des droits de l'antiquité* 37: 117–33

Canter, H. V. 1931. "Digressio in the orations of Cicero," *American Journal of Philology*
52: 351–61

Cerami, P. 1998. "*'honeste et libere defendere*': i canoni della deontologia forense secondo Marco Tullio Cicerone," *Iura* 49: 1–24

Cerutti, S. M. 1996. *Cicero's accretive style*. Lanham

Churchill, J. B. 1999. "*Ex qua quod uellent facerent*: Roman magistrates' authority over *praeda* and *manubiae*," *Transactions of the American Philological Association* 129: 85–116.

Clark, A. C. 1905. *The uetus Cluniacensis of Poggio*. Anecdota Oxoniensia 10. Oxford

Classen, C. J. 1982. "Ciceros Kunst der Überredung" in W. Ludwig, ed., *Rhétorique et éloquence chez Cicéron* (Vandoeuvres-Geneva) 149–84

Clemente, G. 1981. "Le leggi sul lusso e la società romana tra III e II secolo a.c." in A. Giardina and A. Schiavone, eds., *Modelli etici, diritto e trasformazioni sociali* (Rome) 1–14

Cloud, J. D. 1969. "The primary purpose of the *lex Cornelia de sicariis*," *Zeitschrift der Savigny-Stiftung für Rechtsgeschichte* 66: 258–66

1971. "*Parricidium*: from the *lex Numae* to the *lex Pompei de parricidiis*," *Zeitschrift der Savigny-Stiftung für Rechtsgeschichte* 68: 1–66

Corbeill, A. 1996. *Controlling laughter: political humor in the late Roman Republic*. Princeton.
2002. "Rhetorical education in Cicero's youth" in J. M. May, ed. *Brill's companion to Cicero: oratory and rhetoric* (Leiden) 23–48

Corbier, P. 2005. *Nudités romaines*. Paris

Cornell, T. 1981. "Some observations on the 'crimen incesti'," in *Le délit religieux dans la cité antique* (Rome) 27–37

Craig, C. 1993. *Form as argument in Cicero's speeches: a study of dilemma*. Atlanta

Crawford, J., ed. 1994. *M. Tullius Cicero: The fragmentary speeches*. 2nd edn. Atlanta

Crook, J. 1955. *Consilium principis. Imperial councils and counsellors from Augustus to Diocletian*. Cambridge

1995. *Legal advocacy in the ancient world*. London

Culham, P. 1989. "Archives and alternatives in Republican Rome," *Classical Philology* 84: 100–15

Cumont, F. 1922. *After life in Roman paganism*. New Haven

David, J.-M. 1992. *Le patronat judiciaire au dernier siècle de la république romaine*. Rome
1995. "Le tribunal du préteur: contraints symboliques et politiques sous la République et le début de l'Empire," *Klio* 77: 371–85

della Morte, P. M. 1977. *Studi su Cicerone oratore. Struttura della 'Pro Quinctio' e della 'Pro Sexto Roscio Amerino'*. Naples

Devine, A. M., and L. D. Stephens, 2006. *Latin word order: structured meaning and information*. New York

Dickey, E. 2002. *Latin forms of address from Plautus to Apuleius*. Oxford

Diederich, S. 2007. *Römische Agrarhandbücher zwischen Fachwissenschaft, Literatur und Ideologie*. Berlin and New York

Draeger, A. 1866. "Zu Cicero's Reden," *Philologus* 24: 587

Dufallo, B. 2007. *The ghosts of the past: Latin literature, the dead, and Rome's transition to a principate*. Columbus

Dyck, A. R. 1998. "Narrative obfuscation, philosophical *topoi*, and tragic patterning in Cicero's *Pro Milone*," *Harvard Studies in Classical Philology* 98: 219–41

2003. "Evidence and rhetoric in Cicero's *Pro Roscio Amerino*: the case against Sex. Roscius," *Classical Quarterly* 53: 235–46

2009. Review of Hinard and Benferhat 2006, *Mnemosyne* 62: 675–8

Edwards, C. 1993. *The politics of immorality in ancient Rome*. Cambridge

Egmond, F. 1995. "The cock, the dog, the serpent, and the monkey: reception and transmission of a Roman punishment, or historiography as history," *International Journal of the Classical Tradition* 2: 159–92

Epstein, D. F. 1987. *Personal enmity in Roman politics 218–43 BC*. London

Falco, A. 1982. "Alcune osservazioni sulla *iuvenilis redundantia* di Cicerone," *Bolletino di Studi Latini* 13: 223–8

Ferrary, J.-L. 1991. "Lex Cornelia de sicariis et veneficis," *Athenaeum* 79: 417–34

Fleckeisen, A. 1892. "*munitare*," *Jahrbücher für classische Philologie* 83: 211–12

Flower, H. 1996. *Ancestor masks and aristocratic power in Roman culture*. Oxford

Fowler, W. W. 1911. *The religious experience of the Roman people from the earliest times to the age of Augustus*. London

Fraenkel, E. 1968. *Leseproben aus Reden Ciceros und Catos*. Rome

Frazel, T. D. 2009. *The rhetoric of Cicero's "In Verrem."* Göttingen

Freeze, J. H., ed. and tr. 1930. *Cicero: Pro Quinctio, Pro Roscio Amerino, Pro Roscio comoedo, Contra Rullum*. Cambridge, Mass., and London

Freyburger, G. 1986. *Fides. Étude sémantique et religieuse depuis les origines jusqu'à l'époque augustéenne*. Paris

Fugier, H. 1963. *Recherches sur l'expression du sacré dans la langue latine*. Paris

Fuhrmann, M. 1997. "Zur Prozeßtaktik Ciceros. Die Mordanklagen gegen Sextus Roscius von Ameria und Cluentius Habitus" in U. Manthe and J. von Ungern-Sternberg, eds., *Große Prozesse der römischen Antike* (Munich) 48–61

Gabba, E. 1976. *Republican Rome, the army and the allies*. Tr. P. J. Cuff. Berkeley and Los Angeles

Gaudemet, J. 1951. "Utilitas publica," *Revue historique de droit français et étranger* 4th ser. 29: 465–99

Gelzer, M. 1969. *Cicero. Ein biographischer Versuch*. Wiesbaden

Gnoli, F. 1979. *Ricerche sul crimen peculatus*. Milan

Goldberg, S. M. 2005. *Constructing literature in the Roman Republic*. Cambridge

Gotoff, H. C. 1986. "Cicero's analysis of the prosecution speeches in the *Pro Caelio*: an exercise in practical criticism," *Classical Philology* 81: 122–32

Greenidge, A. H. J. 1901. *The legal procedure of Cicero's time*. Oxford

Gruen, E. S. 1968. *Roman politics and the criminal courts, 149–78 BC*. Cambridge, Mass.

Hanssen, J. S. T. 1951. *Latin diminutives*. Bergen

Harries, B. 2007. "Acting the part: techniques of the comic stage in Cicero's early speeches" in J. Booth, ed., *Cicero on the attack: invective and subversion in the orations and beyond* (Swansea) 129–47

Harris, W. V. 1971. *Rome in Etruria and Umbria*. Oxford

216 REFERENCES

Hartman, J. J. 1911. "Cicero: *pro Roscio Amerino* 136," *Mnemosyne* 39: 292

Hartung, H.-J. 1974. "Religio und sapientia iudicum: einige grundsätzliche Bemerkungen zu einem Geschworenenspiegel in Ciceros Reden," *Hermes* 102: 556–66

Haury, A. 1955. *L'ironie et l'humour chez Cicéron*. Leiden

Havet, L. 1927. "Cicéron, *Pro Roscio Amerino*," *Revue des études Latines* 5: 166–8

Heinze, R. 1960. *Vom Geist des Römertums*. Ed. E. Burck. 3rd edn. Darmstadt

Hellegouarc'h, J. 1963. *Le vocabulaire latin des relations et des partis politiques sous la République*. Paris

Hellmuth, H. 1877. *De sermonis proprietatibus quae in prioribus Ciceronis orationibus inveniuntur*. Diss. Erlangen

Helttula, A. 1974. "On *itum ambitum datum*: a formula of *ius sepulchri*," *Arctos* 8: 9–17

Highet, G. 1949. *The classical tradition: Greek and Roman influences on Western literature*. New York

Hinard, F. 1979. "L. Cornelius Chrysogonus et la portée politique du pro Roscio Amerino," *Liverpool Classical Monthly* 4: 75–6

1980. "*Paternus inimicus*. Sur une expression de Cicéron," *Mélanges de littérature et d'épigraphie latines, d'histoire ancienne et d'archéologie*. Hommages à la mémoire de Pierre Wuilleumier (Paris) 197–210

1985a. *Les proscriptions de la Rome républicaine*. Rome

1985b. *Sylla*. Paris

1988. "De la dictature à la tyrannie. Réflexions sur la dictature de Sylla," in F. Hinard, ed., *Dictatures. Actes de la Table Ronde réunie à Paris les 27 et 28 février 1984* (Paris) 87–95

1999. "Dion Cassius et l'abdication de Sylla," *Revue des études anciennes* 101: 427–32

Hinard, F., and Y. Benferhat. 2006. See CITED EDITIONS, p. x

Hofmann, J. B. 2003. *La lingua d'uso latina*. 3rd edn. Ed. L. Ricotilli. Bologna

Holst, H. 1925. *Die Wortspiele in Ciceros Reden*. Symbolae Osloenses Suppl. 1. Oslo

Hutchinson, G. O. 1995. "Rhythm, style, and meaning in Cicero's prose," *Classical Quarterly* 89: 485–99

1998. *Cicero's correspondence. A literary study*. Oxford

2005. "Pope's spider and Cicero's writing" in T. Reinhardt et al., eds., *Proceedings of the British Academy 129: Aspects of the language of Latin prose* (Oxford) 179–93

Imholtz, A. A., Jr. 1971–2. "Gladiatorial metaphors in Cicero's *Pro Roscio Amerino*," *Classical World* 65: 228–30

Jal, P. 1963. "'Hostis (publicus)' dans la littérature latine de la fin de la république," *Revue des études anciennes* 65: 53–79

Jones, C. P. 1987. "*Stigma*: tattooing and branding in Graeco-Roman antiquity," *Journal of Roman Studies* 77: 139–55

Jörgensen, C. 1913. "*Dimissui esse* bei Cicero pro Rosc. Am. §11," *Berliner philologische Wochenschrift* 33: 253–4

Kaster, R. A. 2005. *Emotion, restraint, and community in ancient Rome*. New York

Keaveney, A. 1982. *Sulla: the last Republican*. London and Canberra

Kennedy, G. A. 1963. *The art of persuasion in Greece*. Princeton

　1972. *The art of rhetoric in the Roman world 300 BC–AD 300*. Princeton

Kierdorf, W. 1980. *Laudatio funebris. Interpretationen und Untersuchungen zur Entwicklung der römischen Leichenrede*. Meisenheim am Glan

Kinsey, T. E. 1967. "The dates of the *Pro Roscio Amerino* and *Pro Quinctio*," *Mnemosyne* ser. 4, 20: 61–7

　1968. "Cicero, *Pro Roscio Amerino*, 125," *Mnemosyne* ser. 4, 21: 290–2

　1975. "Cicero's speech for Roscius of Ameria," *Symbolae Osloenses* 50: 91–104

　1980. "Cicero's case against Magnus, Capito and Chrysogonus in the *Pro Sex. Roscio Amerino* and its use for the historian," *Antiquité classique* 49: 173–90

　1985. "The case against Sextus Roscius of Ameria," *Antiquité classique* 54: 188–96

　1987a. "Criminal courts at Rome under the Cinnan regime," *Hermes* 115: 502

　1987b. "Cicero, *Pro Roscio Amerino*, 2," *Latomus* 46: 847

　1988a. "The lacuna in Cicero's *Pro Roscio Amerino*," *Revue belge de philologie et d'histoire* 66: 78–9

　1988b. "The sale of the property of Roscius of Ameria: how illegal was it?," *Antiquité classique* 57: 296–7

Klodt, C. 2003. "Prozessparteien und politische Gegner als *dramatis personae*. Charakterstilisierung in Ciceros Reden" in Schröder and Schröder 2003: 35–101

Klose, F. 1933. *Die Bedeutung von honos und honestus*. Diss. Breslau

Konstan, D. 2001. *Pity transformed*. London

　2005. "Clemency as a virtue," *Classical Philology* 100: 337–46

Kragelund, P. 2001. "Dreams, religion and politics in Republican Rome," *Historia* 50: 53–95

Kroon, C. 1995. *Discourse particles in Latin. A study of nam, enim, autem, vero and at*. Amsterdam

Krostenko, B. A. 2000. "Beyond (dis)belief: rhetorical form and religious symbol in Cicero's *de Divinatione*," *Transactions of the American Philological Association* 130: 353–91

Kurczyk, S. 2006. *Cicero und die Inszenierung der eigenen Vergangenheit*. Cologne, Weimar, Vienna

Landgraf, G. 1878. *De Ciceronis elocutione in orationibus pro Quinctio et pro Sex. Roscio Amerino conspicua*. Diss. Würzburg

　1912. "*Dimissui esse* bei Cicero pro Rosc. Am. § 11," *Berliner philologische Wochenschrift* 32: 1299–1301

La Penna, A. 1990. "La legittimazione del lusso privato da Ennio a Vitruvio. Momenti, problemi, personaggi" in F. Milazzo, ed., *Contractus e pactum: tipicità e libertà negoziale nell'esperienza tardo-repubblicana* (Naples) 251–85

Latte, K. 1960. *Römische Religionsgeschichte*. Munich

　1968. *Kleine Schriften zu Religion, Recht, Literatur und Sprache der Griechen und Römer*. Ed. O. Gigon et al. Munich

Laughton, E. 1964. *The participle in Cicero*. London

Laurand, L. 1911. "Les fins d'hexamètre dans les discours de Cicéron," *Revue de philologie* 35: 75–88

Lebreton, J. 1901. *Etudes sur la langue et la grammaire de Cicéron*. Paris

Letzner, W. 2000. *Lucius Cornelius Sulla. Versuch einer Biographie*. Münster

Leumann, M. 1977. *Lateinische Laut- und Formenlehre*. Munich

Levene, D. S. 2004. "Reading Cicero's narratives" in Powell and Paterson 2004: 117–46

Levy, E. 1933. "Von den römischen Anklägervergehen," *Zeitschrift der Savigny-Stiftung für Rechtsgeschichte* 53: 151–233

Liebs, D. 2007. *Vor den Richtern Roms. Berühmte Prozesse der Antike*. Munich

Lincke, E. 1890. "Zur Beweisführung Ciceros in der Rede für Sextus Roscius aus Ameria," *Commentationes Fleckeisenianae* (Leipzig) 189–98

Lintott, A. W. 1971. "The offices of C. Flavius Fimbria in 86–5 BC," *Historia* 20: 696–701

   2008. *Cicero as evidence*. Oxford

Lo Cascio, E. 2006. "Realtà e rappresentazione: la caratterizzazione degli *homines ex municipiis rusticanis* nella *pro Roscio Amerino*" in G. Petrone and A. Casamento, eds., *Lo spettacolo della giustizia: le orazioni di Cicerone* (Palermo) 49–62

Löfstedt, B. 1963. "Zum lateinischen possessiven Dativ," *Zeitschrift für vergleichende Sprachforschung* 78: 64–83

Löfstedt, E. 1956. *Syntactica*. 2 vols. Lund

Lomas, K. 2004. "A Volscian mafia? Cicero and his Italian clients," in Powell and Paterson 2004: 97–116

Loutsch, C. M. 1979. "Remarques sur Cicéron, pro Sex. Roscio Amerino," *Liverpool Classical Monthly* 4: 107–12

   1994. *L'exorde dans les discours de Cicéron*. Brussels

Lovisi, C. 1999. *Contribution à l'étude de la peine de mort sous la république romaine (509–149 av. J.-C.)*. Paris

Macaulay, T. B. 2008. *The journals of Thomas Babington Macaulay*, ed. W. Thomas. 5 vols. London

MacKendrick, P. 1989. *The philosophical books of Cicero*. London

Madvig, J. N. 1912. "*Dimissui esse* bei Cicero pro Rosc. Am. §11," *Berliner philologische Wochenschrift* 32: 1400

Magdelain, A. 1984. "Paricidas" in *Du châtiment dans la cité* (Rome) 549–70 = 1990. *Jus imperium auctoritas. Études de droit romaine* (Rome) 519–38

Marchetti, S. C. 1986. "L'avvocato, il giudice, il 'reus' (la psicologia della colpa e del vizio nelle opere retoriche e nelle prime orazioni di Cicerone)," *Materiali e discussioni per l'analisi dei testi classici* 17: 93–124

Marinone, N. 2004. *Cronologia ciceroniana*. 2nd edn. Ed. E. Malaspina. Rome and Bologna

Marouzeau, J. 1938. *L'ordre des mots dans la phrase latine, 2: Le verbe*. Paris

Maslowski, T., ed. 1995. M. Tullius Cicero. *Orationes in P. Vatinium testem, Pro M. Caelio*. Stuttgart and Leipzig

Maurin, J. 1984. "*Funus* et rites de séparation," *AION* 6: 191–208

May, J. M. 1988. *Trials of character: the eloquence of Ciceronian ethos*. Chapel Hill

Meiser, G. 1998. *Historische Laut- und Formenlehre der lateinischen Sprache*. Darmstadt

Merguet, H. 1877–84. *Lexikon zu den Reden des Cicero*. 4 vols. Jena

Mitchell, T. N. 1991. *Cicero, the senior statesman*. New Haven

Mommsen, T. 1887–8. *Römisches Staatsrecht*. 3 vols in 5. Berlin
  1899. *Römisches Strafrecht*. Leipzig

Moreau, P. 2006. "*quem honoris causa appello*. L'usage public des noms de personne et ses règles à Rome" in J. Champeaux and J. Chassignet, eds., *Aere perennius: en hommage à Hubert Zehnacker* (Paris) 293–307

Néraudau, J.-P. 1978. "Sexagenarii de ponte (Réflexions sur la genèse d'un proverbe)," *Revue des études Latines* 56: 159–74

Neue, F., and C. Wagener, 1892–1905. *Formenlehre der Lateinischen Sprache*. 3rd edn. 4 vols. Berlin

Nicolet, C. 1966–74. *L'ordre équestre à l'époque républicaine (312–43 av. J.-C.)*. 2 vols. Paris

Nippel, W. 1995. *Public order in ancient Rome*. Cambridge

Nisbet, R. G. M. 1990. "Cola and clausulae in Cicero's speeches" in E. M. Craik, ed., *'Owls to Athens': essays on classical subjects presented to Sir Kenneth Dover* (Oxford) 349–59

Nowak, K.-J. 1973. *Der Einsatz privater Garden in der späten römischen Republik*. Diss. Munich

Offermann, H. 1974. "Cicero, Pro Sex. Roscio Amerino 2,6," *Altsprachlicher Unterricht* 17.2: 65–73

Oksala, P. 1953. *Die griechischen Lehnwörter in den Prosaschriften Ciceros*. Helsinki

Opelt, I. 1965. *Die lateinischen Schimpfwörter und verwandte sprachliche Erscheinungen. Eine Typologie*. Heidelberg

Otto, A. 1890. *Die Sprichwörter und sprichwörtlichen Redensarten der Römer*. Leipzig

Parker, H. T. 1937. *The cult of antiquity and the French revolutionaries*. Chicago

Parker, R. 1983. *Miasma: pollution and purification in early Greek religion*. Oxford

Parkin, T. G. 2003. *Old age in the Roman world*. Baltimore and London

Parzinger, P. 1910. *Beiträge zur Kenntnis der Entwicklung des Ciceronischen Stils*. Landshut

Paterson, J. 2004. "Self-reference in Cicero's forensic speeches" in Powell and Paterson 2004: 79–96

Pericoli, F. G. 1993. "Nota a *Pro Roscio Amerino* 2,6" in M. Bandini and F. G. Pericoli, eds., *Scritti in memoria di Dino Peraccioni* (Florence) 263–6

Petersmann, H. 1996. "From concrete to abstract thinking: the development of moral concepts in Archaic Latin" in H. Rosén, ed., *Aspects of Latin: papers from the Seventh International Colloquium on Latin Linguistics, Jerusalem, April 1993* (Innsbruck) 665–74

Pfeiffer, R. 1968. *A history of classical scholarship from the beginnings to the end of the Hellenistic Age*. Oxford

Pinkster, H. 1969. "A, B and C coordination in Latin," *Mnemosyne* ser. 4, 22: 258–67
  1990. *Latin syntax and semantics*. London and New York

Platschek, J. 2005. *Studien zu Ciceros Rede für P. Quinctius*. Munich

Posch, S. 1979. "Zur Symmetrie und Ausgewogenheit bei Cicero," *Innsbrucker Beiträge zur Kulturwissenschaft* 20: 307–17

Pöschl, V. 1983. *Literatur und geschichtliche Wirklichkeit. Kleine Schriften II*. Ed. W.-L. Lieber-mann. Heidelberg

Powell, J., and J. Paterson, eds. 2004. *Cicero the advocate*. Oxford

Radin, M. 1919. "The lex Pompeia and the poena cullei," *Journal of Roman Studies* 9: 119–30

Rankin, H. D. 1961. "Word-play on prepositional *gratia* in Cicero, Pro Roscio Amerino 16,45," *Hermes* 89: 378–9

Rawson, E. 1991. *Roman culture and society: collected papers*. Oxford

Reichenbecher, M. 1913. *De uocum quae sunt scelus flagitium facinus apud priscos scriptores usu*. Jena Diss. Weitz

Reynolds, L. D., ed. 1983. *Texts and transmission: a survey of the Latin classics*. Oxford

Riggsby, A. M. 1995. "Appropriation and reversal as a basis for rhetorical proof," *Classical Philology* 90: 245–56

  1999. *Crime and community in Ciceronian Rome*. Austin

Risselada, R. 1993. *Imperatives and other directive expressions in Latin*. Amsterdam

Robinson, O. F. 1981. "Slaves and the criminal law," *Zeitschrift der Savigny-Stiftung für Rechtsgeschichte* 98: 213–54

  1995. *The criminal law of ancient Rome*. London

Roloff, H. 1938. *Maiores bei Cicero*. Diss. Leipzig. Göttingen

Roloff, K.-H. 1953. "Caerimonia," *Glotta* 32: 101–38

Rosenberger, V. 1998. *Gezähmte Götter. Das Prodigienwesen der römischen Republik*. Stuttgart

Rotondi, G. 1912. *Leges publicae populi Romani*. Milan

Rüpke, J. 2007. *Römische Priester in der Antike. Ein biographisches Lexikon*. Stuttgart

  2008. *Fasti sacerdotum: a prosopography of pagan, Jewish, and Christian religious officials in the city of Rome, 300 BC to AD 499*. Tr. D. M. B. Richardson. Oxford

Saller, R. P. 1986. "*Patria potestas* and the stereotype of the Roman family," *Continuity and Change* 1: 7–22

  1987. "Men's age at marriage and its consequences in the Roman family," *Classical Philology* 82: 21–34

Santalucia, B. 1999. "Cic. *pro Rosc. Am.* 3, 8 e la scelta dei giudici nelle cause di parricidio," *Iura* 50: 143–51

Sauerwein, I. 1970. *Die leges sumptuariae als römische Maßnahme gegen den Sittenverfall*. Diss. Hamburg

Scherillo, G. 1953. "Appunti sulla 'sectio bonorum'," *Iura* 4: 197–205

Schmidt, P. L. 2000. *Traditio Latinitatis. Studien zur Rezeption und Überlieferung der lateinischen Literatur*. Ed. J. Fugmann, M. Hose, B. Zimmermann. Stuttgart

Schmitz, C. 2000. *Das Satirische in Juvenals Satiren*. Berlin

Schmitz, D. 1985. *Zeugen des Prozeßgegners in Gerichtsreden Ciceros*. Prismata 1. Frankfurt a.M.

Schneider, C. 1967–9. *Kulturgeschichte des Hellenismus*. 2 vols. Munich

Schröder, B.-J. and J.-P. 2003. *Studium declamatorium. Untersuchungen zu Schulübungen und Prunkreden von der Antike bis zur Neuzeit*. Leipzig

Sedgwick, W. B. 1934. "Cicero's conduct of the case *Pro Roscio*," *Classical Review* 48: 13

Shackleton Bailey, D. R. 1979. "On Cicero's speeches," *Harvard Studies in Classical Philology* 83: 237–85

1992. *Onomasticon to Cicero's speeches*. 2nd edn. Stuttgart and Leipzig

Shatzman, I. 1972. "The Roman general's authority over booty," *Historia* 21: 177–205

Solmsen, F. 1968. "Cicero's first speeches: a rhetorical analysis," *Kleine Schriften II* (Hildesheim) 231–45

Solodow, J. 1978. *The Latin particle quidem*. Boulder

Stroh, W. 1975. *Taxis und Taktik*. Stuttgart

2003. "Declamatio" in Schröder and Schröder 2003: 5–34

Suder, W. 1995. "*Sexagenarios de ponte*. Statut juridique des vieillards dans la famille et dans la société romaine. Quelques remarques et opinions," *Revue internationale des droits de l'antiquité* 42: 393–413

Suerbaum, W. 2002. *Die archäische Literatur von den Anfängen bis Sullas Tod* in R. Herzog and P. L. Schmidt, eds., *Handbuch der lateinischen Literatur der Antike* (Munich)

Swain, S. 2007. "Polemon's *Physiognomy*" in S. Swain, ed., *Seeing the face, seeing the soul: Polemon's* Physiognomy *from classical antiquity to medieval Islam* (Oxford) 125–201

Swarney, P. R. 1993. "Social status and social behaviour as criteria in judicial proceedings in the late Republic" in B. Halpern and D. W. Hobson, eds., *Law, politics and society in the ancient Mediterranean world* (Sheffield) 137–55

Szemler, G. J. 1972. *The priests of the Roman Republic*. Brussels

Talbert, R. J. A., ed. 2000. *Barrington atlas of the Greek and Roman world*. Princeton

Taldone, A. 1993. "Su *insania* e *furor* in Cicerone," *Bollettino di studi Latini* 23: 3–19

Taylor, L. R. 1949. *Party politics in the age of Caesar*. Berkeley and Los Angeles

Thomas, Y. 1981. "Parricidium," *Mélanges de l'Ecole Française de Rome. Antiquité* 93: 643–715

Toynbee, J. M. C. 1971. *Death and burial in the Roman world*. London

Treggiari, S. 1969. *Roman freedmen in the late Republic*. Oxford

Vasaly, A. 1993. *Representations: images of the world in Ciceronian oratory*. Berkeley

Visscher, F. de 1963. *Le droit des tombeaux romains*. Milan

Volkmann, R. 1885. *Die Rhetorik der Griechen und Römer in systematischer Übersicht*. 2nd edn. Leipzig

Watson, A. 1967. *The law of persons in the later Roman Republic*. Oxford

1968. *The law of property in the later Roman Republic*. Oxford

Webster, T. B. L. 1960. *Studies in Menander*. 2nd edn. Manchester

Wegner, M. 1969. *Untersuchungen zu den lateinischen Begriffen socius und societas*. Göttingen

Weische, A. 1972. *Ciceros Nachahmung der attischen Redner*. Heidelberg

Weise, O. 1909. *Language and character of the Roman people*. Tr. H. A. Strong and A. Y. Campbell. London

Westermann, W. L. 1955. *The slave systems of Greek and Roman antiquity*. Philadelphia

Wiedemann, T. 1981. *Greek and Roman slavery*. Baltimore and London

Wiesthaler, F. 1956. *Die oratio obliqua als künstlerisches Stilmittel in den Reden Ciceros*. Commentationes Aenipontanae XII. Innsbruck

Wilkinson, L. P. 1963. *Golden Latin artistry*. Cambridge

Wills, J. 1996. *Repetition in Latin poetry: figures of allusion*. Oxford

Winterbottom, M. 2004. "Perorations" in Powell and Paterson 2004: 215–30

Wirszubski, C. 1961. "*Audaces*: a study in political phraseology," *Journal of Roman Studies* 51: 12–22

Wiseman, T. P. 1967. "T. Cloelius of Terracina," *Classical Review* 18: 263–4

    1971. *New men in the Roman senate 139 BC–AD 14*. Oxford

    1983. "*Domi nobiles* and the Roman cultural élite" in M. Cébeillac-Gervasoni, ed., *Les "bourgeoisies" municipales italiennes aux IIe et Ier siècles av. J.-C.* (Paris-Naples) 299–307

Wissowa, G. 1912. *Religion und Kultus der Römer*. Munich

Wölfflin, E. von, 1933. *Ausgewählte Schriften*. Ed. G. Meyer. Leipzig

Wood, N. 1988. *Cicero's social and political thought*. Berkeley, Los Angeles and Oxford

Wright, F. W. 1931. *Cicero and the theatre*. Smith College Classical Studies 11. Northampton, Mass.

Zellmer, E. 1976. *Die lateinischen Wörter auf -ura*. 2nd edn. Frankfurt a.M.

Zielinski, T. 1904. *Das Clauselgesetz in Ciceros Reden*. Leipzig

INDEXES

Unless otherwise indicated, references in the Indexes are to chapter numbers in the Commentary.

1 LATIN WORDS

a te, abs te, Intro. sec. 7
ab, 85
absens, 76
absoluo, 56, 65
abutor pro, 59
accedo, 4, 46
  ad rem publicam, 3
  huc accedit, 104
accido, 16, 42
accipio (see *pars*)
accusator, 28, 35, 53
  bonus, 58
  mutus, 104
accuso, 57
acer, 11, 37, 153
acerbus, 78, 141, 150
actio (see *fides bona*)
acuo, 110
ad, 102
  + acc., Intro. sec. 7, 18, 44
ad-, 121
adamo, 121
adaugeo, 30
adduco rem, 96
adiungo auxilium, 116
adiutor, 23
  + *ad*, 6
adiuuo + *ad*, 6
administer, 77, 102
admitto, 62, 73, 77
adsum, 148
aduersarius, 126
adulescens, 6
adulescentia, 1, 2, 3, 50
adulescentulus, 1
aduocatus, Intro. sec. 5, 1–14, 1, 2, 149
aequus, 7
  aequo animo, 49
aerarium, 125
aes alienum, 39
aetas, 1, 3
affecto iter/uiam, 140
affero, 54
afficio macula, 113
affinis, 18

agito, 66, 67
ago, 8, 73, 152
  actum est, 150
  age, 48, 93, 105
    nunc, 105, 108
  nihil, 26, 130
agrestis, Intro. sec. 5, 39, 74, 75, 143–4
agricola, 143–4
alien(issim)us, 87
aliquando, 83, 140, 145
aliquis, 76, 141
aliquotiens, Intro. sec. 5, 77
allego, 25
alluo, 72
alter . . . alter, 133
altercatio, 40, 54, 73, 92, 94, 96, 120
amandatio, 44
amando, 44
amens, 41
amentia, 29, 33–4, 62, 67
amicitia, Intro. sec. 5, 4
amo, 121
amplificatio, Intro. sec. 7, 9
amplitudo, 2, 83, 136
amplus, 83, 102–3
animaduerto, 137
animus, 10 (see also *aequus*, *nisi*)
  animi causa, 133, 134
  ex animi mei sententia, 129
  patrius, 46
annumero, 144
antequam, 60
antiquus, 26
Antoniaster, Intro. sec. 5
anulus, 144
apertus, 15–29, 116
appendo, 144
appeto, 30, 50
applicatus, 85
appromitto, 26
arbiter datus, 114
  ex compromisso, 114
arbitrium (see *nutus*)
arcesso, 50
architectus, Intro. sec. 7, 132

2 GREEK WORDS

3 GENERAL INDEX

anaphora, Intro. sec. 7, 66, 67, 98, 104, 118, 121, 140, 142, 147, 149, 154

Anaximenes, 71

Ancharius Rufus, C., Intro. sec. 5

animals
  appeal to behavior of, 63
  exposure to as punishment, 71
  rationality attributed to, 56

anticategoria, 17, 79, 83–123, 84

Antistius, 90

Antonius, C., 2

Antonius, M. (orator), Intro. sec. 3, 5 and 7, headnote to Comm., 6

Antonius, M. ("triumvir"), Intro. sec. 3, 6, 132, 137, 154

antonyms, 116

Apollo, 66

apologia, 83–123

aposiopesis, 139

apostrophe, Intro. sec. 7, 144, 146

approval by one's own group as linchpin of defense, 152

Arausio, battle of, headnote to Comm., 15

archaism, Intro. sec. 7, 44, 48

argument (see also *argumentum*)
  a fortiori, 37, 62, 65, 111, 113, 116, 117, 131
  complex, refutation of, 76–7
  cui bono?, 78, 124–42
  Stoic for divine providence, 131

Aristotle, 14, 23, 133

Arpinum, Intro. sec. 5, 2

Artemo of Centuripae, 104

Asconius Pedianus, Q., Intro. sec. 9

assonance, Intro. sec. 7, 5, 16, 67, 87, 103

asyndeton, Intro. sec. 7, 11, 24, 30, 134
  adversative, Intro. sec. 7, 6, 15, 31, 53, 54, 61, 76, 117, 142, 143
  aside in, 25
  examples introduced in, 56
  explicative, Intro. sec. 7, 6, 10, 71, 77, 82, 102
  in lists, Intro. sec. 7
  narrative introduced in, Intro. sec. 7, 25, 84

Athens, 70 (see also *prosecutor(s)*)

Atilius, L., p. 1n.6

Atilius Regulus Serranus, C. (?), 37–82, 43, 50

attentiveness of listeners
  as goal of exordium, 1–14, 10

Automedon, 98

Baccanae, 15

balance, rhetorical, Intro. sec. 7, 12, 50, 54, 62, 137, 148

bronze,
  Corinthian, 133
  Delian, 133

Bruttii, 132

burial, oldest form of, 72

Caecilia Metella (protector of Sex. Roscius jun.), Intro. sec. 5, 4, 13, 15–29, 15, 27, 77, 119, 143–54, 144, 147, 154

Caecilia Metella (wife of Sulla), 27

Caecilii Metelli, Intro. sec. 5, 15, 77

Caecilius Metellus, M. (cos. 115), 147

Caecilius Metellus, M. (pr. 69), Intro. sec. 5, 1, 15, 77, 119

Caecilius Metellus Baliaricus, Q., 27, 77

Caecilius Metellus Caprarius, C., 77

Caecilius Metellus Celer, Q., 77–8

Caecilius Metellus Diadematus, L., 147

Caecilius Metellus Macedonicus, Q., 27, 77

Caecilius Metellus Nepos, Q., 27

Caecilius Statius, 37–82, 46

Caelius Rufus, M., 18

Calabria, 132

Cannae, battle of, 89

Cassius Longinus Ravilla, L., 84, 154

Cato (see *Porcius*)

censors
  adlection to senate by, 8
  violation of sumptuary laws punished by, 134

chiasmus, 1, 6, 10, 12, 19, 23, 31, 38, 39, 62, 68, 71, 78, 83, 119, 145

Cicero, M.
  additions allegedly made to published speech by, p. 19n.55, 3, 22, 131, 152
  anxiety of at the beginning of a speech, 9
  appropriation and reversal of opposing argument by, 11, 39
  appropriation of comic vocabulary by, 6, 9, 12, 26, 43, 128
  aside(s) used by, 150
  assimilation of Roman ideals by, Intro. sec. 6, 50
  assumes large burden of proof, 8, 18, 37, 109
  assumes rôle of omniscient narrator, Intro. sec. 8, 19, 28, 136
  astute observer of opposing counsel, 59
  attitude of toward the *nobilitas*, Intro. sec. 6, 141, 149
  attitude of toward prosecution, 83, 149
  calls for jurors' collaboration, Intro. sec. 5, 10, 36, 153
  characterizes opponents, 6, 8

with consecutive force, 5, 32, 37, 109, 119, 138
with final force, 25, 50, 59, 60, 91, 151
with indefinite antecedent, 24, 34, 38, 51, 54, 55, 60, 119
with limiting force, 17, 59
short, Intro. sec. 7, 60
mirroring sense, 150
clausula(e), 5, 6, 8, 15, 19, 22, 30, 31, 53, 62, 64, 67, 69. 81, 124, 153
clichés, use of legal, Intro. sec. 7
Clodia Metelli, 74
Clodius, P., 27, 83, 91
Cloelius, T., 37–82, 64
Cluentius Habitus, A., 97
Cluny, Intro. sec. 10
colloquialism, Intro. sec. 7, 2, 6, 8, 13, 24, 26, 39, 48, 52, 55, 59, 64, 74, 82, 83, 95, 97, 104, 107, 115, 123, 127, 130, 140, 154
comedy as *imago uitae* (*topos*), 47
characters from as basis for argument, 45–7
commands, means of expressing, 154
comparative adj. or adv.
without explicit standard, 3, 150
conditional sentences
ideal, 56
conspirators, Catilinarian, 139
copious style, characteristics of, 8
Cornelii Scipiones, 15
Cornelius Chrysogonus, L., Intro. sec. 5 and 6, 2, 6, 8, 12, 13, 15–29, 17, 20, 21–2, 23, 24, 25, 26, 34, 35–6, 35, 37–82, 49, 50, 58, 60, 61, 72, 77, 78, 80, 83–123, 84, 86, 93, 94, 95, 96, 99, 105, 105–6, 106, 107, 108, 110, 114, 119, 120, 122, 123, 124–42, 125, 127, 130, 131, 132, 133, 135, 137, 138, 140–2, 141, 142, 143–54, 143–4, 143, 144, 145, 147, 150, 151, 152 (see also *potens*, *potentia*)
cruelty attributed to, 144, 146, 150, 154
shielded from charge of murder, Intro. sec. 5, 6, 124–42
Cornelius Cinna, L., Intro. sec. 3, 5 and 8, 11, 149
Cornelius Lentulus Sura, P., 19
Cornelius Nepos, Intro. sec. 9
Cornelius Scipio Nasica, P., Intro. sec. 5, 1, 15, 77, 119
Cornelius Scipio Aemilianus, P., 102–3
Cornelius Scipio Africanus, P., 151
Cornelius Sulla, P. (C.'s client), 149
Cornelius Sulla Felix, L., Intro. sec. 3, 4, 5, 6, 7 and 8, 6, 11, 13, 15, 16, 19, 20, 21–2,

22, 25, 33, 42, 83–123, 89–91, 91, 94, 105, 110, 124–42, 125, 127, 128, 130, 131, 132, 135, 136, 137, 138, 139, 149, 150, 153
correlatives marking units, 83, 118
court(s), defiling of, 12, 32, 91
difficulty in maintaining, 139
functions of Roman, 36, 154
suspension of, 11, 89–91
voting procedures in, 56
crescendo, rhetorical, 9
crime, deterrence of, 55, 70
relation of to punishment, 116
theory of the genesis of, 75
cruelty in the Roman state, 146 (see also *crudelitas*, *Chrysogonus*)
curia, burning of, 91
Curtius, 90
Curtius, C., 90

danger (theme of speech), 7 (see also *periculum*)
dative
double, 11, 48, 49, 75, 77, 81, 84, 142
ethic, 133
of disadvantage, 2
of possession, 17
predicative, 40
decree, summarized and read out, 25
defense, legalistic, reason for eschewing, 2
delivery,
faults of, 59
gesture, possible use of, 68
demonstrative with following defining clause, 61
Demosthenes, 73, 135
Desmoulins, Lucie Simplice Camille Benoist, Intro. sec. 9
diatribe, 112
digression(s), 29–32, 55–7, 58, 61, 91, 92, 138
dilemma, 30, 41, 73, 88, 123, 124, 152
pseudo-dilemma, 74
diminutives, fondness of Latin for, 115
force of, 120
dog, characteristics of, 57 (see also *prosecutor(s)*)

Egnatius, Cn. 52
elements, four, 71, 72
embassy (see *decem primi*)
Empedocles, 71
enmity, personal, in Roman life and politics, 145
Ennius, Q., 6, 66, 67, 90

Ephesus, 61
Erucius, C., Intro. sec. 3, 5 and 8, 10, 28, 35–6, 37–82, 38, 39, 43, 44, 45, 46, 49, 50, 53, 58, 60, 61, 62, 72, 73, 74, 75, 79, 80, 81, 82, 90, 93, 100–1, 102, 104, 132 (see also *prosecutor(s)*)
  inability of to assign convincing motive, 42, 46, 53, 54, 62, 72, 84
  poverty of the case of, 83
Etruscan (language), 113
euphemism, 93, 97, 154
Euripides, 66
exclamations (see *accusative*)
  acc. + inf. in, 95
exordium, 1–14, 9

Fabius Quintilianus, M. (see *Quintilian*)
Fannius, M., 11, 85
father and son homonymous, 6
Fenestella, Intro. sec. 9
Fides, 95
Flavius Fimbria, C., 33–4, 33, 40, 135
formula
  for holding attention, 129 (see also *patience*)
  summarizing, 9
  transitional, 14, 79, 83, 95, 105, 108, 116, 117
friendship
  caution needed in dissolving, 112
  instrumental, 111
Frontinus, 151
Fulginiae, Intro. sec. 5
Furies, 66, 67
future perfect tense, 84
future tense, "prophetic," 47

Gabinius, A., 135
Gauls, 56
general, authority of, 21–2
genitive
  of quality, 17, 108
  of the rubric, 8, 16, 30, 83, 90, 91, 97, 122, 133, 147, 154
  objective, 80
  partitive, 10
  with expressions of remembering, 95
  with judicial verbs, 53
  with verbs of rating, 46, 115
gesture, use of, 68
gladiatorial imagery (see *imagery*)
goals of the litigants, 7, 8, 143–4
Gracchus, C., 29
greed as motive for prosecution, 1–14 (see also *cupiditas*)

haplography, 24
Hecataeus of Miletus, 102–3
hegemonial states preferred as parallels to Rome, 70
hendiadys, 8, 9, 17, 25, 66, 84, 133
Heraclitus, 71
heritability of friends and enemies, 15, 106
Hermagoras of Temnos, 35–6, 37–82
hermaphrodite(s), treated as a prodigy, Intro. sec. 1
homoeoteleuton, 23, 91
Hortensius, Hortalus, Q., 30, 35, 60, 104
hyperbaton, Intro. sec. 7, 5, 8, 24, 29, 30, 38, 70, 97, 144, 150, 153, 154
hyperbole, 9, 11, 19, 58, 74, 94, 119, 154

Illyrii, 132
imagery
  gladiatorial, 17, 30, 33, 84, 100
  medical, 154
  military, 17, 81, 108
  of spoils, 108
imperative, 154
  "future," 18, 57, 74, 93, 109, 118
imperfect, 50, 54, 58, 119
  for pluperfect, 91
  inceptive, 23
  indicative as present unreal, 64
imperium Romanum as viewed by Romans, 50
increasing members, law of, 50, 117, 136
indicative for subj. (see *imperfect*)
  in expressions of necessity, 37, 53
  in expressions of possibility, 64, 75
indignation, arousal of, 14, 23, 143–54
infinitive
  for finite verb expressing indignation or wonderment, 64
  historical, 110
interpolations, 21, 30, 124
invective, topic(s) of, 46
irony, 1, 6, 16, 23, 33, 39, 51, 52, 58, 78, 84, 104, 120, 133, 134
isocolon, 23
Isocrates, 1
items in series, organization of, 31, 141

Julius Caesar, C., Intro. sec. 5, 33
Julius Caesar, C. (the dictator), 33, 53, 132, 136, 154
Julius Caesar, L., Intro. sec. 3, 33
Julius Caesar Octavianus, C., Intro. sec. 3
Junius, M., Intro. sec. 5, 59
Juno Sospita, 27
Jupiter, Intro. sec. 7, 131
jurors (see also *oath(s)*)